New Mathematics Education Research and Practice

D0813812

New Mathematics Education Research and Practice

Edited by:

Jürgen Maasz and Wolfgang Schloeglmann
University of Linz, Austria

SENSE PUBLISHERS
ROTTERDAM / TAIPEI

A C.I.P. record for this book is available from the Library of Congress.

Paperback ISBN 90-77874-74-7

Published by: Sense Publishers,
P.O. Box 21858, 3001 AW Rotterdam, The Netherlands
http://www.sensepublishers.com
Printed on acid-free paper

TABLE OF CONTENTS

JUERGEN MAASZ AND WOLFGANG SCHLOEGLMANN

INTRODUCTION

The genesis of this book lies in our reflections about the development and current state of research and practice in mathematics education. Looking back at the 1960s and 1970s, education in general was at the centre of political debate. In reaction to the so-called "Sputnik-shock", a powerful movement emerged in the West aiming to change education at all levels, particularly in mathematics and science. Mathematics education came to be dominated by the concept of "New Math", which was to guide mathematics education from the kindergarten to the university.

Behind the New Math was an emphasis (based on an approach by Bourbaki) on the basic structures of mathematics. Thus a philosophy of mathematics provided the guiding idea for reform of curricula. As René Thom (1973, p. 204) wrote: 'In fact, whether one wishes it or not, all mathematical pedagogy, even if scarcely coherent, rests on a philosophy of mathematics'. Interestingly, in that period leading mathematics researchers became involved in the debate about mathematics education at schools and universities (see, for instance, Thom's article, "Modern Mathematics: Does it Exist?" and J. Dieudonne's reply, "Should We Teach 'Modern' Mathematics?").

The guiding principle in the New Math was the careful construction of mathematical concepts, beginning with sets and logic. Precise definitions of mathematical objects and the study of structures such as groups and finite fields became central in mathematics education in schools and universities. The goal of teaching was to give "clean" definitions and a "clean" construction of the mathematical theory. Teachers had to give careful explanations of terms and theory. The language used in classrooms had to be strongly oriented towards definitions and was often "sterile". This orientation was also supported by Piaget's theory of learning with its strong emphasis on Bourbaki's concept of structure.

But this strong emphasis on structure in school mathematics led to resistance. Thom wrote somewhat polemically, "The modernist tendency is grounded on a formalist conception of mathematics – that which was classically expressed in the famous aphorism by Bertrand Russell, 'Mathematics may be defined as the subject in which we never know what we a talking about nor whether what we are saying is true'" (Thom 1973, p. 204). Many teachers, parents and even journalists argued against the New Math. Some of the arguments in a placard-style are collected in the book by M. Kline (1973), "Why Johnny Can't Add: The Failure of New Math". For a much deeper and more detailed analysis we refer to the book written by Howson, Keitel and Kilpatrick (1981).

J. Maasz, W. Schloeglmann (Eds.), New Mathematics Education Research and Practice, 1–6.

One aspect missing in the New Math classroom was the application of mathematics. Thus the strong emphasis on "pure" mathematics was later followed by an orientation towards the application of mathematics. The first volume of ESM contained the Proceedings of the Colloquium on 'How to Teach Mathematics so as to be Useful' organized by H. Freudenthal. B. Booss and M. Niss (1979) published the book, "Mathematics and the Real World". In 1976, W. Dörfler and R. Fischer organized a conference for participants from German-speaking countries, "Application-Orientated Mathematics for Secondary Level II" (Anwendungs-orientierte Mathematik für die Sekundarstufe II).

Nevertheless, if one considers all the papers in mathematics education published at the time, one notices that the content of mathematics together with its presentation was of central importance. Quantitative research methods dominated empirical research at the time, and criteria such as 'representativity', validity, reliability and so on became important for the acceptance and perceived quality of papers.

After the failure of the New Math in mathematics education, many researchers concluded that a strong emphasis on just one philosophical viewpoint of what constitutes the foundation of mathematics was not sufficient to grasp the complexity of the subject, nor moreover, of the process of mathematics learning. Much analysis is required to understand why mathematics learning is important to a society or to an individual, and the answer cannot be found in a single conceptualisation of the foundations of mathematics.

This consensus provoked widespread research and curriculum constructing or changing activity. Careful analysis was carried out to understand the meaning of mathematics in our society. As a consequence of an emphasis on the meaning of mathematics in the industrialised West, an extension to the development and status of mathematics in various cultures (Ethnomathematics) emerged. A further line of research was the clarification of the specification of mathematics. The meaning of signs and representations in mathematics and mathematics learning was put under the microscope of analysis using concepts from philosophy. Extensive analysis of the status of mathematical objects as abstract terms, as well as of the process of abstraction which requires mathematical terms, led to important insights. In the course of this research, concepts from the philosophy of mathematics, the history of mathematics, critical theory and so on were adapted to the needs of mathematics education research.

Learning in general, and mathematics learning in particular, became an important research field. Researchers recognized that deeper understanding of the learning process was indispensable. The mechanisms of learning were studied, beginning with the conceptualisation of learning due to Piaget. Using concepts from cognitive psychology researchers constructed models for the cognitive processes of an individual learner. To study such processes it was necessary to use new research methods. Quantitative methods alone were not sufficient to gain deeper insights into an individual learner's learning process. Hence researchers increasingly used qualitative methods such as interviews as well as observation of an individual learner's mathematics construction process.

In recent times researchers have focussed on a number of aspects, including problem-solving processes for non-routine problems. While studying cognitive processes, researchers became increasingly aware that a purely cognitive position is not sufficient to explain the learning process because affective factors influence the process in a deep way. While at first cognitive as well as stable affective factors such as attitudes and beliefs were thought to be of central importance, studies of the solution process in non-routine problems have led researchers to focus on stronger and short-term affects.

A further important extension of the understanding of mathematics learning was the study of the social conditions of learning. Learning is always a social process, too. On the one hand the classroom is a social place, on the other hand learning is always embedded in a culture.

However, not only is learning a social process, mathematics is also the result of a cultural process and therefore the learning of mathematics is also influenced by cultural developments. In particular, computers and technology in general have had a tremendous influence. New technology opens new opportunities for learning experiments and for using computers as a tool, but it also leads to difficult questions. How should learners use a computer? What should be learned without computers? Which paper-pencil skills should students learn? Moreover, while the use of computers opens many new opportunities for mathematics learning, it also leads to learning problems connected with the tool itself.

Mathematics education research has blossomed into many different areas, which we can see in the programmes of the ICME conferences, as well as in the various survey articles in the Handbooks. However, all of these lines of research are trying to grapple with the complexity of the same learning and teaching process. Although our knowledge of the process is now more extensive and deeper, it seems to be more difficult to specify a conceptualisation of mathematics that should be used by an ordinary teacher in order to handle mathematics learning in the classroom.

To overcome this fragmentation, we have identified six themes:
- Mathematics, culture and society,
- The structure of mathematics and its influence on the learning process,
- Mathematics learning as a cognitive process,
- Mathematics learning as a social process,
- Affective conditions of the mathematics learning process,
- New technologies and mathematics learning.

Let us finish with a few words that extend the discussions to encompass our point of view on the ideas and decisions behind the selection of these themes. Mathematics is a cultural product developed in various cultures over a long period. But mathematics is not a product that we can find in the 'Physical World' in the sense of Popper; not only is its development driven by societal and economic forces but also by an epistemological interest. In this sense mathematics is a product of the human mind and the possibilities of human rational thinking. Many cultures use mathematics to organize their social and economic life; furthermore mathematics is an important tool for many occupations that is often hidden in the context. Therefore we find mathematics in the curricula of all countries and mathematics education is a universal concern even if there are specific problems depending on the cultural and economic conditions.

The capacity for learning is a capacity common to all humans. But this capacity is very general and mathematics learning uses this capacity in a specific form. Therefore it is important to study the structure and nature of mathematics to understand the nature of mathematics learning. Humans have general mechanisms for thinking and learning and mathematical reasoning at their disposal and learning uses this capacity in a specific form. For research in mathematics education a crucial question is to find out what distinguishes mathematics learning from learning other subject matter and this difference must be a consequence of the structure of mathematics.

For a long time, mathematics learning has been seen as a cognitive process and interpreted in the context of an evolving understanding of cognitive processes. Today it seems that the cognitive process is mostly seen as a conscious, constructive mental process. But in this description there exists various interpretations of the meaning of conscious, constructive and mental. Beside these issues in mathematics education research we have to develop a concrete formulation for our questions. What are the objects of mathematical activities? What does 'cognitive' and 'learning' mean in the context of mathematics learning?

This also leads to the question: What are the conditions under which the individual processes of mathematics learning takes place? Mathematics learning is always embedded in the social context. On the one hand mathematics is a cultural product and cultural products always require social learning to introduce an individual into the "culture". On the other hand mathematics learning in school takes place within a social group and discourses and learning conditions within the group are central elements of the learning process.

Mathematics learning as a cognitive process encompasses only one of several central aspects of individual learning. All mental processes are always inseparably combined with affects. There exists no pure cognitive processes on the individual level, these processes are always embedded and strongly influenced by affects, motivation, moods etc. But affects are also a social construction within a social group and group values have a deep influence on learning conditions within a group.

Tools for calculating have a long tradition in mathematics and also in school mathematics. But the new technologies dramatically change the condition for tool use. They include not only widespread possibilities for calculating; they are also tools for thinking. Regarding this situation, we should be alert to new challenges this development brings; the new technologies include a big challenge for mathematics education to rethink the learning process regarding the new tool and to develop new methods to include the new tool if it is useful.

An important decision in this sense was that we should concentrate on research results of our discipline and to leave out questions of curriculum development, the discussion about surveys like TIMSS, PISA or standard tests. A lot of books about these questions exist. Our central aim is to make a contribution towards overcoming the fragmentation in research. The way we brought the fragments together was motivated by our personal history. We had good success with an interdisciplinary conference on "Mathematics as Technology" in the year 1988 (see Maasz/ Schloeglmann 1989), when we invited mathematicians, philosophers, sociologists, teachers and mathematic educators to discuss the new position of mathematics within highly industrialized countries and its consequences for research and education. Based on this experience we invited three researchers per theme to a conference that took place in August 2005 in Strobl (Wolfgangsee, Austria). The aim of this conference was to present and discuss crucial concepts in a theme with researchers in other areas. This book is the result of the presentations given at the conference, as well as the discussions that ensued during the paper preparation process, since all the papers were circulated as drafts amongst the conference participants before being finalised. The teams of three were free to decide how to structure their part of the book. As you can read they found different ways consistent with their own viewpoints.

Finally we would like to thank all the individuals and institutions that supported this book. First of all the authors did much more than write a paper. They worked together in teams of three to design their individual parts and they have read the other parts and edited their text to reach "consistency" in presentation.

Thanks to the publisher, Peter de Liefde, for his valuable support.

The staff of the "Bundesinstitut für Erwachsenenbildung" in Strobl am Wolfgangsee provided a beautiful conference venue and facilities. An important part of the effort invested in the work for this book was motivated by the conference.

The following sponsors helped with their financial support. We would like to say thank you to:

Johannes Kepler Universität Linz

Linzer Hochschulfonds

Magistrat der Landeshauptstadt Linz

Amt der oberösterreichischen Landesregierung

Juergen Maasz and Wolfgang Schloeglmann

Linz, Summer 2006

REFERENCES

Booss, B. & Niss, M. (1979) (Eds.). *Mathematics and the real world.* Basel/Boston/ Stuttgart: Birkhäuser Verlag.

Dieudonne, J. (1973). Should we teach "modern" mathematics? *American Scientist,* 61(1), 16 – 19.

Doerfler, W. & Fischer, R. (1976). Anwendungsorientierte Mathematik in der Sekundarstufe II. Klagenfurt. Verlag Johannes Heyn.

Freudenthal, H. (1969). Proceedings of the colloquium 'How to Teach Mathematics so as to be Useful'. *Educational Studies in Mathematics 1.*

Howson, G., Keitel, C., & Kilpatrick, J. (1981). *Curriculum development in mathematics.* Cambridge: Cambridge University Press.

Klein, M. (1973). *Why Johnny can't add: The failure of new math.* St. Martinn's Press.

J. Maasz, & W. Schloeglmann (1989) (Eds.): *Mathematik als Technologie? Wechselwirkungen zwischen Mathematik, Neuen Technologien, Aus- und Weiterbildung.* Weinheim: Deutscher Studien Verlag.

Thom, R. (1973). Modern mathematics: Does it exist? In: A. G. Howson (Ed.) *Developments in mathematical education.* Cambridge University Press, 194 – 209.

Jürgen Maasz
Universität Linz, Austria

Wolfgang Schloeglmann
Universität Linz, Austria

OLE SKOVSMOSE

INTRODUCTION TO THE SECTION: MATHEMATICS, CULTURE AND SOCIETY

Mathematics, culture and society constitute a vast field of relationships. In addition, 'mathematics', 'culture' and 'society' are open and contested concepts that could be interpreted in very different ways. Any attempt to provide an overview of connecting relationships between these issues is doomed to establish a gross simplification; this introduction as well.

I will address three themes: mathematics and society; mathematics education and society; and mathematics education research and society. On the one hand, one could consider in what way society might influence mathematics, mathematics education, and mathematics education research. On the other hand, one could consider how mathematics, mathematics education and mathematics education research might have a social impact.

Mathematics and society. A Platonic perspective finds the entities of mathematics occupying a region beyond social influence. This ensures that mathematical truths become the closest humanity can get to eternal truths. Also formalism and structuralism present mathematics in such a way that it appears independent of the social. The relationships between mathematical formulas are interpreted as logical, and certainly not socio-logical relationships.

However, the immunity of mathematics to the social has been questioned. For instance, when rationalism presented certainty as an epistemological ideal and searched for an unshakable foundation of knowledge, mathematics was pointed to as an ideal for how to organise knowledge. Nominated as an epistemic paradigm, mathematics assumed a powerful role. And this nomination can be seen as a powerful social act – although during the period of rationalism, it was not thought of in this way. Mathematics can be seen as open to cultural influences in many other ways. Thus, a range of ethnomathematical studies show how mathematics reflects elements of the culture in which it is embedded. The social impact on mathematic can also be analysed within a mathematics-technology-power dynamics. New technologies structure how mathematics is conducted and how the conceptual framework of mathematics is formulated. Thus, in the chapter 'Mathematical Knowledge and Political Power', Christine Keitel analyses how information technologies invoke paradigmatic changes in the mathematical sciences, including their applications.

J. Maasz, W. Schloeglmann (Eds.), New Mathematics Education Research and Practice, 7–10.

The other way around, mathematics exercises an impact on technology. Thus, mathematics was essential for the initial conception and construction of the computer. It is not possible to develop any element of information technology without bringing a huge amount of mathematics into operation. In the chapter 'Materialization and Organization', Roland Fisher analyses the materialisation of the abstract. In this way, he formulates how mathematics as an abstract science, can have an impact, not only on technology, but on social structures in general. In the philosophy of mathematics, abstraction has been analysed in great detail as a concept-generating process. Consideration of the 'materialisation of the abstract', however, opens up for analysis the way mathematics operates in social structures. Another attempt to conceptualise the social impact of mathematics is presented in my chapter 'Challenges for Mathematics Education Research', where I investigate mathematics as action.

Mathematics education and society. While there has been an extensive debate concerning the degree to which mathematics is influenced by, and is influencing, social structures, everyone seems to agree that mathematics education is interacting strongly with social structures. Thus, Keitel analyses the social needs for mathematics education, which immediately leads us to detect the socio-political needs for controlling mathematics education.

Through political efforts, the content of the curriculum, as well as priorities in educational methodology, are influenced. Possible answers to questions like, "Is group work or project work appropriate for learning mathematics or not?" are sought adjusted to political priorities. Society's interest in mathematics education is also expressed through the extension of international comparative studies of students' performance in mathematics. Such studies could naturally serve a clarifying purpose, but they seem to function in quite a different way. The publication of results provides an opening for a deluge of political comments and initiatives. The studies seem to legitimise any kind of political initiative with respect to mathematics education.

Although it is generally recognised that mathematics education is influenced by, and at the same time is influencing, social structures, little agreement exists about the nature of this influence. What is it, in fact, that mathematics education could do to society, and society to mathematics education?

One the one hand, mathematics education can ensure an enculturation in mathematics, and in so doing, propagate a form of thinking and doing which fits the rationality of the 'social order'. As Fisher notices, in modern society, people are socialised in such a way that they "submit themselves voluntary" to the demands of daily life: "they pay the bills, they fill out questionnaires, they accept decisions based on statistic data, they trust the computer". In this way, mathematics education can support the development of 'functional' competencies. On the other hand, mathematics education can play important functions in developing empowering competencies. Like 'literacy', so does 'mathematical literacy' provide a necessary foundation for a well-functioning democracy, as well. And this brings us to the discussion of what 'mathematical literacy for critical citizenship' could mean, a discussion which is taken up by Keitel.

Thus, the possible functions of mathematics education can range from a submissive functionality accepting the social order of the day and fulfilling society's demand for a certain distribution of competencies among pupils and students; to a concern for developing a critical mathematical literacy.

Mathematics education research and society. Although it is generally accepted that research in mathematics education is influenced by economic priorities, it may be assumed that this influence is extrinsic, concerning the quality of research facilities, for example, and not intrinsic, influencing the very theoretical structures produced through research. However, seeing the influence as non-intrinsic might be questionable.

A particular well-resourced and well-functioning mathematics classroom seems to dominate the research literature (see my chapter). It appears that research in mathematics education is, to a great extent, building on empirical material, which is far from representative of the variety of sites of where mathematics is being learned. Thus, we have to be reminded that the mathematics classrooms, positioned in what statistically is referred to as the 'developed world' (USA, Canada, Western and Central Europe, Japan, Australia, New Zealand, and some other countries), includes only 10% of all the children in this world. This could be compared with the fact that 16% of the world's children do not go to school (see, for instance, *Education for All: Statistical Assessment 2000*, Paris: UNESCO). Considering our global community, research in mathematic education might be highly biased. This bias might be reflected in the way students are conceptualised, motives and feelings are formulated, educational relevance of topics is discussed, and in the way in which resources for learning are addressed.

Research in mathematics education might be deeply influenced by the 'affluent' world's priorities. For instance, there is no lack of fascinating investigations clarifying how information and communication technologies (ICT) provide new ways of experimenting, visualising and communicating about mathematics. More powerful ways for learning mathematics are made available. However, even though it is important for research to clarify possible learning-gains that ICT might bring to the classroom, it is also important to ask: What does the identification of the powerful ICT-learning potential mean for that large majority of children and students around the world who have no access to computers? Are we facing a technology-facilitated form of social exclusion?

Not only economic priorities might influence research in mathematics education. Ideological and political priorities could also have an intrinsic impact. At present, a neo-conservative influence, not least in the USA, impedes diversity in educational approaches. Instead, a back-to-basics trend has come to dominate. Certainly, such ideological priorities can influence research in mathematics education and establish limits for what educational possibilities to explore. As is the case with mathematic education, so also could mathematics education research accommodate itself to given social and economic priorities. However, research could also try to establish visions for alternatives to a given social order and, in this way, try to exercise a critical social influence.

Ole Skovsmose
Aalburg University, Denmark

CHRISTINE KEITEL

MATHEMATICS, KNOWLEDGE AND POLITICAL POWER

INTRODUCTION

Mathematics is perceived today as one of the most powerful social means for planning, optimizing, steering, representing and communicating social affairs created by mankind. By the development of modern information and communication technologies (ICT) based on mathematics, this social impact of mathematics came to full power: Mathematics is now universally used in all domains of society, and there is nearly no political decision-making process, in which mathematics is not used as the rational argument and the objective base replacing political judgements and power relations.

For the ordinary citizen, it becomes increasingly difficult and sometimes impossible to follow these developments of mathematics, mathematical applications and ICT, and to evaluate their social use appropriately, because specialisation and segmentation of mathematical applications often are extremely hard to understand. The principal insight into their necessity and a basic acknowledgement of their importance in general are often confronted by a complete lack of knowledge of concrete examples of their impact. Competencies to evaluate mathematical applications and ICT, and the possible usefulness or its problematic effects, however, now are a necessary precondition for the political executive and the democratic participation of citizens. The new challenge is to determine what kind of knowledge and meta-knowledge in a mathematised society is needed and how to gain the necessary constituents.

The development of competencies for decision-making under conditions that include the coding and processing of knowledge by means of systems of symbols (e.g. book-keeping, planning models, calculation of investment or pensions, quality control, theories of risks, IT in banking etc.) and their complete mathematisation, is not only an actual problem. The history offers numerous examples for the fact that similar problems arose at various times, although in historically specific forms and with historically specific solutions. In particular, examples of historically radical breaks in the organisation of decision-making could be referred to, i.e. examples of developments, in which the mutual effect of changes of knowledge systems and innovations in the technology of using information have questioned traditional mechanisms of decision-making as well in the educational and social policy as in policy for scientific development, which in long terms have been replaced by new

J. Maasz, W. Schloeglmann (Eds.), New Mathematics Education Research and Practice, 11–22.

forms. One example with particularly radical consequences is the linking of controllable empirical research and newly developed forms of representations of mathematical theories during the raise of classical sciences in the 16th and 17th century, another example is the raise of modern physics at the beginning of 20th century, in which - like in the first example - not only the changes immanent to scientific research and practice were of importance, but the accompanying complete revision of decision-making processes about the production, the use and evaluation of social and scientific knowledge. In the first case, the consequence was the development of a new organisation of autonomous bodies or systems of sciences, in the second it was the raise of modern, independent and rather autonomous institutions for scientific research only. Both examples are not singular cases.

Studies in the history and philosophy of sciences show that changes of the forms of symbolising and processing of information usually had mutual effects on social organisations and led to new structures of scientific knowledge. (Damerow & Lefévre 1981; Hoyrup & Damerow 2001; Renn 2002) Together with the change of structures of knowledge, characteristic styles of thinking and in particular worldviews were developed, which also effected fundamental changes in the process of political decision-making on general social goals, and on means and measures to pursue them, accompanied by changes in the allocation of resources in a society.

1. HISTORICAL ACCOUNTS OF MATHEMATICS AND POLITICAL POWER

1.1 Mathematics as a Distinctive Tool for Problem Solving in Social Practices and Means of Social Power

Since the beginning of social organisation, social knowledge of exposing, exchanging, storing and controlling information in either ritualised or symbolized (formalised) way was needed, therefore developed and used, in particular information that is closely related to production, distribution and exchange of goods and organisation of labour. This is assumed as one of the origins of mathematics: early concepts of number and number operations, concepts of time and space, have been invented as means for governance and administration in response to social needs. Control of these social practices and the transmission of the necessary knowledge to the responsible agents were often secured by direct participation in social activities and direct oral communication among the members. Ritualised procedures of storing and using information have been developed since Neolithic revolution, during the transition to agriculture and permanent living sites, which e.g. demanded planning the cycles of the year.

The urban revolution and the existence of stratified societies with a strong division of labour induced symbolical storage and control of social practices by information systems based on mathematics, which were bound to domain-specific systems of symbols with conventional meaning. The earliest documents available are the clay tablets from Mesopotamia (Uruk 3000 BC), in which mathematics appears as necessary and useful tool for solving problems of agriculture and economic administration – "bookkeeping" of production and distribution of goods in a highly hierarchically structured slavery based society (Nissen et al. 1990, Høyrup & Damerow 2001). We witness mathematics of that time employed as a technique and a useful and necessary tool. The scribe, who disposed of the appropriate knowledge to handle this tool, became an important man. More generally speaking, the governing class or group disposed of mathematics as an additional instrument of securing and extending its political power and authority.

A new, and eventually most consequential perspective of mathematics emerged in Ancient Greece: Mathematics (more correctly: geometry) as a theoretical system, as a philosophy, as the queen of sciences, and a universal divine mental force for mankind. Greek societies were differentiated into two classes with two distinct social practices: the Non-Greeks or slaves for all practical and technical manual labour necessary for the maintenance and practical life of the society, and the Greek citizens for warfare, physical sport activities as leisure and spiritual activities in politics, philosophy, rhetoric and the other of the seven "liberal arts", mathematics among them. For the Greek therefore mathematics was detached from the needs of managing ordinary daily life as from the necessity of gaining their living. Instead, by scientific search for fundamental, clearly hierarchically ordered bases, creating connections and elements of a systemic characterisation of existing formal mathematical problem solving techniques and devices, independent of any specific practical intention, they reformulated mathematics as a scientific system and philosophy, a (Platonic) ideal theory to be further discovered and constructed by human theoretical thinking and reasoning, not by doing or solving practical problems. This distinction between mathematics as the queen, as a science of formal systems by introducing a structure and defining mathematical thinking as logical reasoning from axioms to concepts and theorems to proofs, in opposition to a view of mathematics as a simple technique or problem solving tool, which is only and simply used: mathematics as the servant, is ascribed to Greek scholars (Snell, 1948). Being able to think mathematically was a sign of those who had political power. By viewing mathematics as the structure underlying the construction of the cosmos and number as the basis of the universe and emphasizing a hermetical character of the mathematical community, the ground was laid for the high esteem of mathematics as a segregation means of political and social power by the Christian church in the middle ages.

1.2. Mathematics as a Human Force for General Scientific and Social Development

Over the centuries, the traces of structuring the world by human rational activity became more numerous, appropriate dealing with it, more imposing. There were several fields in which the mathematisation of the real world and of social life advanced more remarkably, among these notably architecture, military development in both, fortification and armament, mining industry, milling and water-regulation, surveying, and before all, manufacturing and trade. The extension of trade from local business to far distances exchange prompted the emergence of banking, and for the functioning of this an unambiguous form of clear and universal regulation was needed: the system of book-keeping was invented. This was the first consistent, comprehensive mathematical structuring of a whole field of a social practice. (Damerow et al. 1974)

All these endeavours culminated in the period of the European Renaissance with a unique confluence of a wide range of contributions: inventions, discoveries, and human genius. The rediscovery of Greek culture incited a revolutionary change of perceptions and their secularisation, the idea of man as an autonomous individual, and a merging of all of his various capacities and powers in this one notion of the individual genius. A prototype of this new man is Leonardo da Vinci, painter, architect, mathematician, engineer, inventor, scientist, writer, cartographer etc. A key-achievement in renaissance mathematics is linear perspective, and interestingly, it is in this point that renaissance mathematics and art converge. It is not surprising if we identify Leonardo's activity in both, art and mathematics, as visual research. Mathematics as the queen and the servant of sciences, as a practical and theoretical tool, as artful theory and general philosophy and a base for the development of technology and natural sciences, with a worldview to "discover the world" to the benefit of all citizens and "to tame or dominate nature".

1.3. Mathematics as Rationality and Common Sense

By the development of universities, (mathematical) knowledge emancipated from clerical purposes. Renaissance interest in antique culture also contributed to rediscover and re-edit classical texts and old knowledge, and book printing made them available to a wider public. The technology of unlimited reproducibility of knowledge by the revolution of media development by book printing machines – a revolution like the more recent one by modern radio- and television broadcasting and ICT - enabled and demanded to decide about standards and canonical representations of knowledge. The sciences emancipated from religious and philosophical restrictions, as mathematics from religious and philosophical bonds. The abundance of knowledge became itself a subject of analytical reflection and of new philosophical approaches.

The idea of the "rational man" developed: When inventing algebra as the general method for mathematics and rational thinking, Descartes believed that mathematics itself could become so 'easy' or easily understandable, accessible and acceptable by all people that it could be considered as part of "common sense", "le bon sens pour tout le monde". Leibniz, one of the inventors of calculus, shared this perspective of the rational mankind: In evaluating the discovery of calculus, he believed that rational discourse and strict mathematical reasoning had become unlimited and would solve all social and political problems in the world. His call "Calculemus (let us compute!)" encouraged those engaged in a dispute to turn it into computing, and stated that whenever and wherever a dispute arose, calculation should solve it, and finally save the whole world from controversies, from hostile actions and even from war! The application of a mathematical, rational argumentation and calculation was considered as the universal remedy for any personal or social problem, as it solved problems in a way understandable and acceptable for everybody and accessible for rational proceeding. Mathematics and thinking mathematically was considered as the fundament of a 'sane' mind building, as a general reasoning competency, the facilitator and creator of rationality and the rational mankind.

At the same time, mathematics had become more and more a necessary tool for the development of scientific knowledge and craft knowledge, the professional knowledge for practitioners. The increasing importance of trade and commerce demanded extensive computation skills in trade, commercial and banking companies, but also in manufactures, and quality control of production and distribution necessitated new mathematical tools. The availability of Arab-Indian mathematics and their connotation system allowed for written computation with ciphers, decimal fractions, and formal solutions for practical problems of craft, trade and commerce in terms of calculation rules, and appropriate schooling was demanded and propagated. Computation schools served as a secular complement and a necessary element in various kinds of vocational or professional training in practical mathematics.

2. SOCIAL NEEDS FOR MATHEMATICS EDUCATION

2.1 Professionalisation and Specialisation of Knowledge

The achievements of the 15th to 18th century entailed an explosion of trades, crafts, manufacturing and industrial activities with an impressive diversity, ingenuity, and craftsmanship (mostly mechanical) developed and required in numerous professions. The ability of a greater part of the population to appropriately dealing with fundamental systems of symbols like writing and calculating became a condition for the functioning of societies: Elementary (mathematics) education and training was established as reaction to social demands and needs, either prior or during vocational training and various professional practices. Parallel to upcoming educational institutions and in concert with them, mass production for unlimited reproduction of knowledge enabled and asked for standardisation and canonical bodies and representations of knowledge. A reflection and restructuring of existing knowledge on a higher level was demanded: Meta-knowledge had to be developed that offered standards of knowledge and their canonical representations for educational purposes; at the same time meta-knowledge as orienting knowledge became an immanent condition for developing new systems of knowledge, in particular for sciences like mathematics that were perceived to a greater part as independent of immediate practical purposes.

In the 19th century, the competition between the bigger European states, inspired by a strong and fateful ideology of national superiority and ambition, drew attention to "knowledge as power", making public education a central interest of governments. Industrialisation was accompanied by an increasing autonomy of systems of scientific and practical knowledge. To be a mathematician, somebody who does mathematics and nothing else, emerged as a new profession. Mathematics was conceived as an autonomous subject domain, without immediate practical use in other domains, and mathematicians worked as scholars at university or as high-level school teachers.

As in sciences, specialisation and professionalisation of experts were requirements in all branches of economy, as in social services and administration. Constructing and creating new knowledge became a precondition for the material reproduction of society, not a consequence. Specialisation was a condition for creating new knowledge, but at the same time bore the risk of disintegrating more comprising systems of knowledge and making integration in a wider context difficult. Partial knowledge must be generalised and incorporated on a level of meta-knowledge.

2.2 (Mathematics) Education as A Public Task

In the 19th century in many countries, public and state controlled two partite school systems were created: higher education as mind forming for an elite, elementary education to transmit skills and working behaviour for the majority, the future working class.

Humboldt's notion of "Bildung" comprised learning as universal as ever possible with strong emphasise on humanities: Philosophy, history, literature, art, music, but also with an emphasis on mathematics and sciences. The ideal was the completely cultivated, best educated human being, and "Bildung" was not a process ending at the end of one's studies, but just the base laid in the youth to be enlarged and enriched during the whole life, "Bildung" as an attitude and a path as much as an accomplishment. And that was to be conveyed by means of a public education, at special secondary schools and at universities. Mathematics became subject in higher education institution for the elite and governing class because of its formal educational qualities, e.g. educating the mind independent of a direct utilitarian perspective, and fostering general attitudes to support the scientific and science-driven technological development.

In the elementary or general school for workers and farmers, only arithmetic teaching in a utilitarian sense was offered: to secure the necessary skills for the labour force, to secure acceptance of formal rules and formal procedures set up by others. Mathematics education for the few was strictly separated from the skill training for the majority, this corresponded to a separation of mathematics education as an art and science in contrast to mathematics education as a technique, scientific knowledge and conceptual thinking versus technical, algorithmic, machine-like acting.

2.3. Mathematics Education For All

In the 19th and 20th century, mathematics became the driving force for almost all scientific and technological developments: mathematical and scientific models and their transformation into technology had large impact not only on natural and social sciences and economics but also on all activities in the social, professional and daily life. This impact increased rapidly by the development of the new information and communication technologies (ICT) based on mathematics, which radically changed the social organisation of labour and our perceptions of knowledge or technique to an extent that is not yet fully explored.

On the one side, mathematics as a human activity in a social environment is determined by social structures, hence it is not interest-free or politically neutral. On the other side, the continuous application of mathematical models, viewed as universal problem solving procedures, provide not only descriptions and predictions of social actions, but also prescriptions: The increasing social use of mathematics makes mathematical methods and ways of argumentation to quasi-natural social rules and constraints, and creates a mathematised social order effective in social organisations, hierarchical institutions like bureaucracy, administration, management of production and distribution, institutions of law and military etc. Social and political decisions are turned into facts, constraints or prescriptions that individual and collective human behaviour have to follow.

New perspectives of the social role of (mathematical) knowledge and general education were developed that partly gained political acceptance and support: "Mathematics education for All" and "Mathematical Literacy". The concepts were differently substantiated and received different interpretations and supporters: The New Math movement had started to introduce mathematics for all by a formally unified, universally applicable body of theoretical knowledge of modern mathematics exposed to all, but had to be revisited and discarded as a solution. Intensive work in curriculum development created a wide range of different and more and more comprehensive approaches combining new research results in related disciplines like psychology, sociology, and education and developed this vision further (Howson, Keitel, Kilpatrick 1981, Sierpinska & Kilpatrick 1998). A variety of conceptions promised to describe the socially necessary knowledge in a more substantiated form and to integrate scientific mathematical practices and common vocational or professional practices and their craft knowledge, or conceptual and procedural knowledge, or mathematical modelling and application.

However, the most radical development within and outside of mathematics as a discipline was caused by ICT, by the invention of electronic media and the new possibility of data-processing. The immediate consequence, based on the integration of human-mental and sensory-information processing techniques within machines, is the creation of technologies which take over human information processes and independently determine social organisation. This new development is called globalisation of knowledge: the technological integration of new representation forms and the distribution of knowledge in a global net of knowledge represent the greatest challenge for a restructuring of political power and decision making processes about the way, in which information is gained and used, available to anybody everywhere with access to the internet.

Information and communication technologies are the fundament for communication which is an essential aspect of globalisation: access to and exchange of information and knowledge from anywhere in the world, quickly and cheaply. On the one hand, that leads to a general acknowledgement of cultural diversity, but on the other hand also to universalisation and domination by certain languages and cultural positions - e.g. the English language and Euro-American or Western belief systems, encompassing a variety of knowledge traditions and knowledge systems.

2.4.Changing Mathematical Sciences and its Applications by Information Technologies

The social role and impact of mathematics has dramatically changed by the development of modern information technologies based on mathematics. Mathematics is ascribed a new utility value, which has never before been so strongly indubitable as it is now. Illustrating examples for new technological and most effective applications of mathematical methods are numerous, e.g.: Computer-based simulations are applied in most different areas like modelling of climate changes, crash tests, chemical reaction kinetics by building process-oriented technical machines, dynamical system models in macroeconomics and biology. Software packages allow the most complex calculation processes for many applications in forms of black boxes, like statistical processes in quality control, research on market and products, risk theories for portefeuille-management in assurance companies, computer based algebra systems and software for modelling in sciences and engineering. Mathematics as the basis of many technologies is effective although only invisibly, i.e. as theoretical base of formal language in informatics, as fundament of coding algorithms for industrial robots or in the daily used scanners, mobile phones, cash corners or electronic cashiers. New technologies in return have feedback with great impact on mathematics as a discipline itself. Besides traditional applied mathematics new directions combined applied sciences with experimental procedures like techno-mathematics, industrial mathematics, theory of algorithms.

New procedures in some application areas are celebrated not only as new means to ends or a refined methodological repertoire, but furthermore as a new paradigm: In contrast to classical applied mathematics, which was oriented towards and restricted to the representation of mathematical structures of a reality existing completely independent of any subjective intention, new forms of applications do not hide the fact that interests and intentions always guide the construction of a model, as well as specific goals and convictions. The theoretical poverty of such models is interpreted as advantage, as no comprehensive theories of the object have to be presupposed, by some the new paradigm is celebrated as humanisation of modelling and mathematics.

Mathematics and information technology not only provide descriptions and explanations of existing reality, but they also create new reality: As a basis of social technologies like arithmetical models for election modes, taxation models, calculation of interests and investment, calculation of costs and pensions etc., mathematical models are transformed into reality, establish and institutionalise a new kind of reality. This process can be reconstructed and analysed as the development of implicit mathematics: Patterns of social acting and formal structures are transformed via formal languages into algorithms or mathematical models which can be rectified and objectified as social technologies (Davis & Hersh 1986, Davis 1989, Keitel, Kotzmann, Skovsmose 1993).

In models of macro-economy, translations of an ideology into mathematical concepts can be identified, which by enrichment with subtle economical terminology and by internal consistency of the mathematical representation suggest not only progress, but existence as a natural law. In such a way, mathematisations also can be established as unconscious cultural forms and rites and as a kind of language that create a milieu for thoughts, which further creates unquestioned constraints and restrictions of consciousness (Keitel, Kotzmann & Skovsmose 1993).

Such results of applications of mathematics are often encountered in communication situations mainly shaped by conflicting interests where they serve to justify opinions and to stabilise attitudes. Graphical representations of information e.g. are excellently structured, provide sufficient overview and relative universality of readability, but are also appropriate means for accentuation guiding the perception into wrong directions. In such communication processes the possibilities for interaction between interpreters are usually restricted. Even neglecting the fact that credibility is often depending on the prestige of the participants, the prestige of mathematics as such often serves to suggest objectivity and objective goals and intentions. Thus the regulation and democratic control of actual and future research, development and application processes of mathematics and mathematics education demand a specific competence and knowledge as a basis of decision making on the side of the politicians and new knowledge for evaluation and democratic control on the side of the citizens.

2.5. Mathematical Literacy for Critical Citizenship

The pervasiveness of economic thinking and interests have successively created so high a pressure of economic orientation that educational aims and the subject matter are marginalized unless they prove justification in terms of economic interest (Woodrow, 2003). New notions like "Mathematical Proficiency, or Competency or Literacy", "Educational Standards" and "Benchmarks" are expressions of such economic interests. They are a major concern of politicians but also a pressure for educational researchers and practitioners. They are the key issues in the recent political debates and disputes about mathematics education, which broadened after the release of international comparative studies like TIMSS and PISA and their ranking of test results. Proclaiming that the PISA tests are based on "definitions of mathematical literacy" that are underpinned by fundamental and widely accepted educational research results, and that it is absolutely unproblematic to test such kind of competencies or proficiencies on a global scale to rank countries' performances, produced strange and urgent political measures to be taken in some of the countries that did not perform well, called for by the alarmed public and the medias. Results of tests like PISA are used as reference and base for decisions in educational policy, in particular in cases when they show that only a small part of the tested students or adults have reached a higher level of competencies in the international comparison.

The Programme for International Student Assessment (PISA) claims for its test of Mathematical Literacy, that those competencies of young adolescents are measured, which enable them to participate in democratic decision-making processes:

- „Mathematical Literacy is the capacity to identify, to understand and to engage in mathematics and make well-founded judgements about the role that mathematics plays, as needed for an individual's current and future life, occupational life, social life with peers and relatives, and life as a constructive, concerned and reflective citizen" (OECD 2000, 50)

As this definition clearly demonstrates, each attempt to define Mathematical Literacy is confronted with the problem that this can not be done exclusively in terms of mathematical knowledge: To understand mathematised contexts or mathematical applications and to competently use mathematics in contexts goes beyond mathematical knowledge. An early and first research study to explore such cross-curricular competencies by investigating the ways how mathematics is used in a social–political practice had unexpected and surprising results (Damerow et al. 1974).

Conflicting conceptions of Mathematical Literacy are numerous, although not always the conflict is recognised: Jablonka (Jablonka 2003) analysed what research on Mathematical Literacy can and cannot do. She investigated different perspectives on Mathematical Literacy and showed that these perspectives always considerably vary with the values and rationales of the stakeholders who promote them. The central argument underlying each of her investigations is that it is not possible to promote a conception of Mathematical Literacy without at the same time – implicitly or explicitly – promoting a particular social practice of mathematics: be it the practice of mathematicians, of scientists, of economists, of professional practices outside science and mathematics etc. She argues that Mathematical Literacy focussing on citizenship in particular refers to the possibility or need of critically evaluating most important issues of the surrounding society or culture of the students – a society and culture that are very much shaped by practices involving mathematics. In her conclusion, she emphasises that the ability to understand and to evaluate different practices of mathematics and the values behind has to be a component of Mathematical Literacy.

Mathematical Literacy must be understood as functional in relation to pedagogical postulates. But by reducing the concept of Mathematical Literacy to the descriptions of the process of its measurement cannot be justified, while conclusions of these comparisons mostly are formulated in terms of daily language or connected with highly demanding and complex meanings and connotations of the concepts.

The demands and threats of Knowledge Society are referred to in most political declarations and justifications for educational policy. From an international or global point of view, this includes to investigate what approaches towards knowledge perceptions are taken in different countries, at the levels of policy and of practice; what are the most important knowledge conflicts at various social levels, and in particular in the educational systems, e.g. clashes between students' personal knowledge and the knowledge presented by teachers, between knowledge systems, between 'modern/popular' cultures and traditional cultures, between teachers' and students' views (Clarke, Keitel& Shimizu 2006); and on the more general level, e.g. how are global technologies – especially the World-Wide-Web, television and print media – used to promote or diminish diversity, or what effects of inequality are reproduced.

The question how mathematics is perceived and used in political debates and decision-making processes, in particular in decisions that concern mathematics education, is a necessary complement to be studied. We have started case studies to investigate which connections are established between results of comparative studies on mathematical competencies and the attributions of causes and effects deduced from them in the public debate. We collect and analyse which criteria for political decisions and forms of decision-making processes are defined and stated, which kind of controlling mechanisms to secure quality is foreseen or used and on what the credibility of results is based, in particular in the media. We try to reconstruct the origin and history of such studies and confront criteria and decisions for selecting the participating institutions and experts, contrast the official publications of national and international projects and the reconstruction of views and conceptions held by participating experts in interviews. The history of the social reception of these studies is to be interpreted in the light of conflicts of interests and different interest groups. An analysis of published statements of all stakeholders in political decision-making processes and of representatives of interest groups in industry and economy has been started, complemented by interviews with teachers, mathematicians and experts in the ICT-area (Burton 2003). The interpretations of these statements in the light of the factual political interests are re-analysed on the base of the historical accounts of mathematics as means of social power and of the actual account of modern mathematics as a scientific discipline and technology provider. This adds hopefully to a broader and more substantially defined conception of becoming mathematically literate, and to a debate about what and how much mathematics is needed to educate or create well informed and critical citizens for a democratic society.

4. REFERENCES

Burton, L. (2003). *Mathematicians as enquirers. Learning about learning mathematics.* Dordrecht: Kluwer.

Clarke, D., Keitel, C. & Shimizu, Y. (Eds.) (2006). *Mathematics classrooms in 12 countries: The insiders' perspectives.* Rotterdam: Sense Publishers.

Damerow, P., Elwitz, U., Keitel, C., Zimmer, J. (1974). *Elementarmathematik: Lernen für die Praxis? Ein exemplarischer Versuch der Bestimmung fachübergreifender Curriculumziele (Elementary mathematics: Learning for practice? An exemplary attempt to determine cross-curricular goals in mathematics).* Stuttgart: Klett.

Damerow, P., Lefévre, W. (Eds.) (1981). *Rechenstein, Experiment, Sprache. Historische Fallstudien zur Entstehung der exakten Wissenschaften.* Stuttgart: Klett-Cotta.

Davis, P. (1989) Applied mathematics as social contract. In: C. Keitel et. al. (Eds.) *Mathematics, education and society,* Unesco Document Series No. 35, Paris: Unesco, 24-28 .

Davis, P. J. & Hersh, R. (1986). *Descartes' dream.* San Diego: Harcourt.

Ernest, P. (1999). Forms of knowledge in mathematics and mathematics education: Philosophical and rhetorical perspectives. *Educational Studies in Mathematics, 38* (1-3), 67-83.

Gellert, U.; Jablonka, E.; Keitel, C. (2001). Mathematical literacy and common sense in mathematics education. In: B. Atweh et al. (Eds.) *Sociocultural aspects of mathematics education,* New York: Lawrence Erlbaum, 57-73.

Howson, G.A., Keitel, C., Kilpatrick, J. (1981). *Curriculum development in mathematics.* Cambridge: Cambridge University Press

Høyrup, J. & Damerow, P. (Eds.) (2001). *Changing views on ancient near Eastern mathematics.* Berlin: Reimer.

Jablonka, E. (2003). Mathematical literacy. In: Bishop, A., Clements, K., Keitel, C., Kilpatrick, J., Leung, F. (Eds.). *Second international handbook of mathematics education.* Dordrecht: Kluwer, 77-104.

Keitel, C., Kotzmann, E., and Skovsmose, O. (1993). Beyond the tunnel vision: Analysing the relationship between mathematics education, society and technology. In C. Keitel & K. Ruthven (Eds.), *Learning from computers: Mathematics education and technology* . Berlin: Springer, 242-279.

Kline, M. (1985). *Mathematics and the search for knowledge.* Oxford: Oxford University Press.

LPS (2006). http://www.edfac.unimelb.edu.au/DSME/lps/ (Learners' Perspectives Study) (last update February 2006)

Nissen, H., Damerow, P., Englund, R. K. (1990). *Frühe Schrift und Techniken der Wirtschaftsverwaltung im Vorderen Orient: Informationsspeicherung und -verarbeitung vor 5000 Jahren* [Early writing and technologies of the management and administration of economics in the Near East: Information storing and processing 5000 years ago]. Bad Salzdetfurth, Germany: Franzbecker.

OECD (Eds.) (2000). *Programme for international student assessment* (PISA). Paris: OECD.

Renn, J. (2002). *Wissenschaft als Lebensorientierung – eine Erfolgsgeschichte?* Preprint 224, Berlin: Max-Planck-Institut für Wissenschaftsgeschichte.

Sierpinska, A.& Kilpatrick, J. (1998) (Eds.). *Mathematics education as a research domain: A search for identity.* Dordrecht: Kluwer

Snell, B. (1948). *Die Entdeckung des Geistes bei den Griechen.* Hamburg: Claasen & Goverts.

Woodrow, D. (2003). Mathematics, mathematics education and economic conditions. In: Bishop, A., Clements, K., Keitel, C., Kilpatrick, J., Leung, F. (Eds.). *Second international handbook of mathematics education.* Dordrecht: Kluwer, 11-32.

Christine Keitel
Freie Universität Berlin, Germany

ROLAND FISCHER

MATERIALIZATION AND ORGANIZATION:

Towards a Cultural Anthropology of Mathematics

Abstract: *This summary of six articles which have been written in the past fifteen years focus on the question of the social relevance of mathematics on a principal level. The main theses are: Mathematics provides materializations of abstract issues, thereby it supports mass communication. The principles of mathematics are basic for our social organization. The limits of mathematics are limits of organization. But they can be overcome by emphasizing the reflexive potential of mathematics*

This is a summary of six articles which I have written in the past fifteen years. These articles have been collected in the book "Materialisierung und Organisation. Zur kulturellen Bedeutung von Mathematik" (Fischer 2006).

INTRODUCTION

There is a difference between the meaning of mathematics for somebody who does mathematics actively (may he be a calculating pupil in elementary school, a secondary student solving a problem in algebra or a mathematical researcher) and the meaning for somebody who is affected passively by mathematics, its applications, its power of regulation and order. I will deal with the second kind of meaning.

Another important difference concerns the contribution of mathematics to our culture. I make a difference between the contribution to the implicit culture, that means to our norms, value systems, patterns of organization, especially to civilization and regulation of modern societies, and the contribution to our explicit culture, which is processed in the consciousness of people, about which we speak, negotiate and make decisions according to important / unimportant.

Firstly I will speak about the implicit culture, which need not be unconscious, but which is in a certain sense a prerequisite for our daily life (also professional and political lives). Later on I will come to the role of mathematics in our explicit culture.

J. Maasz, W. Schloeglmann (Eds.), New Mathematics Education Research and Practice, 23–32.

MATERIALIZATION OF THE ABSTRACT

The first thesis is, that mathematics is important, because it is materialization of abstract issues, namely those not directly perceivable by the senses. In addition to pure thinking, mathematics provides systems of signs, which eventually are materially fixed and by which abstract issues can be represented and manipulated. These sign-systems begin with calculation stones, with marks for numerating, digits, algebraic notation, graphs of functions, graphs with vertices and edges, flow charts and end with the fixing of abstracts in electronic computers. The laws of physics, starting with the fact that stones do not increase by themselves and ending with the laws of quantum physics, are used for an "outhousing" of thinking – mathematics as applied non-living nature, in a certain sense. The represented abstract issues are numbers, relations, structures, probabilities etc. Behind all these concepts there stands a view of the world, according to which abstract issues are important, especially relations and processes, perhaps more important than those "substances", to which the abstracts are related. This world view is expressed in the Pythagorean dictum "All is Number" and its modern pendant "All is Structure".

The claim to the importance of materializing for mathematics itself is not new, recently it is considered in an intensive discussion about the semiotic character of mathematics, partially following the philosophy of Charles S. Peirce (see OTTE 1994, pp. 382, 383). For this discussion the doing of mathematicians is the starting point. Therefore one has to add that materializations are especially mathematical (in difference to pictures or schematic representations) if they are accompanied by a system of rules for manipulating the materializations. The actions of an active mathematician – again from a calculating elementary student up to a mathematician doing research – is an interplay of representing and operating (with the representations), with more or less creative steps. The point is that it is not necessary to be creative all the time, not even thinking, but it is possible to rely on the rule system. It can also be shown by examples that the prevailing systems of notation – i. e. forms of materializing – have an influence on the kind of theories within even pure mathematics.

THE BENEFIT OF MATERIALIZING

Materializing makes the abstract concrete and thereby perceivable by senses. Thereby it facilitates the process of abstraction and gives reality to the abstracts. In practical life this fact is important, if decisions are to be made. Decisions are, if they are not clear a priori but require deliberation of various arguments, facilitated by abstraction. One formulates abstract principles and criteria, one classifies the concrete issue with respect to an abstract pattern, one possibly evaluates single factors by assigning points and then makes thereby the decision. In this process it is important to forget. One cannot bear in mind all the pros and cons, one has to put aside some aspects of the issue, one has to concentrate on those relevant from the abstract point of view, in order to come to a decision. Material representations facilitate this process. If, in addition, the material representations allow for manipulations and transformations, which generate condensation (if, for example, a mean value is calculated) or directly show the best alternative (in, for example, an optimization problem), the decision process is additionally supported. Of course there exists a back side of the coin: Important aspects can be forgotten, a questionable force of circumstances can be constructed.

What has been said about the importance of materializing so far can be understood as follows: the single human, the individual, is supported in his/her thinking, abstracting and decision making. But materializing the abstract and mathematics become still more important, if social systems or whole societies are under consideration. Firstly abstract issues are of eminent importance for social systems, in which face-to-face-communication is not possible because of their size. Self-description and self-perception of such systems and their ability to act require the development of appropriate abstracts such as the number of people in various subsystems, environmental conditions, consumption of energy, welfare, etc. Gross domestic product, tax- and pension fund systems are materialized abstracts, which cause discussions, decisions and payments. The problems of these reductions are well known, nevertheless modern societies cannot live without them. But even before this the processing of such systems, that means the performing of the interactions between the members of the system, makes certain abstracts necessary, for example money as the materialized potential to get goods or services.

The materialization of these abstracts is important, because thereby they gain that status of existence, which makes them able to be content of communication among many people. Materializing has the function to give existence to the abstracts by borrowing existence from matter – that entity about we have the highest common security of existence. It helps to establish communicative stability, materializing thereby contributes that people have the impression to know what they are talking about. In this specific sense mathematics is an important medium of mass communication.

SYSTEMICITY

Besides materialization there is another aspect of mathematics which is essential for its societal importance. For mathematics is not only an offer of material "tools" and certain transformation rules, it moreover offers a system of concepts, theories, theorems, proofs etc. – partially in form of the transformation rules, but going widely beyond. Even if one, with respect to social relevance, emphasizes the material forms of representation the fact that there exists a system of connections with the claim to totality is significant. Certainly this "total connections" have not been worked out explicitly in all details – mathematical research is working and there is no end in sight – but there are intensive efforts of mathematicians to establish these total connections. Compared with other disciplines in mathematics the striving for connections is rather strong, though there are also strong tendencies to specialization. Additionally there occur permanently enlargements of the system by inventing new subjects, concepts and forms of representation.

One principle to be regarded in this system of total connection is the avoidance of contradictions. Certainly it cannot be guaranteed but it has absolute priority in case of a concrete contradiction. The elimination of contradictions is always possible in mathematics, since mathematics is not obliged to a fixed range of objects outside of it – e. g. nature – that means that one can avoid the contradiction by canceling parts of the content.

What is the relevance of the "systemicity" of mathematics for the society? Besides materialization, the contradiction-free systemic network is a second factor of security. As far as the society tends to consensual synthesis – what of course does not include all aspects of society – mathematics as an intentionally contradiction-free system offers a basis for a minimal consensus.

A further property of mathematics as a system is its beauty, expressed for instance by minimality of descriptions. Maybe the beauty is at the present only accessible by those who do mathematics on a higher level. But, as I think, there is the potential to gain societal relevance also from this aspect of mathematics. Aesthetic appeal is a necessary prerequisite for perceivability. Abstract issues, especially those which arise from complex phenomena, need form in order to be perceived, especially if they shall be perceived not only by individuals but by collectives. This is a category which we seldom take into consideration when social systems are designed; today democratic negotiations of interests dominate. The law system, for example, could be improved if aesthetic categories would be applied, with the benefit of more collective perceivability and thereby of more legal security. One should try out whether mathematics or mathematicians, for whom beauty is important, can contribute.

MEANS AND SYSTEM

At the end of my deliberations about the contribution of mathematics to our implicit culture I point to a duality, which describes the impact of mathematics onto our society: Mathematics is a means which we can use, and simultaneously it is a system, to which we are subject. I now use the term "system" in a slightly different sense than before, when I wrote about the "systemicity", meaning the fact that mathematics is a coherent building of thoughts. Now I mean by "system" the socially implemented system of norms, principles, conventions of representations, rules of decision and forms of organizing, which have to do with mathematics and have become indispensable for modern life. This system comes to expression by the fact, that numbers play an important role, that measuring and calculating occur in many fields, but also in the fact that logical reasoning, formalizing, the generating of rule-oriented and/or hierarchical structures are of high importance in our life. By this importance also those people are affected, who are not dealing with mathematics, they are subject to the system.

In modern societies people are socialized in a way such they submit themselves voluntarily: They pay the bills, they fill out questionnaires, they accept decisions based on statistic data, they trust in the computer. Especially the rise of the computer would not have been possible if mathematics would not on the one hand have provided means for development of technologies and on the other hand have had an impact towards a disciplined society with competence in formal thinking.

What is means and what is system in ambiguous in special cases: The index of prices is a means of description of parts of the economy, simultaneously it is part of the system, if it is used as a parameter within contracts, for example. More precisely: There is a circularity. Permanently new means are developed, especially to handle the complex system, and exactly these means can become parts of the system, thereby increasing its complexity. The interplay of developing instruments of description for economical processes and the implementation of these instruments in legal regulations is an example. In the field of finance markets it is not even necessary to implement into a rule system, it suffices that all, or at least the most important, participants suppose that the others use the mathematical instruments of analysis.

VALUE OF MEANING AND VALUE OF USING

Now I come to the contribution of mathematics to our explicit culture, for the first with a negative diagnosis: The complaint of friends of mathematics about the minor role of mathematical (and in general scientific) contents in our understanding of good education, compared with contents of literature and history, which often can be heard, is legitimate. One has to know the story of Hamlet, the main theorem of calculus can be forgotten after school, if one has it perceived as such actually. But, and now it comes still worse: the complaint is not legitimate in that sense, as it complaints about a fact, behind which these stands a certain reasonableness. What do I mean? Functioning renders discussion superfluous. Mathematical procedures are functioning without to be understood. One can use them – from a simple division-algorithm up to a sophisticated mathematical software – if one correctly handles the "user interface". The reliability of mathematics, based on objective validity, combined with the outhousing by more or less comprehensive materializations, makes possible a division of labor between the creators and the users. This kind of division of labor is not possible in other fields of cultural creation, especially in the humanities. Because of this division of labor it is not necessary to become acquainted with the contents of mathematics as it is with contents of literature, history etc., and can nevertheless get benefits from them.

Further because of the fact that mathematics avoids contradictions and controversies it offers only a small potential for conflicts as motivation for discussion. A cultural asset, which stands as an objective, unassailable block of knowledge, is not interesting. It is clear that for the active mathematician the case is otherwise. It is difficult to get both: acknowledgement for reliable results and discussion about them.

These deliberations are supported by more general considerations in the sociology of knowledge. The German sociologist F. H. TENBRUCK (1975) makes a difference between the value of meaning and the value of using of a discipline, where by "meaning" he means something independent of instrumental using, namely the power to give sense and orientation to humans and the society. He states a "law of trivialization" according to which in the progression of any discipline its value of meaning decreases, though the value of using may increase. TENBRUCK gives evidence to his thesis by considering the development of modern natural science, which, in his presentation, had a high value of meaning in the 18th and 19th century, which step by step decreased. For mathematics the situation is a bit more complicated, but in principle the smallness of the contribution of mathematics to our explicit culture can be understood in these terms.

MEANING OF USING

What I have said so far gives no pleasure to all who would like to see a larger contribution of mathematics to our explicit culture. But one can develop a more optimistic perspective and this is the focus of the rest of the paper. The basic idea is the following: For any discipline with a high value of using a new meaning in the sense of TENBRUCK can be made accessible, if humans refer self-reflexively to the using. To say it otherwise: If mathematics is relevant for our lives, as a system of representations and procedures, as patterns of thinking, as scheme of organization, then we can learn about ourselves by studying mathematics, especially about our social lives. Mathematics as a mirror of mankind in a certain sense.

The central questions of reflection are of the following kind: What does the using of mathematics tell us about us, our intentions, our pre-decisions? What is our will, maybe unconscious, when we use mathematics in a certain way? The aim is self-recognition with the opportunity of new options of action.

Some examples how these very principal questions can be put into more concrete terms:
- What means *measuring* – what do we gain, what do we loose by it?
- What are the opportunities, what the limits of *(algebraic) formalisms*?
- What are benefits and the costs of *reifying visualizations*?
- What means *linearization*?
- What is the benefit of *statistics*, what are the limits?

Partially these questions are dealt with in special disciplines (of mathematics or philosophy), but usually not with that principal openness, which would be necessary in order that the discussion could become part of our explicit culture. For this purpose the questions must be transformed into thesis and anti-thesis which can be understood by educated laymen. I think that this should be possible; it should be a task of schools to introduce into this kind of discussion – its most important task at the upper level.

RULE-ORIENTED SOCIAL SYSTEMS

More fundamentally than in the above mentioned examples of reflective questions one can learn from analogies connecting the mathematical way of thinking and social organization. For me papers and lectures of the Viennese philosopher G.

SCHWARZ (1985) were and are an interesting source of ideas. He established an analogy between Aristotelian logic as a system of thinking and hierarchy as a system of social organization. I extended this analogy by letting mathematics correspond to a type of organization which I would call rule-oriented. The paradigmatic example for this type is bureaucracy; but also the market (in economical sense), large parts of the organization of a modern state and increasingly international networks are rule-oriented systems. All these systems have in common that they are largely governed by rules, maybe even kept together by rules. This is accompanied by the fact that frequently well-defined procedures play an important role and that – partially in order to avoid arbitrariness – the issues are de-personalized and objectivized. Thereby a separation of rule system and motives is established in a way that the rule system is the invariant, which represents the structural framework for various motives, which are brought in by people. The two characteristics of modern societies, namely to allow for individuality and variety at the one hand and to establish commonality on the other hand are realized in this way.

One specialty of this type of systems is that nobody has to care for the "whole", it suffices that the individuals care for their issues – for instance by maximizing their profit as "homines oeconomici" in a market – and observe the rules. The rest is done by an "invisible hand", of the market, but also of a bureaucracy or of political negotiating. That by organizing in this manner not always best results arise, can be seen by considering thought experiments like prisoner's dilemma. I call systems, in which their wholeness is not collectively reflected, "systems without consciousness".

THE "LOGIC OF FUNCTIONS"

In the following the analogy between mathematics and rule-oriented social systems shall be illustrated by an example. The aim will be, that the limits of both parts – mathematics on the one and rule-oriented social systems on the other hand – should become more obvious.

The example starts with the mathematical concept of function: This concept requires two separate entities: a rule for assigning and the area of objects to which this rule is applied, usually called the domain of the function. These entities have to be separated, especially it is not allowed that the elements of the domain define the rule. Certainly by introducing additional parameters and thereby enlarging the domain, it can seem as if this were possible, for instance:

$$f(x) = x^2 \qquad \text{is enlarged to} \qquad f(x, n) = x^n$$

But such an enlargement will never be exhaustive, always an additional (meta-)rule will be required, which is not defined by the elements of the domain. These are in a certain sense "subject" to the rule.

By this phrasing I have already done one step towards social organization. Rule-oriented social systems are designed in a way, that there is a rule system which is put before the members of the system (corresponding to the elements of the domain). This rule system regulates collaboration, for instance with respect to the production of goods and services, and may not be changed, at least not in the last resort, by the members of the system. At least there must exist an invariant kernel of the rule system which can only be changed by an authority standing outside (or above?) the system.

The such described idea of organization is determining for large parts of thinking and acting in business administration. Especially the question, how to govern organizations, usually is answered on the basis of this idea, even if one thinks to have leaved rigid bureaucratic concepts of organization. The "logic of function", as I call it, seems to be compelling: How else should one be able to govern a system, if not some components of the system are fixed? How else could the identity of a social system be constituted, if not by abstraction from the elements towards an invariant mechanism of processing the system? And should not mathematics earn the merit, that by its way of thinking this abstract invariant can be named and perhaps even represented by appropriate concepts?

IRREFLEXIVITY OF MATHEMATICS

Such we have arrived at a fundamental limit. In the field of designing social organization (the disciplines are called "theory of management" or "organization development") since some decades there exist efforts to invent and try out new, alternative models of governing, which are not based on the "logic of function", on the separation of rule system and motives. One speaks about the "eigen-logic" of a system, about "learning systems", about the competence of self regulation, about "coupling up" and "irritating" instead of governing, about "evolutionary management" etc. The aim is to give "more rights" to the systems, to view it not only as subject to the will of a "governor". Most of these concepts integrate the motives in the rule system and simply cancel the elements as not belonging to the system. My approach is different and ends, as a theoretical problem, up to the question, whether another relation between elements and the whole can be conceived, respectively put into practice, than that which is suggested by mathematics respectively brought to the point by mathematics: The elements are less than the whole, the whole arises only when some structure is implemented, at least the comprehension of some elements. Behind this there is a principle of set theory, namely: elements become a set only by being integrated by somebody else, they cannot do it by themselves. I call this the irreflexivity of mathematics.

Is it really possible to think otherwise? One hint stems to Thomas KUCZYNSKI (1987) who in a lecture in Klagenfurt 1987 pointed to Karl MARX's concept of the individual as the "ensemble of social relations" and to Werner HEISENBERG's idea of elementary particles consisting of the relations with all the other particles in the universe. In both cases the point is a dialectical relationship between elements and the whole, a relationship according to with the element is not subject to the whole but, metaphorically spoken, stands face to face with the whole with equal rights. In a certain sense then, not only the element is contained in the whole, but the whole is also contained in the element. This is a relationship which is not allowed in mathematics.

KEEPING VS. OVERCOMING

On the base of a concept of humans, according to which individuality and sociality are related dialectically, mathematics is inhuman. But one has to add that almost no discipline makes contributions to dialectical organization. So mathematics is not in bad company. Still more: In its fundamental considerations it brings the basic assumptions of the dominant disciplines to the point. Going beyond this defensive diagnosis, I dare to claim still more: If one takes the character of mathematics as a means of reflection for serious, one could expect from it to foster dialectical organization.

I mean this in the following way: One can use descriptions with mathematical means in order to keep the described fix or in order to overcome the described. For instance the organigram of a firm is usually used to fix the structure. On the other hand one uses sociograms, that are representations of the relations in a small group (of humans), as an instrument, by which the described structure is changed, namely simply by confronting the group with its image in the mirror named sociogram.

Transferred to mathematics as a whole this means: By its property as a powerful means of representation, which brings to light structures very precisely and clearly, in some cases by transforming the representation letting consequences come to light, mathematics can contribute to change these very structures; namely by provoking decisions which lead to change. Its "decidedness" and precision serve for sharpening, so the limits of given conditions can become obvious. Just by this potential mathematics can, if it is not used in order to dogmatically legitimate the given, contribute to its overcoming. In my opinion, like no other discipline mathematics has the potential to overcome itself. It thereby can foster a process which I would call consciousness of the society.

REFERENCES

Fischer, R. (2006). *Materialisierung und Organisation. Zur kulturellen Bedeutung von Mathematik*. Vienna/Munich: Profil.

Kuczynski, TH. (1987): Einige Überlegungen zur Entwicklung der Beziehungen zwischen Mathematik und Wirtschaft (unter besonderer Berücksichtigung der Entwicklung in der Wirtschaftsmathematik). In: Dörfler, W., Fischer, R. (1987). *Wirtschaftsmathematik in Beruf und Ausbildung. Vorträge beim 5. Kärntner Symposium für Didaktik der Mathematik*. Vienna: Hölder-Pichler-Tempsky, p. 145-166.

Otte, M. (1994): *Das Formale, das Soziale und das Subjektive. Eine Einführung in die Philosophie und Didaktik der Mathematik*. Frankfurt/Main: Suhrkamp.

Peirce, Ch. S. (1932-1965): *Collected papers*, ed. by Ch. Hartshorne and P. Weiss. Cambridge, Mass.: Harvard Univ. Press.

Schwarz, G. (1985). *Die "Heilige Ordnung" der Männer. Patriarchalische Hierarchie und Gruppendynamik*. Opladen: Westdeutscher Verlag.

Tenbruck, F. H. (1975). Der Fortschritt der Wissenschaften als Trivialisierungsprozeß. In: Stehr, N., König, R. (Eds.). *Wissenschaftssoziologie. Kölner Zeitschrift für Soziologie und Sozialpsychologie*, Sonderheft *18*, p. 14-47.

Roland Fischer
Alpen-Adria Universität Klagenfurt in Wien, Austria

OLE SKOVSMOSE

CHALLENGES FOR MATHEMATICS EDUCATION RESEARCH

Abstract: *A modern conception of science is characterised through the assumptions of progress, neutrality, and epistemic transparency, which also have had an impact on research in mathematics education. I try to clarify what it could mean to operate outside these assumptions.*

As a first step, I consider 'mathematics in action' by addressing technological imagination, hypothetical reasoning, justification, legitimisation, realisation, routinising, authorising and ethical filtration. I emphasise that mathematics-based actions are as complex as any other actions. They do not demonstrate any intrinsic connection to progress; they are far from transparent; and they are in need of ethical reflections.

What does it mean for mathematics education research to position itself outside the assumptions of modernity? In order to address this question, four challenges are presented. They concern: (1) the content in mathematics education, in particular with reference to mathematics in action; (2) the context of mathematics education; (3) the agency in mathematics education, in particular the students; and (4) the agency of the researchers in mathematics education.

Any attempt to address such challenges brings us, however, to the notion of uncertainty, which signifies a condition for research and theorising. Challenging the assumptions of modernity means challenging any new 'certainties', including any that might be expressed in the following.

Within research, labelling is a widely celebrated and, to many, also an enjoyable activity. The labelling by means of which we try to express principal aspects of our future compared to the past, leaving the present somewhere in between, seems to have stimulated a sparkling imagination. What we might be entering has been referred to as late-modernity, post-modernity, liquid modernity, reflexive modernity, risk society, hyper-complex society, network society, informational society, information society, knowledge society, learning society, Mode-2 society. l Our past, however, has been referred to in terms of Modernity.

As will soon be revealed, I also enjoy this game of labelling. I will present characteristics of what I refer to as the 'modern conception of science' in terms of the assumptions of progress, neutrality and epistemic transparency. These assumptions have also had an impact on educational ideas, including research in

J. Maasz, W. Schloeglmann (Eds.), New Mathematics Education Research and Practice, 33–50.
© 2006 Sense Publishers. All rights reserved.

mathematics education. Based on this clarification, I will enter the over-labelled regions of the future.

I discuss 'mathematics in action', which opens the way for an understanding of mathematics that leaves behind the modern conception of science. In this way, I try to open a way of looking at the mathematics-science-technology composite as including knowledge-power bundles. This leads us to consider some challenges for mathematics education research. I find that, to the extent to which research is ready to face these challenges, it steps into a future that is, above all, defined through uncertainties.

1. MODERN CONCEPTION OF SCIENCE

There is no lack of suggestions about how to characterise Modernity. But instead of trying to find my own way among this multitude of suggestions, I will limit myself to condensing three assumptions (or theses) that give profile to the modern conception of science.

The assumption of progress claims that science makes progress, and that this progress serves as the motor of social progress in general.[2] This idea was a defining element of the Enlightenment. The primary metaphor was 'light' (which is repeated in German in Aufklärung, in Portuguese in iluminismo, in Danish in oplysning, etc.). Following the path, illuminated by science, the whole of humanity could be safely guided towards improvements and developments in all aspects of life. The celebration of scientific knowledge as the true foundation of progress also reached education. In Education and Democracy, published in1916, John Dewey explicitly states that 'true' and 'genuine' progress is based on scientific insight. Progress is not any, more or less, random process, but can be ensured by deliberate and careful planning, including planning of 'progressive education'. There are no socio-political complications connected to scientific development. This contains an intrinsic righteousness, as the essence of science is social progress.

Second, I want to characterise the modern conception of science by the assumption of neutrality. This assumption states that science must be separated from any expression of moral convictions, political proprieties, cultural biases, religious beliefs or subjective tastes, and that science must be characterised through its ethical neutrality. This thesis was emphasised most emphatically by logical positivism, which recognises ethics as being similar to metaphysics and, therefore, as having no scientific content.[3] When we consider mathematics, the thesis of neutrality appears well founded. In fact, logical positivism found much inspiration in the formalist interpretation of mathematics, which left no cracks for smuggling any ethical elements into the logic-defined edifice of mathematics. The assumption of neutrality ensures that science should not preoccupy itself with socio-political issues, as such issues, due to the very nature of science, are not part of the scientific enterprise.

Third, I find that the modern conception of science includes an assumption of epistemic transparency. According to this thesis, it is possible to delineate, in simple terms, what knowledge is. Such attempts were found in René Descartes' rationalism and in John Locke's empiricism. Later, logical positivism proposed their transparent characteristic of knowledge.4 Only when one tries to identify specific elements of knowledge – in physics, in sociology, in mathematics, etc. – the researcher faces tremendous difficulties. There are no straightforward routes or techniques to identify particular pieces of knowledge. Nevertheless, it was claimed that an overall characterisation of knowledge could be expressed in a transparent way. In the philosophy of mathematics, the dream of providing a simple definition of mathematical knowledge was attempted through the logicist programme (mathematics is a collection of tautologies) and the formalist programme (mathematics is the science of formal systems), two very elegant exemplifications of epistemic transparency.

Brought together, the assumptions of progress, neutrality and epistemic transparency establish what I refer to as the modern conception of science. Although the thesis of progress and the thesis of neutrality appear to contradict each other, they facilitate different ways of talking about science. And this is important: A discourse need not be combined of consistent elements, but of elements that, depending on the context, could be brought into operation. This also applies to the modern conception of science. Thus, the thesis of neutrality can be applied internally within the scientific community, emphasising, for instance, that it is not the task of science education to address socio-political elements. Such elements can be identified as extra-curricular. The proper content of any science, and therefore of any science education, does not include any ethical elements. The thesis of progress can be brought into operation anyway when, for instance, one has to argue for further funding of scientific initiatives.

2. MODERN CONCEPTIONS IN EDUCATIONAL RESEARCH

The modern conception of science has inspired much educational thinking, John Dewey being only one example. Also, much research in mathematics education reflects this conception of science. Let me try to illustrate some features of this reflection.

The thesis of neutrality is included in formal approaches to mathematics. As mentioned, the formalist analysis of mathematics provides a main inspiration for logical positivist analyses of science in general, which resulted in an explicit formulation for the thesis of neutrality. Formalism turned into structuralism, which is also an expression of the thesis of neutrality: a curriculum in mathematics education can be elaborated in pure mathematical terms. More generally, when it is claimed that content-matter issues can be discussed in logical terms and with references to mathematical notions and ideas only, we operate within an assumption of neutrality. In this sense, modern research in mathematics education addresses mathematics as a value-free domain. Socio-political issues are not important for clarifying content-matter issues.

The thesis of epistemic transparency found a most striking interpretation through Jean Piaget's genetic epistemology. Here the development of mathematical knowledge was described through a simple model. The idea of epistemic transparency was further elaborated into a structuralism, which combined the Bourbakian identification of mother-structures in mathematics with Piaget's claimed identification of genetic roots of mathematics.5 Later, epistemic transparency became basic to Jerome Bruner's claim that a complex curriculum can be elaborated around a few basic structures.6 Epistemic transparency assumes that defining features of knowledge can be identified through logical analyses.

The thesis of progress reveals its existence in educational thinking through the claim that general aims of education, and of mathematics education, as well, can be accomplished by concentrating on issues of content matter. Formulations of overall educational aims often include rosy formulations, for instance concerning citizenship and learning for life. At the same time the content of the curriculum can be specified through a list of mathematical topics and issues. From an analytic point of view, this appears to be a conceptual gap, not bridged by any logic. No induction seems to bring us from content to aims, and no deduction from aim to content. However, as if by magic, the thesis of progress establishes a connection by claiming that content, defined in mathematical terms, can be the motor of progress, in whatever terminology we want to express this progress – also when 'progress' is expressed in attractive educational aims. The assumption of progress allows us to decorate any science-based or mathematics-based curriculum with nice-looking goals. The essence of science and mathematics, also when organised in a curriculum, is social progress.

In this way, research in mathematics education could reflect assumptions of progress, neutrality and epistemic transparency. These assumptions impose a certain paradigmatic perspective on research in mathematics education. I find, however, this 'modern perspective' to be problematic, and in the following, I will indicate what it could mean to move beyond this perspective.

3. MATHEMATICS IN ACTION

For a discussion of mathematics education research for the future, it is important to observe what it means to leave behind the modern conception of science. As a first step, I am going to make some observations about 'mathematics in action'. This brings question marks to the assumptions of progress, neutrality and epistemic transparency.7

It has been observed that mathematics can be socially structured. The whole approach of the sociology of knowledge elaborates on this idea, and particular analyses of the social formatting of mathematics have been presented. Analyses addressing the inverse processes, the mathematical formatting of the social, have also been presented. In the following, through a discussion of mathematics in action, I address the last issue. Naturally, the two formatting processes are related, but they need not be simple 'inversions' of each other. One might think of them as intermixing processes.8

In order to summarise the overall idea of the mathematical formatting of the social, one could turn to the philosophy of language. Mathematics has been considered a language, the language of science, and according to the picture theory of language, as suggested by Ludwig Wittgenstein in Tractatus, the principal quality of the formal-mathematical language is to represent facts. The key notion in any picture theory of language is representation. Furthermore, this formal-mathematical language is (still according to Wittgenstein) unique, as it provides the most adequate grammar for representing the scientifically relevant aspects of reality.9 An act of 'representing' is not supposed to include any 'formatting'. A language, including mathematical language, leaves what is described as unchanged. This claim fits nicely a widely accepted way of thinking about mathematical modelling: namely, as being a way of representing aspects of reality in the most accurate way. However, when we turn to speech act theory and discourse theory, we find language characterised in a quiet different way.10 One is acting through language. The use of language includes a change and a reconfiguration of what is addressed. One is constructing not only the content of the speech act but also the contexts within which one is performing this act. One is speech-acting in a speech-acted-out world. Such formulations can also be applied to mathematics (interpreted as language).11 This inspires a mathematics-in-action interpretation, which I shall summarise below.

3.1 Technological Imagination

Mathematics supports what I call a technological imagination. Thus, mathematics can be used in design processes. The Turing machine represents an exemplary case of the idea that, by means of mathematics and formal descriptions, one can conceptualise possible constructions that go far beyond what a common-sense based imagination can create. Before even the first computer was physically constructed, it was possible to analyse principal aspects of its capacity. Such hypothetical constructions can be established in very many domains.

In some sense, technological imagination is related to sociological imagination, presented by C. Wright Mills (1959) as an important sociological concept. A sociological imagination reveals that a given sociological fact could be different. Sociological imagination was conceptualised as an attractive imagination that could help liberate people from traditions and routines, which could be revealed as being contingent, and therefore possible to change. Something different could be done.

A technological imagination might reveal that procedures of production, technological machinery, structures of information processing, etc. are contingent, and that they can be substituted by completely different devises. A mathematics-based technological imagination has a creative power which no common sense-based imagination has the possibility to imitate. Such a technological imagination opens new depths of contingencies. However, while sociological imagination is conceptually related to empowerment and liberation, technological imagination could also bring about disempowerment, domination, controlling, etc.

A technological imagination might be an imagination within limits. Although it certainly goes beyond what commonsense-based imagine might reach, it is elaborated within the limits of formal language. It reflects the grammar of formal language

3.2 Hypothetical reasoning

Possibilities presented as hypothetical constructions through a mathematics-based technological imagination facilitate hypothetical reasoning. One can investigate the stability of a new design of an airplane before embarking on any real construction. One can elaborate a tax system and investigate some to its implications before any economic initiative is implemented. One can propose advertising strategies and make decisions based on model-descriptions of consumers' behaviour before any campaign is launched. More generally, based on a hypothetical construction, one can try to identify implications of realising the construction. In all such cases, mathematics is essential for the hypothetical reasoning.

Such an analysis is based on counterfactuals. One can try to identify implications, Q, of a construction, P, even though P does not yet exist. In all possible processes of technological design, the handling of counterfactuals is important, and to a large extent they are handled through mathematical modelling. In particular, the situation P is supposed to be represented formally by a mathematical artefact which we could call p. The essential element in a hypothetical reasoning is to identify implications, q, of p, and, as p is available only in a mathematical format, all implications, q, are identified through formal manipulations. Naturally, here we find full-size openings for uncertainties; for when one decides to make the real construction, P, then one has only an insight into the real implications, Q, of doing so, through the clarification of q. The realised construction, P, is different from the hypothetical construction, p, and certainly the implications, Q, of the realised construction might show only limited similarity to q. Through the similarity-gap between Q and q, all kind of unexpected consequences emerge, also possible catastrophes. This similarity-gap provides a grandiose portal into the risk society.12 Hypothetical reasoning is powerful, but it also includes blind spots (and in this formulation, 'spot' might in fact refer to a sizeable terrain). Mathematics is crucial, also for fabricating blind spots.

3.3 Justification and legitimisation

A decision about realising a technological design or initiative can be based on a variety of arguments, produced through hypothetical reasoning. It is characteristic for decisions which, when first taken, cannot be changed, to draw heavily on mathematical modelling. Most often traffic planning is based on the analysis of only one model. This fact is pointed out through a Danish investigation of the widespread use of models in political decision-making processes.13 This means that mathematical models, through the way they compose hypothetical reasoning, become used for justifications of decisions. To what extend we are dealing with pseudo-justifications of decisions that have already been made is an open question;

but also in such cases of legitimisation, a mathematic-based hypothetical reasoning can be applied with convincing efficiency.

3.4 Realisation

When decisions are made, and the real constructions completed, we experience a realisation of 'something' initiated by a technological imagination. This could mean a new economic policy; a rationalisation of an industrial production; a decision about outsourcing; a decision about new investments; as well as the production of any kind of technological equipment. We find mathematics-based decisions and design carried out in all aspects of life. In this sense, mathematics becomes realised.14 It forms part of our life-world. We become encapsulated in a mathematically-formatted environment. We could try to imagine what it could mean to 'subtract' mathematics from our everyday life. How, for instance, to proceed with the operations of credit cards, or with any operation based on information and communication technology? We are surrounded by 'packagers' brought into operation, and their packages include many algorithms and other forms of materialised mathematics.15

The notion of 'realisation' is not meant to indicate that any proper 'copy' of the technological imagination has been realised. The process of realisation includes so many factors that one should only think of a technological imagination as an initiation to a process of construction and production, also of contingencies.

3.5 Routinising, authorising and ethical filtration

When mathematics is brought in operation and packages installed, we are able to establish new routines. For instance, the whole business of travelling has become re-routinised. While previously, the price of a ticket was determined by a few explicitly stated parameters, a price is now a function of many more parameters: the day of the reservation, the day of departure, the time of the day, conditions for payment, conditions for cancelling, insurance conditions, etc. This jungle of parameters establishes new routines for the traveller as well as for any travel agency. It is simply not possible to create or to handle such complexities without bringing mathematics into operation. This observation applies not only to the travel business. In all forms of work-practices we could talk about mathematics-based design of routines, operating on top of a wilderness of parameters.

The person operating a mathematics-based system for decision-making is assigned an authority through the system. Many expert systems are operating in hospitals. This displays new authority to the nurses, when they explain to the patients what dose of medicine is 'necessary'. Such a mathematics-supported expertise includes a reconfiguration of authority, and this also includes a reconfiguration of responsibility. What kind of responsibility is in fact accompanying the authority which is assigned to people operating a system? Or should one attribute the responsibility for the actions carried out to the people who invented the systems? Or to those who implement the system? Or within the mathematics-designed system itself? Some kind of ethical filtration seems to take place. It is not easy to identify who are responsible for mathematics-based actions.

4. THE MYTHS OF PROGRESS, NEUTRALITY AND OF EPISTEMIC TRANSPARENCY

Through processes like technological imagination, hypothetical reasoning, justification, legitimisation, realisation, routinising, authorising and ethical filtration, I want to emphasise that mathematics operates in many contexts, and that it does so in a powerful way. In fact, I find that if one wants to explore the relationship between knowledge and power, an exemplary case is found in mathematics in action.16

How does this clarification of mathematics in action fit with the assumptions of progress, neutrality and transparency? Does mathematics in action signify progress? My answer is 'no'. However, this 'no' does not bring us to the opposite assumption: that mathematics in action turns society backwards. Questioning the assumption of progress means refraining from assuming that mathematics-based actions obtain particular 'progressive' values by being mathematics-based. Such actions are as complicated as any other actions. They can be risky, reliable, confidential, controversial, exemplary, surprising, irresponsible, etc. Actions are not neutral; they are carriers of value. When we see language as speech acts and as discourses and interpret mathematics in these terms, then any claim of neutrality loses credibility. Thus, legitimation, routinisation and ethical filtration are all value-loaded actions. The idea of epistemic transparency is also gone. Mathematics in action operates in a complexity which cannot easily be analytically disentangled. We are facing knowledge-power bundles, which obliterate any hope of obtaining epistemic transparency. Thus, the complexity of a process initiated by a technological imagination and turning into a mathematics-based design destroys any dream of maintaining epistemic transparency.

Analyses of mathematics in action bring us beyond the modern conception of science. These assumptions of progress, neutrality and epistemic transparency become revealed as myths. As a further justification of this, I shall mention some general analyses, not carried out with any particular reference to mathematics, that also bring us beyond the modern conception of science.

The assumption of progress is challenged by the many catastrophes and almost-catastrophes accompanying technological development. The emergence of a risk society is characterised not only by what we can call explicit production, but also by implicit production.17 While explicit production results in goods that can be brought to the market and 'priced' according to profit schemes, implicit production is much more difficult to identify. It could take the form of those effects of pollution that might not show themselves immediately, but that only later on, in accumulated forms, turn into possible catastrophes. The economic aspects of implicit production are difficult to grasp; and maybe implicit production only becomes grasped when we are over our heads in its accumulated effects. The emerging of the risk society exposes 'progress' as an illusionary concept.

Let us consider the assumption of neutrality. Mathematics forms part of the whole techno-scientific resource for production, design, management, exploitation, innovation, etc. This applies not only to mathematics, but to science in general. This observation has been elaboration in terms of the Mode-2 Society', characterised by the complexity of science-technology-economy interrelationships. 18 While, previously, universities had provided the institutional framework for more advanced knowledge production, this production is now taking place in a variety of institutions, organisations, programmes and companies; and within universities themselves, there is a trend toward increasing funding of research by private companies. This imposes an intricacy of structuring interests and priorities on knowledge production, and changes the concept of quality of research dramatically. According to the modern conception of science, scientific quality criteria can be expressed in terms of verification, falsification, representation, predictability, etc. – all concepts referring to logical properties of the theories developed. But in a Mode-2 Society, such internal quality criteria operate together with very many other criteria, referring to production, marketability, profit, etc. Such clusters of criteria take us far beyond any claim of the neutrality of science. Considering a Mode-2 Society, the assumption of neutrality appears to be a myth.

Finally, the hope that the assumption for epistemic transparency might have any bearing has been shattered through Michel Foucault's analyses of the relationship between knowledge and power. 19 His point is that the modern conception of science, which provides a most flattering image of science, is also hiding many functions that science might exercise. Formulations of intrinsic qualities of science might highlight only some well-intended and self-congratulating, but also illusionary perceptions of science. If we follow Foucault's analyses, we will realise that power and knowledge operate together in complex bundles. Foucault's examples are chosen with a noteworthy distance to mathematics and natural sciences, but knowledge-power bundles are also operating in these areas. Thus, 'technological imagination' refers to such a bundle, and so do the concepts of 'hypothetical reasoning', 'routinisation', 'realisation', etc. These bundles bring us far beyond any illusion of epistemic transparency. (Naturally, knowledge-power bundling also brings us far beyond the assumptions of neutrality and of progress).

I see the assumptions of progress, neutrality and epistemic transparency as myths. My presentation of mathematics in action points in this direction, and so do the presentations of the risk society, the Mode-2 Society, and the Foucault-inspired knowledge-power awareness. I find it most important that we leave behind these myths and, in particular, consider what challenges research in mathematics education might then face.

5. CHALLENGES

Leaving the myths of progress, neutrality and epistemic transparency means leaving the protective environment established by the modern conception of educational research. So the question is: What does it mean for mathematics education research to position itself outside this protection?20

In order to clarify what this challenge might include, I will make comments about: (1) content master issues, in particular with reference to mathematics in action; (2) the socio-political context of mathematics education; (3) the agents of mathematics education, in particular the students; and (4) the agents of the mathematics education research practice. As conclusion, I return to the notion of uncertainty.

5.1 Content in mathematics education

In Dialogue and Learning in Mathematics Education, Helle Alrø and I analyse different examples of educational practices which could illustrate what it could mean to consider critical reflections regarding mathematics in action as being an educational task. In one of the projects, 'Terrible Small Numbers', the students (14-15 years old) addressed the notion of risk and the meaning of those very small numbers, which are supposed to indicate that certain catastrophic events are almost sure not to happen.21 Previously, in connection with the discussion of the safety of running an atomic power plan, such numbers had entered the public debate. (Bech's analysis of the risk society is related to this discussion.) What does it mean to claim that the likelihood that an accident would take place at a particular power plant during a one-year period can be estimated to be p? How were such numbers identified? How do they operate in decision making?

In the project 'Terrible small numbers', the students were addressing the issue of salmonella-infected eggs. The eggs had the shape of film cases. Such eggs could easily be opened for inspection. Most of the eggs contained a healthy yolk in the form of a yellow piece of plastic. Other contained a blue piece indicating a salmonella infection. The first task for the students was to select samples from a big collection of eggs, brought to the classroom in a trolley. It was known in advance that 10% of the eggs in the trolley were infected by salmonella. The student was to select samples and consider to what extend these samples reflected the 'real' degree of salmonella infection. The students were surprised that samples did not always 'reflect' the 10% degree of salmonella infection – far from always. How could that be? Was the mixing of the eggs in the trolley not done in a proper way?

This activity leads to the discussion of reliability. The initial issue was: How could it be that samples often do not reveal the 'real' distribution? And what to think of a situation where one does not know the real distribution? In fact, in real-life situations, one only has information based on samples. This counts for any kind of quality control. How reliable could such information be? In this way, we wanted to introduce a more general discussion of the reliability of information provided by numbers. The discussion for reliability not only concerns samples, but any situation where mathematics is brought into action.

Later, the project 'Terrible Small Numbers' placed students in a situation where they had to make decisions based on (more or less reliable) numbers. They were presented with two parties of egg (in two different trolleys). The two parties were both infected by salmonella, but to different degrees not known by the students –

and in fact not known to anyone, as the teacher had just randomly added some infected eggs to each party. Each group of students had to assume they were representatives of an egg-import company, which had to decide from which party of eggs to make the import. They had to make a budget for the whole import business, based on information of prices of buying and selling eggs, cost of the salmonella control, etc. Furthermore, they were informed that the eggs opened for inspection were damaged and could not be sold, implying that 'playing safe' by controlling each and every egg was no business at all. The students faced the dilemma that the more extensive they wanted the quality control, the more expensive it would become to make the best choice. How to handle such a situation? What could it mean to act in a responsible way in such a situation?

I find that the issues of reliability and responsibility are of general significance for mathematics education. In particular, it becomes important for mathematics education research to investigate how reflections and ethical considerations with respect to mathematics in action could form part of an educational practice.

5.2 Context of Mathematics Education

One can claim that the task of mathematics education is to provide a supply matrix of competencies, which replicates society's need for man-power. This applies to all levels in the educational system. Thus, given a matrix of demand of man-power – in terms of specialised mathematicians, computer scientists, engineers, operators of any kind, particularly skilled workers – one could see the task of an education system being to make sure that competences are developed and distributed in a supply matrix according to the expected matrix of demand. Such a discourse reflects the idea that mathematics education should be functional, given the social order, and that research in mathematics education should facilitate this functionality. One could however, also try to introduce a critical mode, as one need not accept the demand-matrix as constituting relevant quality criteria for education.

Distinguishing between a functional and a critical mode is a step beyond the assumptions of Modernity. Like mathematics, so also can mathematics education have very many functions depending on the context. Alan Bishop (1990) asks if "Western mathematics" could be "the secret weapon of cultural imperialism"; Wenda Bauchspies (2005) suggests that, in some situations, learning could be interpreted as colonisation; while Arthur Powell and Marilyn Frankenstein (1997) present ethnomathematics as a "challenge to Euro-centrism in mathematics education". Raising such issues challenges the conception of mathematics education as being an intrinsically good activity. This move, however, presupposes that research in mathematic education will become sensitive to the socio-political context of learning.

There are, however, many ways in which research in mathematics education becomes context-blind. When we consider research addressing the mathematics classroom, we can ask what kind of classrooms we are presented with. In other contexts, I have stressed that a prototype mathematics classroom dominates research literature in mathematics education.22 The prototype is characterised by its nice environment: there are not many disturbing, impolite or violent students. Instead most students appear motivated, at least ready to address the mathematical tasks which are presented to them by the teacher or the researcher. They take their time to work with the tasks, apparently without too many irrelevant side remarks – and if so, then at least they make some remarks that add a good sense of humour to the transcripts. The prototype classroom is not overrun by hungry students from desolated neighbourhoods. The classroom is not located in violent areas. There are no police positioned on the school premises. The students do not have to pass through a metal detector before entering the school. The prototype classroom is not located in a war-like zone, where students might suffer from some sort of trauma. All 'disturbing' factors have been eliminated through the process of selecting the site for doing research: data has been sanitised as part of the decisions regarding what to include as data, and what not.23 It appears that very strong paradigmatic priorities are exercised in order to produce the prototype classroom. Much research in mathematics education addresses the prototype mathematics classroom, which is far from representing any major sites for learning mathematics.

This makes it important to consider to what extent theorising in mathematics education might be biased.24 My concern is whether research in mathematics education – through its very notions and theorising – has become biased, and in this way become functional with respect to certain socio-economic priorities. When we leave behind the assumptions of progress, neutrality and epistemic transparency, mathematics education research also comes to face equations like: Could mathematics education, in certain situations, operate as a secrete weapon of Western imperialism? Could learning of mathematics include a form of colonisation? Could it include a Euro-centrism? Depending on the context, mathematics education could become functional or critical. Research in mathematics education comes to face this challenge.

5.3 Agency in Mathematics Education

When we consider mathematics education, we have not only to consider content and context, but also agency. This agency includes not only students, but also teachers, parents, administrators. This being said, I will, in the following, concentrate my comments on the students. I find that one important step in moving beyond the paradigm of modern research in mathematics education is to consider students as acting subjects positioned in a complex socio-political context.

Much research in mathematics education has concentrated on students in a particular transparent format. One could find inspiration for this approach in Piaget's notion of 'epistemic subject', which he distinguishes from the 'psychological subject'.25 In his attempt to identify archetypical steps in the process of learning, he presents the epistemic subject as a learning subject. This way of framing research establishes a particular way of looking at students, and as a consequence, of what is important to include in transcriptions and analyses when one is investigating processes of learning. In this way, the Piagetian perspective has established a rigorous selection scheme for research in learning mathematics.

This scheme reflects the assumption of epistemic transparency, which makes it possible to abstract away the socio-political reality as being irrelevant for understanding the processes of learning mathematics. As mathematical knowledge can be described in a transparent way, so also the learning of mathematics.

In reaction to this conception of the students, Paola Valero has talked about 'realising students', meaning that they should be portrayed as "whole learners, who have multiple motives for learning, and who live in a broad context which influences their intentions to participate in school mathematics practices" (Valero, 2004, p. 48). 26 Such an observation opens the way for questions like: What does it mean for the learning of mathematics that students have to work when they leave school? What does the emerging racism mean for the learning of mathematics for migrant students in Europe? What does poverty mean for students' motives for learning mathematics? In order to address such questions, it is important to consider students in their socio-political, economic and cultural context. Therefore, learning theories of mathematics must be opened to conceptual constructs, through which one may grasp such complexities of learning.27

5.4 The Agency of the Researchers

What is the domain of mathematics education research? What are we looking at? It has been common to address the object of research as including three elements: the content matter, namely mathematics, the students, and the teachers. This triple model has been refined in different ways. It has been emphasised that the content matter issues also include interdisciplinary elements, that the students cannot be considered in isolation, that the communication between students and teachers is important, etc. An important step in leaving the triple-model is to consider the socio-political context of the triple. The importance of making this step is also included in my comments in the section 5.2, but I find one more step to be important.

We can again look at the question: What are we looking at? This sentence contains a 'we'. The 'we' refers to the researchers. My point is that we, as researchers, also must look at the 'we' that is researching. The researcher and the researching form part of the research domain. Thus, abolishing the assumption of epistemic transparency not only concerns the interpretation of what learning mathematics may include, but also what researching might include. Research in mathematics education is an integral part of socio-political conflicts and interests. Addressing this complexity becomes part of the very research process itself.

Including such a reflexive element in mathematic education research has many implications. Here I will only address one more general economical issue. A political economy of mathematics education can include several elements.28 The possible economic significance of mathematics education is expressed through international awareness about performances in mathematics. Naturally, the ranking of countries reflects elements of competition, but one could also assume an economic significance of the ranking. Thus, the portrayal of the information society and the knowledge society suggests that not only 'capital' and 'labour' but also 'knowledge' is an important parameter in the function of production.29 With respect to the knowledge parameter, it becomes important to specify how mathematics and mathematics education might operate. This could help to shed light on the possible economic significance of both mathematics and mathematics education.

To me, observations concerning the political economy of mathematics education indicate that research in mathematics education is operating in an economic context. This research could easily come to serve very different, and also rather particular, interests. It could facilitate the management of large-scale evaluations of competencies, and maybe do so from a neo-liberal perspective, assuming that the task of mathematics education is to make sure that competencies are developed in a functional way, reflecting society's need for man-power. It could reflect particular interests when dealing with learning possibilities provided by new technology, by ignoring the problems that students without access to computers have to face. As researchers, we could act in many different ways. We cannot, however, escape acting as researchers. And this makes it important, also, to address the very process of researching as part of the doing research.

6. CONCLUSION: UNCERTAINTY

I have tried to point out challenges that research in mathematics education might face when leaving the assumptions of Modernity. A discussion of the rationality of mathematics in terms of mathematics in action might help to reveal that this rationality cannot be taken as a simple 'progressive' factor; neither it is neutral, nor transparent. Mathematical rationality is a problematic rationality, as part of mathematics education, as well.

This observation brings us to address a basic uncertainty. The critical mode in education has, to a large extent, been inspired from certain developments after the Second World War in German education. It emerged as an educational aim to prevent any frame of thinking, as exercised to a disastrous extreme during the Nazi regime, from emerging again. Or as Theodor Adorno condenses it: The aim on any education is to prevent a new Auschwitz from happening again.30 One should not forget that mathematics education, during the 1930's in Germany, also placed itself in an accommodating and 'functional' relationship with the Nazi regime.31 It is a permanent reminder that education, and also mathematics education, needs to be critical.

However, this does not bring any simple orientation to our present situation. Shedding the tutelage of the assumptions of progress, neutrality and epistemic transparency, includes a step away from any aspiration of identifying an epistemic position with some 'foundational' solidity. In particular, I find that one needs to give up looking for any solid epistemic foundation for 'being critical', which brings us directly to the notion of uncertainty. Without the protection of the assumptions of modernity, one is left in the open. And let it be like this. But being uncertain does not mean that one is not concerned. The best I can do is to emphasise that, amidst theoretical uncertainties, research in mathematics education can still address the challenges concerning the content, context and agency of mathematics education, as well as the agency of researching.

ACKNOWLEDGEMENTS

I want to thank Miriam Godoy Penteado for critical comments and suggestions for improving preliminary versions of this paper, and Anne Kepple for completing a careful language revision.

REFERENCES

Adorno, T. W. (1971). Erziehung nach Auschwitz. In T. W. Adorno, *Erziehung zur Mündigkeit* (88-104). Frankfurt am Main: Suhrkamp.

Alrø, H and Skovsmose (2002). *Dialogue and learning in mathematics education: Intention, reflection, critique.* Dordrecht: Kluwer Academic Publishers.

Archibugi, D. and Lundvall, B.-Å. (Eds.) (2001). *The globalizing learning economy.* Oxford: Oxford University Press.

Apple, M. W. (2000). Mathematics reform through conservative modernization? Standards, markets, and inequality in education. In J. Boaler (Ed.), *Multiple perspectives on mathematics teaching and learning* (243-259). Westprot (USA): Ablex Publishing.

Austin, J. L. (1962). *How to do things with words.* Oxford: Oxford University Press.

Ayer, A. (1970). *Language, truth and logic.* London: Victor Gollancz. (First edition 1936.)

Ayer, A. (Ed.) (1959). *Logical positivism.* New York: The Free Press.

Bauman, Z. (2000). *Liquid modernity.* Cambridge: Polity Press.

Bauchspies, W. K. (2005). Sharing shoes and counting years: Mathematics, colonalization, and communication. In A. Chronaki and I. M. Christiansen (Eds.), *Challenging perspectives on mathematics classroom communication* (237-259). Greenwich (USA): Information Age Publishing.

Beck, U. (1992). *Risk society: Towards a new modernity.* London: SAGE Publications.

Beck, U. (1999): *World risk society,* Cambridge: Polity Press.

Beck, U., Giddens, A. and Lash, S. (1994). *Reflexive modernization: Politics, tradition and aesthetics in the modern social order.* Cambridge: Polity Press.

Bell, D. (1980). The social framework of the information society. In Forrester, T. (Ed.). *The microelectronics revolution* (500-549). Oxford: Blackwell.

Beth, E. W. and Piaget, J. (1966). *Mathematical epistemology and psychology.* Dordrecht: D. Reidel Publishing Company.

Bishop, A. J. (1990). Western mathematics: The secret weapon of cultural imperialism. *Race and Class 32*(2), 51-65.

Bruner, J. (1960). *The process of education.* Cambridge (USA): Harvard University Press.

Bury, J. B. (1955). *The idea of progress: An inquiry into its origin and growth.* With an Introduction by Charles A. Bead. New York: Dover Publications. (First published 1932.)

Carnap, R. (1937). *The logical syntax of language.* London: Routledge and Kegan Paul. (Original German edition from 1934.)

Carnap, R. (1959). The elimination of metaphysics through logical analysis of language. In A. Ayer (Ed.), *Logical positivism* (60-81). New York: The Free Press. (First published in German in 1932.)

Castells, M. (1996). *The information age: Economy, society and culture. Volume I: The rise of the network society.* Oxford: Blackwell Publishers.

Castells, M. (1997). *The information age: economy, society and culture. Volume II, The power of identity.* Oxford: Blackwell Publishers.

Castells, M. (1998). *The information age: Economy, society and culture. Volume III, End of millennium.* Oxford: Blackwell Publishers.

Dewey, J. (1966). *Democracy and education: An introduction to the philosophy of education*. New York, London: The Free Press. (First published 1916.)

Foucault, M. (1989). *The Archeology of Knowledge*. London: Routledge. (First French edition 1969.)

Foucault, M. (1994). *The order of things: An archaeology of the human sciences*. New York: Vintage Books. (First French edition 1966.)

Gibbons, M., Limoges, C., Nowotny, H., Schwartzman, S., Scott, P., and Trow, M. (1994): *The new production of knowledge: The dynamics of science and research in contemporary societies*. London: Sage Publications.

Keitel, C. (1989). Mathematics and technology. *For the Learning of Mathematics, 9*(1), 7-13.

Keitel, C. (1993). Implicit mathematical models in social practice and explicit mathematics teaching by applications. In J. de Lange, I. Huntley, C. Keitel, M. Niss (Eds.), *Innovation in maths education by modelling and applications* (19-30). New York: Ellis Horwood.

Keitel, C., Kotzmann, E. and Skovsmose, O. (1993). Beyond the tunnel vision: Analysing the relationship between mathematics, society and technology. In C. Keitel and K Ruthven (Eds.), *Learning from computers: Mathematics education and technology* (243-279). Berlin: Springer.

Lyotard, J.-F. (1984). *The postmodern condition: A report on knowledge*. Translated from French by Geoff Bennington and Brian Massuni, Foreword by Fredric Jameson. Manchester: Manchester University Press. (Original French edition 1979).

Mehrtens, H. (1993). The social system of mathematics and national socialism: A survey. In S. Restivo, J. P. van Bendegem and R. Fisher, R. (Eds.) (1993). *Math worlds: Philosophical and social studies of mathematics and mathematics education* (219-246). Albany: State University of New York Press.

Nisbet, R. A. (1980). *History of the idea of progress*. New York: Basic Books.

Nowotny, H., Scott, P. and Gibbons (2001). *Re-thinking science: Knowledge and the public in an age of uncertainty*. Cambridge: Polity Press.

Powell, A. and Frankenstein, M. (Eds.) (1997). *Ethnomathematics: Challenging eurocentrism in mathematics education*. Albany: State University of New York Press.

Qvortrup, L. (1998). *Det hyperkomplekse samfund: 14 fortællinger om informationssamfundet*. Copenhagen: Gyldendal.

Qvortrup, L. (2001). *Det lærende samfund: Hyperkompleksitet og viden*. Copenhagen: Gyldendal.

Restivo, S., Bendegem, J. P. van and Fisher, R. (Eds.) (1993). *Math worlds: Philosophical and social studies of mathematics and mathematics education*. Albany: State University of New York Press.

Searle, J. (1969). *Speech Acts*. Cambridge: Cambridge University Press.

Skovsmose, O. (2004). Research, practice and responsibility. Article presented as part of a Survey Team for the International Congress on Mathematics Education in Copenhagen 2004. http://www.icme-10.dk/ (Click on 'PROGRAMME', then 'ICME-10 Survey Team', and eventually 'ST1'.)

Skovsmose, O. (2005a). Foregrounds and politics of learning obstacles. *For the Learning of Mathematics, 25*(1), 4-10.

Skovsmose, O. (2005b). *Travelling through education: Uncertainty, mathematics, responsibility*. Rotterdam: Sense Publishers.

Skovsmose, O and Yasukawa, K. (2004). Formatting power of 'Mathematics in a Package': A challenge for social theorising? *Philosophy of Mathematics Education Journal*. (http://www.ex.ac.uk/~PErnest/pome18/contents.htm)

Skovsmose, O and Valero, P. (2002a). Mathematics education in a world apart – Where we are all together. In P. Valero and O. Skovsmose (Eds.), *Proceedings of the Third International Mathematics Education and Society Conference* (1-9). Copenhagen, Roskilde Aalborg: Centre for Research in Learning Mathematics, Danish University of Education, Roskilde University Centre, Aalborg University.

Skovsmose, O. and Valero, P. (2002b). Democratic access to powerful mathematical ideas. In L. English (Ed.), *Handbook of international research in mathematics education* (pp. 383-407). Mahwah: Lawrence Erlbaum Associates.

Stadler, F. (2001). *The Vienna Circle: Studies in the origins, development and influence of logical empiricim*. Wien: Springer.

Teknologirådet (1995): *Magt og modeller: Om den stigende anvendelse af edb-modeller i de politiske beslutninger*. København: Teknologirådet.

Tomlinson, M. (2001). New roles fro business services in economic growth. In D. Archibugi and B.-Å. Lundvall (Eds.) (2001), *The globalizing learning economy* (97-107). Oxford: Oxford University Press.

Torfing, J. (1999). *New theories of discouse: Laclau, Mouffe and Žižek*. Oxford: Blackwell Publishers.

Valero, P. (2004). Postmodernism as an attitude of critique to dominant mathematics education research. In M. Walshaw (Ed.), *Mathematics education within the postmodern* (35-54). Greenwich (USA): Information Age Publishing.

Valero, P. (2005). What has mathematics got to do with power? In D. Chassapis (Ed.), *Proceedings of the 4th Dialogue on Mathematics Teaching Issues: Social and cultural aspects of mathematics education* (25-43). Thessaloniki (Greece): Aristotle University of Thessaloniki, Primary Education Department.

Vithal, R. (1998). Data and disruptions: The politics of doing mathematics education research in South Africa. In N. A.Ogude and V. Bohlmann (Eds.), *Proceedings of the sixth annual meeting of the Southern African Association for Research in Mathematics and Science Education* (475-481). UNISA.

Valero, P. and Vithal, R. (1999) Research methods of the 'North' revisited from the 'South'. *Perspectives in Education, 18*(2), 5-12.

Vithal, R. and Valero, P. (2003). Researching mathematics education in situations of social and political conflict. In A. J. Bishop, M. A. Clementsw, C. Keitel, J. Kilpatrick and F. K. S. Leund (Eds.), *Second international handbook of mathematics education* (545-591). Dordrecht: Kluwer Academic Publishers.

Walshaw, M. (Ed.) (2004). *Mathematics education within the postmodern*. Greenwich (USA): Information Age Publishing.

Wittgenstein, L. (1992): *Tractatus logico-philosophicus*. London: Routledge. (First German edition 1921).

Wright Mills, C. (1959). *The sociological imagination*. Oxford: Oxford University Press.

NOTES

1 See, for instance, Bauman (2000); Beck (1992, 1999); Beck, Giddens and Lash (1994); Bell (1980); Castells (1996, 1997, 1998); Gibbons et al. (1994); Lyotard (1984); and Qvortrup (1998; 2001).

2 For a discussion of the idea of progress, see Bury (1955) and Nisbet (1980).

3 See Ayer (1970); Carnap (1959); and Stadler (2001) for a careful presentation and analysis of logical positivism including its conception of ethics.

4 See, for instance, the discussion of knowledge in Ayer (Ed.) (1959).

5 See Piaget's careful analysis in Beth and Piaget (1966).

[6] See Bruner (1960).

[7] For a discussion of mathematics in action, see Skovsmose (2005b).

[8] See, for instance, Keitel (1989, 1993); and Restivo, Bendegem and Fisher (Eds.) (1993).

[9] Carnap (1937) provides a careful analysis of the nature of an adequate scientific language: it must be formal.

[10] See, for instance, Austin (1962); Searle (1969); Torfing (2002).

[11] I find that mathematics is more that a language, but still one can find inspiration from seeing mathematics as (among other things) a language.

[12] One could think of both Q and q as ranges of consequences, and it might well turn out that many of the possible consequences included in Q, have not even been mentioned in q.

[13] See Teknologirådet (1995).

[14] For a discussion of this form of realisation see Keitel, Kotzmann and Skovsmose (1993).

[15] See, for instance, Skovsmose and Yasukawa (2004).

[16] I also find that this case is of such importance that a social theorising cannot find any adequate form if mathematics in action is ignored.

[17] See Beck (1992, 1995).

[18] See Gibbons et al. (1994); and Nowotny et al. (2001).

[19] See, for instance, Foucault (1989, 1994).

[20] This question has been addressed by Valero (2004). See also Valero (2005); and Walshaw (Ed.) (2004).

[21] 'Terrible small numbers' has been developed and analysed in co-operation with Morten Blomhøj, Henning Bødtkjer and Mikael Skånstrøm.

[22] See Skovsmose (2004).

[23] For a discussion of what it could mean to research mathematics education of socio-political conflicts, see Vithal and Valero (2003). For a discussion of 'sanitising data' see Vithal (1998); and Vithal and Valero (1999).

[24] See also Skovsmose and Valero (2002b).

[25] See Piaget's discussion of the relationship between the epistemic and the psychological subject in Beth and Piaget (1966).

[26] See also Skovsmose (2005b).

[27] The notion of students' foregrounds is a proposal for such a construct. See Skovsmose (2005a). Let me add that it is important that not only students but also teachers become 'realised'. Teachers are not simple attachments to curricula and educational principles; they are professionals engaged in teaching, supervision, administrating, collaboration with parents, etc.

[28] Suggestions for a political economy of mathematics education are presented in Skovsmose and Valero (2002a). See also Apple (2000).

[29] Tomlinson (2001) considers the function of production in the form of $Q = Q(C, L, S)$, where C refers to input of capital, L to input of labour, and S to the input of communication and business services. See also Archibugi and Lundvall (Eds.) (2001).

[30] See Adorno (1971).

[31] See Mehrtens (1993).

Ole Skovsmose
Department of Education, Learning and Philosophy
Aalborg University

MOGENS NISS

THE STRUCTURE OF MATHEMATICS AND ITS INFLUENCE ON THE LEARNING PROCESS

INTRODUCTION

First of all, let me make it clear that in this paper the word "structure" should be taken in a wide sense. It is not only meant to refer to the architecture of mathematics (in some version) but also to the nature and characteristics of mathematics as a discipline, both as an edifice and as a system and community of practices. No particular approaches to, or views or philosophies of, mathematics, such as structuralism, nor a particular organisation of the discipline, e.g. Bourbaki's, are meant to be presupposed or invoked by the word "structure".

The focus of this paper is on structural aspects of mathematics that are known or are likely to cause problems or challenges to the learning of mathematics, and hence to its teaching as well. There are numerous such aspects to consider, but I have chosen three themes for the purpose of this paper. They are all related to deep issues in the epistemology and cognition of mathematics: The formation, nature, and role of mathematical concepts; the need for and role of mathematical proof; and symbolism and formalism in mathematics. The way in which these themes are being dealt with here is neither by way of an overview of the research literature for each theme, nor by presentation of original pieces of research, but rather by reflection on significant insights that have been uncovered by research, and on issues that have not yet been dealt with to a sufficient extent. In other words, the genre of this paper can perhaps best be referred to as an analytic essay.

THE FORMATION, NATURE, AND ROLE OF MATHEMATICAL CONCEPTS

Two significant research findings on concept formation have obtained an almost classical status in this area of our field.

The first one is the distinction between "concept definition" and "concept image" as coined and investigated by Vinner and Hershkowitz (1980) and by Tall and Vinner (1981). The notion of "concept definition" consists in the formal definition of a mathematical concept formulated within some theoretical framework containing that definition. In contrast, the notion of "concept image" is the entire set of representations and properties of a concept at issue that is being held by a given individual. The concept image needs neither be coherent nor internally consistent. In case the individual is able to produce a definition of the

J. Maasz, W. Schloeglmann (Eds.), New Mathematics Education Research and Practice, 51–62.

concept (which does not have to be (equivalent to) an "official" one) this definition forms part of that individual's image of the concept.

For an illustration, take the concept of, say, (real) function. In one formal setting, a real function can be defined as a correspondence from a subset A of the real numbers, $\mathfrak{R}$, into the real rumbers such that each element in A is corresponds to exactly one element in $\mathfrak{R}$ (there are alternative, end even more formal, set theoretical definitions at hand, but that is not the important point here). The concept image held by some given student may include all graphs of continuous functions defined on the full real line or on a real interval, as well as all mappings given by only one algebraic expression involving polynomial or trigonometric functions. It may well happen that the student, if asked to provide a definition of function, will give the one just cited, while at the same time discarding, say, the function having the value 0 at all negative numbers and the value 1 at all non-negative numbers as a function, because it is not part of that student's image of the concept of function, since this function is neither continuous in its domain, nor given by a single algebraic expression. For this (imaginary) student there is a discrepancy between his or her image of the concept of function and its definition, including the student's own definition.

It seems that students form their images of a given concept mainly through the set of specific examples of the concept that they have become familiar with through the teaching they have received. So, a significant source of a possible gap between concept image and concept definition occurs if the examples shaping the concept image cover only a limited part of the scope implied by the concept definition. If such a discrepancy exists between image and definition with an individual, research findings show that it is the image that "wins" over the definition, in the sense that in situations involving the concept of function, the student operates on the basis of the image, not on the basis of the range and scope of the formal definition, which is likely to give rise to erroneous work and wrong conclusions. Moreover, the discrepancy between image and definition, if it exists with an individual student, gives rise to severe learning difficulties, and the more severe the greater the discrepancy.

Other examples, worth mentioning, of concepts that tend to give rise to discrepancies between concept image and concept definition are limit, irrational number, and polygon.

The second finding is to do with the formation of those concepts that are formed by reifying (Sfard, 1991) or encapsulating (Tall, 1991) a mathematical process into an entity, object or procept (see also Douady, 1991, for a related but not identical approach; Otte has considered similar aspects under the term "complementarity" since the late 1970's (for an overview, see Otte, 2003)). Objects referred to by such a concept are often themselves taken as elements in a set or are used as ingredients in operations or processes.

A prime example of this duality between process and object is the notion of derivative. Students are taught that the differential quotient of a (differentiable!) function in a given point x0 is defined as the limit value of the difference quotient in x, as x tends to x0. Thus the differential quotient is a number resulting from a limiting process. Moreover, they are further taught how to calculate differential quotients of combined functions of various types (sum, product, quotient, composite, etc.) on the basis of knowledge of the differential quotients of the component functions. Again a number (perhaps taking the shape of an algebraic expression) results from an operation or a process. The step to perceive the differential quotient in a point as an object depending on the point, rather than merely on the process which generated it, represents a demanding cognitive jump. To perceive the correspondence that maps each point in the domain to the differential quotient of the function in that point as an object in itself, i.e. a new function - the derivative of the original one - is an even more demanding jump.

Sfard and others have analysed how the reification of processes into objects constitutes special challenges to learning, as reification itself often requires students to see the reified object as an element of the next stage in the conceptual hierarchy already while the reification process itself is under way and the original process has not yet been reified.

While it is debatable whether any mathematical concept can be seen as an object resulting from encapsulation / reification of a process (I do not think so; take for instance the concept of topological space), there are certainly many key concepts for which this is true. They include, for example, limit, derivative, series, locus, and equation.

In addition to the problems and challenges arising from the concept image / concept definition discrepancy and from encapsulation / reification of processes into objects, there are other obstacles to concept formation that have fundamental epistemological roots. In what follows I shall consider two such obstacles.

The first is to do with concepts that are abstracted from an experiential domain. Let us begin by considering the example of "fraction".

In much mathematics teaching in primary school, the notion of fraction is introduced on the basis of some stylised practical experience. It could be a pizza or a rectangular piece of cardboard, which for various natural n is divided into n congruent parts. Each part is declared as one-n-th of the original object, written $1/n$. This implies that $1/n$ is an operator on some geometrico-physical object - in this case a pizza or a cardboard, but it could also be, say, a line segment – taken as "unity" in the given context. Then m/n is an object created by taking m pieces of $1/n$ (with respect to the unity). This implies that the fraction m/n is introduced as an abstracted operator on magnitudes residing in some experiential domain. As pizzas, rectangular cardboards, line segments, or whatever objects are subjected to the function of the operator, have characteristics and properties of their own, not all of which are reflected in the mathematical abstractions involved in using the operator m/n, there may well be – and research confirms that there often is - interference from the experiential domain on the interpretation of the fraction operator. In fact, there is an act of modelling involved in this interpretation. For instance, it may seem essential to the concept that the primitive pieces $1/n$ are congruent rather than just of equal area (or volume if the unity is, say, a box or a circular cylindrical disc). The reflective student might have doubts about what pizza or cardboard cuts are legal from the perspective of this model.

On the basis of this way of introducing fractions as operators on magnitudes, it is still possible, albeit slightly demanding for the students at this level, to obtain an experientially based justification of the rule

$$(pm)/(pn) = m/n,$$

which requires the identification of two different operators: Taking pm pieces of size $1/(pn)$ gives the same result as taking m pieces of $1/n$ (i.e. p pieces of $1/pn$ equals one piece of size $1/n$), then pm pieces of size $1(pn)$ yield exactly m pieces of size $1/n$. If we go on to establish similar experiential justification of the rules

$$(m/n) \cdot (p/q) = (mp)/(nq), \text{ and } (m/n) : (p/q) = (mq)/(np),$$

we have to invent even more contrived settings from which these can be deduced. This is even more true if we want to establish the notion of fractions of fractions and the rule

$$[(m/n) / (p/q)] = (mq)/(np)$$

in accordance with an experiential interpretation.

The development of the notion of fraction from an operator on more or less idealised magnitudes, taken from students' experiential worlds, to fractions as pure numbers, which are agents in an arithmetico-algebraic game, requires departure from the purely experiential world. This is true, even though the operator conception can be maintained, if the number 1 is taken to represent a unit magnitude (typically a line segment) on which all fractions operate. For instance, the question of dividing one fraction by another fraction is predominantly an algebraic question, and the answer given is predominantly an algebraic answer. We seek the number(s), if there are any, which multiplied by the divisor give(s) the dividend.

In this transition – by abstraction - from an experiential world into the world of numbers, it is neither possible nor desirable to scaffold any conception or arithmetical operation related to fractions exclusively by reference to domains of experience and interpretation. Similar observations hold for negative numbers, functions, probability, and so forth and so on. The mathematical environment of an abstracted concept normally contains traits for which there is no experiential counterpart. This gives rise to cognitively demanding "quantum leaps", and students who insist on the availability of experiential interpretations of all traits of the mathematical concepts they are taught will eventually experience severe learning problems.

By definition, abstracted concepts do not possess all the properties of the concepts from which they have been abstracted. Nonetheless, many students tend to attribute properties of the initial concept to an abstracted concept as well. We may agree to call this "over-generalisation". A classical and very widespread example is over-generalisation of proportionality, both within purely mathematical domains and within the application of mathematics to extra-mathematical domains (cf. e.g. Verschaffel & de Corte, 1997). Other well-known examples of over-generalisation include over-generalisation of additivity (e.g. $(x + y)2 = x2 + y2)$), "squaring a number gives a bigger number", "log (x/y) = logx / log y", "0.3175 > 0.32", "a norm in a finite-dimensional vector space is Euclidean", "a metric in a metric space stems from a norm", "in an algebraic structure there are no non-trivial null-divisors", "multiplication is always commutative".

Another obstacle worth considering is to do with abstract concepts. Abstract concepts are typically represented as objects in some axiomatically defined structure. In contradistinction to what is the case with abstracted concepts, abstract concepts are not a result of an individual abstraction based on a related individual concept, residing at a lower level of the hierarchy of concepts. Rather, what is abstracted here is the entire system to which the concept belongs. In other words, we may define an abstract concept as a member of an abstracted system, which is defined by the elements it contains and the rules that govern it. Examples of this are a matrix, a complex number, a vector, a Boolean algebra, a finite automaton, a σ-algebra, a Hausdorff space. In mathematics even abstract systems, i.e. systems that have not been abstracted from a well-known "lower" level system, are sometimes studied as well, but usually only if links between such systems and other systems whose relevance is taken for granted, can be established.

Particular challenges exist with hierarchies of abstracted mathematical systems, in which, at each level, concepts and terms at that level are borrowed from lower levels. Examples include "divisor" of "prime factor" in some algebraic structure beyond the integers, e.g. a ring of polynomials; "triangle" (Euclidean or spherical or hyperbolic?); "straight line" (in 3-space or in n-space or in, say, spherical geometry?) "open ball" (in 2-3 space or in n-space or in a general metric space?), "zero(-element)" (in a number domain or in a general ring?), "equation" (first degree, algebraic, functional, or differential?)

Again, by definition, not all traits and properties of the experiential domain(s) from which a given system is abstracted carry over to the abstracted system. This constitutes a further cognitive quantum leap. The resulting learning difficulties are aggravated by the fact that the very same set of objects can often be organised in several different ways. For instance, we can introduce several different group compositions on the real numbers. And a given set with more than one element can be organised in at least two different ways (and often many more) as a topological space. Introducing a quotient structure by identification of different elements through an equivalence relation can be interpreted as equating the equivalence relation with the identity relation. The learning difficulties involved in these processes are to do with students' interpretation of the ontology of mathematical objects. Many students tacitly seem to insist that the very nature of the mathematical objects, say the real numbers, entails the kinds of games the numbers can be involved in. For example, they see classical addition and multiplication as canonical to the extent that other compositions are deemed unnatural if not outright illegal.

These considerations and examples lead us to conclude that both abstracted and abstract concepts – or, differently put, abstraction and abstractness – constitute potential learning obstacles, not because of the absence or remoteness of experiential features within abstraction or abstractness, but, on the contrary, exactly because of the very presence and interference of such features in the abstract(ed) domains. In contrast, pure abstractness as found in games such as chess, go, or card games - i.e. abstractness without conceptual relations to any experiential domain, and hence without any obligation to reconcile existing experiences with the state of affairs in the abstract domain – does not seem to constitute cognitive learning obstacles of the same kind as with abstract(ed) systems related to well-known other systems as we have them in mathematics.

THE NEED FOR AND ROLE OF MATHEMATICAL PROOF

Proof and proving have been devoted a fair amount of attention in research during the last couple of decades. From this research three findings (amongst several others) are well known in the community.

Firstly, students have difficulty at coming to grips with the very notion of proof (Hoyles, 1997). What is a proof, really, in contradistinction to other, perhaps weaker, forms of justification? Why do we have it, and what functions does it serve? Many students are struggling with these questions and are somewhat bewildered by most of the answers provided by their teachers. This is a more basic issue than another issue that seems to greatly bother students too, namely "what are the approaches, methods and techniques that are available to us when attempting to prove a statement?" (cf. Harel and Sowder, 1998).

These problems take different shapes in different mathematical contexts. In domains that lend themselves to the use of visual representations, e.g. geometry and calculus, it is often unclear to students why it is necessary to prove statements that are visually obvious to them, such as "in a isosceles triangle the base angles are equal" or "the graph of a quadratic functions has either zero, one or two intersection points with the x-axis". In formal and abstract domains many students tend to activate substantive forms of reasoning borrowed from less abstract domains without understanding why this is not legal according to the rules of the game in the formal context. Students often see each statement as standing alone, and hence tend to check its truth or falsehood on the basis of personal impressions and convictions, without seeing the statement as part of a logico-conceptual network of related statements.

Secondly, although it may come as a bit of a surprise to some mathematicians and mathematics educators, it has been shown by Shlomo Vinner (Vinner, 2004), among others, that to many students the proof and the truth of a statement can be quite unrelated. This happens if students develop, on the one hand, a notion of proof as being a formal game, played according to more or less strange, and usually very restrictive, rules that have been instigated by closed societies of mathematics professionals who have lost contact with everyday common sense reasoning, and, on the other hand, interpret truth as something which is to do with matters empirical and relies on confrontation between claims and reality, something which is not subject to "the rule of rules".

Thirdly, as has been demonstrated by Gila Hanna (Hanna, 2000) and others, when it comes to proof justification and explanation are not always the same.

Instead, we should distinguish between proofs that justify, i.e. deduce the fact that a proposition holds from previously established propositions by means of logical inference, and proofs that explain, i.e. display, in ways that are compatible with general human experience and intuition, why a proposition must be true. It is often the case that one is led to accept the truth of a proposition as a result of a correct deduction without really having obtained an insight into its truth that goes beyond the steps in the formal proof, for instance an insight into why the steps of the proof reveal the truth of the proposition. Similarly, it's is also often the case – perhaps even more frequently – that one is convinced of the truth of a statement without being able to construct or follow a proof that justifies it within some formal framework. In other words, although some proofs not only justify but also explain why a proposition is true, many proofs justify without providing any explanation; and sometimes there are convincing explanations that cannot easily be formalised into valid proofs within a given theoretical framework (e.g. Stokes' theorem in vector analysis).

These findings alone suffice to point to learning problems related to proof and proving for many students. However, there are additional problems and challenges to consider.

To a good many students, proof is to do with propositions and theorems in textbooks, and proving is to do with exercises and problems set by teachers ("prove that such and such is the case…"). Thus to be knowledgeable about proof is to be able to understand and present textbook proofs, and to be knowledgeable about proving is to be able to demonstrate not too complex statements by not too demanding deductive chains in rather ritualised educational settings. The fact that proof and proving are not restricted to propositions and exercises / problems but are to do with all sorts of justification of mathematical claims, whether they appear in theoretical contexts, in problem solving, or in modelling (Niss, 2005), does not seem to be widely acknowledged amongst students (or teachers?). This makes proof and proving a special type of sports in the teaching and learning of mathematics, and not an integral part of almost any kind of mathematical activity. For students to develop a correct view of the roles of proof and proving in mathematics, it is essential to establish a much more multi-faceted and explicit presence of them in mathematics education than is often seen.

Many students do not see or accept the very need for rigorous proof, for this is a point in which mathematics differs fundamentally from almost any other discipline. Imagine a student who asks

"Why is not good enough, in mathematics, to be told by worthy authorities that such and such is the case? In history I have been told by trustworthy people that the French Revolution broke out in 1789. In biology I have been told that there are venomous toads in Australia. And in geology I have been told that the European Alps consist of folded mountains. I am allowed to consider such knowledge true without having witnessed the French Revolution, without having been to Australia or to a toad terrarium, and without having done geological investigations in the Alps. What makes mathematics so different that I, myself, have to go and check its claims? And moreover, even if I give in to the pressure and do accept that I have to convince myself rather than just be told, why am I not allowed to be convinced by checking a large number of cases? And that is not all. Why is it considered illegal to justify mathematical results, say in Euclidean plane geometry, by induction based on empirical measurements, when such an approach is considered perfectly decent in our closest neighbour discipline, physics?"

This suggests that the issue of rigorous proof is deeply rooted in the very nature of mathematics as a discipline, and – above all – in students' perception thereof. The crux of the matter seems to have three components. Firstly, most mathematical statements are non-empirical. The main alternative to rigorous proof by means of deduction would be empirical inspection accompanied by plausible reasoning. However, as the far majority of mathematical statements do not reside in an experiential world allowing for empirical inspection, this is not really an option except in a few cases. Secondly, there is generality. Mathematical statements have to be justified for all the infinitely many instances they cover, which cannot be fully done be empirical inspection, even if it were available. Of course, some degree of justification can be obtained if (epistemological) induction is accepted. But as it is actually possible, in hosts of cases, to obtain results by means of deduction only, for all the instances of a statement, induction has been discarded in favour of deduction, which then, since the ancient Greeks, has become the hallmark of mathematical justification. Finally, the validity and justification of mathematical statements are dependent on precise conditions. If the conditions are changed, the validity and the justification of a statement are likely to change as well. The way in which these ingredients are linked is terribly intricate, in particular in cases where the conditions for a statement appear to be technical, i.e. necessary for carrying through the specific proof considered, without being clearly related to the substantive truth of the statement in an obvious way.

We now come to the final aspect of proof and proving to be dealt with in this paper.

Every mathematics teacher at post-elementary levels has experienced that students often have difficulty at coming to grips with the issue "when is a proof a proof?". This issue actually consists of two sub-issues: "What are we allowed to invoke and make use of as assumptions and prerequisites, both in terms of facts taken as known and in terms of methods and techniques to de adopted, when proving a statement within some mathematical domain?", and "how can we tell when a proof is satisfactorily completed and has been presented with sufficient detail?". With any proof there are endless opportunities for asking "why?" at any step in the proof. What are the stopping criteria at our disposal? All this is not only a matter of how the individual student would answer these questions him- or herself but also of what answers his or her teacher provides, implicitly or explicitly. The issue "when is a proof a proof?" is a challenge to most students, even for those who do accept the relevance of the proof and proving game.

Any proof of a mathematical statement is based on some theoretical framework. Unless this is completely formal, axiomatic, and explicit – which is not the case with most domains in mathematics - it is usually not clear at all what it is legal to assume and to invoke. For example, are we allowed to make use of the real numbers or trigonometry when we prove non-quantitative statements in plane geometry, such as "the medians (or the angle bisectors) in a triangle intersect in one point"? Or when proving that any complex number (defined via pairs of reals) can be written in polar coordinates, what can we safely invoke in the context? Are we, for instance, allowed to make use of plane geometrical representations of vectors, lengths, angles, etc.? In combinatorial proofs – e.g. of the binomial theorem – what theoretical basis is in play? On what grounds can we derive probability distributions in finite sample spaces, e.g. of the sum of the eyes of two dice thrown at random? When accompanying proofs by illustrations, to what extent can we draw inferences from these illustrations?

The theoretical basis of a proof, and the amount of detail provided in a presentation of it, are matters of communicational pragmatism, tradition, and culture. They are not – and cannot be - subject to complete rigour, which is likely to be quite puzzling to students in contexts where we are talking about rigorous proof!

These considerations allow us to arrive at the following conclusion of this section. Proof and proving of statements and claims are at the heart of exercising the discipline of mathematics, both as an academic and as an educational subject, and as a subject to be applied in extra-mathematical contexts. Proof and proving are therefore interwoven with all other aspects of mathematical activity and are linked to the deepest epistemological characteristics of the discipline. This gives rise to immense cognitive demands on students as well as to the need for enculturation into mathematical communities.

SYMBOLISM AND FORMALISM IN MATHEMATICS

Symbolism and theoretical formalism have always been essential in mathematics and have given rise to major problems to learners. Mathematics teachers often locate these problems in students' insufficient mastery of the technical rules of the game(s). Students, teachers observe, have problems doing algebraic manipulations correctly and efficiently. They don't know when to use which algorithms to solve, say, equations, and how to use them. They don't know on what conditions certain types of manipulation and algorithms can be put to use.

I submit that the problems go far deeper. They are to do with the origins and rationales of the whole enterprise of symbolism and formalism. Let us illustrate the points by considering two examples, symbolic notation and equations.

Symbolic notation in mathematics serves a variety of quite different purposes and has a number of different roots, and the relationships between symbols and language are very complex (Drouhard and Teppo, 2004).

Historically, symbolic notation was first used as a short-hand – a system of abbreviations – to cater for easy representation of objects and to make statements short and tractable. This purpose is certainly still a fundamental one. Examples include the equality sign, = ; ordering signs, <, > ; symbols from logic such as $\exists$, $\Rightarrow$; set theoretical symbols, $\subseteq$, $\in$; operations +, ·; etc.

Secondly, symbols are used to make convention-based distinctions so as to facilitate communication. For instance, we normally use i, k, m and n to designate natural numbers, while p and q are integers. Oftentimes a, b, c, d are constants or parameters, whereas s, t, and u are real variables, often used to designate length or time. The letters x, y, and z denote variables, or unknowns in equations. Sometimes z is used for variables in the complex domain. Points in the plane or in 3-space are labelled P, Q, R, S, or T. Functions are denoted f, g, h or φ, ψ. A, B, C are often sets, while A, B , and C are often sets of sets. And in many contexts different alphabets are in play.

Thirdly, symbolic notation is used as an integral part of manipulation or calculation according to specific rules. Examples include arithmetical or algebraic operations; representation of geometrical objects in analytic or algebraic geometry by means of equations or parametrised expressions; matrix algebra; probability; etc.

One tricky aspect here is that these different purposes of symbolic notation are usually mixed in very intricate manners. This is, for instance, the case when short-hand becomes subjected to manipulation rules, like in expressions of formal logic, e.g. $(\exists x \forall y: P(x,y)) \Rightarrow (\forall y \exists x: P(x))$, $\neg(p \wedge q) \Leftrightarrow (\neg p \vee \neg q)$, or when mathematical requirements give rise to conventions, e.g. when we are forced to define a0 = 1, because we want exponents to be added when multiplying power expressions for all integer exponents, and because we have agreed that a-m = 1/am.

Another tricky aspect is that symbolic notation is often transferred unaltered from one domain to another, even though some features disappear and others emerge as a result of the transfer. For example, +, ·, 0, 1 are transferred from number domains to, say, domains of polynomials, matrices, functions, groups, fields, which implies that they designate entirely different operations or objects. Or when we use the notation eM for a matrix or an operator M. It goes without saying that over-generalisation or plain confusion are imminent dangers here.

Our second example is equations. Research suggests that the main problem in solving an equation of a non-routine form is not students' lack of procedural skill or knowledge of relevant formulae. Rather the problem is to come to grips with the very notion of equation and of the different parts played by the "agents" therein. This is true irrespective of the type of equation (algebraic, differential, functional).

What is an equation, really? What kind of object is it? Why is it relevant to seek to establish equations, and to try to solve them?

Antoine Bodin (Bodin, 1993) has shown that amongst students who could successfully and correctly solve the equation $7x - 3 = 13x + 15$, quite a few were not able to tell whether x = 10 is a solution to the equation.

What does it mean that the equation

$$x^2 - 2 = 0$$

has no rational solution, whereas it "suddenly" has two solutions in the real numbers, while

$$x^2 + 1 = 0$$

has no solution within the real numbers, but again, "suddenly", two in the complex domain?

Also, to completely solve the differential equation

$$xy' + ay = 0,$$

apart from understanding the specific notation involved, a fundamental insight into the concept of an ordinary differential equation is needed, and certainly no less so than procedural skills required to solve it.

The conclusion of this section is that many learning problems concerning mathematical symbolism and formalism seem to be closely connected with their fundamental purposes, multi-faceted roles and roots, rather than with the specific procedural rules of the games. Mastery of symbolism and formalism requires students to develop a kind of "controlled schizophrenia" between intuition (and sense-making) and formalism that allows them to switch between the two so as to distinguish between interpretation and meaning, on the one hand, and notation and rules, on the other hand. It seems to be essential for successful learning of mathematics that these facets of symbolism and formalism are put explicitly on the agenda of teaching, instead of being relegated to implicit, tacit learning between the lines.

OVERALL CONCLUSION

The nature and structure of mathematics give rise to fundamental, unavoidable, intrinsic problems and challenges to learning. In this paper we have only looked at three instances of this. There are, indeed, more to consider.

Against the background presented in this paper, there is no royal road to remedying the problems and challenges identified. Students who have successfully been able to learn mathematics have succeeded in overcoming them, either by their own efforts or through the help of excellent teachers. Uncovering and investigating the problems through research and explicitly putting them on the agenda of teaching seem to be necessary, albeit far from sufficient, means to counteract them.

REFERENCES

Bodin, A. (1993). What does to assess mean? The case of assessing mathematical knowledge. In Niss, M. (Ed.).*Investigations into assessment in mathematics eduation.* Dordrecht / Boston / London: Kluwer Academic Publishers, pp. 113-141.

Douady, R. (1991). Tool, object, setting, window: elements for analysing and constructing didactical situations in mathematics. In Bishop, A.J., Mellin-Olsen, S., van Dormolen, J. (Eds.) *Mathematical knowledge: Its growth through teaching*, Dordrecht: Kluwer Academic Publishers, pp. 109-130.

Drouhard, J-P., Teppo, A. (2004). Symbols and language. In Stacey, K., Chick, H., Kendal, M. (Eds.): *The future of the teaching and learning of algebra – The 12th ICMI study.* Boston / Dordrecht / New York / London: Kluwer Academic Publishers, pp. 227-264.

Hanna, G. (2000). Proof, explanation and exploration: An overview', *Educational Studies in Mathematics 44* (1&2), pp. 5-23.

Harel, G. & Sowder, L. (1998). Students' proof schemes: Results from exploratory studies, in Dubinsky, E., Schoenfeld, A.H. & Kaput, J. (Eds.). *Research on collegiate mathematics education, Vol. III*, Providenc, R.I., USA: American Mathematical Society, pp. 234-283.

Hoyles, C. (1997).The curricular shaping of students' approaches too proof', *For the Learning of Mathematics 17*(1), pp. 7-16.

Niss, M. (2005).Modelling and proving as forms of justification, in Henn, H-W. & Kaiser, G. (Eds.) *Mathematikunterricht im Spannungsfeld von Evolution un Evaluation: Festschrift für Werner Blum*. Hildesheim / Berlin: Verlag Franzbecker, pp. 175-183.

Otte, M. (2003). Complementarity, sets and numbers, *Educational Studies in Mathematics 53*(3), pp. 203-228.

Sfard, A.(1991). On the dual nature of mathematical conceptions: reflections on processes and objects as different sides of the same coin, *Educational Studies in Mathematics 26*(3), pp. 191-228.

Tall, D.(1991). Reflections. In Tall, D. (Ed.) *Advanced mathematical thinking*. Dordrecht / Boston / London: Kluwer Academic Publishers, pp. 251-259.

Tall, D. and Vinner, S. (1981). Concept image and concept definition in mathematics with particular reference to limits and continuity, *Educational Studies in Mathematics 12*(2), pp. 151-169.

Verschaffel, L., de Corte, E. (1997). Teaching realistic mathematical modeling in the elementary school: A teaching experiment with fifth graders, *Journal for Research in Mathematics Education 28*(5), pp. 577-601.

Vinner, S., and Hershkowitz, R. (1980). Concept images and common cognitive paths in the development of some simple geometrical concepts, in *Proceedings of the Fourth International Conference for the Psychology of Mathematics Education*, Berkeley, CA, pp 177-184.

Vinner, S. (2004). Mathematics education – procedures, rituals and man's search for meaning, in Fujita, H. et al. (Eds.). *Proceedings of the Ninth International Congress on Mathematical Education*. Norwell, MA, USA: Kluwer Academic Publishers, pp. 207-209. Full paper in press.

Mogens Niss
Roskilde university, Denmark

FRITZ SCHWEIGER

FUNDAMENTAL IDEAS.

A bridge between mathematics and mathematical education

THE SITUATION

The last century saw an increasing gap between mathematics as a scientific discipline and mathematics as a subject taught in schools. As the failure of the 'new maths' movement has shown this gap could not be bridged by a simplification of basic mathematical structures and could not be overcome by introducing exact definitions and proofs which were felt too difficult for students and teachers. But the problem remains and it was during the last ICME that this topic was discussed in a special Thematic Afternoon (see http://www.icme-10.dk/ and look for Programme: Thematic Afternoon C). With the risk of simplifying too much I state the following assertions.

1. The gap between mathematics as a technology for all and mathematics as a science is (almost?) not bridgeable.
2. The structure of present day mathematics has almost no influence on the teaching of mathematics.
3. Several mathematical cultures can be named: Mathematics in every day life or social practice, mathematics as a toolbox for applications, mathematics in school, and mathematics as a science.
4. It is more fruitful to acknowledge these facts than to try in vain to reconcile these different cultures.

The situation of present day mathematics can be easily judged by looking at the book Engquist & Schmid 2001, say or to the Mathematics Subject Classification which covers about 60 pages. On a more philosophical level Bishop 1991 describes the situation by six values attached to mathematical culture. Objectism and rationalism form the background ideology of mathematical culture. Control and progress are the feelings or sentiments which govern mathematical thinking. On the sociological level openness and mystery are discussed. Objectism favours an 'objective' view of reality, a world-view dominated by images of material objects. Rationalism means an attitude against inconsistency, disagreement, incongruity, and loss of certainty. Mathematics empowers us a considerable degree of prediction and control, and as one can recognise we always try to be 'better', i.e. to extend our research activities. Mathematical knowledge is basically shareware, open to everyone who is sufficiently initiated to the appropriate section of mathematical culture but strange enough mathematics is more often felt as a

J. Maasz, W. Schloeglmann (Eds.), New Mathematics Education Research and Practice, 63–73.

basically mysterious subject. However, mathematicians have different feelings about the mystery in mathematics. It could be the strange ontological state of mathematical entities or the amazing beauty of mathematics. A superficial view would find that mathematics is governed by axioms, theorems, and their proofs. It seems not to be possible to link mathematics teaching in schools with contemporary research. Some counterexamples like fractals or chaos theory are not really counterexamples because the rapid development of these disciplines has swept away the connections with research. However, these examples show at least that the idea of mathematics as a living topic has some chances.

These remarks lead me to two claims.

5. The main concern of school mathematics is to provide a skilful use of mathematics as a technology and to promote an understanding that much more mathematics is needed for the functionality of our society.

6. The conception of 'fundamental ideas' can serve both purposes.

School mathematics must deal with the other cultures: mathematics in every day life and mathematics as a toolbox, and to some extent with mathematics as a science. But since school mathematics is a kind of training (or in Bishop's term: playing) situation it will always have its own culture. The contents of school mathematics reflect a certain stage of the historical development of mathematics but will not see great changes in the future. A comparison with the techniques of writing and reading could be helpful: The historical roots are not relevant and the basics of these techniques will not change in the next future.

The use of computers seems to be a new cultural technique which is likely to start a revolution comparable with the invention of writing and reading or later in history with printing techniques. How far it will change the picture of mathematics is an open question. Experimental mathematics or computer assisted proofs could be the key words of such a change. Anyway, an understanding of the fact that mathematics is needed for our society requires an understanding what mathematics is.

In my opinion there is a hierarchy: first come basic skills (algorithmic procedures and interpreting data including some geometric representations, e.g. the map of the traffic net of a city) then come (and should come) understanding. Clearly, basic skills and understanding of concepts are deeply interwoven. There is also a third strand to be named: Preparation for vocational schools and university studies which are mathematically oriented. However, even at this level mathematics very often appears as a mere toolbox which can be used by engineers and natural scientists.

In my opinion a possible answer can be given in terms of the so-called "fundamental ideas" of mathematics.

THE ORIGINS

The origins of this notion are in the work of Jerome Bruner 1960 or even older. Whitehead 1911 complains on the study of mathematics: "...this failure of the science to live up to its reputation is that its fundamental ideas are not explained

...." A quotation from Bruner follows: "It is that the basic ideas that lie at the heart of all science and mathematics and the basic themes that give form to life and literature are as simple as they are powerful." (Bruner 1960:12/13)

Bruner's proposal could be well illustrated by examples from other subjects. Life, love, power ... can be seen as fundamental issues in teaching literature. Nutrition, shape, social organization, procreation ... may be fundamental ideas in biology.

Similar ideas have been issued by several mathematicians. We mention a prominent mathematician's voice: "The best aspect of modern mathematics is its emphasis on a few basic ideas such as symmetry, continuity and linearity which have very wide applications" (Atiyah 1977:73/74). Halmos has written an interesting essay "Does Mathematics Have Elements?" (Halmos 1981a). In this paper he remarks: "No doubt many mathematicians have noted that there are some basic ideas that keep cropping up, in widely different parts of their subject, combining and re-combining with one another in a way faintly reminiscent of how all matter is made up of elements." (Halmos 1981a:147).

Heitele 1975 tries to apply this concept to probability theory. "I have arrived at my list from four angles:
(1) In the frame of Bruner's conception,
(2) By studying the results of developmental psychology with respect to stochastic ideas,
(3) By studying the multifarious failures of adults in stochastic situations,
(4) By studying the history of probability." (Heitele 1975:190).

He also points out to the importance of errors. "There are fundamental ideas, as there are fundamental errors, and both are counterparts of each other. Such errors bridge the centuries, the ages and the cultural layers, and may be criteria of what is really `fundamental'" (Heitele 1975:191).

Schwill 1993 (compare also Schweiger 1984) introduces four criteria which can be summarized as follows. A fundamental idea should have a recurrence within different parts of mathematics. It should recur at various levels within the curriculum. It must be recovered in the historical development of mathematics. It should be anchored in corresponding activities of everyday life. The last point is related to Mac Lane's view that mathematics begins in the human experiences of moving, measuring, shaping, combining, and counting and that these lead, more or less in that order to disciplines such as applied mathematics, calculus, geometry, algebra, and number theory (Mac Lane 1992:11). This view is closely related to Bishop's idea of six basic mathematical activities (Bishop 1991).

The recent introduction of new powerful technology in schools clearly could stimulate again the discussion about the role of fundamental ideas in teaching mathematics.

SOME CATALOGUES

It is clear that mathematicians and mathematics teachers arrive at quite different lists of what they see as 'fundamental' in mathematics. As we will discuss later this does not invalidate my considerations. Let me present a short list of 'catalogues' of fundamental ideas or basic mathematical conceptions.

Bruner (1960) number, measure, probability

Atiyah (1977): symmetry, continuity, linearity

Jung (1978): algorithm, infinity, measuring

Halmos (1981a): universal algebra, size, composition, analogy

Halmos (1981b): algebra ~ size; geometry ~ shape; analysis ~ change

Schreiber (1979): algorithm, exhaustion, invariance, optimality, function, characterisation

Bender and Schreiber (1985): exhaustion, iteration, reduction, map, algorithm, quantity, continuity, optimality, invariance, infinity, ideation, abstraction, representation, space, unity

Tietze, Klika, and Wolpers (1981): algorithm, approximation, modelling, function, geometrisation, linearisation

Bishop (1991): counting ~ discrete aspect; locating ~ topographical features of the environment; measuring ~ continuity; designing ~ imagined form, shape, and pattern; playing ~ imagined and hypothetical behaviour; explaining ~ story telling

MacLane (1992): moving, measuring, shaping, combining, counting

Heymann (1996): number, measuring, spatial structuring, functional dependence, algorithm, modelling

Führer (1997): functional variation, induction, approximation, algorithm, invariance, symmetry, control

In the table below I give a synopsis of some of these proposals.

Comparison of some catalogues						
	Bruner	Jung	Schreiber	Tietze et al.	Mac Lane	Bishop
algorithm		x	X	x		
characterisation			X			
combining					x	
designing						x
exhaustion/approximation			X	x		
explaining						x
function			X	x		
geometrisation				x		
infinity		x				
invariance			X			
linearisation				x		
locating						x

measure, measuring	x	x			x	x
modelling				x		
moving					x	
number, counting	x				x	x
optimality			X			
playing						x
probability	x					
shaping					x	

In this direction we mention the root system of mathematics according to Steen (1990).
- Mathematical structures: numbers, algorithms, ratios, shapes, functions, data
- Mathematical attributes: linear, periodic, symmetric, continuous, random, maximum, approximate, smooth
- Mathematical actions: represent, control, prove, discover, apply, model, experiment, classify, visualize, compute
- Mathematical abstractions: symbols, infinity, optimization, logic, equivalence, change, similarity, recursion
- Mathematical attitudes: wonder, meaning, beauty, reality
- Mathematical behaviours: motion, chaos, resonance, iteration, stability, convergence, bifurcation, oscillation
- Mathematical dichotomies: discrete vs. continuous, finite vs. infinite, algorithmic vs. existential, stochastic vs. deterministic, exact vs. approximate

What Steen calls 'mathematical actions' and 'mathematical attitudes' is closest to the concept of 'fundamental ideas' as presented here, because 'fundamental ideas' are seen as activities or attitudes of mathematicians, teachers, students and anyone who does mathematics.

The last years saw an increasing emphasis on so-called 'standards'. Any list of such 'standards' clearly reflects some ideas of what is seen as 'fundamental'. We present one list as a typical example. We use some of the headlines of the Principles and Standards of School Mathematics (NCTM 2000).
- Number and operations: understand numbers, ways of representing numbers, relationships among numbers, and number systems; understand meanings of operations and how they relate to one another; compute fluently and make reasonable estimates.
- Algebra: understand patterns, relations, and functions; represent and analyze mathematical situations and structures using algebraic symbols; use mathematical models to represent and understand quantitative relationships; analyze change in various contexts.
- Geometry: analyze characteristics and properties of two- and three-dimensional geometric shapes and develop mathematical arguments about geometric relationships; specify locations and describe spatial relationships using coordinate geometry and other representational systems; apply transformations

and use symmetry to analyze mathematical situations; use visualization, spatial reasoning, and geometric modelling to solve problems.

- Measurement: understand measurable attributes of objects and the units, systems, and processes of measurement; apply appropriate techniques, tools, and formulas to determine measurements.
- Data analysis and probability: formulate questions that can be addressed with data and collect, organize, and display relevant data to answer them; select and use appropriate statistical methods to analyze data; develop and evaluate inferences and predictions that are based on data; understand and apply basic concepts of probability.

The list of these Content Standards is supplemented with a list of Process Standards: Problem solving, reasoning and proof, communication, connections, representations. It is worth to be mentioned that the item Connections is described as follows: recognize and use connections among mathematical ideas; understand how mathematical ideas interconnect and build on one another to produce a coherent whole; recognize and apply mathematics in contexts outside of mathematics.

CRITERIA FOR FUNDAMENTAL IDEAS

Looking at this table or the different catalogues one has the uneasy feeling that there is no agreement about fundamental ideas. On the other hand it is evident that almost every item mentioned represents some important feature of mathematics and the different conceptions could be structured into a semantic net. However, following the literature some criteria about the question which conceptions can be attributed as 'fundamental ideas' have emerged (Schweiger 1984, Schwill 1993). There are four descriptive criteria.

Fundamental ideas
- recur in the historical development of mathematics (time dimension)
- recur in different areas of mathematics (horizontal dimension)
- recur at different levels (vertical dimension)
- are anchored in everyday activities (human dimension).

Furthermore at least four normative criteria can be added.

Fundamental ideas should help to
- design curricula
- elucidate mathematical practice and the essence of mathematics
- build up semantic networks between different areas
- improve memory.

The so-called vertical dimension is strongly linked with the problem of curriculum design. The recurrence of an idea at different levels of mathematical abstraction should be reflected by the recurrence at different levels of the curriculum.

A lot of references could be added to illustrate the influence of 'fundamental ideas' on the conception of mathematics teaching. We refer to Führer 1997, Heymann 1996, and Picker 1985.

It is easy to see that most items of the mentioned catalogues meet these criteria to some extent. The human dimension links several levels: Mathematics in everyday life, mathematics as a toolbox, mathematics as a part of our culture, and mathematics as a science. Note that mathematics as a toolbox does not mean just calculating, but also interpreting of results and data. The recognition of geometric shapes or the use of diagrams and maps could also be mentioned here. Bishop's basic activities are reflected in mathematics as a symbolic technology. Speaking metaphorically, we can see mathematics as a tissue composed from two kinds of strands: fundamental ideas and topic areas. The human dimension bridges fundamental ideas with ethnomathematics but it should be emphasized that the time dimension inevitably leads to a certain 'Western' bias if one shapes a catalogue which is influenced by present day mathematics. It should be mentioned that the notion that fundamental ideas should lead to a better understanding of mathematics is closely related to mathematical literacy (see Legnink 2004, Neubrand 1990).

INDIVIDUALIZED CONSTRUCTIONS

In previous work (see Schweiger 1992) I also tried to formulate some candidates for fundamental ideas. I shortly mention some of these proposals.

Language and patterns

There is no doubt that the writing system has been of great importance in the development of mathematics. The thesis is that the written symbols do not just mean mathematical ideas but that the written symbols are patterns which can help to structure mathematics. This observation is related to Dörfler's conception of diagrammatic reasoning (Dörfler, this volume).

An example goes as follows. A basic property is the so-called exponential law for natural numbers, namely $(a^b)^c = a^{bc}$. Then with a suitable identification for sets we also have the relation $(A^B)^C = A^{BC}$. For linear spaces we get $(E^F)^G = E^{F \otimes G}$.

Another example is given by the geometric series. The equation $\frac{1}{1-x} = 1 + x + x^2 + \dots$ is valid for real numbers if $|x| < 1$. However if one inserts $x = -1$ we find $\frac{1}{2} = 1 - 1 + 1 - 1 + \dots$ which can be justified by statistical reasoning (or Cèsaro means). If we take $x = 2$ we find $-1 = 1 + 2 + 4 + 8 + \dots$.

This equation seems to be nonsense but can be transformed into a correct equation within p-adic analysis.

Testing and verification

The basic idea is to look at some properties which are characteristic for some situations. How does one test the freshness of food or the quality of wine? One develops a feeling for some characteristic features. More seriously, medical doctors do a lot of tests to find out the state of your health. We list some examples from mathematics.

The system of n linear equations in n variables $Ax = b$ has a unique solution if and only if $\det A \neq 0$.

A necessary condition that the number p is a local extremum of a differentiable function f is the condition $f'(p) = 0$.

The cubic equation $x^3 + px + q = 0$ has three real solutions if and only if its discriminant is a negative number.

The arithmetical equation $ab = c$ is correct only if the equation $ab = c \bmod m$ is correct. The values $m = 9$ or $m = 11$ lead to nice tests.

Functions, maps, operators

There is no doubt that the making of maps, models, pictures and so on is a common activity. Functions, maps, and operators are basic objects in mathematics. In the connection with "fundamental ideas" we have to look at examples where the introduction of these objects changed the picture. A good example seems to be set theory. The difference between finite or infinite sets has been known since antiquity. The introduction of the concept of equivalence was an important change (two sets A and B are called equivalent if there exists a bijective map $A \to B$). Another example would be the introduction of the dual space i. e. the space of all linear functionals.

– Changing the viewpoint

A lot of progress in mathematics is due to changing the viewpoint, more specifically to make a property a new definition. A natural number $p \geq 2$ is called a prime number if p has no other divisors than 1 and p. Central is the so-called lemma of Euclid: A number p is prime if and only if p/ab implies p/a or p/b.

Prototypes and canonical forms

One of the best illustrations for the interplay between prototypes and normal forms are the conic sections. The three types ellipsis, hyperbola, and parabola are prototypes and supply an almost complete classification.

Iteration and recursion

The observation of repeating cycles is very old. The use of iteration for preparing tools, pottery, canoes and so on is an early activity. Repetition is an important element in artistic production. Mathematical counterparts are: Iteration of functions, approximation, generation of fractals.

– *Repairing and Improving*

This point relates to the fact that many mathematical concepts have been introduced with the aim to save a situation, to fill a gap in a proof, and so on. One example is uniform convergence. The sequence of continuous functions $f_n(x) = x^n$ converges at every point in the interval $[0,1]$. However, the limit function is not continuous. The notion of uniform convergence is introduced to secure that the limit of a sequence of continuous functions is continuous.

The previous list is by far not exhaustive. In my opinion the most important point is that student teachers, teachers, and teacher educators consider the possibility of finding such fundamental ideas. This process clearly should involve a communicative structure and could take place in seminars, during in-service-education, and very important during casual discussions. Such a list will reflect the *personal view of mathematics* and will be open to revision. The awareness of such universal features of mathematical activity should be more central in this connection.

RESEARCH ACTIVITIES

We list some ideas about research activities. The focus could be more 'theoretical' or more 'practical':
- Construction of semantic nets between different fundamental ideas
- Analysis of teaching materials, curricula, and standards along the lines of fundamental ideas
- Connections to other important concepts like mathematical literacy, orientation on applications, orientation on problem solving, orientation on structures, 'genetischer Unterricht'
- Experiments with learning materials which are designed according to this guideline
- Exploring mathematical beliefs (of students and teachers) and fundamental ideas
- Validation of some aspects of the human dimension

SCHWEIGER

It should be mentioned that there are some interesting proposals about the role of fundamental ideas for teaching mathematics like Schupp 1984, Hischer 1888, 2002, and Vohns 2000, 2005.

REFERENCES

Atiyah, M. F. (1997). Trends in pure mathematics. In Athen, H. and Kunle, H. (Eds.). *Proc. Third ICME* Organising Committee of 3rd ICME .

Bender, P. and Schreiber, A. (1985). *Operative Genese der Geometrie.* Wien/Stuttgart.

Bishop, Alan J. (1991). *Mathematical enculturation: A cultural perspective on mathematics education.* Dordrecht: Kluwer.

Bruner, J. S. (1960). *The process of education.* Cambridge, Mass.: Harvard University Press

Dörfler, W.: Inscriptions as objects of mathematical activities. This volume.

Engquist, B. & Schmid, W. (Eds.) (2001). *Mathematics unlimited – 2001 and beyond.* Berlin. Heidelberg. New York: Springer.

Führer, L. (1997). *Pädagogik des Mathematikunterrichts.* Braunschweig: Vieweg.

Halmos, P. (1981a). Does mathematics have elements? *The Mathematical Intelligencer, 3,* 147-153.

Halmos, P.R. (1981b). Applied mathematics is bad mathematics. In Steen, L.A. (Ed.). *Mathematics tomorrow.* New York/Heidelberg/Berlin: Springer-Verlag, 9-20.

Heitele, D. (1975). An epistemological view on fundamental stochastic ideas. *Educational Studies in . Mathematics 6 ,* 187 – 205.

Heymann, H. W. (1996). *Allgemeinbildung und Mathematik.* Weinheim und Basel: Beltz.

Hischer, H. (1998). Fundamentale Ideen" und "Historische Verankerung" dargestellt am Beispiel der Mittelwertbildung, *Zeitschrif fürDidaktik der Mathematik, 21,* 3 – 20.

Hischer, H. (2002). Viertausend Jahre Mittelwertbildung – Eine fundamentale Idee der Mathematik und didaktische Implikationen. *Zeitschrif fürDidaktik der Mathematik, 25,* 3-51.

Jung, W. (1978). Zum Begriff einer mathematischen Bildung. Rückblick auf 15 Jahre Mathematikdidaktik. *Zeitschrif fürDidaktik der Mathematik 1* (1978), 161 – 176.

Lengnink, Katja (2004). Reflektieren und Beurteilen von Mathematik aus der Bildungsperspektive mathematischer Mündigkeit. *Beiträge zum Mathematikunterricht* 2004, 337-340.

Mac Lane, S. (1992). The protean character of mathematics. In Echeverría, J., Ibarra, A. and Mormann, T. (Eds.). *The space of mathematics.* Berlin. New York: Walter de Gruyter.

National Council of Teachers of Mathematics (2000). *Principles and standards for school mathematics.* National Council of Teachers.

Neubrand, M. (1990). Stoffvermittlung und Reflexion: Mögliche Verbindungen im Mathematikunterricht. *Zeitschrif fürDidaktik der Mathematik, 13,* 21-48.

Picker, B. (1985). Mathematikunterricht als Vermittlung von grundlegenden Ideen. *MU, 31*(4) (1985), 6 – 9.

Schupp, H. (1984). Optimieren als Leitlinie im Mathematikunterricht. *Math. Semesterberichte 31,* 59 – 76.

Schreiber, A. (1979).Universelle Ideen im mathematischen Denken - ein Forschungsgegenstand der Fachdidaktik. *Zeitschrif fürDidaktik der Mathematik, 2,* 165 – 171.

Schweiger, F. (1984). Fundamental ideas in mathematics - Can they help to develop positive mathematical attitudes? In: *A collection of papers on pre-service teacher education.* Action Group 6. ICME-5 Adelaide 1984.

Schweiger, F. (1992). Fundamentale Ideen. Eine geistesgeschichtliche Studie zur Mathematikdidaktik. *JMD, 13,* 199 – 214.

Schwill, A. (1993). Fundamentale Ideen der Informatik, *Zeitschrif fürDidaktik der Mathematik, 93*(1), 20-31.

Tietze, U. P., Klika, M., and Wolpers, H. (1981). *Didaktikdes Mathematikunterrichts in der Sekundarstufe II.* Braunschweig: Vieweg.

Vohns, A. (2000). Das Messen als fundamentale Idee im Mathematikunterricht der Sekundarstufe I Hausarbeit im Rahmen der Ersten Staatsprüfung. Universität-Gesamthochschule Siegen. http://www.math.uni-siegen.de/didaktik/downl/messen.pdf

Vohns, A. (2005). Fundamentale Ideen und Grundvorstellungen: Versuch einer konstruktiven Zusammenfassung am Beispiel der Addition von Brüchen. *JMD*, *26*, 52 – 79.

Whitehead, A. N. (1911). *An introduction to mathematics*. London/New York/Toronto: Oxford University Press.

Fritz Schweiger
Universität Salzburg, Austria

MICHAEL OTTE

LEARNING DIFFICULTIES RESULTING FROM THE NATURE OF MODERN MATHEMATICS: THE PROBLEM OF EXPLANATION

INTRODUCTION

In the following paragraphs we shall try and indicate some reasons and examples of learning or teaching difficulties resulting from the historical transformation of pure mathematics and natural science during the $17^{th}/20^{th}$ centuries. It should become manifest, how deeply connected our notions of mathematics are to fundamental questions of our self-image.

The learning difficulties meant, result not the least from the fact that the concept of "explanation" is central to our educational practices and aims, whereas modern science and mathematics do not provide explanations of anything in the sense desired. They are either too hypothetical and abstract or too instrumental and technical.

But we teach mathematics at school because we believe that it will help to establish and legitimate a discourse which everybody of good will can accept in good faith. And such a belief has been at the bottom of all human aspirations for rationality and intelligibility since the times of the Greek. Mathematics could not fruitfully be organized and pursued at school as a primarily professional topic. Mathematical education has, like other subjects, also to contribute to a common search for clarity on fundamental issues.

Now, mathematical explications are based on proofs and a mathematical proof is considered valid because of its form, not its content, since Leibniz at least (Hacking 1980). Few people believe, however, that form can explain anything. Leibniz, for example, did not, as we shall see soon.

I.

Explanation is asymmetric, mathematical calculation or logical proof are not. Aristotle has made this very clear already, thereby differentiating between explanation and logical deduction or mathematical calculation (Post. Anal., Book I, chap. 13, 78a). One can calculate the height of the flagpole from the length of its shadow, but the shadow does not produce the flagpole. If one sees a shadow one looks for a cause and an explanation. If one sees a flagpole there seems to be no

J. Maasz, W. Schloeglmann (Eds.), New Mathematics Education Research and Practice, 75–94.

question whatsoever. "We can explain the length of the of the shadow by reference to the height of the flagpole, and not vice versa" (Newton-Smith 2000, 129)

And worse: a "new light" (Kant) must have flashed on the mind of people like Thales, when they perceived that the relation between the length of a flagpole and the length of its shadow enables one to calculate the height of the pyramid, given the length of its shadow. "For he found that it was not sufficient to meditate on the figure as it lay before his eyes, ... and thus endeavor to get at knowledge of its properties, but that it was necessary to produce these properties, as it were, by a positive a priori construction" (Kant, Critique of Pure Reason, Preface to the Second Edition 1787). And indeed, the flagpole in itself has no positive relationship whatsoever to the pyramid as such. This implies, according to Hume or to Kant, that there do not exist a priori reasons to assume that things or laws must have a certain form, rather than another; and thus generalization of mathematical knowledge becomes a very deep problem.

One might object that mathematics is not concerned with flagpoles, pyramids and the like. But such talk does not help very much, as we have witnessed since Descartes' arithmetization of geometry a gradual destruction of the pre-established harmony between method and object of mathematical inquiry (Boutroux 1920) and have also witnessed an explosive growth and huge generalization of mathematical knowledge during the last 150 years or so. This tremendous and unprecedented growth of mathematical knowledge was not least the result of the discovery of relationships between issues and areas of mathematics that had apparently nothing in common with each other.

Neither mathematics nor modern science are analytic and explanatory in a straight forward sense; nor are they mere formal games, however. Mathematics cannot be reasonably be characterized independently from its applications. The applications of a concept or a theory require, however, pragmatic decisions and do not spring from the "essential" nature of things in themselves. Lebesgue (1875-1941), the great innovator of modern analysis, talking to school teachers once said the following:

"Measure is the starting point of all mathematical applications, and since applied mathematics obviously preceded pure mathematics (mathematical logic), it is usually supposed that geometry originated in the measure of areas and volumes. Furthermore, measure provides us with numbers, the very subject of analysis. Therefore, we discuss the measure of quantities at all three levels of teaching: primary, secondary, and higher" (Lebesgue 1965, 11)

Three observations should be added at this place. First applied mathematics founds pure mathematics, according to Lebesgue. Second pure mathematics is considered by him as synonymous with mathematical logic or with a mere formal language. And third, all teaching requires a philosophy of mathematics such that any teacher needs to consider the problem of mathematical application and explanation. Such an attitude seems attractive to teachers, but it is not without difficulties, concerning the problem of generalization, as we shall see (in the next part).

There exists an extended and unsurveyable discussion about the problem of explanation, showing in particular that there is no universal definition of the term "scientific or mathematical explanation". The traditional and prevailing understanding of the notion comes down to us from Aristotle. Aristotle's Posterior Analytics is the first elaborated theory in the Western philosophical and scientific traditions of the nature and structure of science and its influence reaches well into our times. It had long been accepted with such a degree of unanimity that nobody even thought of imputing special merit to Aristotle for his establishment of it.

Aristotle discusses the difference between knowledge of the fact and knowledge of the reasoned fact by the following example. "Let C stand for planets, B for not twinkling, and A for being near. Then its is true to state B of C ... But it is also true to state A of B; ... Then A must apply to C; and so it has been proved that the planets are near. Thus this syllogism proves not the reason but the fact, for it is not because the planets do not twinkle that they are near, but because they are near they do not twinkle" (Aristotle, Post. Analytic, Book I, chapter 13, 78a-b).

With respect to mathematics and the exact sciences Aristotle's notion of science as explanation became gradually devaluated by the growing interest in the recording of facts and by the hypothetical deductive approach of modern axiomatics, which in its essential tenets is not confined to mathematics at all. It reduces mathematical explanations to mere deductions.

Hence resulted, since some time now, a widespread debate about mathematical explanation and rigorous proof in mathematics education as well as in the philosophy of mathematics (for an overview see Mancosu 2000 and 2001; Hanna 2000). In this discussion over and again a distinction between proofs that prove against proofs that explain has played an important part. But nobody has been able so far to characterize this distinction clearly and without falling back on unreasonable dichotomies, like psychologism vs. Platonism, etc. It has, quite to the contrary in fact, become rather common nowadays to contrast subjective insight and explanation with objective foundation and conviction. Aristotle's model of explanation had relied heavily on the concordance between science and common sense and during the 19th century this conformity broke down.

When in the course of the 19th/20th centuries the humanities (Geisteswissenschaften) were developed by W. Dilthey (1833-1911) and others, it became common to contrast understanding and interpretation, as the basis of the humanities, with scientific and mathematical explanation. This distinction resulted later on in the notion of the "two cultures" (Snow). Snow's basic thesis was that the breakdown of communication between the sciences and the humanities (the "two cultures" of the title) was a major hindrance to solving the world's problems (see C.P. Snow 1993).

II.

Any explanation assumes some foundations or causes. Axiomatics in the traditional sense seemed to furnish these foundations. But when Euclid axiomatized geometry what he really accomplished was the exhibition of the possibility of alternative, non-Euclidean geometries and thus of mathematical generalization.

The common tendency to regard incompleteness as vindicating those who have emphasized the primacy of intuition, as opposed to those who emphasize with Hilbert, Gödel or Kolmogorov the importance of formalism, proves rather superficial, because it ignores "that the very meaning of the incompleteness of formalism is that it can be effectively used to discover new truths inaccessible to its proof-mechanism, but these new truths were presumably undiscoverable by any other method. How else would one discover the 'truth' of a Gödel sentence other than by using formalism meta-mathematically? We have here not only the discovery of a new way of using formalism, but a proof of the eternal indispensability of the formalism for the discovery of new mathematical truths" (Webb 1980, 126/127).

Axiomatics and formal proof have little to do with founding a discipline, even though that could have been the motivation for establishing them. They are simply ways of organizing some field and thus to make its frontiers and alternatives or possible generalizations clearer or even imaginable in the first place. The essence of knowledge is its growth and insight begins at the frontiers of knowledge. Mathematics and science surprise established expectations more often, than they confirm them. Such insights are not always welcome, however, not even among mathematicians.

For instance, when Zermelo explained the "Wohlordnungssatz" by means of a widely used and seemingly inconspicuous "principle", as he called it, the astonishing result, namely the theorem that any set can be well-ordered, stimulated people to look more closely into that principle and it subsequently was transformed into the most important and most controversial axiom of all set theoretical mathematics, namely the Axiom of Choice. After Zermelo had published his proof in Mathematische Annalen in 1905 and had in course of his argument explicitly formulated the axiom of choice, most mathematicians reacted critically to Zermelo's publication, even though many of them had used such choices before, with a greater or lesser degree of awareness in their own research in set theory, analysis and algebraic number theory.

Among the debaters was a group of French constructivists and quasi-empiricist of which Borel and Lebesgue seemed the most critical. In December 1904 Borel had "finished a brief article, requested by David Hilbert as an editor of Mathematische Annalen, on the question of Zermelo's proof" (Moore 1982, 93). Borel's article stimulated an exchange of letters between himself, Hadamard, Baire and Lebesgue, which was finally published in the Bulletin de la Soc. Math. de France (see Hadamard 1905). This sequence of letters "remains a classic statement on the grounds for accepting or rejecting the Axiom" (of Choice) (Moore 1982, 98).

All arguments of these publications were addressed to the problems of an intuitive comprehension of this axiom and nobody bothered himself with the question of its deductive fertility or methodological importance. Today the situation may have changed and the attitude as expressed in the following quotation from the introduction of a well established and widely used university textbook sounds much more familiar to us:

"The fundamental axiom of set theory, the axiom of choice will be freely used throughout this book. In fact, its use is absolutely essential for the success of certain abstract methods. Gödel has shown that, if mathematics is consistent without the axiom of choice, then it remains consistent if this axiom is added" (Loomis 1953, 2).

One should keep in mind, however, that axioms are not arbitrarily designed postulates, but are the result of experience and careful analysis. In conclusion we note that the premises of mathematical arguments have to be presented in such a way as to render them intuitively acceptable and clear, as well as, methodologically productive. This may sound somewhat paradoxical, as it requires conceiving of intuition as simultaneously a means and an object of cognition. Means and objects become quasi indistinguishable when considering the process of generalization in its complete dynamics.

Jerome Bruner (1961) had attributed an important didactical role to the "fundamental ideas" of science and mathematics. On the one hand, these ideas are what the development of an entire theory is devoted to unraveling and to explicating. In mathematics, to understand a concept means to develop a theory, and vice versa, the theory as a whole is logically founded, if it can be understood as an original idea, which has been developed, made concrete, and unfolded. The most far-reaching unfolding of the theory substantiates the original concept, although it is founded on the latter. Hence, these ideas are the goal of theory development.

These ideas are, however, at the same time its beginning and its base. This means that they have to be intuitively impressive, must motivate activity and orient representation. Although by intuition something is only given to us, rather than being apprehended, this presence is essential to begin with as it is an object of activity and motivates it. As long as an object is not in some way incorporated into a conceptual system or theory, it is not really known and we cannot reflect on it. It seems that in the initial states until something is fully understood this something dominates us, rather than the other way around. One must therefore take into account that general ideas and particular incorporations or applications of them are inseparable, transforming these general ideas into processes as just described.

III.

When humanity first tried to explain the world the universe was conceived of in anthropocentric terms, like being a sacred text, which had to be deciphered and interpreted by wise men.

What is the world? What is this or that? Whence does it come from? What does it mean? These were the first questions. And the answers were searched in God. God is the explanation of everything, it was said (Nicolas of Cusa, De docta Ignorantia, II, 3). Nicolas of Cusa (1401-1464), with his Neo-Platonic emphasis on human mental creativity as the image of God's creativity, also united, however, essential concepts and ideas that underlie the dynamic development of later post-Renaissance European science.

Then came the Copernican Revolution! In 1543 Nicolas Copernicus (1473-1543) published his treatise De Revolutionibus Orbium Coelestium (The Revolution of Celestial Spheres) where a new view of the world is presented: the heliocentric model.

The most important aspect of Copernicus' work is that it forever changed the place of man in the cosmos and thereby changed the idea of what it means to explain that cosmos. This change did not occur immediately and when it occurred it was not clearly noticed until Galileo (1564-1642) and Descartes (1596-1650) had begun to outline its epistemological consequences. Copernicus himself had even tried to minimize the philosophical implications, emphasizing that he had merely been led by the search for the "most transparent proofs" ("liquidissima demonstratio"; Dedication of De Revol. to Pope Paul III.). And his friend A. Osiander wrote a foreword in which he assured that Copernicus "has done nothing which merits blame". For it belongs to the job of the astronomer, after observation of the movements of the planets has been completed, "to think up or construct whatever causes or hypotheses he pleases such that ... those same movements can be calculated from the principles of geometry for the past and for the future too".

Now we are not concerned here with the question what Copernicus or his friend Osiander really believed or whether they believed the same, rather futile questions anyway, but we are interested in the type of argument used: mathematical modes of description seemed useful in the investigation of the world, but they were not assumed to provide substantial explanations of that world (for more details see: Hatfield 1990). Kant had quite pointedly emphasized such an attitude, as we have seen already.

It is nevertheless hard to underestimate the importance of Copernicus' work: it challenged the age long views of the way the universe worked and the preponderance of the Earth and, by extension, of human beings. The realization that we, our planet, are quite common in the heavens and reproduced by myriads of planetary systems provided a sobering (though unsettling) view of the universe. All the reassurances of the cosmology of the Middle Ages were gone, and a new view of the world, less secure and comfortable, came into being. Hans Blumenberg in his Genesis der Kopernikanischen Welt describes the Copernican Revolution as follows:

"To translate the notion of the object of astronomy by saying that stars are lawfully moving points of light in the sky in a way into the language of the theology of genesis, that the answer to the question as to which use and for which task God destined the celestial bodies, becomes: motion and shining were their activities, means precisely the liberation of the astronomic object both from an immediate teleology and from the assumption that this huge expense contained some secret message discernible for man. The opportunity for the autonomy of reason consists in the very fact that nature does not have the meaning of a text addressed to man, or of a tool lying in readiness for him" (Blumenberg 1975, 49).

By saying the world is no text addressed to us humans and interpretable from our subjective point of view one might intend to say that not everything in the world has some meaning, that the possibilities of explaining things are therefore restricted and that our knowledge claims are limited. And thereby a more skeptical, de-centered and exploratory spirit arose: What is objectivity? What is knowledge? Does it exist? Can we humans reach truth? Such were now the questions, posed by Descartes, for example, and by others.

After being assured of the existence of true knowledge by its undeniable and everywhere perceivable growth, it was asked how this growth came about. How is knowledge possible? How is pure mathematics possible in particular? What are its conditions? These were fundamental questions formulated by Kant (1724-1804), for example.

All knowledge is, according to Kant, to be considered as relative to the human constitution and answers to the above questions depended thus on an answer to the question: "What is human rationality?"; "What is Man?"

To this in turn a plurality of different answers were given in the course of the last 200 years or so, by philosophy, religion, history, biology, semiotics or sociology and others respectively. Generally it became gradually acknowledged that the question is about the relationship between general and particular as well as that it should be answered from a genetic or evolutionary point of view.

Hence comes the final question of our list: How do humans evolve and grow? How personal representations become generalized? Education, teaching and learning became relevant perspectives in face of this latter question.

Now, what are the main obstacles to generalization? The problem of mathematics education lies, we believe, in an empiricist and reductionistic epistemology. Everyday thinking and theoretical knowledge seem oceans apart. But mathematics and science themselves are also invaded by reductionism, which in certain forms may even be unavoidable. Nevertheless, mathematics, in particular, is difficult for the learner, not because it is rigorous, - calculations should always be more or less exact,- not because of the technical complications of its methods of reasoning, but because we cannot always reduce the unknown to the already familiar and trivially known, and thus "explain" it. We always have to generalize and to widen our vision of reality and to be able to do so, we have to perceive mathematics as a reality sui generis.

IV.

The little child asks: Why does occur X? Wherefrom comes Y? What is Z?

And the mother patiently and continuously goes on to answer all questions and to explain things. If she is an educated person she will try to formulate her explanations in terms of the received views of mathematics and science.

Do science and mathematics provide explanations, however? When the world was still a quasi religious text, it needed authorities to grasp and explain its message. Then people wanted to directly read in the great "Book of Nature". And Galileo's insistence that this Book of Nature was written in the language of mathematics changed natural philosophy from a verbal, qualitative account to a mathematical one.

Nonetheless, as we have said with respect to Copernicus already (and a similar case could be made with respect to Galileo (see Duhem 1991, 43)), neither the status of mathematical explanations nor the notion of mathematical proof were uncontroversial. Euclid, for example, was criticized still in the 16th century, because his proofs did not always give the essence of the matter. When in the proof of Theorem 1 of Euclid's Elements, Euclid shows that an equilateral triangle could be constructed upon a given segment, he uses circles to determine the third vertex. But the circles have nothing to do essentially with the triangle, it was said. And Descartes, also believing that Euclidean mathematics and Aristotelian syllogism serve better to explain things known already, rather than discovering new ones, set out to develop a new mathematics of discovery (Regulae IV). From this resulted then the never-ending debate about analysis and synthesis in mathematics (Israel 1997).

Christopher Columbus still explained the way to the West Indies to a royal committee constituted mainly of religious experts, before discovering them, although he himself never abandoned the belief that he had reached Asia (because it was this what he had explained). The newly discovered lands seemed both a proof of the inadequacy of the traditional conception of science and a stimulus to enter into the search for new types of knowledge.

"But while the experimental philosophers could easily imagine themselves as explorers of the secrets of nature, the case was more difficult for mathematicians. Mathematics, with its rigorous, formal, and deductive structure, appeared to be an ill-suited terrain for intellectual exploration. ..... Mathematicians, it seemed, did not seek out new knowledge or uncover hidden truths in the manner of geographical explorers. Instead, taking Euclidean geometry as their model, they sought to draw true and necessary conclusions from a set of simple assumptions. The strength of mathematics lay in the certainty of its demonstrations and the incontrovertible truth of its claims, not in uncovering new and veiled secrets" (Alexander 2001, 2).

This statement is not completely true, as we have seen already citing Descartes and it severely underestimates the vital importance of mathematical deduction as part of the experimental method (see: Reichenbach 1951). Nevertheless it remains noticeable because it indicates a deep gulf between the logical and empirical, between the analytical and synthetical, which persists in positivistic philosophies of science up to the present day (see, for example, Quine: Two Dogmas of Empiricism).

Mathematics nonetheless became a means to organize knowledge and on this basis to make new discoveries in the hands of people like Descartes, Leibniz, Wallis, Newton and others. The problem was how to reconcile the Aristotelian ideal of scientific explanation of the world with the method of mathematics and inductive science. For the whole of the 17th and most of the 18th century to explain a physical phenomenon meant to give the physical mechanism involved in its production. Descartes by conceiving of nature largely in geometrical terms, as res extensa was able to make use of mathematics and still stick to the ideal of explanation. With the introduction of the notion of force, however, that is, conceiving of motion in dynamical terms, rather than kinematically, the problem grew harder. Leibniz relational notion of space is, for example, absolutely convincing within the kinematical view. As soon as dynamical issues enter, however, things become complicated and Leibniz must explicitly assume a double meaning of the concept of motion. Mathematics in general must acknowledge the reality of hypostatic abstractions, like vector, function, set, etc, that is assume a realistic, rather than a nominalist philosophy. The foundational crisis of mathematics, that began around the turn of the 20th century, was caused essentially by doubts and criticisms of the new Platonic essentialism brought about by Bolzano and Cantor (remember the criticism of Lebesgue).

Already since the 17th century there seemed to remain essentially two options for mathematization. One had either to give up the traditional homogeneity or harmony between object and method – like in the Cartesian arithmetization of geometry -, which was at the base of the classical idea of scientific explanation, or one had to conceive of a more complicated metaphysics and mathematical ontology. Leibniz (1646-1716) essentially followed this way, whereas Newton (1642-1727) opted for the first alternative. Leibniz wanted, like Grassmann after him, to construct a calculus, a characteristica, which allows "to calculate with the things themselves" (Otte 1989, 16ff).

Newton thought that the relationship between mathematics and natural philosophy is methodological, rather than ontological, contrary to Galileo, Huygens or Leibniz (Hacking 1984; Ihmig 2005, 247).

The preface of Huygens (1629-1695) Treatise on Light (written in 1678 and published in 1690) contains "one of the earliest statements of the hypothetic-deductive method in science" (Matthews). "Demonstrations in optics", Huygens wrote, "as in every science where geometry is applied to matter, are based on experimental facts" (quoted from Matthews 1989, 127). Some philosophers have, however, "tried to find the origin and the cause of these facts" and have tried to explain them; this in turn meant to Huygens describe them in terms of matter and motion. Such explanations therefore had to contain hypothetical assumptions.

Leibniz did, like Huygens, not believe that geometry alone could give us absolutely secure optical knowledge (Nouv. Ess., Book IV, chapt. 2+3). And he argued against a merely empirical attitude claiming that the fundamental principle of natural philosophy, "that everything in nature occurs in a mechanical manner" could never be deduced from experience alone. Therefore, in order to refute empiricism as well as Cartesian dualism, Leibniz revived Aristotelian ideas about the notion of "substance". Substances were the subjects of predication, the unities in change and diversity and the true sources of activity. And he called the substances causes of phenomena, that is, "true hypotheses" (Nouv. Ess. Book IV, 13). In this way he established his conviction that knowledge must always be proven knowledge. Leibniz searched for a thoroughly intelligible world, in which even contingent facts would find their explanation, hence his principle of sufficient reason. In his second letter to Clarke he wrote:

"In order to proceed from mathematics to natural philosophy, another principle is requisite, as I have observed in my *Theodicy*: I mean, the principle of a sufficient reason, viz. that nothing happens without a reason why it should be so, rather than otherwise. .... by that single principle, viz. that there ought to be a sufficient reason why things should be so, and not otherwise, one may demonstrate the being of God, and all the other parts of metaphysics or natural theology; and even, in some measure, those principles of natural philosophy, that are independent upon mathematics: I mean, the dynamical principles, or the principles of force" (Leibniz's 2nd letter, Alexander 1956, 15-6).

The principle of sufficient reason was his main argument against "materialists" like Newton, who "confine themselves altogether to mathematical principles, and admit only bodies; whereas the Christian mathematicians admit also immaterial substances" (Leibniz second letter, Alexander1956, 15). Mathematical proofs are formal, and form cannot be an adequate explanation of anything. And nnatural laws, being mere mathematical regularities, are contingent themselves and must be justified by substantial reasons. In his fifth reply to Clarke Leibniz says that a law

"cannot be regular, without being reasonable; nor natural, unless it can be explained by the natures of creatures" (Alexander1956, 94).

Newton, however, wanted to end this metaphysics based, analytical ideal of science and his Principia "marks, conceptually, a radical departure from the then dominant tradition of a mechanical philosophy that explained phenomena, most often qualitatively, by contact forces" (Gingras 2001, 384f). Aristotelian science of the empirical phenomena was descriptive and qualitative. With Newton it was to explain nature in mathematical terms, rather than speculating about the essence of things. Thus physics became "philosophical", but the new "natural philosophy" was to be based on observation and mathematical deduction. Everything that reaches beyond the observable or logical is of a purely hypothetical nature. Hypotheses non fingo, Newton had famously said.

"For whatever is not deduced from the phenomena is to be called a hypothesis; and hypotheses, whether metaphysical or physical, whether occult qualities or mechanical, have no place in experimental philosophy. In this philosophy particular propositions are inferred from the phenomena, and afterwards rendered general by induction. ..... to us it is enough that gravity does really exist, and act according to the laws which we have explained, and abundantly serves to account for all the motions of the celestial bodies, and of our sea" (Newton, Mathematical Principles of Natural Philosophy, Book III, General Scholium).

If the inverse square formula worked, there was no point in speculating about what gravity really was. This would be "metaphysics" in the bad old sense. It is the law itself which counts. Leibniz objected that, no matter what happens or how the data may be, it will always be "possible to find a notion, a rule or an equation", that is, a law, such that they are not violated. "Thus it can be said that however God might have created the world, it would always have been regular and within some general order. But God chose that world that is ... simultaneously the simplest in hypotheses and richest in phenomena" (Leibniz, Discourse on Metaphysics, Manchester Up 1988, 44). Thus the law or the theory must be simpler than the reality it is to describe, otherwise it is useless. If any mathematical representation is admissible it is of no objective value, because anything can be described in some way or other. And if an arbitrarily complex theory is permitted then the notion of "theory" becomes vacuous because there is always a theory.

A comparison with the notion of "computable number" might be useful. By computable numbers we mean since Turing real numbers that we can know or determine as individuals, so to say; not only rational numbers, but even numbers like e or $\pi = 3.1415926...$ that can be computed with arbitrarily high precision, digit by digit on the basis of some computer program or algorithm. Now a real number, as a rule is not computable, because the computable numbers form a countable subset of the real numbers only (presupposing the usual Cantorian definition of real number as well as Turing's thesis about computability). The real numbers form a universe too great and too complex to be described individually. And chance and contingent fact take part in mathematics itself.

Such a world, where nearly everything is contingent and without meaning or explanation, neither Leibniz nor Newton would have accepted. But the very hallmark of natural philosophy – its commitment to the intelligibility of nature – was radically reinterpreted by Newton and since him and mathematics as well as the mathematization of natural phenomena played a fundamental role in this reinterpretation. Mathematics never gives the "essences" of substances. But the foundation of a scientific theory is not to be seen in what it describes or explains, that is, in its conformity with observed phenomena and known facts, but is rather to be seen in its fertility and power to make predictions and to discover new facts. This point of view gained force towards the end of the 19th century only.

Did Newton end metaphysics? Did he make ontological considerations obsolete? Could it even be a reasonable goal of modern science to eliminate everything hypothetical? He certainly did not, as every science reaches in its foundations far beyond the observable or definable. Newton's controversy with Leibniz, as exposed in the Leibniz-Clarke correspondence, shows that questions about the nature of space and of relations, - whether relations are external to relata or not - and, at the heart of the matter, the differences of how Leibniz and Newton respectively conceived of the presence of God, occupied the greatest part of the debate. And Newtons inductivism must be seen in connection with his theological voluntarism as much as Leibniz` rationalism is to be understood as linked to his pantheism (see Blumenberg 1996, p. 164f; see also Hooykaas 1972). If we could enter into the details of these debates, which we cannot do here, we might be able to show how intimately connected seemingly strictly methodological issues are with fundamental philosophical questions, like the nature of Man (or God) and others.

Newton's mathematical philosophy was, during the 17th and 18th centuries, in fact, praised because of its connection with religious attitudes, and at the same time it was much criticized for its formal mathematical presentation. One of the most ardent critics of his conflation of physical and mathematical explanation was probably the Jesuit Castel, who in 1743 published a whole book on the issue. Castel perceived that mathematics was at the core of Newton's physics and he insisted on the distinction to be made between both:

"Geometry is geometry only through the abstract simplicity of its object. Only that makes it certain and demonstrative. The object of physics is much vaster. That is what makes it difficult, uncertain and obscure. But this essential to it: one is not a better physicist because one is the best of geometers" (quoted from Gingras 2001, 401).

The issue at stake becomes very clear reading this statement: A theoretical explanation is worth nothing if it is as complex as the phenomena to be explained. But it will give only mere shadows of phenomena if it is too mathematical and formal. Between these two horns of the dilemma mathematics and mathematical education have oscillated during a long period of time in history. Only recently a mathematical theory – Kolmogorov-Chaitin complexity theory – was designed to explicitly deal with it.

V.

Everything in epistemology revolves around Kant (1724-1804) and Kant's own intellectual development, in fact, reflects the history of epistemology quite well.

Less than fifty years after Newton Kant believed that science and mathematics could no more cope with the pace of times if there could not be clarified this question of how metaphysics is possible. Kant's thoughts on the issue are very interesting because of how they changed over time. In his "Untersuchung über die Deutlichkeit der Grundsätze der natürlichen Theologie und der Moral" of 1764, which was written as a reply to the question – posed by the Royal Academy at Berlin – whether metaphysical truth could be equated with mathematical truth, Kant draws his well-known distinction between analytic and synthetic truths. He classifies mathematics as based on arbitrary definitions and thus as synthetic and affirms that it is, in contrast to mathematics, much too early for metaphysics and natural philosophy to proceed according to the synthetic method. "Only after Analysis has provided us with clearly and extensively understood concepts, synthesis will be able, like in mathematics, to subsume involved knowledge under its simplest elements" (Deutlichkeit ... , Second Consideration).

The empirical method should be nothing but a variant of the analytical one, simply confined to those characteristics, which sound and secure experience detects about things. Its principles are not given, but have to be inferred by analysis of given experiences. This means thus that philosophy finds itself jointly with natural science in one camp and both stand in opposition to mathematics, which is synthetical knowledge.

About 25 years later in his Critique of Pure Reason mathematics and physics become synthetic a priori and thus do not provide genuine explanations in the Aristotelian sense!

What Newton seemed to have said was that physics as well as metaphysics are to be conceived of as completely straightforward rational enterprises, based on the observation of the phenomena and for that very reason, have no need of hypotheses. Kant in his Critique sets out to demonstrate exactly this, by reflecting on the process of human experience and its conditions. In the Introduction to the first edition (1781) he claims that in the sphere of metaphysics "everything which bears the least semblance of an hypothesis must be excluded"; and he adds about six years later in the introduction to the second edition that mathematics and physics "have to determine their objects a priori", because in these fields "the objects must conform to our cognition", rather than the other way around, that is, they must conform to our faculties of perceiving, representing and reasoning.

A "new light" (Kant) must have, in fact, flashed on the mind of Thales, when he perceived that the relation between the length of flagpole and the length of its shadow enables one to calculate the height of the pyramid from the length of its shadow (see part I.). Kant believes, as we have mentioned already, that the idea of knowledge does not lie in the object as such, but is rather based on the conception of the (epistemic) subject. This makes the "objectivity" of the subjective an important question.

The Kant of the Critique believes that the statements of mathematics and exact science are synthetical a priori, rather than analytical (like Leibniz). They are necessary as well as general because we humans cannot reason about things in themselves but have to think in terms of representations (Vorstellungen) of things and must evaluate our judgments relatively to these faculties of representation. Pure mathematics can be true knowledge a priori only because it lies at the basis of our experience. This also implies that all predicates or relations are external, rather than coming from the nature of things in themselves, and all objective judgments are thus synthetical. Kant's epistemology is skeptical in this sense, rather than positivistic. With respect the questions of mathematization and mathematical epistemology, Kant in a sense moved from a Leibnizian to a Newtonian point of view. This seems a very preliminary evaluation only, as Kant fought against simple empiricism as much as against dogmatic rationalism and he transformed the whole notion of objective reality in a profound way. "Reality" means no more something statically given either "out there" or in Platonic 'heaven', but the reality in question consists now of the system of human (cognitive) activity and practice itself. Thus Kantianism produced a third stream, besides positivism (the heirs of Newton) and Leibnizean idealism, a stream from which Pragmatism and Marxism originated and much later also Piaget's genetic epistemology.

The 18th century remained, however, thoroughly dedicated to a belief in the unity and immutability of human reason – and Kant is no exception here (Cassirer 1932). This belief marks the essence of the Enlightenment and its limitations. One key issue would therefore be, when trying to advance from a dichotomic to a complementarist rationality type of mathematical and scientific thinking, to conceive of the notion of epistemic subject in genetic or evolutionary terms.

VI.

Let us reflect a little further in the 18th century, pursuing the issue of explanation and mathematization a little bit more, in order to better understand the epistemological obstacles underneath.

In the great Encyclopédie (1751-1772) of Diderot (1713-1784) and d`Alembert (1717-1783) by the term "Philosophy" were still, and in accordance with the Aristotelian understanding, designated all the sciences which were supposed to provide explanations or foundations for a certain area of knowledge, whereas "history" was called everything which was content with a mere description of facts or data. "Philosopher c`est donner la raison des choses, ou du moins la chercher; car tant qu`on se borne à voir et à rapporter ce qu`on voit, on n`est que historien" (Article "Philosophie").

Philosophy in turn was subdivided between the "Science of Nature", that is, Physics and Mathematics, on the one side, and the "Science of Man", divided into Ethics and Logic, on the other side. Biology, Chemistry, "Celestial wonders", and much more, all that belonged to "Natural History", that is, to the merely descriptive or practical parts of human understanding and knowledge.

This classification, according to which all theoretical science belongs to philosophy, and is devoted to substantial explanations, whereas every work, which is concentrated on relating mere facts, is called history, goes back to Aristotle. Aristotle's Metaphysics counts mathematics and physics, for example, among the philosophical disciplines (Met. VI 1, 1026a).

In the further course of development this contrast between philosophy and history led to an opposition between mathematics, which took the place of philosophy, turning "explanation" into a formal-deductive process, and the empirical sciences, like biology, chemistry, economy etc., which were considered descriptive.

Mathematics, like philosophy, has no objects of its own and both, philosophy like mathematics, could in principle serve equally well as universal modes of explanation. Newton's work helped to turn tables in favor of mathematics and positivism carried this change further on. Nonetheless there have always existed limitations to the mathematical modes of explanation and opposition grew during the Enlightenment. D'Alembert, for example, resigned later from the editorship of the Encyclopédie because he believed that mathematics was a more fundamental science than biology, something to which Diderot strongly opposed.

Diderot had launched a severe and negative criticism of mathematics in his "Reflections about the Interpretation of Nature" of 1753 already, stating that mathematics has come to an end with the works of the great masters of the 18th century, like the Bernoullis and Euler, and Lagrange or d`Alembert. "A great upheaval is imminent in the sciences. In view of the present aspirations of the great minds, I should almost like to claim that there will not be three great mathematicians in Europe within a century" (Diderot 1753, 31). And in February 1758 Diderot wrote a letter to Voltaire, claiming that the "mathematical kingdom does no more exist. The taste has changed. Today natural history and philology rule. D'Alembert, taking into account his age, has no more the conditions to enter into natural history studies ..." In his controversies with d'Alembert, Diderot had over and again indicated the fundamental importance of notions, like transition or transformation and change, claiming that mathematics is incapable of taking these notions into account.

The "death" of mathematics, as predicted by Diderot and even by mathematicians like Lagrange (Misch 1969, 64), did, however, not happen. If "modern" mathematics had an object field proper, than the problems of change would make up the greater part of it. And in fact, contrary of what Diderot had predicted, mathematics soon was to enter into a period of explosive growth and fundamental changes. Diderot, nevertheless, was not completely wrong.

It seems of great interest indeed to see what had caused the double orientation to ever greater abstraction, on the one hand, and to the acknowledgment of the importance of contingent fact as being the main concern of empirical science, on the other hand, that occurred during the 18th century. The main forces that brought about different notions of methodology and theory lay in the new problems and ideas of change, transformation and evolution that beset the new experiences in areas like chemistry and biology, or electricity and thermodynamics and last but certainly not least: economy and social development. The very idea of scientific law, seen as an objective relationship, gained prominence only now.

Chemical change or transformation, for example, is a different and more complicated matter than mechanical motion, which has been the main concern of philosophers and scientists of the 17th/18th centuries, and there must – like in optics - be assumed causes, which can be known by their effects only. This requires subtle ways of forming fertile hypotheses and drawing all possible conclusions from them. Again one should see that in deductive reasoning from hypotheses it is the observation of certain relationships which matter and of the nature of the premises as such. Here as well as in Grassmann's work on electromagnetism and linear algebra lay the roots of modern mathematical axiomatics, in the sense of Peano, Hilbert or Emmy Noether and those for the positivistic program of arithmetization as well. One could certainly argue that the formation of appropriate hypotheses and the drawing of conclusions from there etc. etc. had been essential conditions of Newton's achievements already. This is true, but science entered now into the exploration of much more abstract and remote areas.

Lavoisier introduced a completely new, merely operative conception of chemical element (see Duhem 1991, 128), but he did still not completely replace thinking in terms of substances and their effects by relational thinking. Lavoisier's Traité Elémentaire de Chimie, (1789) contained a clear statement of the Law of Conservation of Mass, and thereby overthrew the theory of phlogiston. His list of substances, however, also included caloric, which he more or less believed to be a material substance. And the theory that heat consisted of a fluid (called caloric), which could be transferred from one body to another, but not "created" or "destroyed" was later replaced by the Law of Conservation of Energy, the most important discovery of the second scientific revolution, which was the work of Robert Mayer (1814-1878), Joule (1818-1889) and others, after Sadi Carnot (1796-1832) had paved the ground through his endeavors to understand and improve the steam engine.

VII.

One of the most influential philosophical results of the 18th century Enlightenment was Auguste Comte's positivism. The immense growth and diversification of knowledge required a kind of synthetic and universal theory of science, much broader in outlook than traditional epistemology and philosophy. The term "Positivism" was first used by Henri de Saint-Simeon, father of sociology and teacher of Comte. After Comte met the social reformer, Saint-Simon, he began writing articles for the Saint-Simon press and became a member of the circle around Saint-Simon, who was interested in the re-organisation of society on a scientific basis. The positive spirit consists, it was said, in substituting the study of the so-called causes of phenomena for that of their invariant regularities,– in a word, in studying the *How* instead of the *Why.*

Comte had, in his "Positive Philosophy" (1830-1842), divided the historical evolution of human knowledge into three great periods, the theological, the metaphysical and the scientific or positive:

> "In the theological state, the human mind, seeking the essential nature of beings. the first and final causes (the origin and purpose) of all effects … supposes all phenomena to be produced by the immediate action of supernatural beings. In the metaphysical state, which is only a modification of the first, the mind supposes, instead of supernatural beings, abstract forces …. inherent in all beings, and capable of producing all phenomena. What is called the explanation of phenomena is, in this stage, a mere reference of each to its proper entity. In the final, the positive state, the mind … applies itself to the study of the laws of phenomena—that is, their invariable relations of succession and resemblance".

Positivism, which is to-day represented by analytical philosophy of science and of mathematics, endorsed a completely instrumental view of mathematics. Pure mathematics, being a mere formal language, has to be founded by applied mathematics, which is in turn used exactly to describe the "invariable relations of succession and resemblance". Comte's positivism in distinction from that of d'Alembert did not more rotate around mathemaics. Comte wrote to Mill, for example, that the great minds should no longer waste their time on pure mathematics, but should turn themselves to social studies instead (Misch 1969, 64). Descartes, Lagrange and Fourier were Comte's greatest heroes because their works had enlarged the areas of truly mathematized science from geometry to Newtonian mechanics and finally to the theory of heat. Mathematization in the end meant arithmetization.

Now, the positivistic affirmation that positive science had eliminated metaphysics was wrong. And its equally strong negation of the objective character of scientific or mathematical hypotheses marked a severe regression even in comparison to Kantinanism. It is therefore not astonishing that the opposition between Newton and Leibniz and the difference between positivistic vs. idealistic views (see above), reproduced itself in the foundational debates of mathematics during the 19th and 20th centuries. There have been, in fact, two different trends in the foundational debate of mathematics since the 19th century, for which the contrasting conceptions of the continuity principle of Cauchy and Poncelet mark a significant expression (Belhoste 1981, Israel 1981, Otte 1989).

One might reasonably claim, as was remarked already, that these differences manifested themselves already in the well-known dispute between Leibniz and Newton (resp. Clarke) concerning the nature of space and continuity and of the nature of relations. But at the time they did not have really an impact on the integrity of the classical episteme. Now, during the 19th century these differences entered into the foundations of quite a number of fundamental concepts, like set, number and quantity or function themselves and thereby enforced that these and other notions be presented in complementary terms (see Otte 2003).

Rather than conceiving of the continuity principle in terms of variation and invariance, Cauchy thought of continuity in arithmetical terms. The program of rigorization by arithmetization searched to solve the foundational problems in a reductionistic manner, by defining all mathematical concepts in terms of some basic entities, ultimately the natural numbers. The axiomatic movement, in contrast tried to employ, so to say, a top-down strategy, solving the foundational problems of mathematics by extending and generalizing its relational structures and its rules of inference. We cannot deal with this matter in more detail here. But whatever side we may take in this controversy, our explanatory concerns shall not be served well, because mathematics becomes either conceived of as mere hypothetic-deductive reasoning or as a formal instrument, ultimately based on arithmetics.

VIII.

Considering it with reference to its social functions, science inclusive mathematics is most often considered as an activity and the scientist as a decision-maker. Whence the recommendation: "When using scientific information, do as the scientists do" (Churchman 1983, 11). This is more general than Bruner`s suggestion to look for the general ideas that organize scientific thought. But it is no less problematic, as scientists are not sufficiently self-conscious to explicitly describe their decision schemes. Explicitness of description would be of little use after all, because it leads to infinite regress. Describing the applications of the procedures of the applications of .... etc.

Science or mathematics then comes down to a certain habit of seeing the world and to a style of reasoning about it. Now education of mathematics became compulsory to everyone and later became an area of academic training and teacher education as soon as this implicit teaching by doing and showing became considered inefficient. Nevertheless the problem remains the same!

"Relational thinking", for example, is one of the notions by which modern mathematics and science has been characterized, since Ernst Cassirer`s famous book, Substanzbegriff und Funktionsbegriff (Substance and Function) of 1910. Relations or functions, however, commonly identified with operative schemes by Neo-Kantians or idealists, like Cassirer, or are considered as mere empirical regularities by positivists, like Comte or Mach, for example. And relational thinking is the great obstacle of everyday knowledge and of the natural attitude of the so called people on the street, who tend, rather positivistically, to identify knowledge with reality or with a mere instrument.

We believe that it is this question addressed, when Thom affirms that the real problem which confronts mathematics teaching is the problem of "the development of meaning, of the 'existence' of mathematical objects" (Thom 1973, 202). And, as we have seen above, it has been the problem of mathematical philosophy since the Scientific Revolution, at least.

I remember the enthusiasm with which we received the first edition of Graeub´s Lineare Algebra (Linear Algebra) published in 1958, and its coordinate free treatment, after having been accustomed to the tedious and clumsy calculations in terms of coordinates and matrixes of the older books. But the weaker or more conservative students and those from physics did not readily follow Graeub´s axiomatic and structural presentation. It is not quite obvious what caused the principal difficulties. It seemed, however, that those students did not really believe in the objectiveness of conceptual arguments or proofs.

These students wanted direct calculations and elementary proofs, that is, proofs that were maximally "self-contained". Such proofs should reveal a theorem to be true by the light of the very terms that contain it, analytically true. No conceptual constructions or additional intuitive hypotheses should be required. R. Skemp had called this type of thinking, instrumental understanding, and had contrasted it with what he called ¨relational understanding¨ (Skemp 1987).

Now among the students devoted to instrumental understanding those from physics did much better than the others, because they had by means of their experimental experience and practice already established a global intuition of the situation.

In any case, what one needs is a practice and an activity, be it conceptual or experimental, to reflect on, because mathematical ontology is constituted by a practice, not vice versa, or, as was stated already, "reality" means no more something statically given either "out there", or in Platonic 'heaven', but the reality in question consists now of the system of human (cognitive) activity and practice itself.

Mathematical education thus cannot abstain from epistemological and historical reflection, but should be careful not to fall back on self-assuring and obscure forms of reductionism and psychologism. In trying to educate the younger generation within to-days technological "knowledge society", it seems worthwhile to remember that knowledge fulfills two major roles in human society: a practical one and a philosophical one. Education is to be based on proven scientific knowledge not the least because "it seems that science came into being with the requirement of [...] coherence and that one of the functions it performs permanently in human culture consists in unifying [...] practical skills and cosmological beliefs, the episteme and the techne [...] despite all changes that science might have undergone, this is its permanent and specific function which differentiates it from other products of human intellectual activity" (Amsterdamski 1975, 43/44).

Amsterdamski`s diagnosis unfortunately seems to be no more than an ideal which we can rarely achieve, but which we should nevertheless not abandon.

But the historical establishment and institutionalization of mathematics education expresses such a desire or endeavor to transform mathematics and technology into instruments of social man, rather than conceiving of the mathematical mind as some isolated product of nature.

This means that mathematics as explanation is the fruit of mathematical education, because explanation is central to social mathematics since the Leibniz-Clarke (Newton) controversy.

REFERENCES

Alexander, A. R. (2001). Exploration mathematics: The rhetoric of discovery and the rise of infinitesimal methods, *Configurations,9*(1), 1-36.

Alexander, H.G. (Ed.) (1956). T*he Leibniz-Clarke correspondence: Together with extracts from Newton's Principia and Opticks.* Manchester University Press.

Amsterdamski, S. (1975). Between experience and metaphysics: Philosophical problems of the evolution of science. Dordrecht: Reidel.

Aristotle (1966 ‹1960›). *Aristotle. Posterior analytics – topica.* Forster, E. S. (Ed.) Cambridge, Mass., London: Harvard Univ. Pr., Heinemann.

Belhoste, B. (1991). *Augustin-Louis Cauchy.* New York: Springer.

Blumenberg, H. (1975). *Genesis der Kopernikanischen Welt.* Frankfurt: Suhrkamp.

Blumenberg, H. (1996). *Die Legitimität der Neuzeit.* Frankfurt: Suhrkamp.

Boutroux, P.(1920). L'idéal scientifique des mathématiciens. Paris: F. Alcan.

Cassirer, E. (1910). *Substanzbegriff und Funktionsbegriff.* Berlin: Verlag Cassirer.

Cassirer, E. (1932). *Die Philosophie der Aufklärung.* Tübingen: Verlag Mohr.

Churchman, C.W. (1983). *Prediction and Optimal Decision.* Holden-Day.

Dilthey, W. (1910/1981). *Der Aufbau der geschichtlichen Welt in den Geisteswissenschaften,* Frankfurt: Suhrkamp.

Duhem, P. (1991). *The aim and structure of physical theory.* Princeton UP.

Gingras, Y. (2001). What did mathematics do to physics. *Hist. Sci., XXXIX,* 382-416.

Hacking, I. (1980). Proof and eternal truth: Descartes and Leibniz. In: *Descartes – philosophy, mathematics and physics,* Stephen Gaukroger (Ed.).Sussex: The Harvester Press. 169-180.

Hadamard J. (1905). Cinq lettres sur la theorie des ensembles. Paris: *Bull Soc. Math. F., 33,* 261-273.

Hanna, G. (2000). Proof, explanation and exploration: An overview. *Educational Studies in Mathematics,* Special issue on "Proof in Dynamic Geometry Environments", *44,* 5-23.

Hart, G. (1990). Metaphysics and the new science. In: D.C. Lindberg and R.S. Westman, *Reappraisals of the scientific revolution.* Cambridge UP, 93-166.

Hooykaas, R. (1972). *Religion and the rise of science,* Scottish Acad. Press.

Ihmig, N. (2005). Newton`s program of mathematizing nature. In: M.H. Hoffmann et al (Eds.). *Activity and sign.* New York: Springer, 241-262.

Israel, G. (1981). Rigor and axiomatics in modern mathematics, *Fund. Scientiae*, *2*, 205-219.

Israel, G. (1997). The analytical method in Descartes' geometrie. In: Otte, M.and M. Panza (Eds.), 3-34.

Kant, I. (1787). *Critique of pure reason.* Preface to the Second Edition.

Lebesgue, H. (1965). *Measure and the integral.* San Francisco: Holden-Day.

Loomis, L.H. (1953). *An introduction to abstract harmonic analysis.* London: van Norstrand.

Mancosu, P. (2000). On mathematical explanation. In: E. Grosholz and H. Breger (Eds.). *The growth of mathematical knowledge.* Dordrecht: Kluwer, 103-119.

Mancosu, P. (2001). Mathematical explanation, *Topoi*, *20*, 97-117.

Matthews, M.R. (1989). *The scientific background to modern philosophy: Selected readings.* Indianapolis: Hackett Publ. Co.

Misch, G. (1969). *Zur Entstehung des franz. Positivismus.* WBG Darmstadt, Reprint der Ausgabe 1901.

Moore, G.H. (1982). *Zermelo's axiom of choice.* Heidelberg: Springer.

Newton-Smith, W.H. (2000). *A companion to the philosophy of science.* Oxford: Blackwell.

Otte, M. (1989). The ideas of H. Grassmann in the context of the mathematical and philosophical tradition since Leibniz, *Hist. Mathematica*, *16*, 1-35.

Otte, M.and M. Panza (Eds.) (1997). *Analysis and Synthesis in Mathematics.* Dordrecht: Kluwer.

Otte, M. (2003). Complementarity, sets and numbers, *Educational Studies in Mathematics*, *53*, 203-228.

Quine, W.O. (1953). Two dogmas of empiricism. In: *Quine, from a logical point of view*, Harvard UP, chap. 2.

Reichenbach, H. (1951). *The rise of scientific philosophy.* Berkeley: University of California Press.

Skemp, R. (1987). *The psychology of learning mathematics.* Lawrence Erlbaum Assoc.

Snow, C.P. (1993). *The two cultures.* Cambridge/USA: Harvard UP.

Thom, R. (1973). Modern mathematics: Does it exist? In: A.G. Howson(Ed.). *Developments in mathematical education.* Cambridge UP, 194-212.

Webb, J. C. (1980). *Mechanism, mentalism and metamathematics.* Dordrecht: Reidel.

Zermelo, E. (1905), Beweis, dass jede Menge wohlgeordnet werden kann, *Math. Ann.*, 514-516.

Michael Otte
Germany

HERMANN MAIER

MATHEMATICS LEARNING AS A COGNI TIVE PROCESS

INTRODUCITION

In my long carrier as researcher in the field of mathematics education I experienced different definitions of learning mathematics, shifting from 'content receptive' across behaviouristic to cognitivistic, constructivist or socio-constructivist approaches. This let me arrive at the question if it really makes sense to continue with passing in the course of time from one uni-dimensional description of learning mathematics to another one. Must we really always look at a particular conceptualisation as the only one, according to which all research is to be designed? Must, e. g. learning of mathematics in terms of pupils' individual constructions and learning in terms of participating in social events or using effects of social life really be regarded as contradictory or exclusive approaches for studying children's learning of mathematics? Should not at least part of the conceptualisations emphasized so far be related to each other, regarding them as particular perspectives or dimensions of a comprehensive concept for the really complex phenomenon with which we are confronted in case of a subject specific learning process? Certainly there are approaches which start from completely different basic assumptions and, for that reason, may be incommensurable. Nevertheless, a kind of holistic view on learning could become a project for future research in mathematics education, and a major factor of innovation as well.

Of course, in the context of a concrete research project the individual researcher has to isolate aspects and to concentrate on a certain point of view. He/she must reduce complexity of the object of investigation in or der to have a real chance of attaining meaningful results. But, such a proceeding remains unobjectionable as long as the researcher subsequently tries to interpret his/her results in the context of the whole complexity of the research object, to integrate them into a broader perspective, and to bring them, as far as possible, consistently together with other researchers' results. In other words: every researcher should look upon his/her own work more as contributive to and less as competitive with other researchers' work in the same field.

In the Strobl conference on "Mathematics Learning" prominent representatives of different perspectives on the process of learning mathematics presented their profiled positions to each other and discussed them extensively. There were researchers who looked at mathematics learning as a process mainly or exclusively

J. Maasz, W. Schloeglmann (Eds.), New Mathematics Education Research and Practice, 95–96.

influenced by the structure of the subject, others who saw it shaped by the pupils' affections respectively emotions. Some participants described this process as a cognitive, others as a social one. But there were also attempts to relate different views to each other, for example a cognitivistic and a socio-constructivist epistemology, affective and cognitive or emotional and social aspects. And, in addition, the discussions might have motivated some participants to see their own position more relatively as a particular contribution to a comprehensive concept of learning mathematics.

In this section we find two contributions to the topic of mathematics learning as a cognitive process, which appears certainly at first as a really restricted approach. But Bert von Oers (Netherlands) discusses in his chapter "An activity theory approach to the formation of mathematical cognition" the absolutism of a purely constructivist or socio-constructivist concept of learning; and he relates individual-psychological concepts to social dimensions. And Willibald Dörfler (Austria) presented his paper "Inscriptions as objects of mathematical activities" explicitly as one possible, subjective perspective on doing and learning mathematics, explicitly surpassing and extending a traditional cognitive view.

After the subsequent reproduction of both chapters I will try to compare the positions which both authors have taken in their chapters, and also to relate them to other approaches appearing in the conference. Questions and positions raised in the plenary discussions of both presentations shall be included.

Hermann Maier
Germany

WILLIBALD DÖRFLER

INSCRIPTIONS AS OBJECTS OF MATHEMATICAL ACTIVITIES

INTRODUCTION

It is a widely shared opinion that basic views about mathematics have a subtle but persistent impact on the content, form and method of mathematics education as a practice in the schools and as a research discipline as well. Those views comprise a great variety of positions with regard to philosophical and epistemological questions which have bothered many scholars throughout history up to now. Among those questions are for instance:

- what is the genetic origin and source of mathematics and mathematical concepts, objects, theories, notations, etc?
- what are mathematical objects?
- which are the referents of mathematical signs? Or: What does mathematics speak about?
- is mathematics invented or discovered?
- why can mathematics be applied so successfully?
- what is, for the general student, important to know about mathematics?
- what is the relation between intuition and more formal reasoning?

These questions and their very differing answers are strongly interrelated. It is not the purpose of this paper even to sketch the more prominent lines of thought in relation to that and there is a vast literature available. Generally it is remarkable that many trials for solutions to those problems have a normative or even dogmatic and sometimes metaphysical character. Very rarely the actual activity of mathematicians is taken as a starting point but rather the codified end-products (natural numbers, sets, etc.) are the phenomena to be explained.

The influence of all that on mathematics education is sometimes overt but mostly, I think, implicit and mediated. Argued programs were for instance Felix Kleins' conceptions, the New Maths movement or the Bourbakian disdain for (geometric) intuition. More modern versions one finds in the "Math Wars" in the US, or imbedded in the conception of "Standards", or even in the tasks of assessment systems like PISA. But besides those more traceable and therefore also debatable reflections of views, positions, assumptions, beliefs, postulates about the quality, character and essence of mathematics and mathematical activities there are implicit, covert and mostly unreflected presuppositions among students, parents,

J. Maasz, W. Schloeglmann (Eds.), New Mathematics Education Research and Practice, 97–111.

teachers and educators. Those influence the content and style of teaching, of text-books, of the tasks, of the exams, in short the whole complex system of mathematics education. In the research area the choice of research problems and methods also depends on many presuppositions (e.g. about what it means to learn and understand mathematics). These statements are not intended as a critique. One always has to start from somewhere and the only sensible demand is to be conscious and aware of the starting point as much as possible, and to regard conceivable alternatives. This then permits deliberate and argued choices, for instance, of teaching/learning contents or research problems. Clearly, those choices and decisions have to be made but they should be viewed also as such and not as unavoidable pre-conditions. For this paper, with these remarks, I wanted to set the scene and present the background of my thinking. After first, in the following, describing what I think is a widespread belief system about mathematics, I will offer a view which puts the mathematical signs, their writing and reading into the centre of mathematical activities of all kind.

A WIDESPREAD BELIEF SYSTEM AND ITS CONSEQUENCES

This section is based on the subjective interpretation and reading of many different sources like school-books, text-books, maths education research papers, books like those by Burton (2004), Lenné (1969), Heintz (2000), Otte (1974), Rotman (1993, 2000), and on widespread experiences from informal talks with many people (laymen, students, teachers, mathematicians, educators). The picture I will paint of a kind of folk-philosophy of mathematics and mathematics learning will be for sure very pointed and partly exaggerated. And I do not assume that there is anybody who subscribes to all the views and positions compiled together by me. But still, I assert, it is a network of ideas, notions, suppositions, and, partly, prejudices which here and there surface in texts and talks even if they usually just lurk in the background. Among the features presented not all have the same strength, importance or impact. To repeat, in the following I describe a contrived system of views and beliefs, parts of which are shared by many and others by less people. But for all components there is also an explicit statement in contributions to philosophy, epistemology or education of mathematics. The latter means all that is not just pure invention by me. Here are the main features.

The objects of study and interest within mathematics and school mathematics are qualified as being abstract without a closer description what this might mean. Rather, by that it is intended to express what mathematical objects are not: they are not accessible to the senses, not palpable, not perceivable, they cannot be shown directly and not communicated. Despite that they enjoy great many properties and relationships and are worth to be investigated. This applies, for instance, to all kinds of numbers as soon as they are no longer counting numbers (expressing n) or measuring numbers but numbers per se. The same applies to (abstract) sets and functions.

Due to this lack of direct accessibility, the mathematical object to become intelligible, learnable, communicable are in need of what commonly are called (external) representations, also termed embodiments, visualizations, materializations and the like. As these notions intimate, they are secondary to what they represent, embody, visualize or materialize. The representations, in this vein, are conceived of as a means either to learn the abstract concept (object) or to investigate the latter. They do not have an independent status and serve predominantly a mediating role (between learner or researcher and abstract object). In the common discourse a strict separation between mathematical object and representation is made. For instance, the learners are admonished to distinguish between numeral and number, the former being a sign or signifier for the latter, the signified. This view is expressed in general by Rotman (1993, p. 20) in the following way:

> "Thus, within this horizon, there is first ontology and being, the inventory of the objects that are or must be in this already-given world; then reference, pointing, and naming whereby language, in an activity external to and after-the-facts of this world, picks out these pre-existent objects; from reference comes sense, the description and meaning of the properties and states of affairs enjoyed by these objects; finally epistemology, the examination of the means of knowing, believing, validating which among the assertions generated by language about these objects is a justifiably "true" description of the states of affairs they take part in. The order of events here – being, referring, meaning, knowing – is a crucial element in the way this framework of what constitutes "knowledge" works to bolster the metaphysics of Platonism."

That in most cases there are different representations supports the view that they all are related to and determined by the unique abstract object. Just consider the case of the function concept, or, the widespread talk about equivalent fractions being just different names for the "same" rational number.

A consequence of such a view is that the representations are on the one hand reduced in school-maths to execute calculations with them (in a mechanistic and algorithmic way) and on the other hand for learning they just have a transient character. They can be disposed of and even be forgotten as soon as the corresponding abstract concept (object) as been developed by the student. Therefore all those representations very rarely become the genuine topic of investigation and exploration since they are judged not to deserve separate and independent attention and interest. At least this is so according to the view which I am here describing (but not subscribing to). I should for the sake of completeness say that over the past years numerous research by scholars like Cobb (1999), Meira (1998), Nemirovsky (1994), Radford (2003), Duval (1995) has taken radi cally different positions much more in accordance with what I will suggest in the second part of the paper. This kind of neglect for a more comprehensive and constitutive role of representations (by reducing them to their representing function) might be among the reasons for the notorious avoidance of them by many students when solving problems (of a purely mathematical character and more applied ones as well): they do not use visualizations even if prompted so. A possible explanation could be that the means for visualizing have to be very familiar to the learner if they are to use them proficiently. I will emphasize this aspect of learning mathematics later in more detail. What is needed is an intimate experience with the sign systems, the notations, the diagrams (in the sense of Peirce, cf. below). But, this necessitates exploration of the "representations" beyond their being means for "representing" and objects of routine calculations.

The common discourse in mathematics and mathematics education posits from the beginning the mathematical objects (numbers of all kind, sets, functions, geometric figures) as abstract ones which one has to learn and understand via all kinds of representations.

I suggest the thesis that this (often implicit and unreflected) discourse is frightening for the students and learners. They often experience that they do not get close to those genuine object which mathematics purportedly is all about, they belief they lack the necessary abilities to think "abstractly", they are convinced that they do not understand what they are expected to understand. They want to reach through the representations to the abstract objects but without success. Failure in maths learning thus predominantly is attributed to deficits within the learner, to a lack of mathematical sense like some are short-sighted and others are deaf. One way out of this dilemma for many is to stick to the more material activity of routine calculations but without paying attention to the relevant features and properties of the objects of calculation (like numerals, algebraic and function terms, etc.). To the contrary, the mathematical expert appears to speak with ease about some abstract realm of objects and he/she thereby of course uses some kind of representations. But the chosen discourse often suggests that the expert relies on some direct and unmediated knowledge which he/she then expresses by a combination of technical language and diagrams. Thus the latter appear do be determined by the genuine mathematical concepts (objects): numbers determine numerals, a function determines its representations. For alternative views compare Krämer (1988), Schmandt-Besserat (1997) or again Rotman (2000).

A central part of the belief system, as I see and experience it, is a specific view on what it means to learn mathematics. This view is based on notions like mental object or internal representation (see, for instance, Goldin and Janvier, 1998). The basic idea is that the learner, by the use of external representations, constructs or develops in his/her mind a mental representation (cognitive structure, schema, or the like) which then permits him/her to think with and about the respective mathematical concept (object). For this process the terms interiorization or internalization are used, or (closer to Piaget) reflective abstraction. An example could be the APOS-theory developed by Dubinsky and his co-workers (Dubinsky and MacDonald, 2001). Here again one recognizes a secondary and auxiliary role ascribed to the (external) representations: as soon as their mental counterparts are constructed they could in principle be discarded since mathematical activities are primarily mental ones. Failure to understand or to use the mathematics then is considered to be caused by flawed or rudimentary mental constructions. The latter to be useful have to show a high degree of fidelity: the mental objects are or should be kind of isomorphic replicas of the mathematical ones. Mathematical thinking then is located in the mind as the mental manipulation of the mental objects (possibly supported by their external representations). What is written or said is (only?) expression of those mental processes. Mathematical objects and activities in these views obtain thus a status of double invisibility: they are abstract and/or mental. In a way, this is a very peculiar mixture of a naïve Platonism with a similarly naïve Intuitionism. Even in its more moderate forms such a view turns mathematics into a very specific endeavour (and as such it is in fact widely perceived) and successful learning of mathematics into a very unlikely event (which in fact it is). My contention to the contrary will be that substituting or at least complementing this "internalism" by "externalism" will offer a better chance for entering mathematical practices. Thereby, generally externalism describes and tries to understand mathematics as the reflected manipulation, exploration and interpretation of what fo r internalism are just representations. This is obtained by switching the roles of what is primary (now the used sign system) and secondary (the concepts, mental and abstract objects). As I see it, this sketched form of internalism also opposes the intellectual to the more material, the (internal/mental) thinking to actions with concrete things (like inscriptions on paper). By the words of Aristotle, mathematics is predominantly viewed as "episteme" and much less as "techné". Needless to say, there are many counterpositions like distributed cognition, situated cognition or situated learning, the theory of scientific inscriptions (Roth, 2003), or the views of authors like Duval (1995), Winslow (2004), Radford (2003), Cobb et al.(1992), Gravemeijer (1999), di Sessa (2000). As a common core of all those one can formulate as an alternative view: mathematics should be considered as a practice of sign use, sign production, sign manipulation and sign interpretation. The second part of the paper will espouse my thoughts about this semiotic approach to maths and maths learning.

A serious consequence of views and beliefs as sketched in the foregoing is the shared belief that mathematics is not (directly) communicable, that it as such cannot be shown to and experienced by students. Therefore much of didactical research was and is devoted to the development of "good" representations which should enable the mental constructions on part of the learner. Over time the expectation that good representations could show to the learner their mathematical meaning has dwindled and now the students are guided to actively construct that meaning. But still the so-called representations very often keep a strong methodological character while not being the "real thing" to be learned. The representations are to mediate between the learner und the to-be-learned but they are not themselves the topic and content of learning. Exceptions, for in stance, are the approaches by Bakker (2004), Cobb (1999) and Gravemeijer (1999).

Closely connected to the issue of "abstract objects" and their roles for learning and doing math is the issue of "ideas", mostly called "deep" or "fundamental ideas". They are said to be also an ultimate goal of mathematics education and kind of prerequisite for genuine and "deep" understanding. Those ideas are to be distinguished sharply from any formalization via a definition or an axiom system which are rather viewed to express the ideas. In a quite loose discourse the ideas have a primary status over, say, symbolizations, diagrammatization or schematization; they are the guiding principle which informs and regulates those processes of mathematization. Further, the ideas are attributed a purely mental status and are widely independent from being expressed by signs of any kind. Thus, they are viewed as difficult to communicate because communicating them of course needs expressing them in one way or the other. In this way, they are similar to "abstract objects". Mac Lane (1986) in a short paragraph discusses the issue of "ideas" in mathematics and points to their necessary vagueness and he says: ideas require formalizations. Thereby he admits that divergent formalizations and explications are rather the rule and especially teaching and communicating is in need of those. Thus, at least in the learning process the direction can, will and should be rather from symbol systems and formal definitions to the "deep ideas". In the learner the "deep ideas" will emerge and grow from an intensive study of the symbolic structures and diagrams which are a "case" of the respective idea. Only in the hindsight and after many pertinent and adequately reflected experiences the "idea" is felt as being expressed by the diagram, the definition or the axiom system. And for this, another sign system, mostly an enriched natural language, is needed (for instance, to describe "linearity" in general terms; but even there a "formula" is of great help, like $L(a + b) = L((a) + L(b))$ And Mac Lance remarks: It seems that we can recognize and name an idea only after it has given rise to one or more formal expressions. Thus the question is legitimate, why bother the learner with "nebulous" (Mac Lane) ideas which only can be understood in their formalized versions.

To end this section: If I am only partly right the described views and beliefs are bound to have an enormous impact on the style and content of teaching and possibly even more so on the attitudes, affects and emotions of the learners.

INTERLUDE

As a kind of bridge to the next section which is concerned with a view which puts the representations as inscriptions (Roth, 2003) and diagrams (Peirce, 1976, 1931) into the centre of attention and of teaching and learning activities I cite two passages from Peirce's writings on mathematics:

"It has long been a puzzle how it could be that, on the one hand, mathematics is purely deductive in its nature, and draws its conclusions apodictically, while on the other hand, it presents as rich and apparently unending a series of surprising discoveries as any observational science. Various have been the attempts to solve the paradox by breaking down one or other of these assertions, but without success. The truth, however, appears to be that all deductive reasoning, even simple syllogism, involves an element of observation; namely, deduction consists in constructing an icon or diagram the relations of whose parts shall present a complete analogy with those of the parts of the object of reasoning, of experimenting upon this image in the imagination, and of observing the result so as to discover unnoticed and hidden relations among the parts. ... As for algebra, the very idea of the art is that it presents formulae, which can be manipulated and that by observing the effects of such manipulation we find properties not to be otherwise discerned. In such manipulation, we are guided by previous discoveries, which are embodied in general formulae. These are patterns, which we have the right to imitate in our procedure, and are the icons par excellence of algebra." (Collected Papers 3.363)

"By diagrammatic reasoning, I mean reasoning which constructs a diagram according to a precept expressed in general terms, performs experiments upon this diagram, notes their results, assures itself that similar experiments performed upon any diagram constructed according to the same precept would have the same results, and expresses this in general terms. This was a discovery of no little importance, showing, as it does, that all knowledge without exception comes from observation." (Peirce NEM IV, 47 f.)

What I take from this is that the (written) inscriptions and their use as diagrams in the sense of Peirce are of pre-eminent importance for all mathematical activities. And, most important is that those inscriptions/diagrams gain thereby the status of the very objects of the activities: they themselves are taught, learned, memorized, investigated, constructed, invented, manipulated, designed, etc. Besides this they keep some of the auxiliary roles as ascribed to the (external) representations. Mathematics turns from a language describing abstract objects, and expressing mental objects or deep ideas, into a "writing science" (compare again Rotman, 2000) where all the former is intricately interwoven with the inscriptions/diagrams.

For the following the Peircean notions of "diagram" and "diagrammatic reasoning" are of pivotal importance. Those are discussed and exemplified in much detail in Dörfler (2004 a,b, 2005, in press), Hoffmann (2003, 2005), Marietti (2005), or Stjernfelt (2000). Thus, I restrict to saying that a diagram is an amalgam composed of an inscription (possibly on a computer screen), a relational structure imposed on it and specific operation rules (including rules for interpretation). Thereby the structure and the operations are mutually constitutive and the source of the "meaning" of the diagram. Diagrams usually are based on compound inscriptions, they are primarily of an iconic character but contain indexical and symbolic elements as well. Diagrams in mathematics occur in mutually interrelated networks and overall they are objects and products of writing and reading. Sources of diagrams are manifold: modelling and mathematization, symbolization of rules and regularities, results of calculations or deliberate design. As examples can serve all those so-called representations: numerals, function graphs and tables, all kinds of formulas, polynomials, matrices, combinatorial graphs, Vern diagrams, the formulas of an axiom systems (like for groups, vector spaces), tools from descriptive statistics, etc. Diagrammatic reasoning then is the investigation, exploration and construction of diagrams. Two simple examples might possibly convey the general intent of that:

1. Explain way, say, $1111 \times 1111 = 1234321$. This can be obtained by observing the diagram based on the multiplication algorithm:

```
1  1  1  1
   1  1  1  1
      1  1  1  1
         1  1  1  1
1  2  3  4  3  2  1
```

2. Explain: $\displaystyle\sum_{i,j=1}^{4} \min(i,j) = 1^2 + 2^2 + 3^2 + 4^2$

```
1  1  1  1
1  2  2  2
1  2  3  3
1  2  3  4
```

This matrix is sliced into layers of a 4×4, a 3×3, a 2×2 and a 1×1 matrix consisting only of ones.

In both examples a great variety of further diagrammatic experiments is possible. It should be clear that diagrammatic reasoning goes far beyond mechanic calculations. As in the first example it rather looks for regularities within, say, algorithmic processes. Wilson (2005) has in a related way underlined the investigation of arithmetic algorithms.

SHIFTING THE FOCUS TO THE DIAGRAMS AND ITS CONSEQUENCES

The thrust of the following is the thesis that it might be of great educational value to present mathematics to the learner as the systematic study of diagrams (presented as inscriptions of many different forms) and all sensible operations with them. This would move those diagrams into the very centre of mathematical learning and teaching. The diagrammatic inscriptions then do not serve just representational purposes but they themselves are the objects of interest, investigation and discussion. The learners have to become aware of this focus on what is written down (or presented on a computer screen) and which thus can be visually analyzed and scanned for relationships and regularities. Learning mathematics to a great extent then consists in familiarizing oneself with the respective diagrams (and many of their usages, for instance in applications). I advance this proposal mainly as an educational and not so much as an ontological/philosophical one. Also in case that the diagrams are taken as representations of otherwise inaccessible mathematical objects the absolute necessity of studying the diagrams persists. But, and that is important, I think, one can do without any metaphysical (or mental) referents and content oneself with the diagrams. To give some more examples, in this vein diagrams are: complex number as 2+5i, continued fractions, fractions, Euclid's algorithm (as a chain of divisions), a differential equation, many proofs, etc. To present those mathematical concepts as diagrams (Dörfler 2004 a,b) makes, I contend, maths better accessible

104

because it thereby becomes demystified. The very objects of interest, of learning and communication are now perceivable and communicable if maths is understood (primarily and initially) as a social practice with, on, about, and through diagrams. It might be difficult and demanding to operate efficiently and creatively with diagrams but one can point to this difficulty and demand. Maths no longer is then a pure episteme (intellectual knowledge about something) but essentially turns into techné, something like a reflected handicraft of working productively with diagrams. This underlines the materiality of mathematics and mathematical activities versus its purported abstractness (which I see as originating from that materiality). I refer the reader again to Rotman (2000) and his emphasis on writing in maths, but also to the publications Cobb et al. (2000), Roth (2003), Gravemeijer et al. (2002), Krämer and Bredekamp (2003) and Hoffmann et al. (2005) where also the importance of diagrams, signs, symbols, ideograms etc. is investigated from many different angles. As one more very impressive phenomenon in support of the proposed "diagrammatization" of learning maths I mention the vastly growing area of experimental mathematics by the use of computers (e.g. Borwein, 2005) where diagrams are manipulated and checked for regularities (formulas, theorems).

DIAGRAMMATIC ACTIVITIES

Diagrammatic activities comprise a great variety:
Basic activities with diagrams are calculations of all forms i.e. manipulating the diagrams according to the diagrammatic operation rules. For instance: matrix multiplication (in different ways), Euclid's algorithm, dividing polynomials, calculating with the integers modulo m, geometric constructions. This base level is important for familiarizing oneself with the diagrams, their structural properties and their operations; it constitutes the technical versatility (like with a handicraft tool or a musical instrument). Already here writing, reading, observing and recognizing relationships are constitutive for the activities which by no means are purely mechanic (though they follow certain rules). The applicability of a rule has to be "seen" which presupposes a kind parsing (of the diagrams) and pattern recognition. I emphasize already here an important role and function of exercise and skill in a reflected way for all kinds of activities with diagrams.

Investigation of diagrams and of the operations with them by analysing the outcomes of certain manipulations (calculations, combinations, transformation). For examples, see Dörfler (2004 a,b, 2005) and the two examples above. Many regularities (recurrent patterns) which then can be phrased as "theorems" thus result from visually inspecting diagrams. Related are the notion of "visual proof" (Nelson, 1993, 2000; Diagrammatic Reasoning Bibliography) and again the whole filed of experimental mathematics. A general attitude behind those diagrammatic activities might be the question: "What happens if …?". The diagrams thereby are considered as objects with as yet undetected or unnoticed properties which can be discovered by carrying out appropriate experiments and observing the outcomes.

Relating different diagrams like various number systems and number line, function representations, graphs and their matrices, figurative numbers and respective formulas, etc. This generally refers to the phenomenon where the common discourse posits a common (abstract) object of which the (essentially) diverse diagrams are taken to be representations. In our context here it might be advisable to speak about the different types of diagrams as representing or modelling each other (one type then becomes the privileged one like possibly the decimal numbers, or $a + ib$ for complex numbers). The various types differ with respect to the operations which are applicable and the relationships which are observable, i.e. the mutual modelling is only a partial one. The various diagrams for the "same object" serve very different purposes and intentions and thus necessitate specific investigations. For instance: fractions/continued fraction; graph/formula for a function.

Inventing and designing diagrams, mostly by using already familiar ones. This is the crux of many proofs as already Peirce indicates with his notion of diagrammatic reasoning (cf. Hoffmann, 2005). Some proofs just use transformations of diagrams which lead from the assumption (expressed by a diagram) to the conclusion (the diagram which results form the transformation). Other proofs need the creative guess (an abduction as Peirce calls that move) of a diagram which not directly is obtainable from the given ones. This might be simply the insertion of new terms into a formula, or the drawing of a line in a geometric figure. Examples abound in any text-book as the reader will know or easily can check by inspection. Beyond this occurrence in proofs the design of diagrams generally serves the purpose of construction (of new "objects" for investigation): transpose of a matrix, Kronecker product of matrices, (hyper)complex numbers, models for non-euclidean geometries, very large natural numbers, like 10^{8000}. The latter cannot be thought of by numerosity since it is just a diagram for which we know in principle how "calculate" with it; decimal numbers with, say, a billion digits have the same purely diagrammatic quality without having a sensible referent (compare Rotmann, 2000, or Dantzig, 1999). For short, many concepts in maths, starting from very simple ones, result from designing, inventing, producing or imagining specific diagrams (see also Krämer, 1988).

One important source for the design and invention of diagrams are processes of modelling and mathematization (most of non-mathematical problems and activities). Several papers in Cobb et al (2000) investigate those processes of "symbolization" in the context of school learning. My focus here but is a more inner-mathematical one so I do not go into any details about that. Similarly I only mention (being aware of its paramount importance) the use of given diagrams for modelling and problem solving outside of mathematics.

Against the background of this short survey of diagrammatic activities (by which I do not assert that everything in maths is diagrammatic) I can point out some features of those activities which might be of great educational/didactical impact (when organizing learning processes):

Writing and reading (of inscriptions) are fundamental activities.

Perceptive processes (observation, pattern recognition, inspection, comparisons) are an integral part.

Diagrammatic reasoning is essentially public and therefore social and sharable because it realizes itself in observable and describable manipulations of diagrams. In a nutshell: you never calculate with numbers but only with numerals and those are perceivable. Diagrammatic activities can be shown, demonstrated and therefore emulated (by a learner or novice). This (partly at least) solves the paradox how knowledge about abstract objects can at all be acquired: it is essentially a practice of working with diagrams.

There is a strong aspect of "technique" in the sense of Aristotle's techné or of a craft.

The diagrams have no fixed referent which gives them sense or meaning. Their meaning resides in the respective operations with them to which belong also referential interpretations of many kinds ("applications"). And this meaning unfolds by experimenting with the diagrams and discovering ever new properties (of the diagrams).

Diagrammatic activities are not only algorithmic/mechanic but very often creative, inventive, explorative and experimental and thus in need of collaboration.

Diagrammatic activities as described above have been and are carried out by mathematicians, learners and users of maths. Thus, in a way, I am telling nothing new. But, the thrust of my paper is to substitute the discursive abstractness of maths by its material diagrammaticity. This is a fundamental change of focus of attention and awareness, I believe.

All these features can for sure be exploited with much profit when designing a framework for learning processes in a classroom: organize it as the development of a shared practice of diagrammatic activities. But there are some potential obstacles and difficulties which will be discussed in the last section.

DIDACTICAL RAMIFICATIONS

All the points listed and discussed in the following concern qualities of diagrams and the activities with them which are of a more didactical interest in the sense that they impact on the process of learning maths as a social practice based on diagrams. Therefore special attention would have to be paid to them when designing learning environments for diagrammatic activities. The chosen order is haphazard since all aspects are equally important.

1. Diagrammatic activities presuppose a growing and intimate familiarity with the diagrams as based on observable inscriptions and rule governed operations. This familiarity develops out of extensive experi ences with diagrams and diagrammatic reasoning of the kinds presented above. The inscriptions and their material handling will be the starting point out of which the diagrammatic practice develops and emerges. This comprises: recognition of an inscription as a specific diagram (depending on the context) and of its relational structure; recognition of the executability of operations and finally of possible abductive choices.

2. An integral part of this familiarity is a comprehensive memory of the respective diagrams. Pattern recognition depends partly on the already memorized patterns. In other words, for expedience in maths one has to know formulas of all kinds and/or know where to find them (and how to use them). This is not rote memory of just the inscriptions but also of potential operations and relations. Studies of experts (like chess masters) clearly point into this direction.

3. Diagrammatic activities in maths demand a high degree of attention, exactness and precision. This is so, since diagrams usually do not tolerate even small "deviations". It is this property which on the other hand enables diagrammatic reasoning to convince of the validity of its outcomes and their generality. One has to observe strictly the rules which do not contradict the necessary creativeness. Clearly, this poses great difficulties to the learners and novices.

4. Diagrammatic activities will always be embedded into a discursive context which offers a rich language to speak about the diagrams and their transformations. This language is a natural language plus a supply of technical terms (like: numeral, digit, place value, fraction, enumerator, graph, differential quotient, integral, arithmetic mean). The novice will have to learn this language simultaneously with her/his development of the diagrammatic practice (which per se is not a language and not a linguistic activity). Like when learning a craft an appropriate language can give guidance, support and focus of attention. But the respective activity cannot be completely described by language, it must be done (and for that observed) and exercised extensively. There is certain autonomy of the diagrams which must be respected. Without pursuing this issue any further I mention that there is a kind of mathematical reasoning which uses linguistic/verbal descriptions of diagrammatic properties. The verbal/linguistic context of diagrammatic activities will also tell about the possible interpretations and usages of the respective diagrams and might even include the talk about abstract objects. But the latter should then clearly be marked as a specific talk about the diagrams.

5. What commonly is called (mathematical) intuition will develop in the learners out of the extensive and intensive diagrammatic activities. Intuition is thus not the condition for (diagrammatic) reasoning but its emergent outcome based on multiple experiences with diagrams and the reflection on them. I think the same holds true for the notorious "deep" or "fundamental" ideas. They mostly reflect very general features of diagrams and diagrammatic operations (like linearity, or average rate) and are themselves often in need of being presented by a diagram (like $L(a + b) = L(a) + L(b)$).

6. The focus on the diagrammatic inscriptions and their manipulations will as well pose many difficulties to the learners (which are now different from the notorious abstractness). One will be the growing structural complexity of the inscriptions (like formulas or figures) which makes it perceptively difficult to recognize the diagrammatic relations (or to impose those). A formula like $(a + b)^2 = a^2 + 2ab + b^2$ appears in many different disguises; or to virtually "see" a specific figure within a given one. There clearly are instants of the

problem of the relation general-particular or type – token which, I think, for the learner is only resolvable by extensive diagrammatic experiences within an appropriate social practice and discursive support. The latter provides a "legend" how to read and use the inscriptions such that they turn into diagrams within the respective practice. There is no other way, I contend, than to start with the inscriptions and successively guide the learner at the development of the diagrams as objects and results of a mathematical practice. Obviously, in this view interiorization or the like does not play a role since a goal of learning is not an internal mental construction but an external, observable activity with diagrams. The latter has its meaning and importance first of all in itself without being void of referential relationships. In a more extreme form: understanding is then not the grasps of abstract objects (based on appropriately constructed mental ones) but the socially accepted expedience with diagrammatic activities.

To sum up, those qualities of diagrams might explain from a different point of view why learning mathematics is very demanding, cognitively and perceptively as well. This is caused by the unavoidable amalgam of writing/reading/perceiving/reflecting which can be found in all diagrammatic activities.

CONCLUSION

The thrust of my paper was twofold. First, I put forward the thesis that the common discourse about mathematics characterizing it as an abstract and mental endeavour might cause much of existing anxieties, misunderstandings and reluctance to engage with maths. Second, as a complementary alternative I suggested to present maths as the systematic study of diagrammatic inscriptions which turns it into a demystified social and public practice of activities with human (material and observable) artefacts. Those then are open to many different interpretations like in the case of Euclid's diagrammatic proof for getting a prime number different from given ones. In a more Platonistic view this is read as: there are infinitely many prime numbers. Thus it is also important to discuss the limitations of what can be justified and reasoned by the use of diagrams (Dörfler 2005).

REFERENCES

Bakker, A. (2004). *Design research in statistics education*. Utrecht: CD- β Press.
Borwein, J.M. (2005). The experimental mathematician: The pleasure of discovery and the role of proof. *International Journal of Computers for Mathematical Learning, 10*, 75-108.
Burton, L. (2004). *Mathematicians as enquirers*. Dordrecht: Kluwer.
Cobb, R., Yackel, E. & McClain K. (Eds.) (2000). *Symbolizing and communicating in mathematics classrooms*. Mahwah: Lawrence Erlbaum.
Cobb, P. (1999). Individual and collective mathematical development: The case of statistical data analysis. *Mathematical Thinking and Learning,1*, 5-43.
Cobb, P., Yackel, E., & Wood, T. (1992). A constructivist alternative to the representational view of mind in mathematics education. *Journal for Research in Mathematics Education, 23*, 2-33.
Dantzig, D.v. (1999). Is $10^{10^{10}}$ a finite number? In Moore, A.W. (Ed.). *Infinity*. Aldershot: Dartmouth.

Diagrammatic Reasoning Bibliography. http://www.hcrc.ed.ac.uk/gal/Diagrams/biblio/html

Dörfler, W. (in press). Mathematical reasoning: Mental activity or practice with diagrams. *Proceedings regular lectures ICME 10*, Copenhagen.

Dörfler, W. (2005). Diagrammatic thinking: Affordances and constraints. In M. Hoffmann et al. (Eds.). *Activity and sign-grounding mathematics education*. New York: Springer, 57-66.

Dörfler, W. (2004a). Diagrams as means and objects of mathematical reasoning. In *Developments in mathematics education in german-speaking countries. Selected papers from the Annual Conference on Didactics of Mathematics 2001*. Hildesheim: Verlag Franzbecker , 39-49.

Dörfler, W. (2004b). Mathematical Reasoning and Observing Transformations of Diagrams. In: Ch. Bergsten and B. Grevholm (Eds.). *Mathematics and language. Proc. MADIF* 4. Linköping: SMDF , 7-19.

Dubinsky, E. & MacDonald, M.A. (2001). APOS: A constructivist the ory of learning in undergraduate mathematics education research. In Holton, D. et al. (Eds.). *The teaching and learning of mathematics at the university level: An ICME Study*. Dordrecht: Kluwer , 273-280.

Duval, R. (1995). *Sémiosis et pensée humaine*. Bern: Peter Lang.

Godino, J.D. Batanero, C. & Rafall, R. (2005). An onto-semiotic analysis of combinatorial problems and the solving process by university students. *Educational Studies in Mathematics, 30*, 3-36.

Goldin, G.A. and Janvier, C. (Eds.) (1998). *Representations and the psychology of mathematics education I, II*. Special Issue of *Journal of Mathematical Behavior,17*(1 and 2).

Gravemeijer , K., Lehrer, R., Oers, B.v. & Verschaffel, L. (Eds.) (2002). *Symbolizing, modelling and tool use in mathematics education*. Dordrecht: Kluwer.

Gravemeijer, K. (1999). How emergent models may foster the constitution of formal mathematics. *Mathematical Thinking and Learning, 1*, 155-177.

Heintz, B. (2000). Die Innenwelt der Mathematik. Zur Kultur und Praxis einer beweisenden Disziplin. Wien/New York: Springer.

Hoffmann, M.H.G. (2005). Signs as means for discoveries. In M.H.G. Hoffmann, J. Lenhard, & F. Seeger (Eds.). *Activity and sign. grounding mathematics education*. New York: Springer.

Hoffmann, M.H.G., Lenhard, J., & Seeger, F. (Eds.) (2005). *Activity and sign. grounding mathematics education*. New York: Springer.

Hoffmann, M.H.G. (2005). *Erkenntnisentwicklung. Philosophische Abhandlungen Bd. 90*. Frankfurt am Main: Klostermann.

Krämer, S., & Bredekamp, H. (Eds.) (2003). *Bild-Schrift-Zahl*. München: Wilhelm Fink Verlag.

Krämer, S. (1988). *Symbolische Maschinen. Die Idee der Formalisierung in geschichtlichem Abriss*. Darmstadt: Wissenschaftliche Buchgesellschaft.

Lenné, H. (1969). *Analyse der mathematikdidaktik in Deutschland*. Stuttgart: Klett.

Mac Lane, S. (1986). *Mathematics. Form and function*. New York: Springer.

Marietti, S. (2005). A semiotic approach to mathematical evidence and generalization. In: M.H.G. Hoffmann, J. Lenhard, & F. Seeger (Eds.). *Activity and sign. grounding mathematics education*. New York: Springer.

Meira, L. (1998). Making sense of instructional devices: The emergence of transparency in mathematical activity. *Journal for Research in Mathematics Education, 29*, 121-142.

Nelson, Roger A. (2000). *Proofs without words. More exercises in visual thinking*. Washington, DC: Mathematical Association of America.

Nelson, Roger A. (1993). *Proofs without words. More exercises in visual thinking*. Washington, DC: Mathematical Association of America.

Nemirovski, R.C. (1994). On ways of symbolizing: The case of Laura and the velocity sign. *Journal of Mathematical Behavior, 13*, 389-422.

Otte, M. (Ed.) (1974). *Mathematiker über die Mathematik*. Berlin: Springer

Peirce, Ch. S. (1976). *The new elements of mathematics (NEM)*, vol. IV (Ed. C. Eisele), The Hague: Mouton.

Peirce, Ch. S. (1931-1958). *Collected Papers I-VIII*. Cambridge, MA: Harvard University Press.

Radford, L. (2003). Gestures, speech and the sprouting of signs. *Mathematical Thinking and Learning*, *5*(1), 37-70.

Roth, W.-R. (2003). *Toward an anthropology of graphing*. Dordrecht: Kluwer.

Rotman, B. (2000). *Mathematics as sign. writing, imagining, counting*. Stanford: Stanford University Press.

Rotman, B (1993). *Ad infinitum ... the ghost in turing's machine*. Stanford, CA: Stanford University Press.

Schmandt-Besserart, D. (1997). *How writing came about*. Austin. University of Texas Press.

di Sessa, A. (ed.) (2000). Meta-representational competence. Special Issue of *Journal of Mathematical Behavior, 19*(4).

Stjernfelt, F. (2000). Diagrams as centrepiece of a Peircean epistemology. *Transactions of the Charles S. Peirce Society XXXVI* (3), 357-384.

Wilson, W.S. (2005). Short response to Tunis's letter to the editor on technology in college. *Educational Studies in Mathematics 58*(3), 415-420.

Winslow, C. (2004). Semiotics as an analytical tool for the didactics of mathematics. *Nordisch Mathematikk Didaktikk (Nomad), 9*(2), 81-100.

Willibald Dörfler
Universität Klagenfurt, Austria

BERT VAN OERS

AN ACTIVITY THEORY APPROACH TO THE FORMATION OF MATHEMATICAL COGNITION: DEVELOPPING TOPICS THROUGH PREDICATION IN A MATHEMATICAL COMMUNITY

"Was du ererbt von deinen Vätern hast,

erwirb es, um es zu besitzen

J.W. Goethe, **Faust** (erster Teil, Nacht).

THE UNENDING QUEST

About 150 years ago, Gregor Mendel did his famous experiments in Austria that led to the discovery of a set of laws that explained heredity. Mendel discovered that biological inheritance was basically an aleatoric process. This was an enormous step in the explanation of heredity, because with Mendel's laws people could explain successfully how individual characteristics would be distributed over the population. However, biologists did not self-contentedly lean back with this successful theory, but kept on asking 'why?' and 'how come?' Through their persistent queries, biologists discovered more precise molecular explanations of heredity, in terms of DNA and RNA etc. The growth of insight is based on an unending endeavour of questioning.

The same is true for our attempts to understand mathematics as a human faculty. There is probably nobody who will disagree with the statement that mathematical problem solving and learning is a cognitive process, but this is a statement at the same level as Mendel's explanation of heredity. Further enquiries should specify what exactly cognitive processes are, which mechanisms are involved; how do they operate?

However, the explanation of mathematical learning and problem solving as a cognitive process has turned out to be tough task, due to the polysemy of the terms used. In the educational domain it is not unequivocally clear what should be considered as 'mathematics' or 'mathematical', and different conceptions are indeed reflected in the mathematics textbooks in schools. However, I will not dwell very long on this complex issue here. The definition of what counts as 'mathematical' is one of the permanent duties of the mathematical community (see

J. Maasz, W. Schloeglmann (Eds.), New Mathematics Education Research and Practice, 113–139.

van Oers, 2001a). For the present purpose I would confine myself to just a general characterisation of what mathematics is, based on the reflections of Freudenthal. In his view, mathematics is the human activity of organising a field (be it experiential or conceptual) with the help of structured symbolic means, which makes it accessible for further analysis (see Freudenthal, 1973, ch 7). This process of organising a field is called 'mathematising' and it strongly emphasises the importance of functionality of the mathematical tools for the particular field that they are meant to organise (or: the specific problem they are meant to solve). Organising an experiential or conceptual field, and studying its structures, validity, and implications is the core of mathematical activity. Mathematics as a discipline encompasses all tools that have been invented during human history for the organisation of such fields, according to the conventions of a mathematical community.

Rather than further specifying what is implied in this starting point (see Freudenthal among others 1973, 1983, 1990, 1991), I prefer to focus on *psychological* issues related to mathematics learning and problem solving, and especially focus on the meaning of the terms 'cognitive' and 'learning'. The use of these terms in explanations of mathematical learning and problem solving is problematic, as their meaning changes with the perspective of the user. In this article I will develop an approach to mathematics as a cognitive process from the perspective of cultural historical activity theory (or socio-cultural theory), and articulate some of its core mechanisms. Finally, I will demonstrate the mechanisms for the domain of mathematical problem solving and learning.

'COGNITION' AS AN ECOLOGICAL CONCEPT

The term 'cognitive' originally referred to events that occur within the Black Box that was created by the Behaviourists for the explanation of human behaviour. The cognitivist orientation among psychologists emerged in the first half of the 20th century and involved a rehabilitation of the mind (or consciousness) as an object of study. Initially, cognitivism was mainly anti-behaviourism. It attempted to open the Black Box and develop theories about cognitive processes and about the ways people retrieve information about the world and accomplish the tasks that are set to them in their interactions with the world. Hence, in this sense all modern theories – ranging from Ausubel, computational cognitive science, situated cognition to Vygotsky and beyond- can be called 'cognitive theories'.

However, the differences among adherents of the cognitive approach concerning the nature of cognition and the methodology needed are considerable. In 1976 Neisser criticised the mainstream approaches of American cognitive psychology. His critique was focused on their reduced conception of both the real world ('task-situation') and the nature of human beings. However, his main argument was that until the mid seventies cognitive psychology had retained one of the basic assumptions of behaviourism that holds that there is a one-way process going from the world to the person. Even when this process was now conceived in terms of information flow, it still assumed the information as given. Cognition, according to

Neisser (1976, p. 11) is 'not just operations in the head, but transactions with the world. These transactions do not merely inform the perceiver, they also transform him. Each of us is created by the cognitive acts in which he engages'.

For Neisser the human mind is a faculty with adaptive power that supports an individual's interactions with the ordinary world. Basically, Neisser repeats what Piaget (1952) and Vygotsky (1925/1982; 1927/1982) have proposed before, be it in different terms. Consciousness (or the human mind) is a faculty that enables a human being to come to grips with a concrete and cultural world and it develops in close connection to the environment (or cultural context) in which it is supposed to function (see also Vygotsky, 1994). Vygotsky goes even further by stating that this context is itself a historically evolving product of the human mind (which he expresses in his notion of 'the social situation of development '- see Vygotsky, 1984). So in our modern language we can summarize this point of view by saying that consciousness and context are co-evolving phenomena that constitute an ecological system, in which the elements are dialectically related and mutually dependent. As far as human interactions with contexts have to do with creating and processing meaning and personal sense, human consciousness manifests itself in a form we can call 'cognition'. Like consciousness in general, cognition (from this point of view) is equally to be seen as an ecological concept: cognition can only be understood in relation to its function of meaningfully relating an individual to its context. The term 'cognitive', then, refers to all psychological processes that are involved in building and maintaining meaningful relationships with the (physical and cultural) world, or in trying to understand the nature and exigencies of this condition.

However, even within this 'ecological' point of view, there are still different specific approaches in the study of cognitive processes. Two dominant approaches in the recent history of learning theory are discussed and compared by Cobb & Bowers (1999). They make a comparative analysis of the 'cognitive' and the 'situated cognition' paradigms (Given the fact that both paradigms are approaches within cognitive psychology, I would suggest to call the first paradigm 'computational' rather than 'cognitive'). Cobb and Bower's analysis makes a strong case for distinguishing both paradigms on the basis of their differing conceptions of basic notions such as 'knowledge', 'context' and the individual. Moreover, the approaches differ with respect to the basic units of analysis that they employ in the analysis and explanation of cognitive processes. The situated cognition paradigm tries to understand the cognitive process in terms of developing meaning and sense, while the computational paradigm tries to construe explanations in terms of transformations of symbolically coded input into task related acts. From the comparison of the two approaches, Cobb & Bowers conclude that both approaches are not easily reconcilable and not entirely satisfactory in their own right. They argue for a third approach that helps us to understand the evolution of cognitive processes in participatory activities in everyday practices (such as mathematics classrooms). The approach they advocate is definitely 'ecological' in the sense defined above. In their view, then, some version of the situated cognition approach deserves preference, particularly a version that can account for both individual and social (collective) processes. According to Cobb & Bowers, the socio-constructivist approach provides such a framework for an understanding of mathematics learning in classroom communities of practice.

THE POVERTY OF SOCIOCONSTRUCTIVISM

Constructivism is one of the attempts to specify the nature of cognition and cognitive processes. Constructivists emphasise the active nature of cognition and maintain that cognitive processes are basically constructive processes that create the contents of the human mind in interaction with the environment. One of the most powerful and popular versions of constructivism nowadays is 'Socio-constructivism'. The socio-constructivist view definitely maintains an ecological conception of cognition. The construction of meanings is conceived as a process that is embedded in a social context. It takes form in close relationships with the characteristics of this social environment and the interactions that take place within that environment. (Socio-) constructivists believe that the process of knowing, appropriation, or knowledge acquisition is not a mere reflection of the experiential world but a process in which new meanings are constructed through interaction and dialogue with others. Indeed, there is a vast body of empirical evidence that demonstrates that the subject has a decisive role in learning. Although the literature sometimes makes a distinction between social constructionism and socio-constructivism (see for example different chapters in Steffe & Gale, 1995), I will not make these distinctions here, because both share the idea that new meaning is constructed in dialogue with others. Exactly these assumptions need to be scrutinised here in order to examine how (if ever) they clarify the notion of cognition.

Does socio-constructivism help us to get a better understanding of cognition or cognitive processes? There are several reasons for doubt about this. One of the main shortcomings of most constructivist theories is that they tend to use 'construction' as an explanatory concept without having a clear explanation of the nature of this process itself. How does the process of 'constructing' proceed? There is not much clarity gained when we just replace 'cognition', by the 'construction of meaning', 'production of constructions', or 'the construction of knowledge'. The addition of a social element to this process by itself does not change much with respect to this blind spot of constructivist theories. Although there are a few positive exceptions (e.g. Anna Sfard's theory of the construction of mathematical objects and Paul Cobb's theory about the chain of signification – I will return to these theories below), most constructivist explanations do not bother about analysing the concept of construction and about giving a detailed theory regarding the process of constructing. As a matter of fact, Confrey's description of the constructivist program is exemplary for this view:

> 'How to obtain an appropriate balance between encouraging students' active
> construction, recognizing and legitimizing diversity in their efforts, and

placing such constructive activity within the framework of guidance and encouragement from more experienced others' (Confrey, 1995, p. 224).

This demonstrates how constructivists tend to use 'construction' in a general philosophical way, like Kant already used it in his explanation of mathematical concept formation (see Kant 1783, edition 1969, p. 18, where Kant himself speaks about 'die Konstruktion der Begriffe' (the construction of concepts)). Like Mendel's conception of heredity, this may not be a false idea, but it does not explain much either about the mechanisms of cognition. Instead of using 'construction' as an explanatory concept, 'construction' is above all the concept to be explained.

Gergen (1995, p. 24 – 25) characterises the situation aptly:

'Social constructionism places the human relationship in the foreground, that is, the pattern of interdependent action at the micro-social level. There is little attempt to explain these patterns by recourse to psychological processes within the person. (...) Thus the constructionist is centrally concerned with such matters as negotiation, cooperation, conflict, rhetoric, ritual, roles, social scenarios, and the like, but avoids psychological explanations of micro-social processes'.

Gergen assumes that an explanation of construction in psychological terms would be seen as a kind of reductionism, placing the social interchange in a secondary role.

It is clear from this that the social dimension in the constructive process is generally considered an essential element in the understanding of construction. As Shotter (1995, p. 43) points out 'all versions of social constructionism now focus on an unbroken, contingent flow of communicative interaction between human beings'. But how exactly are the social and individual related in this view? As many authors already have pointed out, socio-constructivism developed out of radical constructivism that initially tried to explain the construction of knowledge in close harmony with the Piagetian view. Although Piaget never neglected or denied the relevance of the social dimension for development, he conceived it mainly as a trigger condition for knowledge construction. It is clear from Piaget's works that he does not give the social dimension explanatory power: the social dimension for him is mainly a condition that raises conflicts and perturbations, which necessitate the innovation of cognitive structures. It is the thinking subject that is in the last resort responsible for the construction of new knowledge. The focus on the social dimension of the construction process, then, is an attempt to defend constructivism against accusations of individualism (or even solipsism). As Confrey (1995, p. 214) pointed out: "Social constructivism can be viewed as attempting to merge the social dimensions of Vygotsky with radical constructivism'.

Taking a closer look at the relationships between the social and the psychological that is adopted in many constructivist interpretations, we can see that both dimensions often function in a figure – ground relationship, like we see in the words of Thomson (1995, p. 128):

117

'If we agree that social relationships involve individuals, and that individuals are continually involved in social relationships, it is legitimate to take either individuals (as the things related to one another), or relationships (among individuals) as figure and the other as ground, as long as one keeps in mind which is being taken as figure and which is being taken a s ground'

A similar idea is aired by Ernest (1995, p. 481) when he writes that social constructivism (constructionism) ´prioritize the social above the individual'. It is evident that such interpretations of the relationships between the social and psychological (or the social and the individual) still separate both dimensions as distinct categories. So they are ready to accept that individual-psychological processes (like cognition) are essentially influenced by social factors (like interactions, dialogue), but still cannot –from their psychological theory- see that the psychological itself ís a social phenomenon as well. Separating the social from the psychological (or the individual from the group) is a categorical mistake like the belief that we obtain three things when we purchase new shoes: a right shoe, a left shoe, and a pair. Most traditional psychological theories (including the computational cognitivist theories) maintain psychological views that separate the individual (and psychological) from the social. Constructivism seems to adopt this psychological point of view, and is unable to integrate social processes in their explanations. Their emphasis on the social processes unavoidably amounts to neglecting psychological processes. However, it could be that their concern about psychological reductionism is primarily a result of a poor (not to say: defective) psychological theory.

When we take a look at the way social interactions are interpreted in socio-constructivism, then again we can see certain flaws in the arguments. Recent developments of socio-constructivism emphasise the importance of conversation and participation, focusing on face-to-face interactions, and dialogue (see for example Confrey, 1995). The relevance of participating in cultural practices for learning and development is a widely accepted and well-founded idea. For the domain of mathematics learning, for example, it is common wisdom nowadays, to belief that mathematical thinking develops through assisted participation in practices that may lead to mathematising (in the sense of Freudenthal's 'organising fields'). The development of mathematising can then be seen as the interactive constitution of a social practice' (Bauersfeld, 1995, p. 150; see also numerous publications of Paul Cobb and his group). However, for our present goal of clarifying the nature of human cognition, this is still not a very helpful proposition (although generally useful by itself), as it only specifies the context for the occurrence of cognitive processes, but does not spell out precisely which psychological mechanisms are at work. In the wake of Wenger's theory about communities of learners and their role for learning, meaning and identity formation, it seems to become common sense for many socio-constructivists to accept Wenger's statement that 'learning is, in its essence, a fundamentally social phenomenon, reflecting our own deeply social nature as human beings capable of knowing' (Wenger, 1998, p. 3).

This leads to the idea of 'learning as social participation' (Wenger, 1998, p. 4). However, social participation only specifies the conditions under which meaningful learning might take place (sometimes it does not), but does not teach us anything about the cognitive process of learning itself. In the context of Wenger's work, the statement of 'learning as social participation' may be just sloppy language that conceals the true meaning of what he tried to explain. In his work with Lave (see Lave & Wenger, 1991) it was explained that learning is synonymous with changes in the ways that an individual participates in social practices. The formulation of the way of participation in a social practice comes closer to a psychological description of human functioning and learning. Although it is still an open formulation, it does not identify learning with social participation: learning is in the change, not in the participation itself. It is possible to participate and not learn anything (in terms of changed ways of acting), which demonstrates that participation by itself is not yet learning (although it can be a powerful condition that maximises the chances for meaningful learning). So there is nothing wrong with 'viewing individual activity as an act of participation in a system of practices that are themselves evolving' (Cobb & Bowers, 1999, p. 8), but this is still a far cry from explaining the nature of the cognitive aspects involved.

Looking at socio-constructivism, we may conclude that this approach may function as a useful instrument for the organisation of classroom practices, but it does not help us much in fathoming the nature of cognitive processes. Cognitive explanations are either avoided in many socio-constructivist accounts, or framed in general terms. When cognitive accounts are given, it seems that socio-constructivism still tacitly maintains many of the assumptions of its ancestors (Piagetian theory or computational theory), especially with regard to the separation of the psychological from its social context (although the social influence on psychological development is accepted, but as an independent variable).

For a further clarification of human cognitive processes more specific theories are needed that can integrate psychological processes and social processes. Two of such theories were already mentioned above. Anna Sfard developed interesting ideas about the construction of mathematical objects through the use of metaphors and the process of permanent embedded focusing (Sfard, 1994; 2002). Sfard brings us a step closer to understanding the nature of cognition by describing how mental objects are constructed through the attribution of images and metaphors to (discursive) activities. Paul Cobb accounted for the process of mathematisation in sociolinguistic terms in his description of a chain of signification (see Cobb et al., 1997). This explanation is basically an account of mathematics learning as a cognitive process in which signifiers (symbolic means) are related to signified objects. Any signifier-signified unit can be treated as a new (mental) object that can be referred to with new signifiers. Creating chains of signification in the context of communications about a problematic context thus reflects the progress in mathematical meanings development.

Both approaches seem to be plausible approximations of what happens in the cognitive processes in mathematical practices. They go beyond the simple socio-constructivistic approach as they integrate the psychological and the social through their socio-cultural (Vygotskian) view on cognitive processes and they attempt to clarify 'construction' as a functional process of combining meanings and inscriptions within activity systems (practices). Both approaches have adopted a socio-semiotic view on human activity, in which the use of semiotic tools (e.g. language but not only verbal language) plays a key role in how psychological processes proceed. Sfard's account, moreover, gives a beautiful description of the process of abstraction that is going on in mathematics (see also van Oers, 2001b). Cobb and his colleagues give an intriguing account of the progression in mathematical thinking through the use of symbolic means. These approaches are definitely important contributions to the account of cognition in a non-computational way. However, both approaches address only part of the cognitive process, as they confine themselves to describing the problem solving process as an orderly linear process, related to specific tasks. They do not address the deeper levels of meaning construction, development and negotiation, and learning, where construction is not (yet) an orderly, linear process,. At the deeper levels of cognition, thinking manifests itself as a jumpy pursuit, exploring sideways, jumping to previous points, following hunches, accompanied and co-regulated by sense of direction, feelings of uneasiness, joy, impatience, anger etc. In the next sections, I will attempt to broaden the socio-semiotic accounts by adding a new dimension based on the psychological dynamics of the development of meanings within an activity theory approach.

COGNITION AS ORIENTATION WITHIN ACTIVITIES

Let us first take a look at cognition as a psychological phenomenon. From an activity point of view, cognition is seen as a collection of psychological functions that are necessary for the accomplishment of mediated activities, particularly for the participation in cultural practices (socio-cultural activity settings). From this point of view, the function of cognition is basically the regulation and coordination of human activity in accordance with personal, situational and/or cultural requirements (including historical standards and norms). The link between 'cognition' and cultural practices is particularly important as it designates the ecological embeddesness of cognition in a broader activity system, and by so doing articulates both the functional value of cognition and the intrinsic cultural nature of the content and processes of cognition.

However, it must be stressed that this does not exclude the possibility of individual cognition. As was explained by Leont'ev (1975), individual human action (be it cognitive action or concrete real world action) is just a moment of a meta-personal cultural-historically developed activity. So, when a person is reading a book, he accomplishes an individualised version of the cultural practice of reading. Equally: when a person is carrying out a mental calculation for herself, she is realising a personal version of a part of the cultural activity of 'mathematising'.

It is impossible to separate the social from the individual when studying cognition as an essential constituent of cultural practices. We cannot study cultural practices, but through the accomplishments of individuals, and we can never understand individual actions without conceiving these as local (both in time and space) personalised versions of socio-cultural activities (see for example Hedegaard & Chaiklin (2005).

How can we conceive of 'cognition' in the context of activities? Sylvia Scribner once argued that 'Human cognition is culturally mediated; it is founded on purposive activity, and it is historically developing' (Scribner, 1997, 268; italics by Scribner). In a fundamental study of cultural-historical activity theory Gal'perin (1976) had earlier proposed an idea about human cognition that is consistent with Scribner's and actually articulates the nature of cognition in a more detailed way. Gal'perin argues that the essence of the psyche (including cognition) is orientation. Orientation, according to Gal'perin, is a fundamental psychological process through which a person relates to the world. Orientation is a form of exploratory activity that transforms the environment in ideas. On a very basic level, orientation is vital for noticing changes in the environment and preparing for necessary actions. In primitive organisms this can be executed on a reflex basis, but in higher organisms orientational activities not only signal changes, but also identify the nature of the changes, imagine possible actions and goals, anticipate consequences of possible actions, plan execution of selected actions, monitor the process of acting, evaluate outcomes of performed actions etc. According to Gal'perin (1976, p. 84 – 85/ 1980, p 105-106) orientation activities show two general qualities: first they always precede the actual execution of actions and create a model of the actions to be performed, and secondly orientational activities are always focused on finding and giving directions to human activities. Gal'perin writes:

"This orientating activity is an activity in which a subject examines a situation that contains new elements, and either confirms or changes the sense and functional meaning of the objects involved; in this orientation activity the subject accordingly tunes in his actions to the situation or changes them, and anticipates a new course of the execution of his actions; moreover, during the execution of the actions, the subject regulates the course of the actions in accordance with the new, but not yet fixed meanings of the objects" (Gal'perin, 1976, p. 88 – 89/1980, p. 109-110; translation BvO).

When we follow Gal'perin and conceive of the basic function of cognition as 'orientation', it is obvious that the cognitive processes include more than just the execution of operations, accomplishments of the steps in an argument or transformation of inscriptions and meanings. Cognition also includes processes like valuing (emotional, aesthetical, normative etc), production of information, planning, anticipating and predicting, monitoring, evaluating etc. All these processes are carried out in order to find a match between the personalised versions of an activity and the exigencies of the context.

In the phylogenetic and socio-genetic ("cultural") history the orientation activity itself changed as a result of changing tools, strategies, and norms. The biological orientative reflex is still an important mechanism for quick responses to immediate threats, but it is a rigid an uninformed way of reacting to the environment. Over the history of the human species we learned to orient in a more informed way, invented new tools (like walking stick, spectacles, maps, language etc) to assess situations and to accomplish sophisticated actions. But still people have different ways of orienting in a situation. Imagine a situation in which a person wants to furnish a room with a table, two chairs, a desk and a bookcase. This person can explore the situation in different ways when trying to find the optimal design of his room. He can put the furniture in the room and start shifting around the pieces until he has found the optimal arrangement of things. But instead of this material orientation in the room he could also try to imagine what the room looks like in different arrangements and than finally decide which arrangement will be actually created in the room. A third way would be to represent the room with its measures on a paper, and construct different solutions based on different conditions. These latter cases demonstrate how the orientation precedes the actual arrangements of the pieces of furniture in the room, but, what is more important, it also demonstrates that different actions (trials) don't need to be carried out in real, when we can anticipate their outcomes. Therefore, in an orientation activity people can anticipate the outcomes of actions or their consequences, and decide if there is a need to actually carry them out.

Most of human cognitive activities can be properly conceived as orientative activities in which the given ("data", or to use Freudenthal's expression again: a field) is transformed into new symbolic forms that articulate structures in settings and possible actions. Those symbolic actions can be examined before deciding the form of a final action (a real world action, an utterance that answers a question, writing a solution to a mathematical problem etc). Within the context of broader activities (or practices), the outcomes of the orientation activity might be instrumental for further goals, as is the case in the calculation of the rigidity of a steel structure under the pressure of different hypothetical forces, that is needed for the real world construction of a bridge or a tower.

The conception of cognition as an orientation activity has several far-reaching implications. A few of them will be listed here briefly:

(1) It encompasses and broadens the main stream computational conceptions of cognition: in an orientation process it is often necessary to transform symbolic expressions in new symbolic structures. This is exactly how cognition is often described (see for example Bruer, 1993). However, in order to understand the directivity of the process and the levels of abstraction that are often involved, it is necessary to draw from sources that go beyond the purely operational descriptions, and that can deal with meanings and values as well; see also point 4 below that comments this further.

(2) Cognition as an orientative activity is an ecological concept as it is essentially interdependent with other entities in a living activity system: cognition depends on motives of an agent, goals emerging in an activity, rules and tools of a practice; the orientation can take place within the real world (material constructions, communications, etc.), but also within the ideal world of

symbolic systems (as can be the case in mathematical examinations of mathematical structures).

(3) Cognition is a distributed phenomenon: as orientation is related to practices, it is obvious that the quality of the orientation activity is partly based upon the resources that are provided by those practices (tools, resources, co-practitioners). Cognition, then, is not confined within the human skull but is essentially distributed in a cultural practice (see Cole & Engeström, 1993). Individual cognition is a local and personalised version of this distributed orientation and as such, it depends on external resources as well. Although in practice cognition develops trough interpersonal dialogues and interactions with resources, it is through this distributed nature basically a polylogical phenomenon, i.e. cognition develops and is accomplished on the basis of multiple dialogues with actual and virtual others (contemporary and historical).

(4) Ontogenetically, individual cognition develops as an interiorisation of interpersonal orientation activities (following Vygotsky's general law of ontogenesis that says that all psychological functions appear twice: first as s social, interpersonal process, then as a individual intrapersonal process; the reconstruction of the orientation process on an intrapersonal mental level is an example of interiorisation); as the interpersonal orientation is based on polylogical communication (see point 3 above), cognition as an orientation process has a predominantly dialogical structure (Bakhtin, 1981 – see also van Oers, 1996).

In a multi-faceted world, the direction of orientation is never self-evident, but is based on experience and the habits of a particular community of practice. External cues often hint at a certain direction for orientation and often suggest whether the orientation should be mathematical, historical, aesthetical, political, linguistic etc. Symbolic codes (like words, inscriptions, diagrams etc) become imbued with special meaning within a particular social community. These social representations focus a person's attention into a certain direction. Moscovici (1973) described social representation as:

> "Systems of values, ideas and practices with a two-fold function: first to establish an order which will enable individuals to orientate themselves in their material and social worlds and to master it; secondly, to enable communication to take place amongst members of a community by providing them with a code for social exchange and a code for naming and classifying unambiguously the various aspects of their world and their individual and group history"

Both in ontogenesis (development of the individual) and in microgenesis (learning processes) a person appropriates a certain orientation (e.g. a mathematical orientation) to reality through external directives implied in social representations. Participation in a certain practice creates a shared pool of common values that enables the participants to communicate and to expand the set of meanings that are taken as shared. Take a classroom for example: both the appearance of the books and the specific vocabulary suggest to pupils that a mathematical (or other) orientation is required.1 The initial orientation is the beginning of an abstraction process, which follows a course of embedded more specific foci, and finally leads to forms of abstract thinking (see van Oers, 2001b).

(5) 'Learning' in an activity theory approach is the extension or improvement of the repertoire of actions, tools, meanings, and values, that increases a person's abilities to participate autonomously in a sociocultural practice. The orientation within learning processes is focused on the accomplishments of the actions and the successful promotion of ways to improve them (see van Oers, 1996). The increased ability to participate in sociocultural practices can be reached through the improvement of concrete actions (e.g. writing, using calculator, reading tables etc), or through the improvement of the orientations process with the help of newly developed mental strategies or meanings. One important type of learning processes is the process in which concrete actions are translated into mental form. Gal'perin has demonstrated that this learning reaches its optimal stage when a person can anticipate the outcomes of actions without actually having to perform the actions themselves. It is enough to think of the action instead of performing it (Gal'perin, 1969; 1979). In that case, the actions have transsubstantiated into a symbolic existence, and can be used in orientation activities. An example of this can be seen in the concrete act of measuring with material blocks (units), which can develop via a number line into flexible operations with numbers. From that moment on there is no necessity to act out in reality the combination of collections of elements (when adding numbers like $5 + 6$), or carry out the steps on the number line, since we can anticipate the outcome. Thinking of the outcome of this action will be sufficient for using it in the orientations of space, symbolic systems, or virtual realities.

(6) Initial orientation always includes the articulation (explicitly or implicitly) of a topic with new dimensions which are produced through communication (internal or external). The development of the topic into new extended forms is the core process of what we can call the construction and negotiation of meaning. As Vygotsky (1987, ch 7) has argued, this process of topic development is very important for the understanding of interiorisation and the progress of thinking. In the next section, I will focus on this process and will describe cognitive processes involved in the construction of meaning in terms of this process of topic development. The process of topic development is basically a process of adding new aspects to a shared topic that may anticipate future results of discussion or action. As such, topic development is a form of orientation that prepares for potential actions in an activity.

Summarizing the above argument, we can say that cognition is to be conceived as a practice based orienting activity that values the situation and transforms it into a topic for further consideration and analysis. Through the analyses, new qualities are discovered that might become included into the topic for the anticipation of future states, events or action results. *This process of topic development is to be conceived as a description of the process of meaning construction in psychological terms*, and consequently as an explanation of thinking as a cognitive process. In the next section, I will present a theoretical description of this process, starting out from Vygotsky's theory of thinking (Vygotsky, 1987). Although this process can be considered crucial for thinking as a cognitive process and can be seen as a further articulation of cognition, it must be admitted that the theory is still in its early stages of development and probably gives only a partial description of cognitive processes. Future analyses from this perspective may shed new light on cognition and cognitive processes.

THE CONSTRUCTION OF MEANING THROUGH TOPIC-PREDICATE STRUCTURES

A fundamental assumption behind this view on thinking as a cognitive process is that it is based on development of meanings with the help of symbols. It must be kept in mind, though, that symbols do not "possess" meaning in any absolute sense. The meanings of symbols have to be created in a particular context and from a particular intention. In many cases, the creation of meanings has been processed frequently in relatively stable situations, so that the process of re-construction of meaning is automatised and strongly abbreviated. In those cases, it might seem as if the symbol immediately triggers the meaning, and so to say manifest this meaning from itself. In the present view, this is considered as an illusion that is a result of the psychological process of abbreviation (see for example van Oers, 1996 for further explanation). Behind this extremely abbreviated process we suppose a micro-genetically older form of meaning construction that is based on valuation and a gradual process of articulation of already available meanings.

The valuation process is basic to the course of the meaning making process and is a result of an orientative process of focussing on a particular object from a particular point of view. The valuation process is the stage in the orientation that determines the part of an environment that deserves predominant attention (for whatever reason: aesthetic, emotional, intellectual, economical, political etc). It results in the agent's focusing on a certain topic that is for the moment the centre of attention, and in the agent's choice for a perspective from which that topic will be considered. The exact process of valuing needs a detailed analysis but I will not undertake that analysis here. Social representations (Moscovici) probably have an important role in this process. In educational situations the choice of the topic and the perspective is mostly determined by the teacher or the textbook (pupils for instance get mathematical assignments described in the textbook). Sometimes the topic emerges out of the activities and interactions between teacher and pupils. The main problem usually exists in the process of giving new meaning to the topic and developing this meaning into new knowledge.

For the description of this latter process, we can use an idea that was adapted by Vygotsky from linguistics. Vygotsky (1934/1987) demonstrated that speech and thinking are closely related processes. In his view, thinking is based on an interiorisation of speech, and thinking maintains many of the structures of the external dialogue and syntactical organisation. In the explanation of the dialogical structure of thinking Vygotsky remained rather vague and speculative, saying that thinking is based on an inner dialogue (a thesis that was also aired by Bakhtin). According to Vygotsky, inner dialogical thinking retains the fundamental characteristic of linguistic expressions: it is a process of construing new predicates (comments) regarding a topic of attention.

Psychologically the process remained rather unclear, though. About 50 years later Kuÿinskij further specified this theory in his study of the relationships between dialogue and thinking (Kuÿinskij, 1983). Kuÿinskij pointed out that Vygotsky's notion of dialogue was insufficiently elaborated and probably limited as far as he defines dialogue in terms of two individuals communicating. The essence of dialogue according to Kuÿinskij (and he follows Bakhtin at this point) is that two or more different points of view meet and start interacting. Kuÿinskij aptly uses the term 'meaning position' ("smyslovaja posicija", Kuÿinskij, p. 20), which refers to a particular point of view on the object (theme) of the discourse. He argues that the interaction between different meaning positions is the essence of dialogues (p. 30). Of course, different meaning positions can be taken by different persons, but within one person different meaning positions can also emerge and compete. Through the analysis of problem solving processes in dyads and individual problem solving (with thinking aloud protocols) he demonstrated that problem solving could indeed be described as a competition between different meaning positions that exchange alternative possibilities for solution.

Like an external dialogue, inner dialogues often take the form of question-answer or statement – reaction cycles. On an inner plane, each meaning position is alternatingly defended and the problem solver tries to reach a consensus between the positions. According to Kuÿinskij each dialogue is characterised by a theme, a core issue that is being talked about. The presence of a shared theme is essential for a dialogue, for this theme is the shared focus of attention, the integrating and harmonising entity that regulates the dialogue. The aim of the dialogue can also be seen as a collaborative attempt to build a common text about this theme based on propositions that have been uttered from the different meaning positions and that are being made an object of argument and evaluation. Therefore, the text finally summarizes what can legitimately be said about the theme at hand (according to the participants in the dialogue).

In the dialogue, the theme is usually being developed along different lines (Kuÿinskij, p. 67):
new points of view may emerge that become a new 'meaning position' in the dialogue;
within a theme new subthemes (points of predominant attention) emerge that refocus the dialogue (for a while);
the theme becomes a subtheme of another larger theme

The theme and its developments are expressed in the ongoing text production in the dialogue. The communality of the theme for the participants in a dialogue, and definitely for the 'meaning positions' within a thinking pe rson, causes the disappearance of the direct references to theme in the dialogue. Most of the time there is no need or even necessity to explicitly repeat the theme in the (internal or external) dialogue. The theme is always implied in the utterances of the dialogue that mainly suggest new propositions about the theme. These new propositions suggest new dimensions of the theme, comment the theme, articulate new aspects etc. In terms of linguistic theory, we can say that the dialogue and its textual result basically follow the syntax of topic – predicate structures: the theme (topic of dialogue) is expressed in series of predicates that tell something new about the topic. Predicates are assumed to be related to this topic and aim at specifying the growing understanding of the topic, as well as –at the same time- distinguishing this topic from other topics. Imagine the situation that you see a bird flying high in the sky. From the moment that this bird is the focus of your attention, you can try to specify your understanding of this bird by adding new propositions ("predicates") to this topic, for example by saying: "It is a buzzard". There is no need to say: the bird that is flying up there in the sky is a buzzard. You can imply this topic by just referring to it by this word 'it'. And even the word 'it' can be left out when we assume that everybody knows what you are referring to. Then it is enough to utter the predicate: 'A buzzard!' With this predicate you add something more specific to the topic-notion of bird and at the same time you distinguish this bird from a 'falcon', a 'vulture' or a 'lark' etc.

In most dialogues a statement like 'it is a buzzard' will definitely call forth new statements that challenge this proposition or elaborate it. For this reason, Kuÿinskij (p. 26) designated the text as a product of dialogue and described it as a 'system of predicates'. The German linguist Hörmann thoroughly analysed this activity of understanding (Verstehen) of someone else's attempts at expressing intentions concerning an issue. Hörman also points to the fact that often the topic remains unspoken, but is nevertheless shared by a group of communicating people (Hörman, 1976). During communication the participants assume that there is continuity in meaning ("Sinnkonstanz", Hörman, 1976, p. 206 – 212), even though this cannot be substantiated at every moment by all participants. Such intuitively shared issue is the basis of all coherent communication. Hörman writes:

> "The entanglement of a retained basis and predicates that build upon it, is a basic characteristic of verbal actions. The importance of this cannot be evaluated high enough: when people say something, claim something or ask something, they always tie up with what was already available in their consciousness" (Hörmann, 1976, p. 165; translation BvO).

According to Hörmann (p. 505) 'predication' is a central organising factor of the utterance. Predication is the mechanism for the elaboration of a (common) understanding of the pregiven topic.

Doblaev (1982) also developed the idea of the text as a system of predications further. In order to study the structure of textbooks and how students understand them (or fail in understanding them), Doblaev elaborated the theory of topic – predicate structures further.2 He explains that the topic is the issue under discussion, and the predicate is the entity (linguistic or other) that tells something new about the topic and answers the question 'what is being said about this topic?' Doblaev demonstrates that topic – predicate structures are a powerful means for analysing and understanding texts. In most texts, however, they form complex dynamic systems. As an example we could use a small text analysed by Doblaev:

"Animals from the steppe have colours that look like dried-out grass".

In this sentence 'animals from the steppe' is the topic and the new thing that is said about them (the predicate): 'they have the colour of dried-out grass'. However, when the sentence was a part of a longer text, the situation can be different:

"Animals from the steppe have colours that look like dried-out grass. This protects them against natural enemies, and it enables them to imperceptively creap up on their prey"

In this case, the 'colour of the animals from the steppe' is the subject and the propositions that follow are utterances that predicate this topic.

Doblaev analysed only text fragments from textbooks on factual subject matters (like history, literature, geography etc.), but it is not difficult to imagine examples from the area of mathematics:

"Numbers have very important cultural values. They can help people to make complex calculations and even can be used for example for encrypting messages. Especially prime numbers are powerful means for encryption"

This latter example shows clearly that even within a short utterance the topic can shift during the whole utterance (from number to encryption). This is what happens in most texts, according to Doblaev. He refers to this process as topic-modification. When a certain topic is elaborated with a new predicate, it is always possible that this predicate will be picked up as a new topic for examination and discourse. The next predicates, in that case, attempt to clarify the previous predicate, turning the previous predicate into a new topic. The understanding of a text (or discourse) is based on the ability to follow the course of topic modifications and the topic-predicate structures (Doblaev, 1982, p. 31).

Doblaev distinguishes four types of topic modifications: repetition, splitting, precision, introducing new objects. The emergence of one type of modification or the other depends on the context, the aim of the argument and/or the intentions of the participants in the discourse. Repetition of a topic in a new example can have the function of emphasizing the topic's significance in the eyes of the speaker/author. Splitting a topic into constituents can serve as a method for explanation of the original topic. Specifying the topic (like happened in the maths example above) can have the function of being more precise about the first topic (e.g. the value of numbers). Finally, the author can also close the discussion of a topic and introduce a new topic that fits into a wider plan of the author.

A further and very important issue discussed by Doblaev is the relationship between the topic and the predicate. In his view there are three types of relationships between topic and predicates (Doblaev, 1982, p. 51):

concretisation: the predicates give a more concrete example of the issue referred to in the topic: 'Especially the prime numbers are powerful means for encryption' in the math text above is an example of this. It concretises the value of numbers for encryption;

conclusion: the predicates give the major and minor premises of the argument. Take for example the famous syllogism that takes as a topic the statement that Socrates will die at some point in time:

all human beings are mortal (P)

Socrates is a human being (P)

Socrates is mortal (T)

definition: the predicates clarify elements of the topic (which is the definiendum); in this case, the relationship between the topic and the defining predicates is strongly related to the context in which the topic and the clarifying terms of the predicates are embedded. Defining 'prime numbers' for example could be a follow up of the math example above. This definition, however, assumes that the terms of the predicates are taken from a context in which 'numbers' are also a part.

If the text indeed can be seen as a system of predications or topic-predicate structures, then the dialogue that represents the text in statu nascendi can be expected to manifest that same character. In that case, the dialogue can be seen as a 'plant of predications or topic-predicate structures'. And given the dialogical nature of human thinking, we may wonder if thinking also manifests this structure.

However, Kuÿinskij suggested that human thinking contains many more types of utterances that cannot easily be characterised as statements of topic or predicates. Most of the time topic and predicates seem to be the result of exploratory processes based on questioning, answering, hypothesing, arguing, probing, analysing, comparing etc. In a written text, most of these latter actions are often not described and the final text product then can be analysed indeed in terms of topics and predicates. In the analysis of real thinking, however, we also have to deal with these exploratory and arguing actions that examine the validity of proposed topic or predicates. This is, by the way, consistent with the view of cognition as an orienting activity. The exploratory actions of questioning, arguing, trying etc. are orienting actions that try to figure out what legitimately can be said about the world. The statement of the predicates is the end result of this orienting process; it specifies what the person thinks can be said legitimately about the topic.

As we have pointed out above, Kuÿinskij (1983) demonstrated different aspects of this process. He builds on the works of Vygotsky. Vygotsky was one of the first who acknowledged the importance of predicates and topic-predicate structures as a framework for the analysis of human thinking. According to Vygotsky (1934/1987, ch 7), humans often think in predicates as they do not have to mention the topic for themselves. Through this thinking in predicates, human thinking gets its typical private, shorthand character. He claims that the analysis of human thinking in terms of topic-predicate structures will finally disclose the nature of human thinking and cognitive processes.

For the application of this view to thinking activity, Vygotsky, however, warns against confusing this type of psychological analysis with a purely linguistic analysis. The topic should not be confused with the grammatical subject, as they are different concepts. The topic refers to what the speaker or writer has in her/his mind, and what constitutes the object of attention. A grammatical subject just describes the formal relationships between the subject of a sentence the verb and its further constituents. Look at the following utterance:

Three is a prime number. Prime numbers are defined as numbers that can only be divided by two natural numbers, viz. by one and by themselves

In the first sentence 'three' is grammatically the subject of the sentence. However, it is not the topic. Considering the whole utterance, it is clear that 'prime numbers' is the real topic. The best way to employ this topic-predicate-analysis is to look at it from the point of orientative activities. What is the field the speaker obviously tries to orient himself in? That is obviously the world of number, specifically prime numbers, and not in the world of 'three'. It is important to keep in mind that topic-predicate structures are psychological means of orientation in a symbolically represented world.

Understanding thinking as an orienting cognitive process of assembling topic-predicate structures is, then, a major challenge for psychology. I have argued that this idea is useful for the understanding of mathematical activity and learning (see van Oers, 2000). Learning now implies that a certain predicate is consummated by the topic, and is taken to be an integral part of the unspoken background in the predicate production process. In the next section, I want to apply the theoretical framework described above to some examples of mathematical activity, in order to illustrate this framework and its value for understanding mathematical cognition. I will confine myself to the analysis of transcripts of dialogical processes or thinking aloud episodes. The main objective will be twofold: on the one hand, I will present examples that illustrate some of the processes described above, on the other hand I will try to demonstrate that cases of learning indeed can be identified when we analyse the mathematical activity in terms of this topic – predicate structures.

THE CONSTRUCTION OF MEANINGS IN A MATHEMATICS CLASSROOM

– *Illustrating the framework: Making a kite*

Two 14-year-old boys are wondering if they can make a kite with two lightweight sticks (80 cm each) and a piece of lightweight string of 2.30 meter. The material is not yet available, so they cannot find the solution by just trying. They have to orient in the field of symbolically represented materials.

#	Speaker	Utterance	Interpretation
1	A	'Let's put the sticks like a cross, like this.... in the middle'	**Topic 1** (is the kite and its measures)
2	B	'OK, but how much string do we need then?'	Question, introduce **topic 2**
3	A	'We can't measure it' Mmm....'	Predicate

4	B	'no, right, eh….but wait…this side must be forty and this side must be forty too, so this side [*pointing to the hypotenuse*] must be more than forty, let's say fifty. All these sides are the same, so together they are four times 50, *is 200 and 2.30 meters, so it works*	Argument for the production of **predicate to topic 2** Referring to pregiven topic (kite and its measures); abbreviated reasoning (*italics*) through the use of predicates
5	A	"What if it is not fifty but more?	Questioning predicate about predicate ('let's say 50') – **refocusing on topic 2**
6	B	'Well eh……., OK, let's try 60 then. Four times sixty is two hundred and forty. That's ….Ay, that is too much. Is there a way of calculating it more precisely?	New predicate to topic 2 Reasoning and questioning; introducing **new topic** (3) ('calculating')
7	A	'Can't we use Pythagoras?	Predicate to topic 3 (= **Pythagoras' theorem**)
8	B	'yeah let's try, how to do it? What was the formula?'	**Turning predicate into** new topic 4 **(Pythagoras) Questioning topic 4**
9	A	This one is 40, this one is 40 too…….'square these sides and…..'	(implying topic 4) **predicating**
10	B	Yes that's right, so that 40 square and 40 square, that is………..40 times 40	**Predicate turned into new topic (5),** production of new predicate about previous predicate (specifying)
11	A	Sixteen hundred	**New predicate** (about predicate in (9) and topic 3 and 4 implicit)
12	B	Sixteen hundred and sixteen hundred is…… thirty two hundred. Is this side 3200?	(topic 3 and 4 implicit) **predicate** to topic 4
13	A	'We definitely don't have enough of the string'	Return to topic 2, predicate to topic 2
14	B	'No wait, we squared those sides, so we have found the square of this side. That's Pythagoras !	Predicate to topic 5 **(topic 3 implicit)**
15	A	'You mean we have to take the root of 3200?'	**New topic (6)**
16	B	'how do we do that, we have no calculator'	Questioning topic 6
17	A	'must be between 50 and 60'	**Predicate to topic 6** (topic 3 implicit see line 19)
18	B	'We already figured that out'	Comment to predicate
19	A	'No I mean 50 square is 2500 (it's too small) and 60 square is 3600 (it's too big)	**Predicate to predicate**
….	……..	[the boys seem to be stuck here, they talk a bit about other things]	…………………
20	B	'When we divide 230 by 4 we find how long each part can be at the maximum. [calculates on a piece of paper 230: 4]	New topic 7 **(find max length)**
21	A	'57,5 cm'	**Predicate** to new topic 7
22	B	'Should we square this one?'	Questioning predicate, turning it into **new topic 8** (squaring), topic 4 and 5 implicit)
23	A	'We need a calculator' [anyway, he starts calculating 57,5 x 57,5 on paper]	Comment about topic
24	B	'I hope I haven't made a mistake, it is 3306.25	**Predicate** to topic 8
25	A	'What does it mean? For the kite I mean'	Questioning predicate
26	B	'Mmm…..(pause)…..yes you know, the square of this side was 3200, so 3306 is too much….	Conclusive predicate to topic 1
27	A	'So the answer is that it won't work!'	Conclusion as a predicate to basic topic (kite and its materials)
28	B	'I think so'	

It is clear that the boys finally drew the wrong conclusion, probably due to the fact that they have not clearly interpreted (and discussed) the predicate "3306" in the light of topic 3. We have no clear evidence of this, so we can just speculate. What makes this example more interesting at this moment is, that we see the jumpy flow of topic – predicate structures as a framework of the dialog, intervened by hesitations and reflections (questions, comments, arguments), which are supposed to strengthen the validity of the proposed predicates, or turn predicates into new topics. At several moments in the dialogue, we see indeed that the topics remain unspoken and the discourse tends to become predicative. An interesting phenomenon can be seen in utterance 4. The statement betrays that the topic includes a number of implicit ideas. It is evident that the topic here includes the idea of triangles, but also the related fact that the length of the hypotenuse of an orthogonal triangle is longer that each of the other sides. This is a clear demonstration of a previous learning process. The facts and ideas have become an implicit part of a topic. Moreover, it is probably a piece of collective knowledge, as the speaker was not queried about it by his partner. Similarly, no exact formulation of the theorem of Pythagoras is uttered. Obviously both boys had learned this (and hence included in the inscription 'Pythagoras').

– *Analysing arguments*

Shaping arguments is an important and outstanding feature of mathematising (see for example Krummheuer, 1995, 1997; Forman et al, 1998). According to Krummheuer (1997), mathematical argumentation can be conceived of as a narrative process in which participants try to convince others (or themselves) of the correctness of a conclusion. In his view argumentation is a social process in which 'cooperating individuals try to adjust their intentions and interpretations by verbally presenting the rationale of their actions' (Krummheuer, 1995, p. 229). Krummheuer's narrative starting point regarding the presentation of an argument (Krummheuer, 1997) makes his point of view consistent with the topic-predicate view described in the present article. However, Krummheuer employs a different method for the description of arguments and it seems worthwhile to examine how his view can be translated into a topic-predicate description. Following Toulmin (1969) he sees an argument as a narrative structure that attempts to endorse a conclusion with the help of data, warrants and backings. He uses the following analytic model:

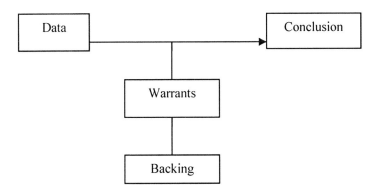

In general, the arguing starts with the presentation of the data (like two sticks, a string and a question). The conclusions (probably not yet the final conclusion) that are drawn on the basis of these data can be seen as an attempt to utter something new about the data set. So this conclusion is basically a predicate on the topic given. However, the conclusion drawn is often not self-evident or clear, therefore the conclusion then is turned into the new topic for reflection and discourse, predicated by the data set and the question. But as a conclusion, this topic includes (in our academic culture) the urge for reasons (in terms of Grice's theory of conversational logic we could interpret this urge for reasons as one of the conversational implicatures of an academic discourse, see Grice, 1975). Hence, we can say that the utterance of warrants is an attempt to make the conclusion acceptable; it explicates something new about the conclusion and therefore predicates the conclusion (in addition to the data). Finally, the warrants also need further support to certify them as genuine and valid reasons for the conclusion. The warrants are backed up by articulating one implicit characteristic of these warrants that may put them beyond doubt. In the 'Backing' part of the argument people give additional reasons to proof the validity of the reasons as a support for the conclusion. So given the topic (conclusion), the backing part of the argument, predicates the warrant-predicate as a valid argument. Schematically the argument runs as follows:

$TOPIC_1$ ----- $Predicate_1$

$TOPIC_2$ ------------- $predicate_{2,1}$ (data & question)

$predicate_{2,2}$(warrant)------$predicate_{2,2,1}$
(backing)

In the transcript given above we can see this figure in the beginni ng of the argument (lines 1 – 14). The change to a new topic (topic 3) occurs in line 6, then this topic is predicated in line 9, where the data are repeated and a suggestion for solution is given. An intermediate solution is given in 14, with the reasons ('squaring') and the backing ('That's Pythagoras!').

This analysis shows that the Krummheuer-analysis is certainly a powerful instrument for describing the general line of arguments. However, the description remains at the level of logic of the argument construction process. At a deeper level we can see that the whole process is far more complex that the argument scheme seems to suggest. At the deeper level we can see how the process of stepwise meaning making takes place as an assembly of topic – predicate structures.

Building a narrative about batteries

As a final example, I want to focus on an argument about batteries that was transcripted in a project of Paul Cobb and his team (see Cobb, 2002; McClain, 2002). In a seventh grade classroom a data-set was introduced that represented the longevity of two brands of batteries. The presentation of the data with a computer-based minitool provided the students with a means to explore the data set in order to figure out which brand of batteries they would recommend. The argument (as described in McClain, 2002, p 171 – 173) can be analysed as a flow of topics and predicates. Looking at the first 50 lines of the discourse we can see the topic flow from composition of the group of batteries that last longest, then the topic shifts to the range to the lower limit, to the consistency (of the batteries). The whole discourse can be seen as an orientation in a symbolic space of data ("data exploration") in order to figure out what can legitimately be said about the two brands of batteries. Can we really say that one brand lasts longer that the other? We see the classroom involved in an activity of building an acceptable narrative about the batteries.

A detailed analysis of the episode in terms of topics and predicates would take a lot of space here, and actually repeat what was already demonstrated in the previous sections. Instead of repeating this argument I will rather focus on those aspects of the discourse that articulate new dimensions of the theory.

First, let us take a look at the role of the teacher (Kay). Her role was mainly that of questioning and revoicing. The following fragment from the transcript demonstrates that (lines 30 – 40 in original transcript, after Blake's request to put the value bar on the computer screen on value 80):

Interesting is also statement 37 when Blake is still trying to find the right expression for the predicate of the topic 'consistency'. There is a lot of tacit knowledge in this statement. He is trying to give a statistical explanation of 'consistency' and implicitly refers to the collection of data as a sample from a larger population. Obviously for him 'consistency' has a statistical meaning and he makes this explicit. It seems to me that this is a clear evidence of learning. After Blake's statement the teacher checks the understanding of this among other pupils, and it is obvious that many students have really understood what Blake meant (they repeat his argument correctly and in their own words). They have learned that for the identification of the best brand of batteries, they shouldn't just look at the best performances (looking at the top 10 best performing batteries is what they did in the beginning of the discourse), but also take into account the proportion of low performing batteries. They integrated this predicate into their topic of 'consistency' and there was no need to repeat it explicitly, except when the teacher asks for it. I take this as an example of the process of learning, i.e. integrating explicit predicates into tacit knowledge inherent in a topic.

Line nr	Speaker	Utterance	Comment
30	Blake	'Now, see, there's still green ones behind 80, but all of the Tough Cell is above 80. So I'd rather have a consistent battery that I know that'll get me over 80 hours than one that just try to guess'	Blake predicates one brand (Always ready) as 'the green ones' (referring to the colour of this brand on the screen); the real topic (Always ready remains unmentioned as it is collectively shared); moreover: he predicates the Tough Cells 'above 80' and 'consistent'
31	Kay	'Why? Why are you picking 80?'	Teacher Query, turning Blake's predicate ('Tough cell is above 80') into a new topic
32	Blake	'Well, because most of the Tough Cell batteries were all over 80'	
33	Kay	'Ah, OK, so it's like a lower limit for you. OK. Questions for Blake? Yes, Jamie?'	Revoicing ; introducing new predicate ('lower limit')
34	Jamie	'Um, why wouldn't the 'Always Ready' batteries be consistent?'	Turning Blake's predicate ' consistent'(see line 30) into a new topic
35	Blake	'Well, because all your 'Tough Cell' is above 80, but you still have 2 behind that are in the 'Always Ready'	
36	Jamie	'I know but that's only 3 out of 10	
37	Blake	'No, but see, they only did, what, 10 batteries? So the 2 or 3 will add up. They'll add up to more and more batteries and all that'	
38	Kay	' Oh, I see; as you get more and more batteries, it's going to get more and more bad ones if that's representative. OK, is that....Jamie?...'	Revoicing
39	Jamie	'So why wouldn't that happen with the Tough Cell batteries?'	
40	Blake	'Well, because the way that those 10 batteries show on the chart that they're all over 80 that means that it seems to me that they would have a better quality'	

From McClain, 2002, p. 172

CONCLUSION: THE FORMATION OF MATHEMATICAL COGNITION

In this article I tried to argue for a view on mathematical cognition as an assembly process of topics and predicates, and go beyond the unarticulated notion of 'construction'. The development of mathematical meanings is then a process of elaborating a topic by the formation and integration of predicates, and constructing arguments (based on new topic – predicate structures) that evaluate the tenability of the proposed predicates as attempts to clarify and develop the topic and (by the same token) distinguish it from other topics. This process turns out to be a jumpy process with many tacit ideas, going back and forth between new predicates and old topics. It is definitely not a linear, orderly process, but a chaotic activity, that is kept in track by a (more or less shared) sense of directionality, suggested by the topic and the orientation from which the topic is viewed.

The formation of mathematical cognition, then, is to be seen as the production of rich mathematical topics that have consummated mathematical predicates which can be made explicit (when required) and functional in the organisation of a field , i.e. in the orientation in a concrete or symbolic domain from a mathematical point of view. As could be seen in two of my examples, this is basically a distributed process that goes beyond the individualistic notion of cognition. The appropriation of the abilities and topics that are needed for mathematical orientation necessarily takes place in close harmony with a mathematical community that provides the social representations and tools for the orientation process. In the classroom, the teacher has an important role to play in keeping the process in harmony with the mathematical community, and even in taking care that the process will wind up being a polylogue, rather than a collection of mutual dialogues.

The analysis of (mathematical thinking) and collective reasoning in terms of topic–predicate assembly brings the complex nature of the dynamics of (mathematical) thinking to the surface. Future studies should cast more light onto the complexities of the dynamics of this process. We can speculate that predicates can have different functions for the speaker or the discussing community, ranging from specifying the topic, generalising the topic, extending the topic to giving arguments and backings, or even falsifying a topic. Moreover, the ways of integration of a predicate in a discussed topic probably can be diverse, ranging from associative integration to logical integration by interpreting the topic as a specimen of a more general category (see Williams, 2001). Further studies are needed to sort this out.

It is important to note that the approach described here is an elaboration of an activity theory approach to human thinking, learning and development and as such, presupposes the tenets of the activity approach regarding activity, action, orientation, transsubstantiation, meaning, learning, the social essence of the individual etc. Activity theory provides us with an apparatus for analysis of cognition that goes beyond the general descriptions of 'cognition as construction'. Hopefully in the near future we can transcend this Mendelian level of analysis of cognition and better understand how the meaning making process in our students evolves or stumbles.

REFERENCES

Bakhtin, M. (1981). *The dialogical imagination.. Four essays by M.M. Bakhtin.* (Ed. M. Holquist). Austin: University of Texas Press.

Bauersfeld, H. (1995). The structuring of the structures: development and function of mathematizing as a social practice. In: L.P. Steffe & J. Gale (Eds.), *Constructivism in education*. Hillsdale: Erlbaum, 137 - 158.

Bruer, J. (1993). *Schools for thought. A science of learning in the classroom*. Cambridge MIT.

Cobb, P. (2002). Reasoning with tools and inscriptions. *Journal of the Learning Sciences, 11*(2 & 3), 187-215.

Cobb, P., Gravemeijer, K., Yackel, E., McClain, & Whitenack, J. (1997). Mathematizing and symbolizing: The emergence of chains of signification in one first-grade classroom. In: Kirshner, D., & Whitson, J.A. (Eds.), *Situated cognition. Social, se iotic, and psychological perspectives*. Mahwah: Erlbaum,151- 233.

Cobb, P. & Bowers, J. (1999). Cognitive and situated learning perspectives in theory and practice. *Educational Researcher, 28* (2), 4-15.

Cole, M. & Engeström, Y. (1993). A cultural-historical approach to distributed cognition. In G. Salomon (Ed.), *Distributed cognitions. Psychological and educational considerations*. Cambridge: Cambridge University Press.

Confrey, J. (1995). How compatible are radical constructivism, sociocultural approaches and social constructivism? In: L.P. Steffe & J. Gale (Eds.), *Constructivism in education*. Hillsdale: Erlbaum, 185-225.

Doblaev, L.P. (1982). *Smyslovaja struktura uÿebnogo teksta i problemy ego ponimanija* [The meaning structure of a learning text and the problems of their understanding]. Moscow: Izd-vo Pedagogika.

Ernest, P. (1995). The one and the many. In L.P. Steffe & J. Gale (Eds.), *Constructivism in education*. Hillsdale: Erlbaum, 459-486.

Forman, E., Larreamendy-Joerns, J., Stein, M.K., Brown, C.A. (1998). "You're going to want to find out which and prove it": Collective argumentation in a mathematics classroom. *Learning and Instruction, 8* (6), 527-548.

Freudenthal, H. (1973). *Mathematics as an educational task*. Dordrecht: Reidel.

Freudenthal, H. (1983). *Didactical phenomenology of mathematical structures*. Dordrecht: Reidel.

Freudenthal, H. (1990). *Weeding and sowing. Preface to a science of mathematics education*. Dordrecht: Reidel.

Freudenthal, H. (1991). *Revisiting mathematics education*. Dordrecht: Kluwer.

Gal'perin, P.Ja. (1969). Stages in the development of mental acts. In M. Cole & I. Maltzman (Eds.), *A handbook of contemporary Soviet psychology*. New Yok: Basic Books, 249-273.

Gal'perin, P. Ja. (1976). *Vvedenie v psichologiju* [Introduction to psychology]. Moscow: Izd-vo Moskovskogu Un-ta. German translation: Zu Grundfragen der Pychologie. Berlin: Volk und Wissen, 1980.

Gal'perin, P. Ja. (1979). Das Lernen als Problem de Pychologie. In P.Ja Gal'perin & A.N. Leont'ev (Eds.), *Probleme de Lerntheorie*. Berlin: Volk und Wissen, 29-42.

Gergen, K.J. (1995). Social construction and the educational process. In L.P. Steffe & J. Gale (eds.), *Constructivism in education*. Hillsdale: Erlbaum, 17-39.

Grice, H.P. (1975). Logic and conversation. In P. Cole & J.L. Morgan (Eds.), *Syntax and semantics. Volume 3: Speech acts.*. New York: Academic Press, 41-58.

Hedegaard, M. & Chaiklin, S. (2005). *Radical-local teaching and learning*. Aarhus: Aarhus University Press.

Hörman, H. (1976). *Meinen und Verstehen. Grundzüge einer psychologischen Semantik*. Frankfurt am Main: Suhrkamp.

Kant, I. (1783/1969). *Prolegomena zu einer jeden künftigen Metaphysik*. Hamburg: Felix Meiner Verlag.

Krummheuer, G. (1995). The ethnography of argumentation. In P. Cobb & M. Bauersfeld (eds.), *The emergence of mathematical meaning: interaction in classroom cultures* . Hillsdale, NJ.: Erlbaum, 229-269.

Krummheuer, G. (1997). *Narrativität und Lernen. Mikrosoziologische Studien zur sozialen Konstitution schulischen Lernens*. Weinheim: Beltz.

Kuÿinskij, G.M. (1983). *Dialog i myŝlenie* [Dialogue and thinking]. Minsk: Izd-vo BGU.

Lave, J., & Wenger, E. (1991). *Situated learning. Legitimate peripheral participation.* Cambridge: Cambridge University Press.

Leont'ev, N.A. (1975). *Dejatel'nost', soznanie, liÿnost'* [Activity, consciousness, Personality]. Moscow: Politizdat.

McClain, K. (2002). Teachers' and students' understanding: The role of tools and inscriptions in supporting effective communication. *Journal of the Learning Sciences, 11*(2 & 3) 163 – 185.

Moscovici, S. (1973). Foreword. In C. Herzlich (Ed.), *Health and illness: A social psychological analysis.* London: Academic Press.

Neisser, U. (1976). *Cognition and reality.* San Francisco: Freeman

van Oers, B. (1996). The dynamics of school learning. In J. Valsi-ner & H-G. Voss (Eds.), *The structure of lear-ning processes.* New York: Ablex, 205-229.

van Oers, B. (2000). The appropriation of mathematical symbols. A psychose-miotic approach to mathematics learning. In P. Cobb, E. Yackel, & K. McClain (Eds.), *Symbo-lizing and communi-cating in mathema-tics class-rooms. Perspectives on discourse, tools, and instructional design.* Mahwah: Erlbaum, 133-176.

van Oers, B. (2001a). Educational forms of initiation in mathematical culture. *Educational Studies in Mathematics, 46*(1-3) 59 – 57.

van Oers, B (2001b). Contextualisation for abstraction. *Cognitive Science Quarterly, 1*(3/4), 279- 306.

Piaget, J. (1952). *The origins of intelligence in children.* New York: International Universities Press.

Scribner, S. (1997). A sociocultural approach to the study of mind. In E. Tobach, R.J. Falmange, M Brown Parlee, L.M.W. Martin & A. Scribner-Kapelman (Eds.), *Mind and social practice. Selected writing of Sylvia Scribner.* Cambridge: Cambridge University Press, 266 – 280.

Sfard, A. (1994). Reification as the birth of metaphor. *For the learning of mathematics, 14* (1), 44-55.

Sfard, A. (2002). The interplay of intimations and implementations: Generating new discourse with new symbolic tools. *The Journal of the Learning Sciences, 11*(2&3), 319-358.

Shotter, J. (1995). In dialogue: Social constructionism and radical constructivism. In: L.P. Steffe & J. Gale (eds.), *Constructivism in education.* Hillsdale: Erlbaum,41-56.

Steffe, L.P. & Gale J. (Eds.). (1995).*Constructivism in education.* Hillsdale: Erlbaum.

Thomson, P.W. (1995). Constructivism, cybernetics, and information processing: implications for technologies of research on learning. In L.P. Steffe & J. Gale (eds.), *Constructivism in education.* Hillsdale: Erlbaum, 123-133.

Toulmin, S. (1969). *The uses of argument.* Cambridge: Cambridge University Press.

Verschaffel, L., Greer, B., & De Corte, E. (2000). *Making sense of word problems.* Lisse: Swets & Weitlinger.

Vygotsky, L.S (1925/1982). Soznanie kak problema psichologii povedenija [Consciousness as a problem of the psychology of behavior]. In L.S. Vygotsky, *Sobranie soÿinenij.* T. I,. Moscow: Pedagogika, 78-97.

Vygotsky, L.S. (1927/1982). Istoriÿeskij smysl psichologiÿeskogo krizisa [The historical significance of the crisis in psychology]. In L.S. Vygotsky, *Sobranie soÿinenij.* T. I,. Moscow: Pedagogika, 291-436.

Vygotsky, L.S. (1984). Problema vozrasta [The problem of age]. In L.S. Vygotsky, *Sobranie soÿinenij.* T. IV. Moscow: Pedagogika, 244-268.

Vygotsky, L.S. (1987). *Thinking and speech.* New York: Plenum Press. [Original Vygotskij, L.S., Myŝlenie i reÿ. Moscow, 1934.]

Vygotsky, L.S. (1994). The problem of the environment. In R. van der Veer & J. Valsiner (eds.), *The Vygotsky reader.* Oxford: Blackwell, 338-354.

Wenger, E. (1998). *Communities of practice. Learning, meaning, and identity.* Cambridge: Cambridge University Press.

Williams, S.R. (2001). Predication of the limit concept: An application of repertory grids. *Journal For Research In Mathematics Education, 32*(4), 341-367.

Bert van Oers
Vrije Universiteit Amsterdam, The Netherlands

NOTES

[1] The famous 'How old is the captain?'-problems are a clear proof of this process. These problems basically go like this: "A captain crosses the river with 5 sheep and 7 goats in his boat. How old is the captain?" Different versions of this type of problems can be constructed with more or less (irrelevant) data. Experience demonstrates that pupils start calculating anyhow (i.e. they assume a mathematical orientation), probably as a result of the fact that the problem looks like the mathematical tasks they are used to, or because of the fact that the problem was presented in the math lesson or both (see Verschaffel et al., 2000 for an overview of this research).

[2] Actually Doblaev uses the expression subject – predicate (like many linguistically oriented authors do). However, given the different meanings of the term 'subject' (like subject-matter, grammatical subject, person or agent) I will avoid confusion and consequently use 'topic' instead of subject when referring to the issue that is the object of our attention and verbal expression.

HERMANN MAIER

COMPARISONS

First I will try to compare the chapters of Willi Dörfler and Bert van Oers under different aspects, namely:
Which are their respective definitions of 'cognitive processes'?
On which philosophy of mathematics is their conceptualisation based?
What do both authors particularly say about the learning of mathematics?
Finally I will try to relate these chapters to other approaches raised in the conference

ABOUT COGNITIVE PROCESSES

First of all it seems striking that Dörfler's and van Oers' texts both use, with reference to the concept of 'cognitive processes', the term 'activity' (already in their titles). This may remind of Jean Piaget as one of the first psychologist who related mathematical cognition and thinking to action. Acting with concrete material appeared him to be the genetic source also for the building up e. g of number concepts. However, he saw children in the course of their cognitive development getting independent, step by step, from concrete actions. They become able to carry out these actions in their imagination, i. e. mentally or internally and that way arrive at abstracts concepts. Briefly said, Piaget regarded mathematical thinking as an internalized acting with concrete objects.

At the first glance, van Oers' conceptualisation of cognitive processes may appear similar to Piaget's, when he talks about the objects of peoples' acting. Actually, however, van Oers draws upon the activity theory of Leont'ev, which makes a distinction between activity and action. Activity refers to the broad cultural category of human enterprises, while action refers to the ways these activities are realised by individuals in a certain situation. Looking for orientation in the reality, people can act with concrete objects, with imaginations of concrete objects, or with graphical respectively symbolic representations. By means of orientation activities "people can anticipate the outcomes of actions or their consequences, and decide if there is need to actually carry them out." In most cases the given situation, therefore, "is transformed into new symbolic forms that articulate structures in settings and possible actions". Distinct from Piaget van Oers sees concrete, imaginative and symbolic acting not as steps in children's ontogenesis but as alternative ways of acting at any age level within the context of cultural activities. People have different ways of orienting in a particular situation

J. Maasz, W. Schloeglmann (Eds.), New Mathematics Education Research and Practice, 141–146.

and can in their acting use different objects. The fundamental assumption behind this concept of cognition is to see thinking as a process based on development of meaning with the help of symbols; and the meaning of symbols has to be started form a particular intention and created in a particular context. Therefore, van Oers includes in his concept of cognition also valuating and emotional processes, what makes it much broader than Piaget's.

Dörfler develops a concept of action which seems less broad as that of Piaget and also of van Oers. In fact it is radically different from traditional cognitivistic views, based on mental models and information processing. According to him, mathematical cognition is mainly based on and restricted to acting with diagrams. With reference to Peirce he speaks of 'diagrammatic reasoning'. Thereby, he uses the term "diagram" in a very broad meaning, including different kinds of "objects and products of writing and reading", e. g. numerals, function graphs and tables, algebraic formulas, polynomials, matrices, etc. Diagrams own a relational structure and are to be treated according to specific operation rules. They gain for Dörfler "the status of the very objects of the activities", like calculations, investigations, relating of different diagrams to each other, inventing or designing diagrams, e. g. for processes of modelling and mathematisation. Cognition in mathematics rises on the basis of diagrams of a certain structural quality by understanding them not just in a figurative but in a relational sense and applying rule-governed operations on and with them.

ABOUT PHILOSOPHICAL AND EPISTEMOLOGICAL BASES

Dörfler characterizes his conceptualisation of mathematical cognition as an 'externalistic' one, since he regards diagrammatic inscriptions by themselves as the objects of interest, investigation and discussion. He contrasts it to the wide spread 'internalistic' position, according to which diagrams are not more than representations (visualisations, embodiments, materialisations) for an abstract, only mentally existing and separate content of mathematical thinking and reasoning. "Math no longer is then a pure episteme (intellectual knowledge about something) but essentially turns into techné, something like a reflected handicraft of working productively with diagrams." It turns into a 'writing science'. The operations can be carried out without permanent respect to a referential meaning of the diagram, to metaphysical or mental referents. Nevertheless, they must and should not be of a just mechanistic or purely algorithmic manner. They go far beyond mechanic calculation, and really can and should be imaginative and creative.

In the subsequent plenary discussion some people questioned this externalistic position by asking, if diagrammatic reasoning can be seen as logical reasoning and, therefore, could really be 'doing mathematics'. It was argued that Dörfler might go back to the behaviouristic position and conceive thinking as a black box event. Other people questioned more the exclusiveness of using diagrams claimed by Dörfler. Questions as follow appeared: Are there not things in mathematics which cannot be represented in a diagram? Is it sensible to speak of a diagram; are there not often isomorphic diagrams for the same mathematical object (e. g. functions are represented in graphs, formulas and equation s)? When we nowadays represent many mathematical objects and operations on the computer screen, can that also be seen as diagrammatic reasoning? What means "understanding", e. g. in reference to the representation of numbers; can the number notation be sufficient for building up a concept in the pupils mind?

Dörfler claimed again, that most of mathematics has a diagrammatic character and structure. Thus, inscriptions and their use as diagrams "are of pre-eminent importance for all mathematical activities." According to him, symbolism constructs the concepts and operating with diagrams must be sufficient for mathematical cognition. However, he admitted also that in fact not everything in mathematics is diagrammatic. Isomorphism of diagrams exists, but various diagrams for the 'same object' "serve very different purposes and intentions and thus necessitate specific investigations." Possibly it has to be decided about a privileged diagram. Finally, media have changed and different diagrams may be used, but the problem is to choose the adequate one.

Van Oers' view on mathematics seems at first similar to Dörfler's, when he quotes Freudenthal's description of mathematics as a human activity of organizing an experimental or conceptual field with the help of structured symbolic means, making it accessible for further analysis. But it turns out that in this case the work with symbolic means – with diagrams – is not so much regarded as a matter in itself, but as a tool for mathematizing a field of reality. Thus, van Oers' approach to the concept of cognition focuses on the function of acting. Referring to Gal'parin he wants most of all cognitive activities to be conceived as 'orientative activities'. Human beings identify by them the nature of signal changes, "imagine possible actions, monitor the process of acting, evaluate out comes of performed actions, etc". The 'orientative activities' precede the actual execution of actions and create a model of actions to be performed. In addition they are always focused on finding and giving direction to human acting. In the plenary discussion van Oers rejected the idea of referring, in connection with orientative activities, to Piaget's concepts of assimilation, adaptation and accommodation, as the latter are mere mechanisms that happen under specific circumstances, while orientation is a human activity that is carried out by intentional and cultural human beings.

Cognitive processes not only include the execution of actions, accomplishments of their steps in an argument or in the transformation of inscriptions and meanings; they include also "processes like valuing (emotional, aesthetical, normative, etc), production of information, planning, anticipating and predicting, monitoring, evaluating etc." Besides their symbolic structure they can deal with meanings and values. Valuation processes determine which part of the environment deserves prior attention, and "it results in the agent's focusing on a certain topic that is for the moment the centre of attention and in the agent's choice for a perspective from which that topic will be considered". In the dialogue about a topic the participants form utterances that suggest new propositions on it and result in a system of predicates. They can modify the topic, e. g. by splitting, precision or introducing new objects. Van Oers follows here Doblaev who points out three types of relationship between topic and predicate: concretisation, conclusion and definition.

143

In summary we arrive at a topic-predicate structure (not to be understood in a grammatical meaning, but as "psychological means of orientation in a symbolically represented world") which characterizes the dialogue between hu man beings, manifesting itself, because of its dialogical nature, also in human thinking. In the analysis of thinking processes one has to deal with "exploratory and arguing actions that examine the validity of proposed topic or predicates".

ABOUT THE LEARNING OF MATHEMATICS

Dörfler's and van Oers' conceptualization of learning mathematics is rather far from traditional cognitivistic learning theories as for example developed by Aebli on the basis of Piaget's psychology (see e. g. Aebli, Hans: Denken das Ordnen des Tuns, Band I – Kognitive Aspekt der Handlungstheorie (1980) and Band II – Denkprozesse (1981) Stuttgart: Klett/Cotta).

With reference to the learning of mathematics Dörfler does not appreciate the idea that mathematical objects, fundamentally regarded as abstract and only mentally present ideas, have to be understood by the pupils as mental representations via the use of different external and well selected ('good') representations. Learning happens in the course of a "systematic study of diagrams (presented as inscriptions of many different forms) and all sensible operations with them. This is an activity which demands a high degree of attention, exactness precision, and strict observation of the rules of treatment. The pupils have to familiarize themselves with diagrams which refer to the respective mathematical concept by extensive experiences with diagrammatic reasoning. "An integral part of this familiarity is a comprehensive memory of the respective diagrams." But also intuition will develop as a result of extensive and intensive diagrammatic activities. Finally diagrammatic activities should always happen in a discursive context. The pupils have to speak about diagrams and their transformations in "a natural language plus a supply of technical terms". And they will learn to develop this language 'simultaneously' with the growing diagrammatic practice.

In the framework of his broad activity approach van Oers defines learning as "the extension or improvement of the repertoire of actions, tools, meanings, and values that increase a person's abilities to participate autonomously in a socio-cultural practice." The orientation activity "includes the articulation (explicitly or implicitly) of a topic with new dimensions which are produced through communication (internal or external)." In the process of topic development cognition not only values a given situation, but adds new aspects to a topic, transforming it for further consideration and analysis. In psychological terms this can be described as a process of meaning construction which explains thinking as a cognitive process. In addition, the initial orientation activity becomes the beginning of an abstraction process, "which follows a course of embedded more specific foci, and finally leads to forms of abstract thinking".

In an example van Oers demonstrated his research method of analysing pupils' thinking processes based on the interpreting transcripts of classroom conversation.

This analysis practice was then also the main issue in the subsequent discussion of his paper in the plenary. Typical questions were: How can be decided, what topic and predicate of a discussion really are? Which is the relative topic for the individual pupil and how can his/her predicate change the topic? Is the researcher willing and able to refer to what words might mean? Van Oers wanted all that to be seen as a matter of interpretation, which can sometimes be really difficult, and needs much experience and understanding of the context. The focus on predicates may be strongly influenced by mathematical practice. After all it has to be discussed about different possibilities to interpret the same utterances. Asked if "topic" is not too simple a concept for conceiving the whole dynamic of a discussion process, van Oers pointed out it might be simple enough to enable the researcher for a meaningful analysis. From an activity theory perspective 'a topic' is the mental counterpart of 'the object' of acting.

Two questions addressed the theory which might have a central place in the exemplified analysis. Van Oers reclaimed openness for different tools which could be used. With reference to the concept of "meaning" he quoted again Leont'ev.

ABOUT THE RELATION TO OTHER ASPECTS OF MATHEMATICS LEARNING

Certainly, neither Dörfler nor Van Oers talked in their papers about emotional or affective aspects of learning mathematics, strongly promoted by other presenters of the conference. Asked in the plenary discussion, van Oers admitted that 'for the moment' he does not look at connected affects or emotions. But this dimension appears to him of mayor importance in the moment when doing mathematics is related to the aspect of valuation in the orienting activity.

However, both chapters about cognitive process come near to sociological approaches to mathematics learning. For Dörfler the use of signs and diagrams is from the very beginning a public and shareable endeavour. Distinct from abstract ideas, diagrams permit collaborative work since according to the externalistic view the objects of interest can be perceived and communicated. And diagrammatic activities need intensive cooperation if they are to become creative, inventive, explorative and experimental. Even in case they are carried out as individual work, this heavily depends on socially shared 'rules', which have been learnt in the course of commonly constructing, investigating or interpreting diagrams. Thus, mathematics can be understood "as a social practice with, on, about, and through diagrams."

Van Oers attributes to cognition both an individual and a social character. He is looking for a position equidistant to the purely individualistic one of cognitivism and to the purely collectivistic one of social constructivism. Linking cognition and cultural practices to each other, he sees cognition ecologically embedded in a broader activity system. He thinks that "so doing articulates both the functional value of cognition and the intrinsic cultural nature of the content and processes of cognition." He definitely does not want to exclude the possibility of individual cognition. But he looks at it as a local and personalised version of a distributed phenomenon, depending also on external resources. "Cognition as an orientation process has a predominantly dialogical structure." In a facet rich world, the direction of orientation is based on experience and the habits of a particular community of practice. "Symbolic codes (like words, inscriptions, dia grams, etc) become imbued with special meaning within a particular social community." Van Oers quotes Leont'ev, describing individual human action just as a moment of a meta-personal, cultural-historically developed activity. For him the study of cognition cannot separate the social from the individual. "We cannot study cultural practices, but through the accomplishment of individuals, and we can never understand individual actions without conceiving these as local (both in time and space) personalised versions of socio-cultural activities."

Herman Maier
Germany

PAUL COBB

MATHEMATICS LEARNING AS A SOCIAL PROCESS

INTRODUCTION

In their chapters, Anna Sfard and Steve Lerman both note that several different theoretical perspectives characterize mathematical learning as a social process. They go on to clarify that the perspectives that they propose fall within the sociocultural tradition most closely associated with Vygotsky and Leont'ev. My goal in this short introduction is to place Anna's and Steve's contributions in historical and theoretical context. To this end, I first outline Vygotsky's and Leont'ev's seminal contributions to sociocultural theory. I then discuss a second perspective, distributed cognition, that treats learning as a social process. Like sociocultural theory, distributed cognition has become increasingly influential in mathematics education research in recent years. In the course of the discussion, I consider the potential usefulness of both sociocultural theory and distributed cognition to mathematics education researchers.

SOCIOCULTURAL THEORY

Vygotsky (1962; 1978; 1981) made his foundational contributions to sociocultural theory during the period of intellectual ferment and social change that followed the Russian revolution. In doing so, he was profoundly influenced by Marx's argument that it is the making and use of tools that serves to differentiate humans from other animal species. For Vygotsky, human history is the history of artifacts such as language, counting systems, and writing that are not invented anew by each generation but are instead passed on and constitute the intellectual bequest of one generation to the next. In formulating his theory of intellectual development, Vygotsky developed an analogy between the use of physical tools and the use of intellectual tools such as sign systems (Kozulin, 1990; van der Veer & Valsiner, 1991). His central claim was that just as the use of a physical tool serves to reorganize activity by making new goals possible, so the use of sign systems serves to reorganize thought. He viewed culture as a repository of sign systems and other artifacts that are appropriated by children in the course of their intellectual development (Vygotsky, 1978). It is important to stress that for Vygotsky, children's mastery of an artifact such as a counting system does not merely enhance or amplify an already existing cognitive capability. He instead argued that children's ability to reason numerically is created as they appropriate the counting systems of their culture. This example illustrates Vygotsky's more general claim

J. Maasz, W. Schloeglmann (Eds.), New Mathematics Education Research and Practice, 147–152.

that children's minds are formed as they appropriate sign systems and other artifacts. This contention is central to the strong social viewpoints that Anna and Steve develop in their chapters.

In the most well known series of investigations that he conducted, Vygotsky attempted to demonstrate the crucial role of face-to-face interactions in which an adult or more knowledgeable peer supports the child's use of an intellectual tool such as a counting system (Vygotsky, 1981). However, there is some indication that shortly before his premature death in 1934, he began to view the relation between social interaction and cognitive development as a special case of a more general relation between cultural practices and cognitive development (Davydov & Radzikhovskii, 1985; Minick, 1987). This aspect of sociocultural theory was subsequently developed by a group of Soviet psychologists, the most prominent of whom was Alexei Leont'ev. Although Leont'ev (1978; 1981) acknowledged the importance of face-to-face interactions, he saw the encompassing cultural practices in which the child participates as constituting the broader context of his or her development. This general viewpoint is apparent in both Anna's and Steve's chapters. They identify historically-developed mathematical discourse as the more encompassing cultural practice in which children initially participate with the support of more knowledgeable others. Following Leont'ev, they argue that children's progressive participation in mathematical discourse is integral to the development of their mathematical thinking. Intellectual development is, for them, synonymous with the process by which children become full participants in mathematical discourse. They therefore consider the cognitive capabilities that children develop to be inseparable from the cultural practices that constitute the context of their development. Like Leont'ev, they view these capabilities to be characteristics not of the child per se but of the child-in-culture-practice.

In my view, sociocultural theory has thus far been of limited usefulness in mathematics education research when actually formulating and improving instructional designs for supporting students' mathematical learning. The contributions of Davydov (1988a, 1988b) notwithstanding, it is in fact difficult to identify instances of influential designs whose development has been primarily informed by sociocultural theory. In my view, this is because the notion of cultural practice employed by sociocultural theorists typically refers to ways of talking and reasoning that have emerged during extended periods of human history. The task facing both the mathematics teacher and the instructional designer is therefore framed as that of supporting and organizing students' induction into a specific discourse practices that have emerged during the discipline's intellectual history. Although the importance of the goals inherent in this framing is indisputable, it provides only the most global orientation for design. A central challenge of instructional design is to develop, test, and refine conjectures about both the classroom processes in which students might participate and the nature of their mathematical learning as they do so. Sociocultural theory has thus far been of limited usefulness because it has failed to develop theoretical constructs that produce detailed analyses of classroom learning situations that can feed back to inform the improvement of instructional designs.

Extending our purview beyond the classroom, a body of scholarship developed within the sociocultural tradition has proven to be highly relevant to the interests of mathematics education researchers. This line of work has compared mathematical reasoning in school with that in various out-of-school settings such as grocery shopping (Lave, 1988), packing crates in a dairy (Scribner, 1984), selling candies on the street (Nunes, Schliemann, & Carraher, 1993; Saxe, 1991), playing dominoes and basketball (Nasir, 2002), woodworking (Millroy, 1992), and sugar cane farming (de Abreu, 1995). These studies document that people develop significantly different forms of mathematical reasoning as they participate in different cultural practices that involve the use of different tools and sign systems, and that are organized by different overall motives (e.g., learning mathematics as an end in itself in school versus doing arithmetical calculations while selling candies on the street in order to survive economically). As Steve discusses in his chapter, this approach of contrasting the forms of reasoning inherent in different cultural practices bears directly on issues of equity in students' access to significant mathematical ideas. An emerging line of research in mathematics education documents that the out-of-school practices in which students participate can involve differing norms of participation, language, and communication, some of which might be in conflict with those that the teacher seeks to establish in the mathematics classroom (Boaler & Greeno, 2000; Gutiérrez, 2002; Martin, 2000; Moschkovich, 2002). In my view, work of this type has the potential to inform the development of designs in which the diversity in the out-of-school practices in which students participate is treated as an instructional resource rather than an obstacle to be overcome.

DISTRIBUTED COGNITION

Sociocultural theory initially developed largely independently of mainstream western psychology. In contrast, distributed cognition has developed in reaction to mainstream cognitive science and incorporates aspects of Vygotsky's and Leont'ev's work. Several of the most important contributors to distributed cognition such as John Seeley Brown (1989), Alan Collins (1992), and James Greeno (1997) achieved initial prominence as mainstream cognitive scientists before substantially modifying their theoretical commitments. In concert with sociocultural theory, the distributed perspective challenges mainstream cognitive science's foundational assumption that cognition is bounded by the skin and can be adequately accounted for solely in terms of internal processes. Distributed cognition theorists instead see cognition as extending out into the immediate environment such that the environment becomes a resource for reasoning. However, whereas sociocultural theorists usually frame people's reasoning as acts of participation in relatively broad systems of cultural practices, distributed cognition theorists typically restrict their focus to the immediate physical, social, and symbolic environment. Empirical studies conducted within the distributed tradition therefore tend to involve detailed analysis of either a specific person's or a small group's activity rather than analyses of people's participation in established cultural practices.

In developing to this position, distributed cognition theorists have been influenced by sociocultural investigations that demonstrate that people develop significantly different forms of mathematical reasoning as they participate in different cultural practices. Part of the reason that distributed cognition theorists attribute such significance to these investigations is that they capture what Hutchins (1995) refers to as cognition in the wild. This focus on people's reasoning as they engage in both everyday and workplace activities contrasts sharply with the traditional school-like tasks that are typically used in mainstream cognitive science investigations. In addition to questioning whether people's reasoning on school-like tasks constitutes a viable set of cases from which to develop adequate accounts of cognition, several distributed cognition theorists have also critiqued current school instruction. In doing so, they treat the mathematical practices that constitute the social situation of students' learning as emergent phenomena that are co-constructed by the teacher and students in the course of their classroom interactions. This focus on locally constituted mathematical practices is a primary point of contrast with sociocultural theory. In my judgment, the distributed perspective has thus far proven to be more useful in informing the formulation, testing, and revision of designs at the classroom level. A number of design research studies have in fact been conducted from this perspective in which researchers both develop designs to "engineer" novel forms of mathematical reasoning, and analyze the process of students' learning in these designed learning environments together with the means by which that learning is supported (Cobb, Confrey, diSessa, Lehrer, & Schauble, 2003; Confrey & Lachance, 2000; Design-Based Research Collaborative, 2003; Gravemeijer, 1994). In doing so, they construe the means of supporting students' mathematical learning relatively broadly to include instructional tasks, classroom norms, the nature of talk, and the ways in which notations and other types of tools are used. As a consequence, design from the distributed perspective focuses on the physical, social, and symbolic classroom environment that constitutes the immediate situation of the students' mathematical learning.

Given my generally positive assessment of the usefulness of the distributed perspective, it is also important to note a potential limitation that concerns the scant attention typically given to issues of equity. The focus of researchers who develop and refine designs at the classroom level usually centers on students' individual and collective development of particular forms of mathematical reasoning. Pragmatically, it is essential that students come to see classroom activities as worthy of their engagement if the designs are to be effective. However, the process of supporting students' engagement by cultivating their mathematical interests is rarely an explicit focus of inquiry. As a consequence, differences in students' engagement that might reflect differential access to the instructional activities used and to the types of discourse established in the classroom can easily escape notice. In my view, this limitation stems from an almost exclusive focus on the classroom as the immediate context of students' learning. This focus precludes a consideration of tensions that some students might experience between aspects of this social context and the out-of-school practices in which they participate. This limitation might be addressed by coordinating the distributed perspective with a sociocultural perspective that situates students' activity not merely with respect to the immediate learning environment, but also with respect to their history of participation in the practices of out-of-school groups and communities.

CONCLUSION

Sociocultural theory characterizes the individual as a participant in established, historically evolving cultural practices. Analyses of learning developed within this theoretical tradition therefore account for learning by focusing on the process by which people become increasingly substantial participants in various cultural practices. I have questioned the contributions that sociocultural theory has made thus far to the development of instructional designs at the classroom level, but also indicated the relevance of analyses of the out-of-school practices in which students participate to the issue of equity in students' access to significant mathematical ideas.

The distributed perspective emerged in response to the limited attention given to context, culture, and affect by mainstream cognitive science (De Corte, Greer, & Verschaffel, 1996). In contrast to sociocultural theorists' focus on people's participation in established cultural practices, distributed theorists usually conduct detailed analyses of a specific person's or a small group's activity. In doing so, they typically emphasize that the person or group use aspects of the immediate physical, social, and symbolic environment as cognitive resources. Although the distributed perspective has thus far made more significant contributions than sociocultural theory to the formulation of designs at the classroom level, distributed cognition theorists have given only limited attention to issues of equity in students' mathematical learning.

REFERENCES

Boaler, J., & Greeno, J. G. (2000). Identity, agency, and knowing in mathematical worlds. In J. Boaler (Ed.), *Multiple perspectives on mathematics teaching and learning*. Stamford, CT: Ablex, 45-82.

Brown, J. S., Collins, A., & Duguid, P. (1989). Situated cognition and the culture of learning. *Educational Researcher, 18*, 32-42.

Cobb, P., Confrey, J., diSessa, A. A., Lehrer, R., & Schauble, L. (2003). Design experiments in education research. *Educational Researcher, 32*(1), 9-13.

Collins, A. (1992). Portfolios for science education: Issues in purpose, structure, and authenticity. *Science Education, 76*, 451-463.

Confrey, J., & Lachance, A. (2000). Transformative teaching experiments through conjecture-driven research design. In A. E. Kelly & R. A. Lesh (Eds.), *Handbook of research design in mathematics and science education* (pp. 231-266). Mahwah, NJ: Erlbaum.

Davydov, V. V. (1988a). Problems of developmental teaching (Part I). *Soviet Education, 30*(8), 6-97.

Davydov, V. V. (1988b). Problems of developmental teaching (Part II). *Soviet Education, 30*(9), 3-83.

Davydov, V. V., & Radzikhovskii, L. A. (1985). Vygotsky's theory and the activity-oriented approach in psychology. In J. V. Wertsch (Ed.), *Culture, communication, and cognition: Vygotskian perspectives*. New York: Cambridge University Press, 35-65.

de Abreu, G. (1995). Understanding how children experience the relationship between home and school mathematics. *Mind, Culture, and Activity, 2*, 119-142.

De Corte, E., Greer, B., & Verschaffel, L. (1996). Mathematics learning and teaching. In D. Berliner & R. Calfee (Eds.), *Handbook of educational psychology*. New York: Macmillan, 491-549.

Design-Based Research Collaborative. (2003). Design-based research: An emerging paradigm for educational inquiry. *Educational Researcher, 32*(1), 5-8.

Gravemeijer, K. (1994). Educational development and developmental research. *Journal for Research in Mathematics Education, 25*, 443-471.

Greeno, J. G. (1997). On claims that answer the wrong questions. *Educational Researcher, 26*(1), 5-17.

Gutiérrez, R. (2002). Enabling the practice of mathematics teachers in context: Toward a new research agenda. *Mathematical Thinking and Learning, 4*, 145-189.

Hutchins, E. (1995). *Cognition in the wild*. Cambridge, MA: MIT Press.

Kozulin, A. (1990). *Vygotsky's psychology: A biography of ideas*. Cambridge: Harvard University Press.

Lave, J. (1988). *Cognition in practice: Mind, mathematics and culture in everyday life*. New York: Cambridge University Press.

Leont'ev, A. N. (1978). *Activity, consciousness, and personality*. Englewood Cliffe, NJ: Prentice-Hall.

Leont'ev, A. N. (1981). The problem of activity in psychology. In J. V. Wertsch (Ed.), *The concept of activity in Soviet psychology*. Armonk, NY: Scharpe, 37-71.

Martin, J. B. (2000). *Mathematics success and failure among African-American youth*. Mahwah, NJ: Erlbaum.

Millroy, W. L. (1992). An ethnographic study of the mathematical ideas of a group of carpenters. *Journal for Research in Mathematics Education, Monograph No. 5*.

Minick, N. (1987). The development of Vygotsky's thought: An introduction. In R. W. Rieber & A. S. Carton (Eds.), *The collected works of Vygotsky, L.S.* (Vol. 1). New York: Plenum 17-38.

Moschkovich, J. (2002). A situated and sociocultural perspective on bilingual mathematics learners. *Mathematical Thinking and Learning, 4*, 189-212.

Nasir, N. S. (2002). Identity, goals, and learning: Mathematics in cultural practice. *Mathematical Thinking and Learning, 4*, 213-248.

Nunes, T., Schliemann, A. D., & Carraher, D. W. (1993). *Street mathematics and school mathematics*. Cambridge: Cambridge University Press.

Saxe, G. B. (1991). *Culture and cognitive development: Studies in mathematical understanding*. Hillsdale, NJ: Erlbaum.

Scribner, S. (1984). Studying working intelligence. In B. Rogoff & J. Lave (Eds.), *Everyday cognition: Its development in social context*. Cambridge, MA: Harvard University Press, 9-40.

van der Veer, R., & Valsiner, J. (1991). *Understanding Vygotsky: A quest for synthesis*. Cambridge, MA: Blackwell.

Vygotsky, L. S. (1962). *Thought and language*. Cambridge, MA: MIT Press.

Vygotsky, L. S. (1978). *Mind and society: The development of higher psychological processes*. Cambridge, MA: Harvard University Press.

Vygotsky, L. S. (1981). The genesis of higher mental functions. In J. V. Wertsch (Ed.), *The concept of activity in Soviet psychology*. Armonk, NY: M.E. Sharpe.

Paul Cobb
Vanderbilt University Peabody, USA

ANNA SFARD

PARTICIPATIONIST DISCOURSE ON MATHEMATICS LEARNING

In the last decade or two, the claim that mathematics learning is a social process can be heard with such frequency that it became almost a cliché. And yet, those who declare their belief in the social nature of learning have an important statement to make: They signalize that in the ongoing debate between cognitivist and sociocultural research communities they side with the latter. This paper is devoted to explicating theoretical and practical consequences of this message.

These days, being explicit about what one means while claiming "the social nature of learning" seems a necessity. In spite of the omnipresence of the word "social" in the current literature – or perhaps just because of it! – there is much confusion about how this term should be understood when applied in conjunction with learning.1 To avoid undesirable connotations, I use a different terminology. Due to the metaphor for learning underlying the particular family of sociocultural discourses to be presented on the following pages, I call these discourses participationist. To bring the special features of the participationism in fuller relief, I present it against the contrasting background of the more traditional acquisitionist approach. The origins of participationism can, indeed, be traced to acquisitionists' unsuccessful attempts to deal with certain long-standing dilemmas about human thinking. After surveying some of these resilient puzzles and presenting basic participationist tenets, I show how the claim that participationism, if followed in a disciplined way, leads to the claim that human thinking originates in interpersonal communication. I finish with a few remarks on the consequences of the participationism for theory and practice of mathematics education and demonstrate how it helps in dealing with some of the questions that acquisitionism left unanswered.

1. ACQUISITIONISM AND ITS DILEMMAS

The roots of acquisitionist discourse on learning, which is usually seen as originating in the work of Piaget, go in fact much deeper. The underlying metaphor of learning as an act of increasing individual possession - as an acquisition of entities such as concepts, knowledge, skills, mental schemas – comes to this scholarly discourse directly from everyday expressions, such as acquiring knowledge, forming concepts or constructing meaning. To get a sense of the impact of the metaphor of acquisition on one's interpretation of human

J. Maasz, W. Schloeglmann (Eds.), New Mathematics Education Research and Practice, 153–170.

mathematical activities, let me take a look at the following episode, featuring young children talking with grownups about numbers. The brief scene is the beginning of a series of conversations about numbers between my colleague Irit Lavi and two young girls: 4 year old Roni, Irit's daughter, and 4 year 7 months old Eyant, Roni's friend. The event took place in Roni's house.2

Episode: Comparing boxes with marbles

Speaker	What is said	What is done
1. Mother	*I brought you two boxes. Do you know what is there in the boxes?*	*Puts two identical closed opaque boxes, A and B, on the carpet, next to the girls.*
2. Roni	Yes, marbles.	
3a. Mother	Right, there are marbles in the boxes.	
3b. Mother	I want you to tell me in which box there are more marbles.	*While saying this, points to the box A close to Eynat, then to box B.*
3c. Eynat		Points to box A, which is closer to her.
3d. Roni		*Points to box A*
4. Mother	In this one? How do you know?	*Points to box A*
5. Roni	Because this is the biggest than this one. It is the most.	*While saying "than this one" points to box B, which is close to her*
6. Mother	Eynat, how do you know?	
7. Eynat	Because... cause it is more huge than that.	*Repeats Roni's pointing movement to box B when saying "than that"*
8. Mother	Yes? This is more huge than that? Roni, what do you say?	Repeats Roni's pointing movement to box B when saying "than that"
9. Roni	That this is also more huge than this.	*Repeats Roni's pointing movement to box B when saying "than that"*
......	......	......
10a. Mother	*Do you want to open and discover? Let's open and see what there is inside. Take a look now.*	

10b. Roni		*Abruptly grabs Box A, which is nearer to Eyant and which was previously chosen as the one with more marbles.*
11. Roni	*1.. 1.. 1.. 2, 3, 4, 5, 6, 7, 8.*	*Opens box A and counts properly.*
12. Eynat	1, 2, 3, 4, 5, 6.	*Opens box B and counts properly.*
13. Mother	So, what do you say?	
14. Roni	*6.*	
15. Mother	Six what? You say 6 what? What does it mean "six"? Explain.	
16. Roni	That this is too many.	
17. Mother	That this is too much? Eynat, what do you say?	
18. Eynat	That this too is a little.	
19. Mother	That it seems to you a little? Where do you think there are more marbles?	
20. Roni	I think here.	*Points on the box , which is now close to her (and in which she found 8 marbles)*
21. Mother	You think here? And what do you think, Eynat?	
22. Eynat	Also here.	

The episode is likely to leave the acquisitionist researcher unimpressed. The girls' mastery of counting would only confirm what she knows only too well from previous studies: 4 and 5 year old children are usually advanced enough in their "acquisition of the concept of number" to be able to count properly (for a summary of the relevant research see e.g. Nunes & Bryant, 1996, Dehaene, 1997). Nor will the acquisitionist researcher be stricken by the fact that in spite of their well developed counting skills, the girls did not bother to count the marbles or even to open the boxes when asked to compare these boxes' invisible contents. Extensive acquisitionist research on early numerical thinking, in which young children have been observed implementing different versions of Piagetian conservation tasks, has shown that at this age, this behavior is quite normal: "Children who know how to count may not use counting to compare sets with respect to number" (Nunes & Bryant, 1994, p. 35).

And yet, knowing what children usually do not do is not enough to account for what they actually do. An unprejudiced observer, whose analysis is not biased by the sole interest in the girls' ability to "operate with numbers", is likely to ask questions to which the acquisitionist researcher may have no answers. Thus, the young interviewees' apparently arbitrary response to the question "Which box has more marbles?" cannot be accounted-for simply by the reference to 'underdeveloped number schemes'. Similarly, the fact that the girls agreed in their surprising decisions does not seem to have much to do with insufficiency of their "conception of number". Finally, one should rather not count on acquisitionist explanation while wondering what made the children "justify" their choice in a seemingly adequate way in spite of the fact that they had no grounds for the comparative claims, such as "this is the biggest than this one", "It is the most" ([5]) and "it is more huge than that" ([7]). If there is little in the past research to help us account for this kind of phenomena, it is probably because the acquisitionists, while watching their interviewee, attended to nothing except for those actions which they classified in advance as relevant to their study. For them, the conversation that preceded opening the boxes would be dismissed as a mere 'noise'. The analysis of the remaining half of the event might even lead them to the claim that the girl's had a satisfactory command over numerical comparisons, although this is not the vision that emerges when the second part of the episode is analyzed in the context of the first.

Probably the main reason for the shortcomings of acquisitionists' accounts is these researchers' belief in the invariability of learning processes across different contexts. In their research, they are tuned to cross-situational commonalities rather than differences. For them, individual minds are the principal source of their own development, whereas the task of the researcher is to discover the universal blueprint of the process. In result, acquisitionist discourse is ill equipped to deal not just with inter-personal and cross-situational differences, but also with those changes in human processes that transcend a single life span. Indeed, as long as human learning is seen as originating in the individual, and as long as this process is thought of as practically impermeable to other influences, notably those coming from interactions with other individuals, one has no means to account for the fact that human ways of doing, unlike those of other species, evolve over history. Within the confines of acquisitionist discourse, there is no cogent explanation for the fact that the outcomes of the ongoing transformations accumulate from generation to generation, constantly redefining the nature and extent of the individual growth.

2. PARTICIPATIONISM AND ITS SOLUTIONS TO ACQUISITIONIST DILEMMAS

Although usually traced back to the work Vygotsky and other founders of Activity Theory,[3] participationism has, in fact, a more extensive genealogy. As a confluence of ideas coming from areas as diverse as philosophy, sociology, psychology, anthropology, linguistics, and more, [4] this relatively new school of thought is a mélange of approaches rather than a single research discourse. Some of these approaches depart from the acquisitionism only marginally, in that they merely add social considerations to the traditional individualist account. Lave (1993) speaks about 'cognition plus' whenever referring to the talk about the 'social' mounted on the top of an acquisitionist discourse. The basic claim that motivates the more radical form of participationism is that *patterned, collective forms of distinctly human forms of doing are developmentally prior to the activities of the individual*. Whereas acquisitionists view the individual development as proceeding from personal acquisitions to the participation in collective activities, strong particpationists reverse the picture and claim that people go from the participation in collectively implemented activities to similar forms of doing, but which they are now able to perform single-handedly. According to this vision, learning to speak, to solve mathematical problem or to cook means a gradual transition from being able to take a part in collective implementation of a given type of task to becoming capable of implementing such tasks in their entirety and on one's own accord. Eventually, a person can perform on her own and in her unique way entire sequences of steps which, so far, she would only execute with others. The tendency for individualization[5] – for turning patterned collective doings into activities for an individual – seems to be one of the hallmarks of humanness, and it is made possible by our capacity for overtaking roles of others.

The difference between the acquisitionist and the participationist versions of human development is thus not just a matter of "zoom of lens," as it is sometimes presented (Rogoff, 1995; Lerman, 1998). Above all, it manifests itself in how we understand the origins and the nature of human uniqueness. For acquisitionist, this uniqueness lies in the biological makeup of the individual. While participationism does not deny the need for special biological pre-requisites - such as, for example, the special voice cords and the ability to discern certain sounds, both of which are the basis for effective human communication - this approach views all the uniquely human capacities as resulting from the fundamental fact that humans are social beings, engaged in collective activities from the day they are born and throughout their lives. In other words, although human biological givens are what makes this collective form of life possible, it is the collective life that brings about all the other uniquely human characteristics, with the capacity for individualizing the collective – for individual reenactments of collective activities - being one of the most important. Human society emerges from the participationist account as a huge fractal-like entity, every part of which is a society in itself, indistinguishable in its inner structure from the whole.[6]

Another notable change that happens in the transition from acquisitionist to participationist discourse is in the unit of analysis. It is this new unit which I had in mind while speaking, somewhat ambiguously, about "patterned collective doings". Other eligible candidates for the participationist unit of analysis are *form of life*, suggested by Wittgenstein (1953), and *activity*, the pivotal idea of the Activity Theory. The nowadays popular term *practice* is yet another viable option (see e.g. Wenger 1998; Cobb 2002). Although all these terms are used in the current literature in numerous ways, with the differences between one use and another not always easy to tell, each of them is good enough for my present purpose. Indeed, all I want, for now, is to describe participationist innovation according to those central characteristics which remain basically the same across different renderings. Whatever name and definition is given to the participationist unit of analysis and whatever claims about humans are formulated with its help, the strength of this unit is in the fact that it has both collective and individual 'editions.'

Armed with this flexible analytic focus, participationists have a chance to address the question of change that exceeds the boundaries of individual life. While speaking about human development, participationists do not mean a transformation in people, but rather in forms of human doing. This non-trivial discursive shift is highly consequential, as it removes the sharp acquisitionist distinction between development of an individual and the development of collective. The developmental transformations are the result of two complementary processes, that of *individualization of the collective* and that of *collectivization of the individual.* These two processes are dialectically interrelated and, as a consequence, both individual and collective forms of doing are in a constant flux, resulting from inevitable modifications that happen in these bi-directional transitions.

So far, I have shown how participationism deals with the dilemma of the historical change in human forms of doing. In the rest of this paper I show how it deals with questions about mathematics learning that acquisitionism left unanswered.

3. CONSEQUENCES OF PARTICIPATIONISM
FOR THE DISCOURSE ON MATHEMATICS THINKING AND LEARNING

3.1 What is Thinking?

Although thinking appears to be an inherently individual activity, there is no reason to assume that its origins are any different from those of other uniquely human capacities: like all the others, this special form of human doing could only develop from a patterned collective activity. This claim is far from intuitively obvious. After all, whatever we call thinking is usually done by each one of us alone and is generally considered as inaccessible to others in the direct manner. It is thus not readily evident which 'visible' human activity might be the collective version of thinking. In fact, one has good reasons to doubt whether such collective edition exists at all. More than any other human activity, thinking appears biologically determined and growing 'from inside' the person. Still, participationist tenets speak forcefully against this deeply rooted conviction. The next thesis to explore is that interpersonal communication is the collective activity that morphs into thinking through the process of individualization.

A powerful, even if indirect, argument comes to mind immediately when one tries to substantiate this conjecture. The ability to think in the complex way people do is absent in other species – and so is the human highly developed ability to communicate. At a closer look, communication, like thinking, may be one of the most human of human activities. This is not to say that the ability to communicate is restricted to people. At least some animals do seem to engage in activities that one may wish to describe as communication. And yet, human communication is special, and not just because of its being mainly linguistic – the feature that, in animals, seems to be extremely rare, if not lacking altogether. It is the role communication plays in human life that seems unique. The ability to coordinate our activities by means of interpersonal communication is the basis for our being social creatures. Our very survival, not to speak about our distinctive forms of living, depends on our being always a part of a group. And since communication is the glue that holds human collectives together, even our ability to stay alive is a function of our communicational capacity. We communicate in order to ascertain the kind of mutuality and collective doing that provides us with what we need and cannot attain single-handedly. The list of human needs that would remain unsatisfied without interpersonal communication is long and multifarious, and it includes not just the most advanced and complex cultural needs, but also the most primitive biological ones, of the kind that most animals are able to take care of by themselves, with only marginal collaboration of other individuals. In the view of all this, it is not surprising that Leont'ev (1930), one of the founding fathers of participationism, declared the capacity for communication as the hallmark of humanness: "[W]e do not meet in the animal world any special forms of action having as their sole and special end the mastery of the behavior of other individuals by attracting their attention" (p. 59).

All this, as important as it may sound, is not yet enough to substantiate the claim that thinking could be defined as a form of communicating. In fact, the current discourses go directly against this vision when they present these two basic human activities as separate, even if tightly connected. This, indeed, is how thinking and communicating are pictured in colloquial forms of talk, through expressions such as 'communicating one's thoughts' or 'putting thoughts in words'. Our speaking about thoughts as being conveyed (or expressed) in the act of communication implies two distinct processes, that of thinking and that of communicating, with the former slightly preceding the latter and constantly feeding into it. According to this vision, the outcomes of thinking, pictured as entities in their own right, are supposed to preserve their identity while being "put in other words" or "expressed somehow differently".

Whereas acquisitionists have been working with this dualist vision of human cognition for centuries, participationists are likely to view the idea of 'thought-conveyed-in-communication" as but a direct result of an unhelpful objectification. With Wittgenstein (1953), they believe that "Thought is not an incorporeal process which lends life and sense to speaking, and which it would be possible to detach from speaking" (p. 108). Having accepted this claim, one can also see that it remains in force when the somewhat limiting word speaking is replaced with the more general term communicating. Consequently, thinking stops being a self-sustained process separate from and, in a sense, primary to any act of communication, and becomes an act of communication in itself, although not necessarily interpersonal. All this justifies the claim that thinking may be usefully defined as the individualized form of the activity of communicating, that is, one's communication with oneself. Of course, this self-communication does not have to be in any way audible or visible, and does not have to be in words.7 In the proposed discourse on thinking, cognitive processes and processes of inter-personal communicating are thus but different manifestations of basically the same phenomenon. To stress this fact, I propose to combine the terms cognitive and communicational into the new adjective commognitive.8 The etymology of this last word will always remind us that whatever is said with its help refers to these phenomena which are traditionally included in the term cognition, as well as to those usually associated with interpersonal exchanges.9

To complete the task of defining thinking as an individualized form of communication, I need yet to explain how this latter term should be understood in the present context. Since the patterned nature of communication is due to the fact that different people act in similar ways, communication needs to be considered as a collective activity, and should thus be described in terms of its global patterns. Restricting the field of vision to a single node, or to single pair of 'sender' and 'recipient', as is done in the majority of known definitions, would be as unproductive as trying to understand the rules of chess from the individual moves of one checker. The following formulation seems to fulfill this requirement: Communication is a collectively-performed rules-driven activit that mediates and coordinates other activities of the collective. More specifically, individuals who participate in the activity of communicating perform actions that are customarily followed by a certain type of re-action of other individuals. The re-actions may be either practical actions or other communicational moves. By practical actions, I mean actions resulting in a change in the physical environment. Opening a window or adding a brick to a wall while building a house are good examples of practical actions. Communicational actions are those that affect members of community and have no direct impact on the environment, although some of them may, in the end, lead another person's practical (re)action. In human activities, communicational and practical actions are usually simultaneously present and inextricably interwoven. Clearly, communication is what enables inter-person coordination needed for the collective implementation of complex practically-oriented activities, form preparing foods and garments to building houses, publishing newspapers, producing films, transporting goods, etc. This said, let me add that it is also typical of humans to have long chains of purely communicational interactions, in which every re-action is, in itself, a communicational action bound to entail yet another communicational re-action. In this process, the participants alternate between the roles of actors and re-actors, often playing both these parts in one communicational move.

Let me finish this introduction to the participationist discourse on thinking with a number of remarks. First, the definition of communication speaks about rules that regulate communication (and thus the commognition in general). It is important to stress that these rules are to be understood as observer's constructs, and not as guiding principles, followed by individual actors in a conscious, deliberate way. Another fact to remember is that the rules of commognition, are not in any sense "natural" or necessary, as nothing "in the world" can possibly necessitate the given types of associations between actions and re-action. The source of the patterns is in historically established customs. This contingent nature of communicational patterns is probably the reason why Wittgenstein (1953) decided to speak about communication as a kind of game.10 Second, because of its being rules-driven, commognition has dynamics of its own, and it would not be possible without the natural human tendency for alignment. This said, it is equally important to note that in commognition, like in any other historically established activity, human players do have agency. Communicative action almost never determines a re-action. More often than not, both action and re-action are a matter of construction, to be performed according to rules that constrain but do not dictate. Third, whereas practical actions are direct actions on objects, commognitive actions are about objects, that is, they focus interlocutors' attention on an object. Fourth, commognitional actions are performed with the help of mediators, which can have auditory, visual or even tactile effects on individuals. In humans, language, which has both vocal and visual editions (as in the case of written exchanges) is the principal, although not the only, form of commognitive mediator.

Finally, just as there is a multitude of games, played with diverse tools and according to diverse rules, so there are many types of commognition, differing one from another in their patterns, objects, and the types of mediators used. Like in the case of games, individuals may be able to participate in certain types of communicational activity and be unable to take part in some others. The different types of communication that bring some people together while excluding some others will be called discourses. Given this definition, any human society may be divided into partially overlapping communities of discourses. To be members of the same discourse community, individuals do not have to face one another and do not need to actually communicate. The membership in the wider community of discourse is won through participation in communicational activities of any collective that practices this discourse, be this collective as small as it may.

3.2 What is Mathematics?

Given participationist vision of thinking as a form of communication, mathematics can be seen as a special type of discourse, made distinct, among others, by its objects, mediators and rules.11 Let me be more specic.

A discourse counts as mathematical if it features mathematical words, such as those related to quantities and shapes. The conversation between Roni, Eynat and Roni's mother, presented in the beginning of this article, is replete with such mathematical terms as number-words and comparison-words (e.g. more, bigger), and can thus count as a case of mathematical discourse. This, however, is just one out of several possible types of mathematical communication. While many number-related words may appear in non-specialized, colloquial discourses, mathematical discourses as practiced in schools or in the academia dictate their own, more disciplined uses of these words. As will be argued below, neither Roni nor Eynat is using any of the mathematical words the way they are used by mathematically versed interlocutors (and I do not mean just the grammatical imperfections of the girls' talk).

Visual mediators used in mathematical discourses tend to be quite unlike those used in many other types of discourses. While colloquial discourses are usually mediated by images of material things, that is, by concrete objects that are identified or pointed to with the nouns or pronouns and that may be either actually seen or just imagined, mathematical discourses often involve symbolic artifacts, created specially for the sake of this particular form of communication. Such symbolic mediation, however, is still absent from the incipient numerical talk of our young interviewees. Quite understandably, the only form of visual mediation that can be found in our data is concrete rather than symbolic: The mathematical task performed by the girls is described in terms of sets of marbles provided by Roni's mother, and is visually (and tangibly) mediated by these sets.

Endorsed narratives are sets of propositions that are accepted and labeled as true by the given community. Mathematical narratives, to be endorsed, have to be constructed and substantiated according to a set of well-defined rules, specific to this discourse. In the case of scholarly mathematical discourse, these endorsed narratives are known as mathematical theories, and this includes such discursive constructs as definitions, proofs, and theorems.6 In addition to the generally endorsed "abstract" narratives such as those listed above, one can speak about more specific narratives that pertain to concrete objects and may be endorsed in a given situation. The aim of Roni and Eynat's activity, at least in the eyes of the grownups, is to create such locally endorsable narratives: The girls are supposed to explore the boxes with marbles and to come up with endorsable statements that answer the Mother's question "Which of the boxes has more marbles"?

Routines are well-defined repetitive patterns characteristic of a given discourse. Specifically mathematical regularities can be noticed whether one is watching the use of mathematical words and mediators or follows the process of creating and substantiating narratives about number. In fact, such repetitive patterns can be seen in almost any aspect of mathematical discourses: in mathematical forms of categorizing, in mathematical modes of attending to the environment, in the ways of viewing situations as "the same" or different, which is crucial for the interlocutors' ability to apply mathematical discourse whenever appropriate; and in production of narratives and their further substantiation. Routines may be algorithmic, and thus deterministic, or just constraining. The canonic routine of numerical comparison, which, in our example, the mother expects her daughter to perform, is an example of algorithmic routine.

3.3 What Is Mathematics Learning?

Learning mathematics may now be defined as individualizing mathematical discourse, that is, as the process of becoming able to have mathematical communication not only with others, but also with oneself. Through the process of individualization, the personal creativity of the learner comes in.

Let me now go back to the Comparing sets of marbles episode and see whether this definition helps to make a better sense of children's actions. It is now natural to assume that the observed phenomena are related to the fact that the children have not yet individualized the numerical discourse – they did not yet turn this form of talk into a discourse for themselves.12 Indeed, there are many signs showing that the girls are probably at the very beginning of the process. The first evidence can be found in the fact that the girls do not use the compare-by-counting procedure on their own accord: The question "[I]n which of the boxes [are there] more marbles?" ([3b]) is clearly not enough to get them started, and nothing less than a clear hint by the mother ("Do you want to open and discover?", [10a]) would help. Further, the children need mother's scaffolding in order to perform the procedure in its entirety (note, for example, that they stop after having counted the marbles and they need to be prompted in order to draw the conclusion; see mother's question [15]). It is thus clear that if the girls participate in the numerical discourse, it is on other people's accord and according to other people's rules. This can be summarized in the following way: What for the grownups is the routine of exploration, geared toward enhancement of one's arsenal of "factual knowledge" (endorsed narratives), for the children is a ritual – a game played with others for the sake of the togetherness that game playing affords. Note that touching the marbles one by one while also pronouncing subsequent number words is not unlike incantation of meaningless rhymes which is often a part of children's play. What is now but a ritual, will turn into exploration in the course of individualization.

The fact that the girls' participation in the numerical discourse is ritualized and undertaken for the sake of connecting with others becomes even more evident when children's actions in the second part of the episode are compared with what they do in the first. When the conversation begins, the girls spontaneously respond to the mother's query with pointing to one of the identical boxes. Evidently, the question "[I]n which of the boxes [are there] more marbles?" when first asked, is not received as a prompt for a conversation on numbers but rather as an invitation to what the children usually do on their own accord and willingly: to choosing one of the boxes for themselves. Making choices, unlike numerical comparisons, is the kind of activity which the girls have already individualized. It will yet take time until the two types of routines – those of choosing and those of comparing – combine one with the other into an individual activity of the child.

It is reasonable to assume that a certain proficiency in a discourse is a prerequisite for its individualization. Roni and Eynat do not yet exhibit sufficient fluency in numerical talk. For example, they have yet to change their use of number words. Right now, these words are for them but a part and parcel of counting. In the future, the words will be used in many different types of sentences and in multiple roles, as adjectives and as nouns, among others. Above all, the use of these words will become objectified: More often than not, expressions such as one, two or two hundred will be used as if they referred to self-sustained, extra-discursive entities. Similarly, the children's use of connectives such as because will change dramatically. Right now, this use is clearly ritualized: If the girls answer mother's why questions in a seemingly rational way (see Roni's utterance [5] and Eynat's utterance [7], which both begin with the word because), it is obviously due not to their awareness of the relations between boxes but to their familiarity with the form of talk which is expected by the grownups in response to this kind of question. At this point, the girls are already aware of how to talk when answering request for explanation, but are not yet fully aware of when – under which circumstances – it is appropriate to apply them. At this point, the mere appearance of the word why in the interlocutor's question may be enough to prompt an utterance that begins with because and then simply repeats, in a somewhat modified form, what the question was asking about. It seems reasonable to conjecture that in the process of individualization, the awareness of how discursive routine should be performed usually precedes the ability to tell when such performance would be appropriate. One may even hypothesize that it is the ability to make independent decisions about when to apply a given discursive procedure which is the ultimate sign of its individualization.

The manner in which all these changes in the girls' numerical discourse 13 are supposed to happen is implicated in the very claim that learning mathematics is the process of individualization of mathematical discourse: Discursive change can only originate in communicating with experienced interlocutors. This vision is quite different from the one professed by the acquisitionist who assumes, if often only tacitly, that learning results from the learner's attempts to adjust her understanding to the externally given, mind independent reality. Contradicting the participationist belief in the primacy of the collective, this latter version implies that learning, at least in theory, could take place without participation of other people.

Not every mathematical conversation is an opportunity for learning. For a discursive change to occur, there must be some discrepancy – a communicational conflict – between interlocutors. Such conflict arises whenever different participants seem to be acting according to differing discursive rules. The difference may express itself in a disparity in the interlocutor's uses of words, in the manner they look at visual mediators or in the ways they match discursive procedures with problems and situations. More often than not, these differences find their explicit, most salient expression in the fact that the different participants endorse differing, possibly contradicting, narratives. 14 The dissimilarities between Roni and Eynat's numerical discourse and the numerical discourse of the grownups express themselves in different uses of words and disparate routines, and thus constitute a good example of communicational conflict, likely to result in considerable learning. 15

In order to fully individualize numerical discourse Roni and Eynat will have to overcome this conflict. This is not going to be easy. If the child is to ever use the numerical discourse in solving her own problems, she must be aware of the advantages of the relevant discursive procedures. For example, she needs to realize that she may benefit from choosing according to number. And yet, in order to become aware of these advantages, she has to already use the numerical discourse. The process is thus inherently circular. The next question to ask is what can possibly motivate the child to engage in the demanding task of overcoming the circularity.

3.4 Why Do We Learn Mathematics?

The circularity implies that learning mathematics requires readiness to engage in the new discourse even before one can see its problem-solving potential and inner logic. In other words, the child needs to be prepared to participate in the numerical discourse in a ritualized way before she is able to practice the discourse while engaging in self-initiated explorations. The child's motivation for such ritualized action is its immediate social reward: Roni and Eynat perform the ritual as an act of solidarity with the grownups and in the attempt to win their approval. Giving the answer that is expected by the interlocutor may be read as an act of pledging allegiance.

More generally, when the child first engages in mathematics learning, it is because of her overpowering need for communication, which grows out of the even more fundamental need for social acceptance. This social concern can clearly be seen all along the conversations with the girls. The way Roni monitors her mother's face, talks to her and follows her lead clearly indicates that getting the parent's attention and approval is the girl's main concern. This wish competes, and is successfully combined, with an equally strong need to belong with the peer. While making their choices, Roni and Eynat are careful to stress that their decisions are shared (in the further parts of our transcripts, this need for solidarity with the friend is further evidenced by Roni's repetitive use of the word we, through which she asserts the joint ownership of solutions.)

To sum up, the children have different goals than those envisioned by the grownups. While counting and comparing, the girls are in fact preoccupied with the delicate social fabric of their little group, and the conversation on boxes with marbles is, for them, as good an occasion for inter-personal engineering as any other. While grownups count in order to get closer to the truth about the world, the children count to get closer to the grownups. The "exploratory" activities of the young participants are therefore a form of community-building ritual.

4. CONSEQUENCES OF PARTICIPATIONISM FOR THE PRACTICE OF MATHEMATICS TEACHING AND LEARNING

Our ability to make sense of what we see depends on our uses of words. As illustrated above, the interpretation of the notion "social" that gave rise to the commognitive framework made a significant difference in our vision of learning and in this vision's theoretical entailments. In particular, it allowed to account for phenomena that escaped acquisitionist' explanations and it offered alternative explanations for some others. Thus, for example, what acquisitionists interpreted as showing children's unawareness of the "conservation of number" became, in our interpretation, the result of the simple fact that in the situation of choice, young learners had no reason to privilege the ritual of counting over other routines that they had already on their disposal.

Perhaps the most dramatic difference between the acquisitionists' and participationists' visions of mathematical thinking is in their respective messages about the origins of mathematical learning. Whereas acquisitionists views learning as resulting from the learners' direct efforts to arrive at a coherent vision of the world, participationists sees learning as arising mainly from one's attempt to make sense of other people's vision of this world. The former perspective implies that learning, at least in theory, could take place without participation of other people. In contrast, the idea of mathematics as a form of discourse entails that individual learning originates in communication with others and is driven by the need to adjust one's discursive ways to those of other people.

Participationism also provokes second thoughts about some common pedagogical beliefs. For instance, it casts doubt on the current call for "learning with understanding," at least insofar as this call is interpreted as the exhortation to never let the student practice routines which she cannot properly substantiate. According to the present analysis, students' persistent participation in mathematical talk when this kind of communication is for them but a discourse-for-others seems to be an inevitable stage in learning mathematics. If learning is to succeed, all the interlocutors must agree to live with the fact that the new discourse will initially be seen by the newcomers as a game to be played with others, and that it will be practiced only because of its being a discourse that others use and appreciate. It is thus now time to rehabilitate the learning that is based on ritualized action and on thoughtful imitation of the grownups' ways with words. Trying to figure out and then to meet the expert participants' expectations is sometimes the only way to initiate the long process of individualization of discourses. Making sense of other person's thinking is not any less demanding (or respectable!) than the direct attempts to understand reality. Indeed, entering "foreign" forms of talk (and thus of thought) requires a genuine interest and a measure of creativity. To turn the discourse-for-others into a discourse-for-oneself, the student must explore other people's reasons for engaging in this discourse.

REFERENCES

Bakhtin, M. (1981). *The dialogic imagination.* Austin, TX: University of Texas Press.

Bauersfeld, H. (1995). "Language games" in mathematics classroom: Their function and their effects. In P. Cobb & H. Bauersfeld (Eds.), *The emergence of mathematical meaning: Interaction in classroom cultures.* Hillsdale, NJ: Lawrence Erlbaum Associates, 271-292.

Blumer, H. (1969). *Symbolic interactionism: Perspective and method.* Englewood Cliffs, NJ: Prentice-Hall.

Cobb, P. (2002). Reasoning with tools and inscriptions. *Journal of the Learning Sciences, 11,* 187-216.

Cobb, P. & Bauersfeld, H., Eds. (1995). *Emergence of mathematical meaning: Interaction in classroom cultures.* Hillsdale, NJ: Lawrence Erlbaum Associates, 25-129).

Cobb, P., Wood, T. & Yackel, E. (1993). Discourse, mathematical thinking, and classroom practice. In E. Forman, N. Minick, & A. Stone (Eds.), *Contexts for learning: Sociocultural dynamics in children's development.* New York: Oxford University Press, 91-119.

Dehaene, S. (1997). *The number sense: How the mind creates mathematics.* Oxford, UK: Oxford University Press.

Edwards, D. (1997). *Discourse and cognition.* London: Sage.

Engeström, Y. (1987). *Learning by expanding: An Activity-theoretical approach to developmental research.* Helsinki: Orienta-Konsultit.

Ernest, P. (1993). Conversation as a metaphor for mathematics and learning. *Proceedings of the Day Conference.* Manchester, UK: Manchester Metropolitan University, 58-63.

Ernest, P. (1994). The dialogical nature of mathematics. In P. Ernest (Ed.), *Mathematics, education and philosophy: An international perspective*. London: The Falmer Press, 33-48.

Garfinkel, H. (1967). *Studies in ethnomethodology*. Englewood Cliffs, NJ: Prentice-Hall.

Goffman, E. (1958). *The presentation of self in everyday life*. Edinburgh: University of Edinburgh, Social Sciences Research Centre.

Greeno, J.G. (1997). On claims that answer the wrong question. *Educational Researcher, 26*(1), 5-17.

Harré, R., & Gillett, G. (1995). *The discursive mind*. Thousand Oaks, CA: Sage.

Holquist, M. (1990). *Dialogism. Bakhtin and his world*. London: Routledge.

Krummheuer, G. (1995). The ethnography of argumentation. In Cobb, P. & Bauersfeld, H. (Eds.), *The emergence of mathematical meaning. Interactions in classroom culture*. Hillsdale, New Jersey: Erlbaum, 229-269.

Lave, J. (1988). *Cognition in practice*. Cambridge: Cambridge University Press.

Lave, J. (1993). Situating learning in communities of practice. In L. B. Resnick, J. M. Levine, & S. D. Teasley (Eds.) *Perspectives on socially shared cognition*. Washington, DC: American Psychological Association, 17-36.

Lave, J., & Wenger, E. (1991). *Situated learning: Legitimate peripheral participation*. Cambridge: Cambridge University Press.

Leontiev, A.N. (1930). Studies in the cultural development of the child. II. The development of voluntary attention in the child. *Journal of Genetic Psychology, 37*, 52-81.

Leontiev, A. N. (1947/1981). *Problems of the development of mind*. Moscow: Progress Press.

Lerman, S. (1998). A moment in the zoom of a lens: Towards a discursive psychology of mathematics teaching and learning. In A. Olivier & K. Newstead (Eds). *Proceedings of the twenty-second annual meeting of the International Group for the Psychology of Mathematics Education*, Stellenbosch, South Africa, Vol 1, 66-81.

Marková. I. (2003). *Dialogicality and social representations: The dynamics of mind*. Cambridge, UK: Cambridge University Press.

Nardi, B., Ed. (1996). *Context and consciousness: Activity Theory and human-computer interaction*. Cambridge, MA: MIT Press.

Rogoff, B. (1995). Observing sociocultural activity on three planes: Participatory appropriation, guided participation, and apprenticeship. In J. V. Wertsch, P. Del Rio, & A. Alvarez (Eds.), *Sociocultural studies of mind*. New York: Cambridge University Press, 139-164.

Schutz, A. (1967). *Collected papers: The problem of social reality*. Hague, Netherlands: Martinus Nijhoff.

Sfard, A. & Lavie, I. (2005). Why cannot children see as the same what grownups cannot see as different? – early numerical thinking revisited. *Cognition and Instruction, 23*(2), 237-309.

Voigt, J. (1985). Patterns and routines in classroom interaction. *Recherches en Didactique des Mathematiques, 6(1)*, 69-118.

Vygotsky, L. S. (1987). Thought and speech. In Rieber, R. W. & Carton, A. S., *The collected works of L. S. Vygotsky*, Vol. 1. New York: Plenum Press.

Wenger, E. (1998). *Communities of practice*. New York: Cambridge University Press.

Wittgenstein, L. (1953). *Philosophical investigations*. Oxford: Blackwell.

Anna Sfard
The University of Haifa, Israel

NOTES

[1] To illustrate, let me just mention two differing interpretations of the word 'social' to be found in the context of the famous dichotomy *individual vs. social,* that lies at the very heart of the current controversies on human development. At a closer look, those who contrast "the social" with "the

individual" may have two different distinctions in mind. In one of these dichotomies, the term *social* means that whatever is described with this adjective has been done or attained *by an individual* through interaction with others. In this case, the *social* could probably be replaced with *interactional*. The other dichotomy that hides behind the opposition *social versus individual* regards not so much the 'technicalities' of individual learning as the nature and origins of what is being learned. This time, the issue at stake is that of the ontological-epistemological status of knowledge, with the word *individual* functioning as almost synonymous with *natural* or *genetically necessitated*, whereas the *social* is tantamount to *human-made*. It is this latter, strong interpretation of the "social" that seems to have spurred Vygotsky's famous criticism of the Piagetian doctrine (the fact of which Piaget was likely to be aware only partially, if at all).

[2] The study from which the vignette is taken has been reported in Sfard & Lavie (2005).The conversation was held in Hebrew. While translating to English, I made an effort to preserve the idiosyncrasies of the children's word use.

[3] For Activity Theory see, e.g. Leontiev (1947/1981), Nardi (1996), Engeström (1987).

[4] In this context, one should mention the significant influence of Wittgenstein, as well as that of two inter-related, but still distinct schools in sociology: The *symbolic interactionism* usually associated with Mead (1934), Goffman (1958), and Blumer (1969); and the *ethnomethodological* approach initiated by Garfinkel (1967). Of relevance in this context is also the *sociological phenomenology* that originated in the philosophical thought of Husserl's and was founded in the first half of 20th century by Schutz (1967). The direct influence of this latter school of thought on psychology and education can be seen in the work of German and American researchers – see e.g. work by Bauersfeld (1995), Voigt (1985), Krumheuer (1995), and Cobb and his colleagues (Cobb et al., 1993; Cobb & Bauersfled, 1995). All these schools, be them diverse as they are, share a number of basic assumptions, which can also be found in most of the current versions of participationism. They all take the inherently social nature of humans as their point of departure and agree that actions of the individual cannot be understood unless treated as part and parcel of collective doings. The patterned collective activities, in turn, are objects of their participants' sense-making efforts. The different schools begin to diverge only when it comes to their respective responses to the question of where the regularities come from and whether the observed patterns are in any real sense 'real," as opposed their lying exclusively in the eyes of sense-making insiders.

[5] The terms *individualization* and *collectivization* may be viewed as strong participationist versions of what Vygotsky and Activity Theorists call *internalization* and *externalization*. The important advantage of the present terminology is that it is free of acquisitionist undertones of the traditional vocabulary. In result, the proposed version of strong participationism does not imply that thinking and behavior are two ontologically different types of processes but rather promotes the idea that they are two forms of basically the same phenomenon, which may be termed simply as 'individual human doing.' These two forms differ only in the degree of their visibility to others.

[6] One should not, of course, take this metaphor too far. Not every collective activity can be fully individualized (reenacted by a single person). Suffices to think about building bridges or performing complex surgeries. And yet, whatever distinctly human activity has been mastered by a person, the source of this ability is in this person's earlier participation in its collective implementations.

[7] This definition resonates well with the conversation metaphor of mind to be found in Ernest (1993, 1994), Mead (1934), Bakhtin (1981), Holquist (1990) and Marková (2003). See also the idea of discursive psychology in Harré & Gillett (1995), Edwards (1997).

[8] The act of coining my own neologism is certainly rather daring, and I feel I owe an explanation. While trying to give a name to the just defined discourse on thinking I could, of course, follow the usual practice of employing a word that already exists in the English language. In fact, after having said that thinking is an individualized form of communication, I could use the word communication to encompass both categories – that of thinking, and that of inter—personal communication. Indeed,

many other human activities that begin as collective and are liable to individualization do not change their names as a result of individualization: the individually performed mathematical problem solving is still called *problem solving* and the task of complex data processing is called *data processing* whether it is implemented by a single individual or by a group.. However, calling thinking (individualized form of) *communication* would require the users to overcome our deeply entrenched habit of using the words *thinking* and *communicating* as denoting different, non-overlapping types of activities. In introducing the new name I was motivated by the conviction that our view of communicating as being collective *by definition* may be too strong to be removed by a mere act of redefining.

[9] At this point, a skeptic can bring yet another argument against the idea of thinking as individualized form of interpersonal communication. The dilemma of relations between thinking and speech has been stirring one of the most persistent and encompassing debates in the history of human thought. Considering the fact that no solution, not even those offered by the most revered of thinkers, managed to bring about a durable consensus, it may be difficult to understand why the simple statement "thinking is (can be usefully defined as) a form of communication" should now be accepted as an answer. In response, let me stress two differences between my present attempt and most of those undertaken in the past. First, what I did has been framed as an act of *defining*, not as an attempt to find out what thinking "really is." Thus, the agreement may be possible provided I manage to convince others about the usefulness of the proposed *thinking* = *self-communicating* equation. The second difference stems from the fact that the time-honored dilemma which, for centuries, has been boggling philosophical minds is that of the relations between thinking and *language* (or *speech*), whereas the proposed definition links thinking with *communication*. The relation between thought and speech has been, indeed, a leitmotif of philosopher's musings about thinking. This is easily explicable, considering the centrality of verbal communication in specifically human forms of life and the resulting tendency to equate human communicating with talking. Speech and communication, however, although related, are not the same: The former is but a special case of the latter. There are numerous non-verbal forms of communication, and all of them must be considered. Thus, the descriptions of thinking as "talking to oneself" or as "inner speech" are more restrictive than the communicational definition proposed above and as such, they do not make full justice to the phenomenon we wish to fathom. If the attempts to capture the gist of human thinking have been invariably deemed futile, it was probably because of the fact that the problem has been restricted to the issue of relations between thinking and language.

[10] More precisely, Wittgenstein (1953) spoke about *language games*. The metaphor of game, however, is clearly applicable also to non-verbal forms of communication.

[11] Equating mathematics to discourse should not be confused with the time-honored, and often contested, claim that mathematics is a language. The word *language* is usually understood as referring to a tool for representing objects, with this objects being external to, and independent from, the language itself. Therefore, the statement "mathematics is a language," unlike its discursive counterpart, could imply that the objects of mathematics are not a part of mathematics itself. Second, discourses involve many mediators, not just language.

[12] The term *discourse-for-oneself* is close to Vygotsky's idea of *speech-for-oneself*, introduced to denote a stage in the development of children's language (see e.g. Vygotsky 1987, p.71). Our terms also brings to mind the Bakhtinian distinction between *authoritative discourse*, a discourse that "binds us, quite independently of any power it might have to persuade us internally"; and *internally persuasive* discourse, one that is "tightly woven with 'one's own world.' (Bakhtin, 1981, pp. 110-111.)

[13] Since the only way to actually observe such changes is by watching the child in mathematical conversation with others rather than with herself, we will need to remember that whatever is found has been informed by the other participants as well. Still, with an appropriate analyses and the

sufficient amount of observations, we may be able to make conjectures about some general properties of the child's participation, as well as of the individualized form of this child's discourse, if any.

[14] Since discursive conflict arises in face of differences in meta-discursive rules, a mere difference in narratives cannot count as a sufficient evidence for such conflict; for example, if one objects to the claim that "The weather is beautiful today", it is indicative of the conflict of opinion, not of discourses

[15] The notion of communicational conflict, although reminiscent of the acquisitionist idea of *cognitive conflict*, is in fact a different type of theoretical construct: Communicational conflict results from a disparity between student's and teacher's discourses rather than from a clash between the learner's vision of the world and the real state of affairs; it is indispensable for learning rather than optional; and it is resolved through students' acceptance and rationalization of the discursive ways of an expert interlocutor and not via their direct, independent reasoning about the world.

STEPHEN LERMAN

CULTURAL PSYCHOLOGY, ANTHROPOLOGY AND SOCIOLOGY: THE DEVELOPING 'STRONG' SOCIAL TURN

A few years ago I wrote a chapter in Jo Boaler's (2000) collection in which I argued that there has been a trend towards the social in research in mathematics education. I suggested that the trend began in the mid-80s and has grown in impact and in the range of theoretical frameworks upon which researchers have drawn. Following Kilpatrick (1992), I marked the shift as the move away from individualistic psychology or mathematics itself as explanatory and predicting frameworks for addressing issues of pupils' learning of mathematics and for addressing teaching. From 2001 to 2003 I co-directed[1] a project which examined systematically the research productions of the mathematics education community through analysing a sample of the publications of two major journals, *Educational Studies in Mathematics* (ESM) and *Journal for Research in Mathematics Education* (JRME) and the *Proceedings of the International Group for the Psychology of Mathematics Education* (PME), partly in order to see if those claims were substantiated. Indeed we found some evidence of the trend although it varied over the years.

In this paper I will do three things: I will first examine the extent of the reach of the social turn. This will call for some discussion of what constitutes sociocultural theories, with a focus especially on how they relate to mathematics teaching and learning and on what is meant by the term 'strong' in the title. I will look to the work of the later Wittgenstein to help me set out that perspective. I will then speculate on the future trends in sociocultural research in mathematics education. I will refer to work on identity and on Activity Theory and then, returning to Wittgenstein, look at the development of what might be called an ethnography of mathematical practices in schools and elsewhere. Finally, given that the focus of the perspective of this part of the meeting, 'Mathematics learning as a social process', is just one of the sub-fields being addressed, I will make some comments, drawing on Basil Bernstein's discussion late in his life on knowledge discourses (Bernstein, 2000), about the advisability or even possibility of achieving the aim of the conference, which is 'to work out a unified view of the didactics of mathematics'.

J. Maasz, W. Schloeglmann (Eds.), New Mathematics Education Research and Practice, 171–188.

THE UBIQUITY OF THE SOCIAL AND ITS MEANINGS

It is now commonplace in our field to find a recognition that the social conditions of mathematics learning have 'a deep influence on learning processes in school situations', to quote, again, from the proposal of this conference. Few would argue with the notion that classroom organisation, cultural values, poverty and deprivation, affect, and other such issues must be taken into consideration when examining learning. For many, though, these are seen as disturbances to what might be thought of as true learning of an accepted body of knowledge, even if it is admitted that recognising learning is far from easy. If one deals with these disturbances in some way (e.g. the provision of breakfast clubs in poor areas of London) then true learning can take place. However the three theoretical fields in the title, cultural psychology, anthropology and sociology, take the notion of 'social' much further, they are a *strong* use of the term, arguing for the situatedness of knowledge, of schooling as social production and reproduction, and of the development of identity (or identities) as always implicated in learning.

To talk of social conditions or of social factors is to imply that there are conditions or factors that are not social. What, then, might be thought to be outside of social factors? One can certainly say that, prior to socialisation we are born with a genetic inheritance but they should be seen as genetic propensities, and whether these are realised or not, whether the opportunities arise to fulfil them or not, are contingent on the life experiences of that individual. The evolutionary biologists claim that all human behaviour can be explained in terms of survival and optimal propagation of the species, and there are the rare cases of 'wolf children' who exhibit only instinctive behaviour. Those primitive aspects of human behaviour aside, it can be argued that all behaviour is the result of socialisation in a range of historical, cultural practices and communities. Vygotsky identified two separate sources of development, the biological and the social, but he too argued that anything beyond the most basic behaviour is overlaid by culture. This includes what constitutes and is accepted as appropriate behaviour that we call *knowing*.

Cognition is often contrasted against sociocultural theories but this is to misunderstand the role of theories of human development, which is to investigate the origins of the individual's knowing. A more appropriate contrast is that of cognition resulting from the individual's efforts and cognition resulting from internalisation from the social plane.

The social theories that are increasingly being used in educational research in general and in mathematics education research in particular offer languages for describing learning as development within socio-cultural historical practices, and that see meaning, thinking, and reasoning as products of social activity. The socio-cultural perspective thus sees all meanings as socially produced, physical experiences too being interpreted through the local cultural practices. Individuality is the expression of the unique set of socio-cultural experiences, gender, class, ethnicity etc. I have elaborated these ideas elsewhere (Lerman, 1996; 2000a; 2000b). I want just to emphasise here that I am putting a strong case of the effects of social life. I think we are best served either by studies of children's learning of mathematics in terms of their individual constructions, or studies of how children's mathematical ways of thinking are brought into alignment with those of the teacher and the authority of mathematics itself, but not both together. In these general terms I am sure the term 'sociocultural' is by now well known and I will not, therefore, extend this discussion. What is required, though, is a breakdown of the term into its elements and I will discuss this in the next section. The title of this chapter contains three theoretical fields, and I want briefly to investigate the commonalities between them, that of Marxism which proposes that consciousness reflects relations to the means of production, in this case of symbolic production, and hence of access to material control. Certainly Vygotsky's programme was to develop a Marxist psychology, providing a framework for demonstrating how consciousness develops in the social context and through socialisation. Vygotsky's theory was a materialist one, building on behaviourism rather than opposing it totally. Proposing the mediation of culture between the stimulus and response link offers a materialist account that incorporates the higher thinking that psychological behaviourism cannot address. Whilst anthropological theories in general cannot be said to be driven by the same orientation, Jean Lave's work, which has been very influential in mathematics education research, was originally Vygotskian inspired and she references Marx in her 1988 book. Marx's work can certainly be said to have been the major influence in sociology. The fact of this commonality indicates again the strong sense of social to which I am referring in this chapter.

I want to make some remarks here about mathematical knowledge, a response, if you like, to the constant cry of reviewers in mathematics education research journals and conferences, "Where's the mathematics?" It has a unique place in the history of culture because of its perceived timelessness and certainty, and its abstract nature. It is therefore possibly the most challenging of tests for any theory of learning. This is because, if one thinks of mathematical fields such as analysis, or earlier (in schooling terms) concepts such as multiplication and division, the perception that learning is coming to understand these abstract ideas, for those few, in regard to analysis, who are able, is very familiar, almost 'natural'. The mathematician/teacher transmits and the individual either comes to understand or, in most cases does not. That view of learning mathematics was challenged many years ago by Piaget and the constructivists who saw the process of learning as cognitive re-organisation, with individuals reaching higher levels of mathematical constructions through reflective abstraction. Transmission of knowledge from one to another makes no sense, they argued. The individual creates meanings of her/his own world; it is the individual who has to do all the work.

Given the distinction I have briefly argued above between constructivism and sociocultural theories, how then does sociocultural theory explain the acquisition of abstract mathematical knowledge? All sociocultural theories, I have argued, are based on a reproduction theory of the development of a distinctly human consciousness, and indeed that consciousness is dependent on the historical, social and cultural settings in which the individual is immersed from birth (if not before). How, then, is 'understanding' anything to be understood, and understanding mathematics in particular? I will turn to the later Wittgenstein for a number of reasons. First, he is perhaps the prime mover of the social turn in the 20th century, shifting the focus from his early picture theory of knowledge to the role and function of language in use. Second, he had much to say about the nature of mathematics in particular. Third, I will be drawing on his ideas both in discussing mathematical meanings here and below in looking at the turn to ethnography as a recent and developing perspective in research on mathematics teaching and learning.

As often quoted, Wittgenstein locates meaning in use. His concern is for us to describe how actors make sense of behaviour and utterances (Bloor, 1983).

> Every sign *by itself* seems dead. *What* gives it life? – In use it is *alive.* Is life breathed into it there? – Or is the *use* its life? (Wittgenstein, 1958, Remark 432, emphasis in the original)

As an example of what it means to understand the meaning of something, rooted in the use of language, he says:

> Do I understand the word 'perhaps'? – And how do I judge whether I do? Well, something like this: I know how it's used, I can explain its use to somebody, say by describing it in made-up cases. I can describe the occasions of its use, its position in sentences, the intonation it has in speech. – Of course this only means that 'I understand the word "perhaps"' comes to the same as: 'I know how it is used etc.'; not that I try hard to call to mind its entire application in order to answer the question whether I understand the word. (Wittgenstein, 1974, p. 64)

A key concern for Wittgenstein in the notion of understanding is that of rule following, but not just following, being able to go beyond. Rules, like writing reports, giving orders, playing chess, are uses or institutions (Remark 199). He says:

> Teaching which is not meant to apply to anything but the examples given is different from that which *'points beyond'* them. (Remark 208).

Being able to go beyond is first shown (by the teacher), then followed, and then the learner is let go (Remark 208), a description strikingly similar to Vygotsky's description of the operation of the zone of proximal development. In interpreting going beyond, it is important for Wittgenstein to explain it in terms of use.

> But is that *all*? Isn't there a deeper explanation; or mustn't at least the *understanding* of the explanation be deeper? – Well, have I myself a deeper understanding? Have I *got* more than I give in the explanation? - But whence the feeling that I have got more? (Remark 209)

Wittgenstein seems to be saying that we often have the feeling that understanding must be more than following rules, which are conventions, and knowing how to go beyond, but on examination there is no more to be said. This leads on, of course, to his argument against private languages.

Try not to think of understanding as a 'mental process' at all. – For *that* is the expression that confuses you. But ask yourself: in what sort of case, in what kind of circumstances do we say, "Now I know how to go on," when, that is, the formula *has* occurred to me? – In the sense in which there are processes (including mental processes) which are characteristic of understanding, understanding is not a mental process. (A pain's growing more or less; the hearing of a tune or a sentence: these are mental processes.) (Remark 154)

Finally, in relation to mathematics he gives the following example of how understanding is about use:

It seems clear that we understand the question: "Does the sequence 7777 occur in the development of π?" It is an English sentence; it can be shown what it means for 415 to occur in the development of π; and similar things. Well, our understanding of that question reaches just so far, one might say, as such explanations reach. (Remark 516)

In these several quotes we have a philosophical account that corresponds, I would argue, with the psychological account of Vygotsky. Their accounts are rooted in use, in language, and therefore potentially in time, location, culture, class etc. These latter are concerns of ours at the end of the twentieth and the start of the twenty-first centuries: the manner in which to work with sociocultural perspectives is mapped out for us by these two thinkers. We too can 'go beyond'.

I have presented a fairly extensive set of quotations from Wittgenstein's later work in order to establish the way in which his social linguistic turn offers a perspective on the acquisition of mathematical, and all, knowledge, what it means to know and to understand. Whilst there are particular features of mathematics that pose interesting problems for researchers the call for a special case to be made for mathematics in knowledge and in learning is not supported by the above quotes and discussion. My interpretation of Wittgenstein's work rests on others with much greater knowledge of course (e.g. Bloor, 1983; 1997).

The extent of sociocultural theories

I will make some comments now about the growth of the use of sociocultural theories in mathematics education research over the recent decades, about which I made speculative comments and offered a broad-brush overview in my (Lerman, 2000b) chapter. In our study (Tsatsaroni, Lerman & Xu, 2003) we mapped the development of sociocultural theories in ESM and JRME and in the Proceedings of PME between 1990 and 2001. Table 1 shows that evidence.

Some 30% of articles in JRME and close to 40% in ESM we classified as of one kind of sociocultural theory or another. As might be expected, there is a smaller percentage in PME papers. We set out the results in two periods, 1990 to 1995 and 1996 to 2001 to show changes over the period taken into the study. The increase in percentages is evident.

To extend the PME analysis, Table 2 shows the use of sociocultural theories from the first conferences until 2004. Those theories are grouped under four headings:

1. cultural psychology, including work based on Vygotsky, activity theory, situated cognition, communities of practice, social interactions
2. ethnomathematics
3. sociology, sociology of education, poststructuralism, hermeneutics, critical theory
4. discourse, to include psychoanalytic perspectives, social linguistics, s
5. emiotics.

Table 1: Theory Types

	PME				ESM				JRME			
	90 -95		96 - 01		90 - 95		96 - 01		90 - 95		96 - 01	
	No.	%	No.	%	No.	%	No.	%	No.	%	No.	%
Traditional psychological & mathematics theories	49	73.1	49	60.5	52	63.4	49	51.6	34	54.8	44	57.9
Psycho-social, including re-emerging ones	8	11.9	8	9.9	8	9.8	19	20.0	4	6.5	10	13.2
Sociology, Sociology of Ed, socio-cultural studies & Historically orientated studies	2	3.0	8	9.9	3	3.7	11	11.6	1	1.6	6	7.9
Linguistics, social linguistics & semiotics	0	0.0	2	2.5	1	1.2	5	5.3	2	3.2	6	7.9
Neighbouring fields of Maths Ed, science ed and curriculum studies	1	1.5	0	0.0	0	0.0	0	0.0	1	1.6	0	0.0
Recent broader theoretical currents, feminism, post-structuralism and psychoanalysis	1	1.5	0	0.0	8	9.8	1	1.1	0	0.0	1	1.3
Philosophy/philo of mathematics	0	0.0	3	3.7	0	0.0	3	3.2	1	1.6	1	1.3
Ed theory and research	2	3.0	0	0.0	1	1.2	1	1.1	2	3.2	0	0.0
Other	0	0.0	0	0.0	1	1.2	1	1.1	2	3.2	0	0.0
No theory used	4	6.0	11	13.6	8	9.8	5	5.3	15	24.2	8	10.5
Total	67		81		82		95		62		76	

Table 2: Numbers of Research Reports classified as socio-cultural

PME meeting	Total no of Research Reports	Categories				Total	Percentage
		1	**2**	**3**	**4**		
PME2 1978	26						
PME3 1979	49						
PME4 1980	58						
PME5 1981	74						
PME6 1982	60						
PME7 1983	74						
PME8 1984	53						
PME9 1985	76	2				2	3
PME10 1986	82	2				2	2
PME11 1987	153	2				2	1
PME12 1988	73	1				1	1
PME13 1989	102	3				3	3
PME14 1990	111	6	1		2	9	8
PME15 1991	126	7	1	3	2	13	10
PME16 1992	91	10	3	1	2	16	18
PME17 1993	88	9	1	1	2	13	15
PME18 1994	157	15	3	3	2	23	15
PME19 1995	77	12	1	1	2	16	21
PME20 1996	77	9			2	11	14
PME21 1997	122	12		1	7	20	16
PME22 1998	119	8	1	5	1	15	13
PME23 1999	136	7	3		4	14	10
PME24 2000	117	4	1		1	6	5
PME25 2001	171	8		1	4	13	8
PME26 2002	165	7		3	1	11	7

PME27 2003	176	6	3	5	1	15	9
PME28 2004	198	23		2	4	29	15
PME29 2005	130	14	1	5	8	28	22

The evidence is of course limited to just 3 English language sources in the earlier research and just one, PME proceedings, in this most recent work (to appear in Lerman, forthcoming). To carry out a more comprehensive study was beyond our budget. Nevertheless I think one can fairly conclude that the extent of the use of sociocultural theories is substantial and growing. In this analysis we have, to some extent, broken down the umbrella term of 'sociocultural' into separate parts. I will discuss these different elements in the next section as a precursor to speculating on the future directions of sociocultural research in our community.

FUTURE DIRECTIONS

Some years ago Anna Sfard (1998) wrote of two distinct orientations in mathematics education research perspectives: the acquisition metaphor and the participation metaphor. Anna argued that we need both. I think this was a useful analysis and one that contrasted with the argument I proposed in Lerman (1996) and subsequently in the debate in JRME (Steffe & Thompson, 2000; Lerman, 2000a), that we are faced with choices and that these two metaphors are at least partly incommensurable perspectives or discourses (see below). These two positions, Anna's and mine, were partly responsible for the choice of the theme of the Plenary Panel at PME in Haifa in 1999 on learning theories and the special issue of ESM that followed, published later as a book (Kieran, Forman & Sfard, 2003). In that, as metaphors, one can research how these orientations are taken up, debated, and used in research, Anna's proposal allows one to take a step back from the theories and engage, as a researcher, with the take-up and application of these metaphors within the community. As metaphors for epistemological descriptions, however, I would suggest we are still faced with choices. Interestingly, 'acquisition' is used by Bernstein (e.g. 2000) as the term for whatever process takes place that leads to the student gaining knowledge, and 'transmission' as the term for what the teacher conveys. 'Transmission' and, to a lesser extent, 'acquisition' are loaded terms in education communities, conveying images of traditional teaching which is almost universally demonised but, through Bernstein's use of these terms we can see the regulating effects of power relations, which may be masked by other terms. I have suggested elsewhere that it is worth noting that all or almost all of the present generation of mathematicians and mathematics educators were taught by traditional methods and that such methods are, therefore, perhaps worthy of further investigation. I will not pursue this here, though.

In the analysis above I broke down sociocultural theories into sub-sections: (1) cultural psychology, including work based on Vygotsky, activity theory, situated cognition, communities of practice, social interactions; (2) ethnomathematics; (3) sociology, sociology of education, poststructuralism, hermeneutics, critical theory; and (4) discourse, to include psychoanalytic perspectives, social linguistics, and semiotics. These mirror the categories we presented in Lerman & Tsatsaroni (1998)

Figure 1: Pedagogic modes

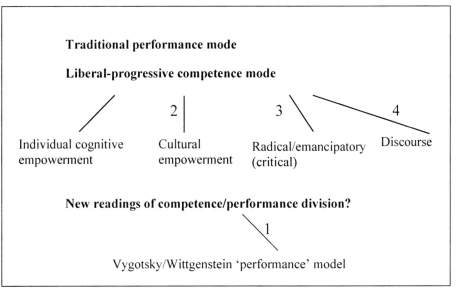

Drawing on Bernstein's description of the turn from traditional performance pedagogy to a liberal-progressive competence pedagogy in the late 1950s, we proposed that this latter could be subdivided into: an individual cognitive focus, that is, Piagetian/reform/constructivism; a social or cultural focus, for example ethnomathematics (as in (2) above); and a critical focus, such as a Freirian approach (as in (3) above). We also suggested that there is evidence of a linguistic turn, to include social linguistics, critical discourse analysis and psychoanalytical approaches (as in (4) above), and, further, an emerging new performance model, quite different from the traditional, based on Vygotskian theories (as in (1) above). If indeed there is a new performance model, we must be conscious of the dangers of the accountability regime in many Western countries. Focusing on performance can be misinterpreted and draw us back into old performance models. This framework formed the basis of our discourse analytic tool (see Tsatsaroni *et al*, 2003), and these latter four constitute the four sub-sections of what I have called sociocultural theories in the extended PME analysis.

As regards future directions in the realm of sociocultural theories, a question I posed in the title of this paper, I believe we will see great attention paid to three issues: that of learning as identity formation; the application of third generation activity theory; and also a greater focus on ethnography. All three can be seen as related to Anna's participation metaphor, although there is a danger that the metaphor masks power relations, and can therefore beg the question of equity. I would add that a key issue will need to be addressed in whatever theoretical perspective is used, is that of equity. Who succeeds and who fails, and why, are critical issues in mathematics especially, given its function in society and in education as a key to entry into privileged studies and careers, often even when they are non-mathematical fields. An under-represented sub-field of research in mathematics education is that of policy (Lerman & Tsatsaroni, 2005); taking account of power and regulating mechanisms calls for greater engagement in critical positions on educational policy.

IDENTITY

There has been a growing interest in identity (Boaler & Greeno, 2000; Boaler, Wiliam & Zevenbergen, 2000; Boaler, 2002; Lerman, 2005; Sfard, 2005) as a focus of analysis of the learning process in mathematics classrooms, in subjectivity as produced in the framing of pedagogic codes (Dowling, 2001) and in the production of regimes of truth (Walkerdine, 1998). In some senses these are complementary, the one a focus on agency, with the dangers of fixed notions of identity, the other on structure, with the dangers of losing sight of the potential for choosing the discourse from which to speak out. Subjectivity focuses on how individuals are both the *subject* in the sense of the actor in a discourse but are also *subjected to* the possibilities and limitations, the affordances and constraints, of that discourse. Identity is therefore produced in discourses and the notion of subjectivity captures that regulation.

One might ask why use the notion of identity? First, it has become a common focus of attention in the social sciences in general. In 1996 Stuart Hall said, "There has been a veritable explosion in recent years around the concept of 'identity'", to which Zygmunt Bauman (2001) added, "The explosion has triggered an avalanche."

Second, the anthropological perspective of Jean Lave has become a powerful influence on research in our community and she shifted the language of learning from cognition to that of identity.

We have argued that, from the perspective we have developed here, learning and a sense of identity are inseparable: They are the same phenomenon. (Lave & Wenger, 1991, p. 115)

One cannot but be aware of the manifestations of identity in students' lives, whether it be in the clothing they wear, to conform, to identify with a sports team or sports star, or with a media star, or in the music they listen to, through which, in their choice, they express conformity to one group or another, or resistance to conformity. There are racial and cultural styles of dress, speech and gestures which students may adopt, sometimes independent of whether they 'belong' to that social group or not. 'Belonging' is perhaps best judged by the person, not by an observer.

In the outward expression of religion, through dress, we again are strongly aware of identity and identification.

Research studies of gender, ethnicity, social class etc. demonstrate the struggle for identity, acceptance and, sometimes, just a peaceful path through childhood and adolescence and through schooling in particular (see e.g. Kehily, 2001; Reay, 2002).

Boaler (1997; 2002; Boaler & Greeno, 2000, Boaler, Wiliam & Zevenbergen, 2000) has done the most extensive work on identity in mathematics education research in a series of studies and publications. Others include: Bibby (2000); Mendick (2003); Graven (2003); Bartholomew (2005); and Sfard (2005), as well as my own (Lerman, 2005). In my talk I examined a number of areas of theory in relation to identity. In the literature of reflexive modernity (e.g. Beck, Giddens & Lash 1994) some writers claim that individuals are more free to write their own life scripts in this period of late modernity than in previous periods that they call traditional and early or first modernity. In these earlier periods people's identities were typically determined by family life and location, and by occupation and social class respectively. Giddens and Beck particularly claim that now individuals can choose who they wish to be. In Boaler and Greeno's (2000) study female students' choices not to go on to study mathematics at University because the identity of mathematicians is perceived by them to be one that does not fit with their perception of their own identity is perhaps an example of identity work in late modernity. Others argue that structures, such as gender, continue to play dominant roles in identity formation, and question whether we are seeing a de-traditionalisation or indeed a re-traditionalisation whereby old roles are changed and extended but do not disappear.

In examining identity we should also take note of the effects that the regulatory systems of the state play in the identity of teachers and pupils, and this formed a second area of literature I touched on in my talk. Ball (2001), for example, uses the notion of 'performativity' to describe the ways in which people are having to respond to the dominating official regulation in the UK. He describes a self-regulation that differs from the panopticon of poststructuralism:

Instead it is the uncertainty and instability of being judged in different ways, by different means, through different agents; the 'bringing-off' of performances – the flow of changing demands, expectations and indicators that make us continually accountable and constantly recorded. (p. 211/212)

He quotes from Jeffrey and Woods' (1998) interviews to illustrate the impact of regulation on teachers' identities:

I don't have the job satisfaction now I had once working with young kids because I feel every time I do something intuitive I just feel guilty about it. 'Is this right; am I doing it the right way; does this cover what I am supposed to be covering'. (p. 213)

My first reaction was 'I'm not going to play the game', but I am and they know I am. I don't respect myself for it; my own self respect goes down. Why aren't I making a stand? (p. 215)

Pupils' identities in mathematics classrooms are strongly affected too, of course, not least of all by their teachers' perceptions of their own roles.

Studying the identities of learners of mathematics or of teachers requires, I suggest, an engagement with these, and other, bodies of literature. They present perspectives that are at play in classrooms and have effect on developing identities. The development of a mathematical identity, better called a school-mathematical identity, is yet another layer that we, as teachers of mathematics, attempt to lay over these other aspects of multiple identities, many of which, such as coping with surviving socially (Kehily, 2001; Reay, 2002), are probably much more important to pupils.

There are dangers in researching 'voice', as Arnot & Reay (2004) discuss, drawing on Bernstein's work. There is a potentially unstoppable spiral of ever more fragmented voices. What we require as researchers is to be able to talk about how these voices are produced if we are also to be able to see how things can change. One cannot ignore the relationship between the researcher and the person being interviewed, that is, the issue of the pedagogic relationship producing/regulating 'voice'. Seen as produced in pedagogic relations, voice is the power to constrain whereas message has the potential to transform.

ACTIVITY THEORY

The second area of theory in our field that I anticipate will develop is often called CHAT, cultural-historical activity theory (see van Oers, this volume). Based on Vygotsky's Marxist thesis that human consciousness develops through mediation and developed into its second generation by Leont'ev, Engestrom has extended the theory into a developed programme for studying how social systems work, the identification of the tensions and contradictions inherent in the system and proposing how working through these tensions leads to a progressive cycle of further activity systems (Leont'ev, 1981; Engeström, 1987, 1991, 1999). One person who has used this work extensively and very fruitfully in studies of mathematical activity is Clive Kanes (see e.g. Kanes, 2002, 2003) but others are using the CHAT perspective too (e.g. Daniels, Williams, Noss, Hoyles, Goodchild). For example, in examining the double-binds inherent in the place of numeracy in the school curriculum as described by Noss (1998), Kanes (2002) indicates how an activity theoretical approach can offer different ways of seeing numeracy. He writes (Kanes, 2002):

At the heart of the activity theoretic framework is a transformation of our understanding of the tensions among visible, useable and constructible numeracies. These should not be viewed as extrinsic eventualities, that is, potentially correctable by suitable means or ways of thinking about numeracy. Instead they are better seen as intrinsic to the nature of numeracy in its current state of cultural development. In other words, Noss' double-bind situations are not anomalies to be overcome so much as keys to understanding the cultural basis of numerical activity. In activity theory language, these anomalies afford primary contradictions underscoring efforts to move numeracy in any given direction. (p. 392)

In his current work Kanes is using activity theory to conceptualise how to align assessment practices with the other features of school mathematics (Kanes, 2005).

ETHNOGRAPHY

The third direction in which I expect to see sociocultural research develop is in what one could call ethnography (Clive Kanes, personal communication). With studies of Brazilian market children (Nunes, Schliemann & Carraher, 1993), candy sellers (Saxe, 1991), newspaper sellers (Santos, 2004) and others the distinction between practical knowledge and formal knowledge has become much fuzzier. The privileged formal knowledge can in fact be seen as, in some ways, another form of practical knowledge, having tacit as well as explicit features of its practice and forms and degrees of participation and identity. We have already seen a number of studies, developing those mentioned above, of the uses of mathematics (at least that's how we as mathematicians would describe it) in workplaces (e.g. Hoyles, Noss, & Pozzi, 2001; Kanes, etc.). It is of no help to pathologise the errors as bad mathematics, they must be seen as potentially life threatening errors in nursing, or money-losing errors in motel and airline industries, etc. Mathematics classrooms too, as in studies of identity/subjectivity, are sites in need of ethnographic engagement to make sense of learning, as we know from the many studies of Cobb and his colleagues and many others. Wittgenstein (the few quotations above can only point to his orientation) was concerned with the triadic relationship between language, action, and social reality, and indeed with the circularity of these three (Kim, 2004). There is no outside standpoint from which to pin these down. Thus the focus of future work in mathematics classrooms will not be so much on learning as cognitive development but ethnographic work on learning as developing appropriate school-mathematical identities. However, to refer back to the problems of voice research mentioned above, there are dangers of slipping back to weak notions of 'social' in ethnographic research. Theorising power relations, identifying regulatory processes and pedagogic identities, and careful elaboration of recognition and realisation rules within research are necessary features of a new ethnographic turn in studies on learning mathematics.

UNIFICATION?

In the description of the goals for the conference is contained the proposal 'to work out a unified view of the didactics of mathematics' and at the recent meeting of PME in 2005 the research forum "Theories of Mathematics Education" was set up to examine the same concern, the proliferation and the use of theories in our field. It is to this issue that I finally turn. I will draw on the sociological theories of Basil Bernstein (e.g. 2000) to ground my comments.

In discussing knowledge discourses Bernstein draws on two notions: hierarchy and verticality. Discourses are described as hierarchical where knowledge in the domain is a process of gradual distancing, or abstraction, from everyday concepts. Hierarchical discourses require an apprenticeship; they position people as initiated or apprenticed. Clearly academic and indeed school mathematics are examples of hierarchical discourses. Research (Cooper & Dunne, 2000) shows that setting mathematics tasks in everyday contexts can mislead some students, namely those from low socio-economic background, into privileging the everyday context and the meanings carried in them over the abstract or esoteric meanings of the discourse of academic mathematics. Bernstein would argue that such students have not had the opportunity to acquire that knowledge (he describes it in terms of language: elaborated or restricted codes) and it is the possibility and indeed the responsibility of schools to invest the resources into providing appropriate opportunities.

His second notion, verticality, describes the extent to which a discourse grows by the progressive integration of previous theories, what he calls a vertical knowledge structure, or by the insertion of a new discourse alongside existing discourses and, to greater or lesser extent, incommensurable with them. He calls these latter horizontal knowledge structures. Bernstein offers science as an example of a vertical knowledge structure and, interestingly, both mathematics and education (and sociology) as examples of horizontal knowledge structures. He uses a further distinction that enables us to separate mathematics from education: the former has a strong grammar, the latter a weak grammar, i.e. with a conceptual syntax not capable of generating unambiguous empirical descriptions. Both are examples of hierarchical discourses in that one needs to learn the language of, say, linear algebra or string theory just as one needs to learn the language of radical constructivism or embodied cognition. It will be obvious that linear algebra and string theory have much tighter and specific concepts and hierarchies of concepts less susceptible to interpretation than radical constructivism or embodied cognition. Adler and Davis (forthcoming) point out that a major obstacle in the development of accepted knowledge in mathematics for teaching may well be the strength of the grammar of the former and the weakness of the latter. Where we can specify accepted knowledge in mathematics, knowledge about teaching is always disputed.

As a horizontal knowledge structure, then, it is typical that mathematics education knowledge will grow both within discourses and by the insertion of new discourses in parallel with existing ones. Thus we can find many examples in the literature of work that elaborates the functioning of the process of reflective abstraction, as an instance of the development of knowledge within a discourse. But the entry of Vygotsky's work into the field in the mid-1980s (Lerman, 2000b) with concepts that differed from Piaget's did not lead to the replacement of Piaget's theory (as the proposal of the existence of oxygen replaced the phlogiston theory). Nor did it lead to the incorporation of Piaget's theory into an expanded theory (as in the case of non-Euclidean geometries). Indeed it seems absurd to think that either of these would occur precisely because we are dealing with a social science, that is, we are in the business of interpretation of human behaviour. Whilst all research, including scientific research, is a process of interpretation, in the social sciences, such as education, there is a double hermeneutic (Giddens,

1976) since the 'objects' whose behaviour we are interpreting are themselves trying to make sense of the world.

Education, then, is a social science, not a science. Sociologists of scientific knowledge (Kuhn, Latour) might well argue that science is more of a social science that most of us imagine, but social sciences certainly grow both by hierarchical development but especially by the insertion of new theoretical discourses alongside existing ones. Constructivism grows, and its adherents continue to produce novel and important work; models and modelling may be new to the field but already there are novel and important findings emerging from that orientation. One might refer to these developments as 'normal science' (Kuhn, 1978)

I referred above to the incommensurability, in principle, of these parallel discourses. Where a constructivist might interpret a classroom transcript in terms of the possible knowledge construction of the individual participants, viewing the researcher's account as itself a construction (Steffe & Thompson, 2000), someone using socio-cultural theory might draw on notions of a zone of proximal development. Constructivists might find that describing learning as an induction into mathematics, as taking on board concepts that are on the intersubjective plane, incoherent in terms of the theory they are using (and a similar description of the reverse can of course be given). In this sense, these parallel discourses are incommensurable. I suggest that the boundaries between discourses with weak grammars are more permeable, however, than those with strong grammars. Hence attempts to merge discourses will be found in education, but rarely in mathematics.

Finally, I will comment on concerns about the effectiveness of educational research in a time of multiple and sometimes competing paradigms, described here as discourses. 'Effectiveness' is a problematic notion, although one that certainly figures highly in current discourses of accountability. It arises because by its nature education is a research field with a face towards theory and a face towards practice, what Bernstein has called a region (Bernstein, 2000). This contrasts with fields such as psychology in which theories and findings can be applied, but practice is not part of the characteristic of research in that field. Research in education, in contrast, draws its problems from practice and expects its outcomes to have applicability or at least significance in practice. Medicine and computing are similar intellectual fields in this respect.

What constitutes knowledge is accepted or rejected by the criteria of the social field of mathematics education research. Typically, we might say necessarily, research has to take a step away from practice to be able to say something about it. Taking the results of research into the classroom calls for a process of recontextualisation, a shift from one practice into another in which a selection must take place, allowing the play of ideology. To look for a simple criterion for acceptable research in terms of 'effectiveness' is to enter into a complex set of issues. Indeed 'effectiveness' itself presupposes aims and goals for, in our case, mathematics education. To ignore the complexity is to lose the possibility of critique and hence I am not surprised by the multiplicity of theories in our field and the debates about their relative merits, nor do I see it as a hindrance. I think our field gains by the multiplicity of theories, although the development within theories is equally of importance. I am more troubled by how those theories are used. Our research (Tsatsaroni *et al*, 2003) indicated that it is rare for researchers to allow data to interrogate theory in the sense of revisiting the theory one has used in order to develop it, re-examine it or whatever. Too often theories are taken to be unproblematically applied to a research study. I am particularly troubled by the attacks on educational research as an inadequate shadow of a fetishised image of scientific, psychological or medical research, as we are seeing currently in the USA, increasingly in the UK, imminently in Australia and, I expect in other countries too.

REFERENCES

Adler, J. & Davis, Z. (forthcoming). Opening another black box: Researching mathematics for teaching in mathematics teacher education.

Arnot, M. & Reay, D. (2004). Voice research, learner identities and pedagogic encounters. Paper presented at Basil Bernstein Conference, Cambridge.

Ball, S. (2001). Performativities and fabrications in the education economy. In C. Husbands, C. & D. Gleeson (Eds.) *The performing school: Managing, teaching and learning in a performance culture*). London: Falmer, 210-226.

Bartholomew, H. (2005). Top set identities and the marginalisation of girls. In M. Goos, C. Kanes & R. Brown (Eds.) *Proceedings of the Fourth International Mathematics Education and Society Conference*, Centre for Learning Research, Griffith University, Queensland, Australia.

Bauman, Z. (2001). *The Individualized Society*. Cambridge: Polity Press.

Beck, U., Giddens, A. & Lash, S. (1994). *Reflexive modernization: Politics, tradition and aesthetics in the modern social order*. Cambridge: Polity Press.

Bernstein, B. (2000). *Pedagogy, symbolic control and identity* (revised edition) Maryland: Rowman and Littlefield.

Bibby, T. (2001). Primary school teachers' personal and professional relationship with mathematics. Unpublished PhD Thesis, King's College, University of London, London.

Bloor, D. (1983) *Wittgenstein: A social theory of knowledge*. New York: Columbia University Press.

Bloor, D. (1997) *Wittgenstein: Rules and institutions*. London: Routledge Kegan Paul.

Boaler, J. (1997) *Experiencing school mathematics: Teaching styles, sex and setting*. Buckingham, UK: Open University Press.

Boaler, J. (Ed.) (2000). *Multiple perspectives on mathematics teaching and learning*. Westport, CT: Ablex.

Boaler, J. (2002). The development of disciplinary relationships: knowledge, practice and identity in mathematics classrooms. *For the Learning of Mathematics, 22*(1), 42-47

Boaler, J. & Greeno, J. G. (2000). Identity, agency and knowing in mathematical worlds. In J. Boaler (Ed.) *Multiple perspectives on mathematics teaching and learning*. Westport, CT: Ablex, 171-200.

Boaler, J., Wiliam, D. & Zevenbergen, R. (2000). The construction of identity in secondary mathematics education. In J.-F. Matos & E. Fernandes (Eds.) *Investigação em educação matemática: Perspectivas e problemas*. Universidade de Madeira: Associação de Professores de Matemática, 192-202.

Cooper, B., & Dunne, M. (2000). *Assessing children's mathematical knowledge* Buckingham, UK: Open University Press.

Dowling, P. (2001). Mathematics education in late modernity. In W. Atweh, H. Forgasz & B Nebres (Eds.) *Socio-cultural aspects in mathematics education: An international perspective*. Mahwah, NJ: Lawrence Erlbaum & Associates, 3-17.

Engeström, Y. (1987). *Learning by expanding: An activity-theoretical approach to developmental research*. Helsinki: Orienta-Konsultit Oy.

Engeström, Y. (1994) Teachers as collaborative thinkers: Activity-theoretical study of an innovative teacher team. In G. Handal & S. Vaage (Eds). *Teachers' minds and actions: Research on teachers' thinking and practice.* London: Falmer.

Engeström, Y. (1999). Expansive visibilization of work: an activity-theoretical perspective. *Computer Supported Cooperative Work, 8,* 63-93.

Giddens, A. (1993). *New rules of sociological method* (2nd ed.). New York: Basic Books.

Graven, M. (2003) Investigating mathematics teacher learning within an in-service community of practice: the centrality of confidence. *Educational Studies in Mathematics 57*(2), 177-211.

Hall, S. & Du Guy, P. (Eds.) (1996). *Questions of cultural identity.* London: Sage.

Hoyles, C., Noss, R. & Pozzi, S. (2001). Proportional reasoning in nursing practice. *Journal for Research in Mathematics Education 32*(1), 4-27.

Jeffrey, B. & Woods, P. (1998). *Testing teachers: The effects of school inspections on primary teachers.* London: Falmer.

Kanes, C. (2002) Towards numeracy as a cultural historical activity system.). In P. Valero & O. Skovsmose (Eds.) *Proceedings of Third International Mathematics Education and Society Conference.* Centre for Research in Learning Mathematics, Danish University of Education, 385-394.

Kanes, C. (2003). Developing numeracy. In J. Stevenson (Ed.) *Developing vocational expertise.* Crow's Nest, Australia: Allen & Unwin, 81-109.

Kanes, C. (2005). In M. Goos, C. Kanes & R. Brown (Eds.) *Proceedings of the Fourth International Mathematics Education and Society Conference.* Centre for Learning Research, Griffith University, Queensland, Australia, 340-350.

Kehily, M. J. (2001). Issues of gender and sexuality in schools. In B. Francis & C. Skelton (Eds.) *Investigating gender: Contemporary perspectives in education.* Buckingham: Open University Press, 116-125.

Kieran, C., Forman, E., & Sfard, A. (Eds.) (2003). *Learning discourse: Discursive approaches to research in mathematics education.* Dordrecht: Kluwer.

Kilpatrick, J. (1992). A history of research in mathematics education. In D. A. Grouws (Ed.) *Handbook of research on mathematics teaching and learning.* New York: MacMillan, 3-38.

Kim, K-M. (2004). Critical theory criticized: Gidden's double hermeneutic and the problem of language game change. *Cultural Studies⇔Critical Methodologies 4*(1), 28-44.

Kuhn, T. (1978). *The Structure of Scientific Revolutions.* Chicago: Chicago University Press.

Lave, J. & Wenger, E. (1991). *Situated learning: Legitimate peripheral participation.* New York: Cambridge University Press.

Leont'ev, A. N. (1981). *Problems of the development of the mind.* Moscow: Progress

Lerman, S. (1996). Intersubjectivity in mathematics learning: A challenge to the radical constructivist paradigm? *Journal for Research in Mathematics Education, 27,* 133-150.

Lerman, S. (2000a). A case of interpretations of social: A response to Steffe and Thompson. *Journal for Research in Mathematics Education, 31,* 210-227.

Lerman, S. (2000b). The social turn in mathematics education research. In J. Boaler (Ed.) *Multiple perspectives on mathematics teaching and learning.* Westport, CT: Ablex,19-44.

Lerman, S. (2005). Learning mathematics as developing identity in the classroom. Keynote lecture to annual meeting of the Canadian Mathematics Education Study Group, University of Ottawa.

Lerman, S. (forthcoming). Socio-cultural research in mathematics education: A study of the research in PME. To be published in Proceedings.

Lerman, S. & Tsatsaroni, A. (1998). Why children fail and what mathematics education studies can do about it: The role of sociology. In P. Gates (Ed.) *Proceedings of the First International Conference on Mathematics, Education and Society (MEAS1).* Centre for the Study of Mathematics Education, University of Nottingham, 26-33.

Lerman, S. & Tsatsaroni, A. (2005). Policy and Practice in Mathematics Education. In M. Goos, C. Kanes & R. Brown (Eds.) *Proceedings of the Fourth International Mathematics Education and*

Society Conference. Centre for Learning Research, Griffith University, Queensland, Australia, 228-237.

Mendick, H. (2003). Choosing math/doing gender: a look at why there are more boys than girls in advanced mathematics classes in England. In L. Burton (Ed.). *Which way for social justice for mathematics education.* Westport, CT: Praeger,169-187.

Nunes, T., Schliemann, A. & Carraher, D. (1993). *Street mathematics & school mathematics.* New York: Cambridge University Press.

Reay, D. (2002). Shaun's story: Troubling discourses of white working-class masculinities. *Gender and Education, 14*(1), 221-234.

Santos, M. (2004). Encontros e esperas com os ardinas de Cabo Verde: Aprendizagem e participação numa prática social. Unpublished Doctoral thesis, Universidade de Lisboa.

Saxe, J. (1991) *Culture and cognitive development: Studies in mathematical understanding.* Hillsdale, NJ: Lawrence Erlbaum Associates.

Sfard, A. (1998). On two metaphors for learning and on the dangers of choosing just one. *Educational Researcher, 27*(2), 4-13.

Sfard, A. (2005). Identity that makes a difference: Substantial learning as closing the gap between actual and designated identities. In H.L. Chick & J.L. Vincent (Eds.) *Proceedings of the Twenty-ninth Meeting of the International Group for the Psychology of Mathematics Education* (Vol. 1). Department of Science and Mathematics Education, University of Melbourne, Victoria, Australia, 37-52,.

Steffe, L. P., & Thompson, P. W. (2000). Interaction or intersubjectivity?: A reply to Lerman. *Journal for Research in Mathematics Education, 31,* 191-209.

Tsatsaroni, A., Lerman, S., & Xu, G. (2003). *A sociological description of changes in the intellectual field of mathematics education research: Implications for the identities of academics.* Paper presented at annual meeting of the American Educational Research Association, Chicago. ERIC# ED482512.

Walkerdine, V. (1998). *Counting girls out (2nd Edition).* London: Falmer.

Wittgenstein, L. (1958). *Philosophical investigations.* Oxford: Blackwell.

Wittgenstein, L. (1974). *Philosophical grammar.* Oxford: Blackwell.

Stephen Lerman
London South Bank University, UK

NOTES

[1] My co-director was Anna Tsatsaroni. For papers from the project see
http://myweb.lsbu.ac.uk/~lermans/ESRCProjectHOMEPAGE.html

PAUL COBB

DISCURSIVE PERSPECTIVES ON MATHEMATICAL LEARNING: COMMENTARY ON SFARD'S AND LERMAN'S CHAPTERS

In this commentary on Anna's and Steve's chapters, I first identify several cross-cutting themes and then elaborate on key ideas proposed in each of the chapters. In doing so, I acknowledge that any commentary necessarily reflects a particular position or point of view. My own work is grounded in design research that involves formulating, testing, and revising designs for supporting students' mathematical learning. As a consequence, my primary concerns when considering the ideas that Anna and Steve present center on the extent to which they might contribute to either the formulation of instructional designs or to the development of classroom analyses that can feed back to inform the improvement of designs. In the context of this work, I have drawn heavily on central constructs of sociocultural theory but have typically found it necessary to adapt them to the purposes of design research. As a consequence of these adaptations, the theoretical position that I typically adopt is closer to the distributed cognition perspective outlined in the introduction to this section on mathematics learning as a social process. I therefore see value in constructivist analyses of individual students' mathematical reasoning, but consider it critical to situate such analyses in social context by viewing students' reasoning as acts of participation in communal classroom mathematical practices.

COMMONALITIES

As Anna and Steve both note, it is widely accepted that the social conditions of mathematics learning have a deep influence on learning processes. They are therefore careful to differentiate their theoretical viewpoints from what might be termed weak social perspectives on mathematical learning. Anna critiques such perspectives when she discusses what she terms "cognition plus" approaches. These approaches account for learning in terms of internal cognitive processes, but acknowledge that cognition is influenced by social interactions with others and, to a lesser extent, by the tools that people use to accomplish goals. In his critique, Steve extends the range of external factors considered in "cognition plus" approaches to include cultural values, poverty and deprivation, and affect. As he clarifies, these factors are treated as disturbances to be overcome if "true learning" is to occur. Thus, as Anna and Steve both point out, although the cognition plus

J. Maasz, W. Schloeglmann (Eds.), New Mathematics Education Research and Practice, 189–201.

view expands the conditions that must be taken into account when developing adequate explanations of cognition and learning, it does not reconceptualize the basic nature of cognition. They both challenge the assumption that social and cultural processes can be neatly partitioned off from cognitive processes and treated merely as external conditions for them. In doing so, they follow Vygotsky in arguing that children's minds are formed as they appropriate aspects of the social and cultural practices in which they participate. Thus, in their view, social and cultural processes do not merely condition internal cognitive processes. Instead, they are fundamental to the very development of cognitive processes. Anna is particularly explicit on this point when she clarifies that researchers who adopt a strong social perspective view "all the unique human capacities as resulting from the fundamental fact that humans are social beings, engaged in collective activities from the day they are born and throughout their lives".

In developing their strong social perspectives, Anna and Steve both find inspiration in Wittgenstein's later writings. Anna emphasizes Wittgenstein's claim that thinking cannot be separated from speaking, and goes on to develop her basic proposition that thinking can be viewed as the individualized form of interpersonal communicating. For his part, Steve highlights Wittgenstein's closely related claim that the meaning that particular words (including mathematical terms) have for people is synonymous with how they use them. Anna and Steve both question the widely held assumption that we first formulate our thoughts without language and then express those thoughts in language. In doing so, they reject the view that thinking precedes and is primary to speaking and, more generally, to communication. This position might easily be dismissed as a variant of psychological behaviorism. However, this summary judgment would misrepresent their intent. This become clear once we note that the goal of the approaches they propose is to account for people's actions rather than their observed behavior. As Taylor (1995) clarifies, behavior is concerned with physical responses, including speaking, whereas actions are concerned with the intentionality of observed behavior. This concern for intentionality immediately focuses attention on the very phenomena that were banished from analysis by psychological behaviorism, meaning and understanding.

On my reading, Anna's and Steve's intent is to propose alternative analytical approaches that reject the traditional separation between thinking and communicating while simultaneously accounting for the development of meaning and understanding. Rorty (1979), himself an admirer of Wittgenstein's later philosophy, terms explanatory schemes of this type epistemological behaviorism precisely because they question the assumption of internal cognitive process isolated from speaking and communicating. Anna emphasizes this epistemological behaviorist stance by introducing the term commognitive to indicate that, in her view, cognition and communication are but different aspects of a single process. The proposals that she and Steve make are radical, particularly in a field in which the notion of internal, mental concepts is employed as a basic explanatory construct and is assumed to underpin what students say and do. However, as the sample analysis that Anna presents makes clear, their proposals are radical not because they eschew a focus on meaning, but because of the manner in which they attempt to account for meaning.

In developing their positions, Anna and Steve are both explicit in characterizing communication as a rule-driven activity. Anna emphasizes that rules regulate communication, and Steve argues that understanding can be accounted for in terms of following and adapting rules. They also describe these collective rules in similar ways. Anna refers to them as historically established customs and Steve calls them conventions. In my view, these formulations are open to misinterpretation. In everyday discourse, we speak of conventions when we have the sense that particular norms or rules could be modified and attribute their source to tradition or custom. Mathematical norms or standards do not appear to fit this everyday view of conventions. We collectively act towards the norms of mathematics as ahistorical truths whose source we attribute not merely to custom but to the way the world stands. Davis and Hersh (1981) argue forcefully that in engaging in mathematics, we necessarily act as Platonists who are investigating a timeless mathematical reality.

The distinctions that Much and Shweder (1978) draw between qualitatively different types of rules or norms are helpful in resolving the apparent clash between the claim that mathematical norms are customs or conventions, and our experience of them as ahistorical truths. Much and Shweder focus on those moments when a norm is perceived to have been breached and note that accusations are typically followed by accounts that attempt to make the perceived transgression more understandable. As they demonstrate, the consequence of breaching a convention is social disapproval, whereas the consequence for breaching a norm is error in how the world stands. In light of Much and Shweder's analysis, I offer a friendly amendment to Anna's and Steve's proposals: The rules of mathematics are historically contingent, human-made norms that have the quality of truths rather than merely of conventions or customs. This formulation is, I believe, entirely consistent with the central trust of Wittgenstein's arguments.

As a second elaboration, I want to unpack the notion of people following rules. Anna makes an important observation in this regard when she clarifies that the rules of communication "are to be understood as observer's constructs, and not as guiding principles, followed by individual actors in a conscious, deliberate way." This clarification echoes Blumer's (1969) observation that people respond to the material and social world as they understand it, not to theoretical constructs that researchers project into their worlds when analyzing their activity. Bauersfeld (1980) emphasized this crucial point by differentiating cases in which people's observed activity fits rules posited by an observer from cases in which rules actually guide people's actions. To illustrate this point, I take as an example a relatively common pattern of classroom interaction called the elicitation pattern identified by Voigt (1985). This pattern consists of four phases:

• The teacher asks an open-ended question or poses an open-ended task and elicits responses from the students.

• The students present their responses and the teacher does not evaluate their contributions but instead calls on other students who indicate that they have developed different solutions.
• The teacher begins to give increasingly explicit cues about the solution process that he or she has in mind until a student produces the desired solution.
• The teacher gives a reflective summary of the exchange that explicitly relates the desired response to the original question or task.

This description of the elicitation pattern specifies rules for the teacher's and students' activity in each of the phases. However, Voigt clarifies that the teacher and the students are typically not aware of either the pattern in their joint activity or the rules that comprise it. The pattern and rules are observer constructs. The teacher and students instead know how to act moment by moment in the course of their ongoing interaction as informed not by the observer's rules but by their understanding of each other's expectations. In my view, the most that can be claimed is that the teacher's and students' actions fit the rules posited by the observing researcher. To account for how the teacher and students collectively regenerate the pattern, Voigt also found it necessary to take account of their ongoing interpretations of each other's actions. This acknowledgement of people's interpretive activity and thus of agency has the added benefit of making it possible to account for the process of going beyond rules to which Steve refers.

Having identified and commented on several themes that are common to the two chapters, I now focus on the ideas advanced in each chapter commencing with Anna's contribution.

PARTICIPATING IN PARTICIPATIONIST DISCOURSE ON MATHEMATICAL LEARNING

In her chapter, Anna develops the position that thinking can be usefully defined as the individualized form of the activity of communicating. In doing so, she makes the important observation that children learn not by attempting to make sense of what Dewey (1929/1958) disparagingly referred to as brute reality, but by attempting to make sense of other people's vision of the world. She argues that, in the case of mathematical learning, this sense making involves a process of individualizing collective, historically developed mathematical discourse. In the introduction to this section of the book, I questioned the usefulness of research conducted thus far within the sociocultural perspective for mathematics educators interested in issues of instructional design and teaching. Against this background, Anna's chapter makes a critical contribution. Sociocultural theorists repeat the claim that thinking originates in social action with such regularity that it sometimes takes on the quality of a mantra. In contrast, examples of solid empirical analyses that document how specific forms of thinking originate from specific forms of collective activity are few and far between. Further, the few convincing analyses typically deal with relatively global cognitive functions such as reflection rather than with discipline-specific forms of thinking.

Anna goes a long way towards rectifying this situation by specifying the collective activity, mathematical discourse that might be individualized in the course of mathematical learning. In delineating what makes a discourse mathematical, she does not limit her focus to particular words and their use but also includes visual mediators as well as routines and endorsed narratives. This is important from the point of view of instructional design given that the development of physical materials, text and computer-based graphics, and conventional and non-standard notation systems are all means of supporting mathematical learning. In addition, Anna makes good on her claims about the usefulness of her perspective by presenting a convincing analysis of an adult attempting to support two young children's arithmetical learning. In doing so, she illustrates that the inferences she makes delineate the nature of the individual children's discourses or, in other words, the nature of the game for them, as well as the specific meanings that number words might have for them. This analysis provides a compelling response to a charge that Steve notes is often leveled against sociocultural theorists, "Where's the mathematics?"

Having acknowledged the contribution of Anna's commognitional viewpoint, I want to raise several points of potential clarification. The first concerns the process of individualizing collective mathematical discourse such that it becomes a discourse for oneself. Anna states that this process occurs as learners attempt to make sense of other people's visions of the world and stresses the importance of communicational conflicts. In presenting the sample analysis, she goes on to clarify that the aim of the activity at least for the adult is that the two girls will create statements that the adult would endorse as legitimate responses to the question, "Which of the boxes has more marbles?" The issue that remains unclear for me is that of how the children actually make sense of the adult's vision of the world and create endorsable statements. On my reading, these references to creating and making sense leave space for analyses that focus on the development of the individual children's interpretations or, as Anna would prefer to say, their individual discourses. Although it will probably be an anathema to Anna, I think that it is worthwhile to consider adapting constructs from constructivist accounts of mathematical learning when addressing this issue. More generally, I contend that such a space opens up as soon as an analytical approach moves beyond social and cultural determinism, as is the case with the viewpoints that Anna and Steve both develop.

The second point of clarification concerns the notion of community. Anna indicates that mathematical discourse is but one of many types of discourse within a society, and that these discourses can be distinguished in terms of the four characteristics that she proposes (i.e., words and their use, visual mediators, routines, and endorsable narratives). She then draws the immediate implication, namely that "any human society may be divided into partially overlapping communities of discourses." Anna is well aware that these wide communities of discourse should not be confused with what I would term local communities of practice: "membership in the wider community of discourse is won through participation in communicational activities of any [local] collective that practices this discourse, be this collective as small as it may."

The issue that arises for me is the relation between these local communities and the broader discourse into which children are being inducted. Anna appears to view this relation as relatively unproblematic. On my reading, she considers the role of a more knowledgeable other (e.g., a parent or a teacher) to be critical in the local collective and characterizes this more knowledgeable other as a representative of historically established mathematical discourse. In the sample analysis, the adult's activity is framed as mediating between mathematical discourse and the two children's individual discourses. In my view, it would be useful to include an additional level of analysis to this analytic approach that currently focuses on 1) the more knowledgeable as a representative of mathematical discourse, and 2) children's individual discourses or, in my terms, their individual interpretations. This additional level would focus on the local discourse that is jointly established by the members of the local collective in the course of their ongoing interactions. This elaboration of the analytic scheme is important because the local discourse in which children participate constitutes the immediate social setting of their learning. As we know only too well, the forms of discourse jointly constituted by the teacher and students in a classroom can depart significantly from historically established mathematical discourse.

This proposal instantiates Vaughn's (1992; 2002) argument concerning the importance of coordinating analyses at what she terms the macro, meso, and micro levels. The institutionalized mathematical discourse on which Anna focuses corresponds to Vaughn's macro level, and individual children's discourses correspond to the micro level that comprises interpretations of ongoing interactions and events. The meso level that I content would augment Anna's analytic framework comprises taken-for-granted assumptions originating in practical activity that create and recreate routines that constitute the culture of the local collective. Vaughn indicates that her proposal is an elaboration of Bourdieu's (1977) notion of habitus. Crudely put, a habitus consists of a system of dispositions that function as categories of perception and assessment as well as organizing principles for action. Consistent with Wittgenstein's metaphor of historically established discourses as language game, Bourdieu spoke of a habitus as a feel for a social game that had been embodied and turned into second nature. Bourdieu proposed this notion as a microsociological complement to institutional theory that would link individual activity and historically established discourses. Against this background, Vaughn (2002) draws on a series of empirical analyses to illustrate the importance of the meso level in theories of practical action. As she puts it, the discourses of a local collective vary from institutionalized discourses "such that they become specifically tailored to practical activity in everyday life, reproducing universalistic symbol systems in the environment, but elaborating them in locally particularistic ways" (2002, p. 48). In my view, Vaughn's argument applies to Anna's as well as to Bourdieu's analytic scheme.

The third point of clarification builds directly from the second and concerns the need to distinguish between different local elaborations of mathematical discourse.

In her chapter, Anna takes on the challenge of differentiating mathematical discourse from other forms of discourse in society, particularly everyday discourse and other disciplinary discourses. For this purpose, it is quite reasonable to delineate a single, institutionalized discourse. However, I predict that it will be essential to make additional distinctions between different forms of mathematical discourse if Anna extends her approach to also focus on the discourses constituted by local collectives such as the teacher and students in particular classrooms. These local discourses clearly differ in terms of the way in which mathematical words are used and thus their locally normative meanings. In addition, numerous studies of the classroom microculture document that the very nature of the mathematical game or, in other words, what it means to know and do mathematics can vary significantly from one classroom to another.

As an illustration, an analysis in which I was involved some years ago revealed that the normative mathematical activities constituted in most American elementary classrooms have the quality of either instructions or conventions rather than truths in Much and Shweder's (1978) terms (Cobb, Wood, Yackel, & McNeal, 1992). In this regard, mathematics as it was established in these classrooms differed in fundamental ways from the historically developed mathematical discourse delineated by Anna. In contrast, the normative mathematical activities constituted in a classroom in which we conducted a design experiment were better aligned with institutionalized mathematical discourse in that they had the quality of mathematical truths. The findings of this and other studies indicate the necessity of differentiating between historically developed mathematical discourse on the one hand and various forms of school mathematical discourse on the other (cf., Richards, 1991). These distinctions are critical in my view in that students are actually being inducted into the local discourses as they interact with other members of local collectives.

In concluding this discussion of Anna's chapter, I want to reiterate that, in my judgment, the commognitional perspective she is developing has the potential to overcome some of the most critical limitations of sociocultural theory as it has been applied to issues of mathematical learning and teaching. It is clear from a reading of Anna's recent papers that this perspective is still a work in progress that she continues to refine and elaborate. I consider this line of work to be one of the most important current developments in mathematics education research. The relatively detailed nature of my comments should be interpreted as a compliment (and not a back-handed one). Anna's work deserves too be widely read and discussed.

ELABORATING THE 'STRONG' SOCIAL TURN

In her chapter, Anna proposes a specific scheme for analyzing mathematical learning. In contrast, Steve presents a broad overview of approaches that draw on sociocultural theory and makes a number of observations about theorizing in mathematics education. With one exception, I agree with his observations and will, for the most part, merely elaborate on the issues that he introduces.

195

The one point of significant disagreement concerns Steve's claim that "we are best served either by studies of children's learning of mathematics in terms of their individual constructions, or studies of how children's mathematical ways of thinking are brought into alignment with those of the teacher and the authority of mathematics itself, but not both together." Steve goes on to clarify that he takes this stance because constructivism and sociocultural theory are what he terms parallel discourses that are grounded in incommensurable epistemologies. I think that he is surely correct on this latter point. Nonetheless, I contend that it is worthwhile to appropriate and adapt ideas from different theoretical perspectives including constructivism and sociocultural theory as we pursue our concerns and interests as mathematics educators. In commenting on Anna's chapter, for example, I indicated that it is reasonable to consider adapting constructs from constructivist accounts of mathematical learning when accounting for how children make sense of others' visions of the world. The key term in this approach is adaptation in that it implies that the process of appropriating particular constructs from either constructivism or sociocultural theory can involve epistemologically recasting those constructs. As an illustration, I have found it useful to draw on conceptual analyses of students' reasoning in specific mathematical domains that have been developed from a constructivist perspective (e.g., Konold, Pollatsek, Well, & Gagnon, 1997; Thompson & Thompson, 1996). These analyses delineate what Anna might term students' visions of the world at particular points in their development and attempt to account for those inferred visions in terms of mental processes such as schemes, conceptual operations, and so forth. It is the inferences about students' visions of the world that I have found valuable. On my reading, Anna makes inferences of this type in her sample analysis when she attempts to document the two children's individual discourses. The epistemological recasting involves stripping away the account of these visions in terms of internal mental constructs and instead frames students thinking as acts of participation in (locally) collective practices that involve the use of various visual mediators.

The proposal that we view different theoretical perspectives as potential sources of ideas that we can appropriate and modify for our purposes as mathematics educators resonates with Gravemeijer's (1994b) description of instructional design as a process of bricolage.

[Design] resembles the thinking process that Lawler (1985) characterizes by the French word bricolage, a metaphor taken from Claude Levi–Strauss. A bricoleur is a handy man who invents pragmatic solutions in practical situation. [T]he bricoleur has become adept at using whatever is available. The bricoleur's tools and materials are very heterogeneous: Some remain from earlier jobs, others have been collected with a certain project in mind. (p. 447)

Similarly, I suggest that rather than adhering to one particular theoretical perspective, we act as bricoleurs by adapting ideas from a range of theoretical sources. This is clearly an issue on which Steve and I will have to agree to disagree for the present. It should, however, provide grist for future conversations.

Toward the end of his chapter, Steve draws on Bernstein's distinction between vertical and horizontal knowledge structures to challenge the feasibility of attempting to develop a single, unified theoretical perspective in mathematics education. He instead predicts that "mathematics education knowledge will continue to grow both within [theoretical] discourses and by the insertion of new discourses in parallel with existing ones." Steve's formulation provides a useful antidote to the tendency to portray theoretical developments in mathematics education as a linear, historical sequence of perspectives, each of which overcomes the limitations of its predecessors. As Guerra (1998) notes, narratives of this type are based on the implicit metaphor of theoretical developments as a relentless march of progress. Guerra also clarifies that such narratives are historical reconstructions that edit out tensions and conflicts between co-existing perspectives. I would only add to Steve's account that new theoretical discourses typically emerge in opposition to existing perspectives. In the case at hand, for example, Steve and Anna both indicate that the viewpoints they propose have emerged in opposition to cognitive and developmental psychology in general, and to Piagetian theory in particular.

It is worth clarifying that Steve's remarks about the likelihood of a unified theoretical perspective emerging do imply a state of intellectual anarchy in which adherents to different paradigms remain trapped in isolated theoretical enclaves, doomed to talk past each other. In their chapters, Anna and Steve both clarify their theoretical stances by taking cognitive theory as a point of contrast. In doing so, they illustrate Feyerabend's (1975) observation that we cope with incommensurability in both theoretical and everyday settings by attempting to draw comparisons and contrasts. This process of attempting to communicate across theoretical perspectives can be further aided by aligning concrete concerns and interests. The sample analysis that Anna presents is a case in point in that she consciously adjusts to the concerns of cognitive and developmental psychologists who seek to understand young children's numerical thinking. As a second illustration of the alignment of concrete concerns and interests, cognitive information-processing psychology was the most prominent perspective in US mathematics education 15 years ago. I was quite critical of both this general perspective and the laboratory studies of students' mathematical reasoning conducted by its proponents. A number of these researchers subsequently began to conduct studies in which they worked in classrooms to test and revise instructional designs to support students' learning. I found that I had much to discuss with these researchers as a consequence of our shared interest in instructional design at the classroom level even in cases where there continued to be fundamental differences in our underlying theoretical stances. The lesson I took from this experience is that the alignment of concrete concerns and interests is at least as important as the alignment in theoretical perspectives. This acknowledgement of the specific practices in which researchers engage as they conduct empirical studies, and the concerns and interests that motivate those practices, is of course entirely consistent with a sociocultural perspective on communication in any field including mathematics education.

In his chapter, Steve argues that research needs to take a step away from practice to in order to say something about it. As he indicates, the goal of research is to produce generalizable knowledge. The stepping away inherent in the generation of such knowledge necessarily involves employing theoretical constructs to frame instances of practice as cases of broader classes of phenomena. In my experience, the challenge of stepping away from practice while still having something relevant to say about it is far from trivial. It is, for example, easy to slide into a separate, self-contained theoretical discourse structured by unrelated concerns and interests. I can best illustrate one approach to this challenge by teasing out the relations between theory and practice implicit in classroom-based design research.

One of the central problems with which I and my colleagues have struggled is that of accounting for students' mathematical development as it occurs in the social situation of the classroom in a manner that is specifically tailored to the demands of instructional design. The interpretive framework we developed while addressing this problem emerged over a period of several years as we attempted to understand specific events in the classrooms in which we worked (Cobb & Yackel, 1996). The relation between theory and practice implicit in the framework is therefore reflexive. On the one hand, theory as exemplified by the interpretive framework grew out of our efforts to support students' mathematical learning. On the other hand, interpretations of classroom events organized in terms of the emerging framework fed back to inform the ongoing instructional development effort. A central feature of this process is that theoretical constructs evolve in response to problems and issues encountered in the classroom. As a consequence, the resulting constructs do not stand apart from instructional practice but instead remain grounded in it.

Similar remarks can be made about the development of Realistic Mathematics Education (RME) design theory in that it emerged from and yet remains grounded in the activities of designing and experimenting in classrooms over a 25-year period (Gravemeijer, 1994a; Streefland, 1993; Treffers, 1987). The key point to note in both cases is that theory did not emerge from classrooms per se, but instead from the activity of experimenting in classrooms. As a consequence, the interpretive framework and the RME design theory both reflect the concerns of participants in the learning-teaching process rather than those of a disinterested spectator to classroom events. For example, the interpretive framework is grounded in our interpretive routines as we attempted to make sense of specific classroom episodes while planning for subsequent classroom sessions. Similarly, the design theory captures regularities in the process of designing a variety of specific sequences of instructional activities. The design theory and the interpretive framework both describe in general terms a way of coming to grips with and making judgments in concrete cases. I suggest that this approach to theory development helps ameliorate the tendency for theorizing to become an end in itself rather than a means to the end of contributing to the improvement of mathematics learning and teaching.

CONCLUDING REFLECTION

The final comment that I want to make concerns an issue that Steve raises at several points in his chapter that of equity in students' access to significant mathematical ideas. In my view, the circularities that Anna argues is inherent to mathematical learning have potentially far-reaching implications, particularly for equity. Anna uses her sample analysis to illustrate this circularity, contending that if the two children are ever to use institutionalized numerical discourse to solve their own mathematical problems, they must be aware of the advantages of the relevant discursive procedures. However, in order to become aware of these advantages, they already have to use the numerical discourse. It is in this sense that Anna contends that mathematical learning is inherently circular. Anna then goes on to draw the logical implication, namely that students initially need to be prepared to participate in the mathematical discourse in a ritualized way. She suggests that students' motivation for doing so is a need for communication, which grows out of the even more fundamental need for social acceptance. I would add that, for older students, the reasons for initially participating in mathematical discourse in a ritualized way might include attaining ends other than social acceptance by the teacher and the school, and might include entry to college and future high-status careers. D'Amato (1992) calls rationales of this type in which learning mathematics in school is a means of attaining other ends structural significance. It has been well documented that not all students have access to a structural rationale. R. Gutiérrez (2004, August) observes, for example, that many urban students do not see themselves going to college, hold activist stances, have more pressing daily concerns (e.g., housing, safety, healthcare), or do not believe that hard work and effort will be rewarded in terms of future educational and economic opportunities. D'Amato (1992), Erickson (1992), and Mehan, Hubbard, and Villanueva (1994) all document that students' access to a structural rationale varies as a consequence of family history, race or ethnic history, class structure, and caste structure within society. The immediate implication of Anna's analysis is therefore that there are inherent inequities in students' motivation to learn mathematics in school that are associated with the extent to which they have access to a structural rationale. Given the disquieting nature of this conclusion, part of me hopes that aspects of Anna's analysis might require modification. At a minimum, Anna highlights the importance of cultivating students' mathematical interests as an explicit goal of both design and teaching.

REFERENCES

Bauersfeld, H. (1980). Hidden dimensions in the so-called reality of a mathematics classroom. *Educational Studies in Mathematics, 11*, 23-41.

Blumer, H. (1969). Symbolic interactionism: Perspectives and method. Englewood Cliffs, NJ: Prentice-Hall.

Bourdieu, P. (1977). *Outline of a theory of practice.* Cambridge: Cambridge University Press.

Cobb, P., Wood, T., Yackel, E., & McNeal, G. (1992). Characteristics of classroom mathematics traditions: An interactional analysis. *American Educational Research Journal, 29*, 573-602.

Cobb, P., & Yackel, E. (1996). Constructivist, emergent, and sociocultural perspectives in the context of developmental research. *Educational Psychologist, 31*, 175-190.

D'Amato, J. (1992). Resistance and compliance in minority classrooms. In E. Jacob & C. Jordan (Eds.), *Minority education: Anthropological perspectives*. Norwood, NJ: Ablex, 181-207.

Davis, P. J., & Hersh, R. (1981). *The mathematical experience*. Boston: Houghton Mifflin.

de Certeau, M. (1984). *The practice of everyday life*. Berkeley: University of California Press.

Dewey, J. (1929/1958). *Experience and nature*. New York: Dober.

Emirbayer, M., & Mische, A. (1998). What is agency? *American Journal of Sociology, 103*, 962-1023.

Erickson, F. (1992). Transformation and school success: The policies and culture of educational achievement. In E. Jacob & C. Jordan (Eds.), *Minority education: Anthropological perspectives.*. Norwood, NJ: Ablex, 27-51.

Feldman, M. S., & Pentland, B. T. (2003). Reconceptualizing organizational routines as a source of flexibility and change. *Administrative Science Quarterly, 48*, 94-118.

Feyerabend, P. (1975). *Against method*. London: Verso.

Garfinkel, H. (1967). *Studies in ethnomethodology*. Englewood Cliffs, NJ: Prentice Hall.

Gravemeijer, K. (1994a). *Developing realistic mathematics education*. Utrecht, The Netherlands: CD-ß Press.

Gravemeijer, K. (1994b). Educational development and developmental research. *Journal for Research in Mathematics Education, 25*, 443-471.

Guerra, J. C. (1998). *Close to home: Oral and literate practices in a transnational Mexicano community*. New York: Teachers College Press.

Gutiérrez, R. (2004). The complex nature of practice for urban (mathematics) teachers. Paper presented at the Rockefeller Symposium on the Practice of School Improvement: Theory, Methodology, and Relevance, Bellagio, Italy.

Jahnke, H. N. (1989). Mathematics and systematic thinking: A historical note on an acute problem. In L. Bazzini & H. G. Steiner (Eds.), *Proceedings of the First Italian-German Bilateral Symposium on Didactics of Mathematics*. Pavia, Italy: Universita di Pavia, 59-71.

Konold, C., Pollatsek, A., Well, A., & Gagnon, A. (1997). Students' analyzing data: Research of critical barriers. In J. B. Garfield & G. Burrill (Eds.), *Research on the role of technology in teaching and learning statistics: Proceedings of the 19996 International Association for Statistics Education Roundtable Conference*. Voorburg, The Netherlands: International Statistics Institute,151-167.

Lawler, R. W. (1985). *Computer experience and cognitive development: A child's learning in a computer culture*. New York: Wiley.

Mehan, H., Hubbard, L., & Villanueva, I. (1994). Forming academic identities: Accommodation without assimilation among involuntary minorities. *Anthropology and Education Quarterly, 25*, 91-117.

Much, N. C., & Shweder, R. A. (1978). Speaking of rules: The analysis of culture in breach. *New Directions for Child Development, 2*, 19-39.

Richards, J. (1991). Mathematical discussions. In E. von Glasersfeld (Ed.), *Radical constructivism in mathematics education*. The Netherlands: Kluwer, 13–52.

Rogoff, B. (1995). Observing sociocultural activity on planes: participatory appropriation, guided participation, and apprenticeship. In J. V. Wertsch, P. del Rio, & A. Alvarez (Eds.), *Sociocultural studies of mind*. New York: Cambridge University Press, 139-164.

Rorty, R. (1979). *Philosophy and the mirror of nature*. Princeton, NJ: Princeton University Press.

Searle, J. R. (1983). *Intentionality*. Cambridge: Cambridge University Press.

Steffe, L. P., & Thompson, P. W. (2000). Teaching experiment methodology: Underlying principles and essential elements. In A. Kelly & R. Lesh (Eds.), *Handbook of research design in mathematics and science education*. Mahwah, NJ: Erlbaum, 267-307.

Streefland, L. (1993). Fractions: A realistic approach. In T. P. Carpenter, E. Fennema, & T. A. Romberg (Eds.). *Rational numbers: Integrating research*. Hillsdale, NJ: Erlbaum, 289-325.

Suchman, L. A. (1987). *Plans and situated actions: The problem of human-machine communication*. New York: Cambridge University Press.

Taylor, C. (1995). *Philosophical arguments.* Cambridge, MA: Harvard University Press.

Thompson, A. G., & Thompson, P. W. (1996). Talking about rates conceptually, part II: Mathematical knowledge for teaching. *Journal for Research in Mathematics Education, 27,* 2-24.

Treffers, A. (1987). *Three dimensions: A model of goal and theory description in mathematics instruction - The Wiskobas Project.* Dordrecht, The Netherlands: Reidel.

Vaughan, D. (1992). Theory elaboration: The heuristics of case analysis. In C. R. H. S. Becker (Ed.), What is a case? *Exploring the foundations of social inquiry.* New York: Cambridge University Press.

Vaughan, D. (2002). Signals and interpretive work: The role of culture in a theory of practical action. In K. A. Cerulo (Ed.). *Culture in mind: Towards a sociology of culture and cognition.* New York: Routledge, 28-54.

Voigt, J. (1985). Patterns and routines in classroom interaction. *Recherches en Didactique des Mathematiques, 6,* 69-118.

Paul Cobb
Vanderbilt University Peabody, USA

GILAH C LEDER

AFFECT AND MATHEMATICS LEARNING

INTRODUCTION

Exploring the interaction between affect and mathematics learning raises a number of important challenges. What should be regarded as the boundaries of this topic? The long standing and continuing interest in the affective domain in mathematics education has yielded a multitude of distinct and overlapping descriptions of affect, highlighting its multi-faceted and somewhat elusive nature. To what extent do instrument limitations influence how and what aspects of affect are measured, recognized, and discussed in the literature?

The many elements subsumed under the heading of affect can not be measured directly but need to be inferred from the ways in which an individual responds to specially designed instruments or cues, or behaves in certain situations. In the early years of psychology, research on the more stable aspects of affect (attitudes and beliefs), measured most commonly by self report paper-and-pencil measures, was most prevalent. Over time, as more refined and robust measurement techniques were devised, increased attention has been directed as well to the more volatile aspects of affect (emotions and values). Is affect worthy of research attention *per se* or is the extent to which achievement in mathematics is influenced by affective factors of primary concern? In this respect McLeod's (1992) summary is worth noting: "Research on affect has been voluminous, but not particularly powerful in influencing the field of mathematics education. It seems that research on instruction in most cases goes on without any particular attention to affective issues" (p. 590). What theoretical frameworks optimally explain or predict how affect facilitates or inhibits mathematical thinking and learning?

In the remainder of this chapter and in the two chapters that follows, issues such as those cited above are addressed in more detail.

AFFECT DELINEATED

In daily life, many terms are used to describe affect. Within the research literature, the affective domain is often conceptualized in terms of attitudes, beliefs, values, emotions, and feelings. Descriptors such as interests, opinions, moods, and motivation are often also included. Aiken, an influential contributor to research on the affective components of mathematics education stated that descriptors such "as attitudes, interests, opinions, beliefs, and values can all be viewed as personality

J. Maasz, W. Schloeglmann (Eds.), New Mathematics Education Research and Practice, 203–208.

characteristics or motivators of behavior" (1996, p. 169). These terms, he continued, are often used loosely and interchangeably.

Research on affect, in common with educational research more generally, is carried out in many countries and is certainly not limited to those who write in English. Language issues can confound intellectual exchanges: subtle distinctions in common meanings of the various terms subsumed under affect can be exaggerated or lost when translated into other languages. Goldin (2004) has argued bluntly that we still do not "have a precise, shared language for describing the affective domain, within a theoretical framework that permits its systematic study (p. I -109). Mandler's (1989, p. 3) description of affect comprises one example:

> The term affect has meant many things to many people, acquiring interpretations that range from "hot" to "cold". At the hot end, affect is used coextensively with the work *emotion*, implying an intensity dimension; at the cold end, it is often used without passion, referring to preferences, likes and dislikes, and choices.

Aiken's description of attitudes serves as another example. An attitude, he postulated, "consists of cognitive (knowledge of intellect), affect (emotion and motivation), and performance (behavior or action) components" (1996, p. 168). More recently, Goldin (2002) described a number of other subtle operational differences:

> In the individual we can distinguish certain subdomains of affective representation ...: (1) *emotions* (rapidly changing states of feeling, mild to very intense, that are usually local or embedded in context), (2) *attitudes* (moderately stable predispositions toward ways of feeling in classes of situations, involving a balance of affect and cognition), (3) *beliefs* (internal representations to which the holder attributes truth, validity, or applicability, usually stable and highly cognitive, may be highly structured), and (4) *values, ethics, and morals* (deeply-held preferences, possibly characterized as "personal truths", stable, highly affective as well as cognitive, may also be highly structured). (p. 61)

Both theoretical orientation and measurement options have often determined how affect is operationally defined and which aspects attract research interest.

MEASUREMENT OF AFFECT

Early attempts to measure aspects of affectivity focussed on "cold" affect, to use Mandler's terminology, and – as already mentioned above - relied heavily on self report paper-and-pencil measures, including Thurstone, Likert, Guttman, and Osgood's semantic differential scales. Because of their now recognized doubtful validity, Thurstone scales have lost their popularity in recent years. Guttman scales, which are rather difficult to construct, have always been used sparingly. Osgood's semantic differential scales, which rely on participants' responses to lists of bipolar adjectives covering evaluative, potency, and activity aspects, enable measurement congruent with the cognitive, affective, and behavioural components of attitudes and beliefs captured in definitions such as the one favoured by Aiken and cited in an earlier section. Likert scales, which consist of a series of statements about the attitude object or activity of interest, represent a common approach to the measurement of affect, and in particular attitudes.

Several decades ago mathematical affect was often, and simplistically, equated with mathematics anxiety and attitudes to mathematics, typically inferred from Likert scales such as those devised by Fennema and Sherman (1976). An article published by the latter authors (Fennema & Sherman, 1977) in which their then newly constructed Fennema—Sherman mathematics attitudes scale [MAS] was used to explore a link between gender differences in mathematics achievement, spatial visualization and affective factors, has since spawned much research. Indeed, this article has been identified as among the most frequently cited publications in mainstream journals of educational psychology (Walberg & Haertel, 1992), and the MAS, partly or in full, as a particularly commonly used measure of attitude.

IMPACT OF AFFECT

McLeod (1992, p. 575) has argued that "affect is a central concern of students and teachers, (but) research on affect in mathematics education continues to reside on the periphery of the field". Yet references to the importance of engaging students, affectively as well as cognitively, are found in many curriculum documents. Well over two decades ago Cockcroft (1982) wrote in his influential *Mathematics counts*:

> It is to be expected that most teachers will attach considerable importance to the development of good attitudes among the pupils whom they teach... Attitudes are derived from teachers' attitudes... and to an extent from parents' attitudes. ... Attitude to mathematics is correlated ... with the peer-group's attitude. (p. 61)

In a similar vein, the powerful National Council of Teachers of Mathematics [NCTM] argued:

> Students' understanding of mathematics, their ability to use it to solve problems, and their *confidence in*, and *disposition toward*, mathematics are all shaped by the teaching they encounter in school. The improvement of mathematics education for all students requires effective mathematics teaching (NCTM, 2000, pp 16-17). (Emphasis added)

More recently, those conducting the Programme for International Student Assessment [PISA] concluded that data gathered as part of this large scale study revealed "how motivation, self-related beliefs and emotional factors are linked to the adoption of effective learning strategies, and thus can help students become life long learners" (OECD, 2004, p.12).

It is widely acknowledged that those concerned with gender and mathematics learning have recognized, more often than colleagues focussing on other variables influencing mathematics learning, the importance of affective factors and have included affectivity in their research designs. A brief overview of major developments in this field illustrates the importance of the role played by affect.

Impact of Affect – Gender

During the early years of research on gender and mathematics, the 1970s and 1980s, much effort was spent documenting gender differences in performance on mathematical tasks and in participation in mathematics once this subject was no longer compulsory. Differences found were typically attributed to inadequate educational opportunities, social barriers, or biased instructional methods and materials (Leder, Forgasz, & Solar, 1996). The removal of school and curriculum barriers, and if necessary the resocialisation of females, were initially thought to be fruitful paths for achieving gender equity. Male (white and western) norms of performance and participation levels were largely accepted as appropriate for all students. Accordingly, special interventions and programs were mounted so that, in line with the tenets of *liberal feminism*, females might attain achievements equal to those of males (Leder, 1992; Fennema & Hart, 1994; Hanna, 1996). Thus textbooks began to include female friendly settings, special single sex programs were put in place, successful (contemporary) female mathematicians and users of advanced mathematics were used as role models in schools, and the importance of mathematics for entry to an extensive range of courses and occupations was stressed. When such initiatives were evaluated, it appeared that they were often followed by changes in students' beliefs about mathematics and about themselves as learners of mathematics (Forgasz, Leder, & Kloosterman, 2004).

Over time, the earlier crude comparisons between groups of females and males became more refined: gender differences between – as well as within – groups began to be acknowledged. No longer was it thought appropriate to ignore the value and diversity of different ways of knowing, nor the harm done in the past, to individuals as well as to larger groups, of denying this diversity. The focus moved to a possible reconsideration of the nature of mathematics itself and a reexamination of the pedagogical methods used in mathematics. Thus beliefs about mathematics and its teaching began to be examined within a framework more accepting of females. The concerns of *social feminism* and *radical feminism* began to shape new initiatives to encourage women to study mathematics, to question traditional beliefs about mathematics, about users of mathematics, and indeed about working and life expectations. Curricular materials and instructional strategies introduced during the 1980s and 1990s reflected these changes (Rogers & Kaiser, 1995; Jacobs, Becker, & Gilmer, 2001).

Contemporary reviews of gender differences in academic performance and participation in education sketch quite a different picture from that obtained 30 years earlier: Cox, Leder, and Forgasz (2004) report data highlighting females' superior performance in recent (Australian) mathematics examinations, including the most challenging mathematics subjects. Again such findings are not confined to Australia, with many examples pointing to boys' poorer performance in a large range of subjects now emanating as well from the UK and the USA.

The body of research with a dual focus on gender and mathematics and beliefs about mathematics, contains many examples of planned interventions which have been followed by changes in beliefs (e.g., about those most likely to enjoy mathematics, be good at mathematics, and find it interesting) and changes in behaviour (e.g., electing to take a mathematics course when it is no longer compulsory, or to persist with a challenging problem). Thus changes in the delivery of mathematics and in individual and societal perceptions of mathematics have lead to changes in affectivity, performance, and behaviours.

THEORETICAL FRAMEWORKS

In the early years of psychological research, and the dominance of behaviourism, observable facets of human behaviour were of particular interest. In recent years, with increased theoretical and measurement sophistication, more recognition is given to aspects of affectivity which rely on high levels of inference. Speculations about the interplay between cognition and affectivity have fuelled research throughout the decades and have led to many attempts at terminological precision. Such attempts are discussed in more detail in the two chapters which follow.

REFERENCES

Aiken, L. R. (1996). *Rating scales and checklists: Evaluating behavior, personality, and attitudes*. New York, USA: John Wiley.

Jacobs, Becker, & Gilmer (2001).

Cockcroft, W. H. (1982). *Mathematics counts*. London: Her Majesty's Stationary Office.

Cox, P. J., Leder, G. C., & Forgasz , H. J. (2004). Victorian certificate of education: Mathematics, science and gender. *Australian Journal of Eduction, 48*(1), 27-46.

Fennema, E., & Hart, L. E. (1994). Gender and the JRME. *Journal for Research in Mathematics Education, 25*, 648-659.

Fennema, E., & Sherman, J. (1976). Fennema-Sherman mathematics attitude scales. *JSAS: Catalog of selected documents in psychology, 6*(1), 31 (Ms. No. 1225).

Fennema, E. & Sherman, J. (1977). Sex-related differences in mathematics achievement, spatial visualization and affective factors. *American Educational Research Journal, 14*, 51-71.

Forgasz, H. J., Leder, G. C., & Kloosterman, P. (2004). New perspectives on the gender stereotyping of mathematics. *Mathematical Thinking and Learning, 6*(4), 389-420.

Goldin, G. (2004). Characteristics of affect as a system of representation. In M. J. Høines & A. B. Fuglestad (Eds). *Proceedings of the 28th conference of the International Psychology of Mathematics Education* (pp. 1-109-1-114). Bergen: Bergen University College

Goldin, G. (2002). Affect, meta-affect, and mathematical belief structures. In G. C. Leder, E. Pehkonen, & G. Törner (Eds.), *Beliefs: A hidden variable in mathematics education?* (pp. 59-72). Dordrecht, The Netherlands: Kluwer.

Hanna, G. (Ed.) (1996). *Towards gender equity in mathematics education. An ICMI study*. Dordrecht, the Netherlands: Kluwer Academic Publishers.

Jacobs, J. E., Becker, J. R., & Gilmer, G. F. (Eds.) (2001). *Changing the faces of mathematics*. Reston, Virginia: National Council of Teachers of Mathematics.

Leder, G. C. (1992). Mathematics and gender: Changing perspectives. In D. A. Grouws (Ed.), *Handbook of research on mathematics teaching and learning.* New York: Macmillan, 597-622.

Leder, G.C., Forgasz, H.J., & Solar, C. (1996). Research and intervention programs in mathematics education: A gendered issue. In A. Bishop, K. Clements, C. Keitel, J. Kilpatrick, & C. Laborde (Eds.), *International handbook of mathematics education.* Dordrecht, The Netherlands: Kluwer, 945-985.

McLeod, D.B. (1992). Research on affect in mathematics education: A reconceptualization. In D. A. Grouws (Ed.), *Handbook of research in mathematics teaching and learning.* New York: MacMillan, 597-622.

Mandler, G. (1989). Affect and learning: Causes and consequences of emotional interactions. In D. B. McLeod, & V. M Adams (Eds.), *Affect and mathematical problem solving. A new perspective.* New York: Springer-Verlag, 3-19.

National Council of Teachers of Mathematics [NCTM] (2000). *Principles and standards for school mathematics.* Reston, VA: Author.

OECD (2004). *First results from PISA 2003. Executive summary.* Paris: Author.

Rogers, P. & Kaiser, G. (Eds.) (1995). *Equity in mathematics education: Influences of feminism and culture.* London: Falmer Press

Walberg,H. J., & Haertel, G. D. (1992). Educational psychology's first century. *Journal of Educational Psychology,* 84, 6-19.

Gilah C. Leder
La Trobe University, Australia

MARKKU S. HANNULA

AFFECT IN MATHEMATICAL THINKING AND LEARNING

Towards Integration Of Emotion, Motivation, and Cognition

INTRODUCTION

Human behaviour is a complex topic to study. Reid (1996) has distinguished between an effort to create theories *of* and theories *for* a topic of interest. It is not likely that we can ever develop a single theory of affect in mathematics education that would accurately represent all relevant aspects of affect. Instead, we can build theories for understanding affect in mathematics education that can inform practice and future research. When summarising a research field one must be open to multiple perspectives and tolerant to different paradigms of research. Yet, some focus is necessary. One of the choices in this chapter is to focus on the level of the individual student. The theoretical frameworks elaborated consider an individual rather than their interactions as the level of analyses. The theories are, broadly speaking, psychological, rather than biological or sociological.

The multiplicity of research traditions is reflected in the diverse vocabulary used in the field and different definitions given to concepts. Affect will be used, here, as a general term that includes all emotional and motivational phenomena. Under this general term, we include two main concepts, namely emotion and motivation. Unlike in some traditions, we shall not make a distinction between motivation and volition or between emotion and mood.

The reader will be introduced to the theme of this chapter with brief examples of two main traditions of research on affect in mathematics education. The first tradition is concerned with measuring different elements of affect to identify characteristics of affect that predict future achievement. The second tradition is interested in analysing the role of different affective states in the processes of mathematical learning and problem solving.

The main critics to prevalent research traditions of the past will be reviewed. Attitude and beliefs have the longest tradition, but they lack clarity and instruments used to measure these need refining.

Next, the nature of affect as a research topic will be analysed. Affect is simultaneously physiological, psychological, and social. Yet, a research methodology or a theoretical framework cannot easily bend to these different approaches at the same time. Despite the chosen individualistic approach, one must

J. Maasz, W. Schloeglmann (Eds.), New Mathematics Education Research and Practice, 209–232.

be aware of the importance of classroom culture, social and sociomathematical norms as well as the social context of the student and the school.

In the latter part of the chapter we shall elaborate more closely the nature of emotion and motivation, and their interactions with each other and cognition. The focus is on affective processes, including the meta-level of affect. To date, insufficient attention has been paid to how different emotional and motivational states influence mathematical thinking in characteristic ways. Some implications for teaching and research are also considered.

Why affect is relevant to mathematics teaching?

There are two main traditions to examine affect in mathematics education. The first tradition is to measure relatively stable affective traits and their relation to achievement. Ma and Kishor (1997) synthesised 113 survey studies of the relationship between attitude towards mathematics (liking mathematics) and achievement in mathematics. The causal direction of the relationship was from liking mathematics to achieving in it. Although the correlations were weak in the overall sample, they were stronger throughout grades 7 to 12, and in studies that had performed separate analyses for male and female subjects.

Also more generally, educators are interested in the possible causal relationship between affect and achievement. Based on a literature review of self-concept and achievement in learning, Chapman, Tunmer and Prochnow (2000) suggested a developmental trend for their causal relationship. During the first school years the causal relation appeared to be from achievement to self-concept, for the next years there seemed be a reciprocal relationship, and in the upper secondary school the causal relationship was from self-concept to achievement.

Some evidence for this developmental trend in mathematics has been found (e.g., Linnanmäki, 2002; Hannula, Maijala & Pehkonen, 2004), but further systematic research is needed to confirm it. Gender differences in self-confidence favouring males have been well confirmed (e.g. Leder, 1995), and some studies indicate that also the relationship between self-confidence and achievement is affected by gender (e.g. Hannula et. al. 2004).

These findings highlight the importance of developing sound self-confidence in mathematics during the early years of schooling. They also point to the importance of gender as a mediating factor. However, they do not directly reveal how to promote positive affect among those whose achievement is not good in the early years. Neither do such findings inform us how to help those who already have low self-confidence in their struggle to learn mathematics.

Another research tradition has been looking at affect as an important aspect of mathematical problem solving. In *Mathematical Problem Solving* Schoenfeld (1985) defined an individual's beliefs or "mathematical world view" as shaping how one engages in problem solving. For example, those who believe that mathematics is no more than repetition of learned routines would be more likely to give up on a novel task than those who believe that inventing is an essential aspect of mathematics. Looking at more rapidly changing affective states, Goldin (2000)

210

explained in detail how experiences may lead students to adopt either positive or negative affective pathways (established sequences of states of feeling that interact with cognition). Such pathways serve important functions for experts as well as novices – providing useful information, facilitating monitoring, and suggesting heuristic problem-solving strategies. A slightly different approach has been to consider how teaching approaches or characteristics of a problem influence the affective experience of the learner. For example, Liljedahl (2005) describes tasks that allow *Chain of discovery* and sustained engagement. One teacher student of his study describes her experience as follows:

> Of all the problems that we worked on my favourite was definitely the pentominoe problem. We worked so hard on it, and it took forever to get the final answer. But I never felt like giving up, I always had confidence that we would get through it. Every time we got stuck we would just keep at it and suddenly one of us would make a discovery and we would be off to the races again. That's how it was the whole time – get stuck, work hard, make a discovery – over and over again. It was great. I actually began to look forward to our group sessions working on the problem. I have never felt this way about mathematics before – NEVER! I now feel like this is ok, I'm ok, I'll BE ok. I can do mathematics, and I definitely want my students to feel this way when I teach mathematics ... (Liljedahl, 2005)

These examples show that both relatively stable emotional traits as well as rapidly changing emotional states have an important role in mathematical thinking and learning.

CRITIQUE OF EARLIER RESEARCH

Multiple concepts have been introduced in research of affect in mathematics education. Most of the concepts have ambiguous definitions and it has been justifiably argued that the field needs more coherence. (Leder, this Issue)

Research on affect has typically focussed either on classifying affect as one of the few predetermined types, or to measure the strength of affect on a one-dimensional scale. Anxiety measures have been used extensively in mathematics education research in the 70's and somewhat later the trend was to identify students' attitudes on a positive-negative dimension (Zan, Brown, Evans & Hannula, In print). Educational psychology has been interested in motivation, where a typical approach has been to distinguish between different categories of motivation, e.g. intrinsic vs. extrinsic motivation or mastery vs. performance vs. ego-defensive orientation (Murphy & Alexander, 2000).

Such a descriptive approach to classifying/measuring affect has charted the field and sketched the main trends of the affective field. We know that mathematics-related attitudes, beliefs and motivations are relatively stable, yet they are susceptible to influence through interventions. We know that gender, ethnicity and achievement in mathematics are correlated to attitudes, beliefs and motivation. With respect to the causal relations we are less certain. Although these findings have predictive power, they do not provide an understanding of how affect is developing on a personal level – or how to change affect.

For example, attitude towards mathematics is often defined as an inclination to evaluate mathematics favourably or non-favourably ('I like ...', 'It is important',..). (An alternative three-component view of attitude will be presented a little bit later in the chapter). Attitude (defined as liking) may be affected by situation variables (e.g. teacher behaviour), automatic emotional reactions of the student (based on some traumatising event(s) in the past), expectance of outcome (beliefs), goals of the student (e.g. career aspirations), or social variables (attitudes of the family). Different causes for a negative attitude would call for different actions, but a single attitude measure would not suffice. (Hannula, 2002a)

Belief is another frequently used concept in mathematics education research. Belief research has distinguished different objects of beliefs (e.g. McLeod, 1992), and each of these has its own significance. Beliefs about the nature of mathematics, for example, relate to girls' "quest for meaning" (Boaler, 1997). Beliefs about self (e.g. self-efficacy beliefs) are psychologically central and often difficult to change once formed. Beliefs about teaching mathematics include beliefs about social context but also social and sociomathematical norms (see Yakel & Cobb, 1996). Furthermore, students often hold different views about different domains of mathematics, such as algebra or problem solving. Belief research has accumulated a vast body of findings, such as a robust gender difference in self-confidence in mathematics (e.g. Leder, 1995). Yet, when Furinghetti and Pehkonen (2002) analysed the different characterisations used by researchers in this field, they concluded that there is a lack of agreement on what beliefs are. There are, for example, different views about how much are emotions part of beliefs.

Motivation has been less frequently used in mathematics education, but in educational psychology it has been an important concept. The naïve view assumes that higher motivation would automatically lead to higher achievement. Unfortunately the issue is not that simple.

> "[I]nstructional efforts that lead to positive learning outcomes do not always produce sustained motivation, and conversely, instructional efforts to boost motivation of students without simultaneously improving their learning processes or competencies do not always produce sustained achievement" (Zimmerman & Schunk, 2004, p.323)

Critique of mainstream motivation has raised two main needs of improvement: acceptance of the importance of the unconscious in motivation (Murphy & Alexander, 2000) and focusing on motivational states and processes rather than traits (Dweck, 2002).

Conceptual frameworks

McLeod's (1992) classification of affect constructs in mathematics education is well known and frequently used (Figure 1). In addition to providing a classification

212

for concepts used in this field, it also characterised their nature on an affective-cognitive continuum and assigned different levels of stability to them.

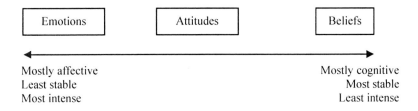

Figure 1. McLeod's (1992) classification of the concepts of the affective domain.

The middle concept, attitude, has been divided in social psychology into beliefs, emotions and behaviour (Figure 2). This conceptualisation has also been used frequently in mathematics education (see Di Martino & Zan, 2001 for an elaboration of the concept 'attitude' and its use in mathematics education research).

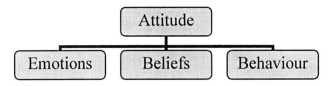

Figure 2. Subconstructs of attitude.

Combining these two well-established approaches is problematic. Emotions and beliefs are in one approach, subconstructs of affect together with attitude, while in the other approach emotions and beliefs are subconstructs of attitude. Clearly, more coherence is needed.

WHAT KIND OF BEAST IS AFFECT? ONTOLOGICAL, EPISTEMOLOGICAL, AND METHODOLOGICAL ASSUMPTIONS

Affect as a research topic can be analysed based on Popper's idea of three worlds. Popper distinguished three ontologically different worlds: the world of physical objects (1), the world of subjective experience (2), and the world of human creation (3) (Popper & Ecceles, 1977). In this elaboration, the world of human creation is seen in its broadest sense. All expressions (word, smile, gesture etc.) that may be observed and interpreted by another human are part of this world. Because these worlds differ in their ontology, research in each of these worlds is of a different nature. If we use the different inquiry paradigms described by Lincoln and Guba (2000) we may make a reasonable claim that, in general, the postpositivist paradigm is the most appropriate one for research in the world of physical objects, the constructivist paradigm for research in the world of subjective experience, and the critical theory paradigm for research in the world of human creation. Hence, quite different approaches can be adopted to explore affect as a research topic.

If we take the subjective experience as the starting point, we need to acknowledge the inevitable ontological and epistemological assumptions related to it (subjectivist perspective). We can also perceive the human mind as a 'biological machine' and approach affect thorough neurobiological activity in the brain (biological perspective). Alternatively, we, as researchers, may choose to perceive human affect as an element in social interaction (social perspective).

Affect as Subjective Experience

The oldest solution for accessing affect and other experiential states is introspection; to reflect upon one's own subjective experience. However, there are several problems with this approach. For example, the act of introspection alters the experiential state, much of our own mind is inaccessible to introspection and this method does not allow us to understand anything about minds that are different from our own.

Behaviourists did not accept introspection as a method. The unavoidable problem is that we cannot directly access someone else's experiences either. We need to rely on observable changes in associated physiological processes or expressions of affect in social interaction. Yet, only through our own experiences can we understand the qualities of affect.

Affect as Physiological Process

The scientific tradition has approached subjective experiences through physiology (physical objects). This line of study has, for example, been able to identify which areas of the brain are activated in emotions, and how different neurochemicals are related to our emotions (see, e.g. Buck, 1999). Despite the scientific accuracy of the research results, the biological processes cannot be interpreted as experiences. In the case of human subjects, we also have the verbal expressions of their feelings; objects of human creation that are based on their subjective experiences. Thus, we have moved beyond the limits of the world of physical objects, and we need to take into account the different epistemological assumptions of these different worlds. Although the research on physiological processes alone gives an extremely limited view into subjective experiences, this approach has greatly enhanced our understanding of the psychological processes of affect.

Affect As Social Text

Most of the research done on subjective experiences has relied on studying objects created by humans: people's behaviour, their verbal and facial expressions. This approach has led to the use of interviews, observations, think-aloud protocols, tests, and questionnaires as methods of enquiry. It has a long tradition and it has accumulated a huge amount of important results. However, we need to take into consideration the epistemological assumptions of this social approach. People are socially positioned, and this will inevitably influence how and whether they express their emotions (e.g. Evans, 2000, this issue).

Furthermore, even if we assume our subject to be expressing a genuine experiential state, there is the problem of interpreting this as subjective experiences. Unlike with physiology, we all learn to do this interpreting automatically from early childhood (at least within our own culture). We see people around us behaving and expressing, and we learn to interpret those actions as emotions and thoughts. This is possible because we share biology, language, and experiences with the people around us. We see tears and we remember how we felt when something made us cry. A friend tells how happy he is and his words echo in our own experience and we think we understand.

However, there are limits to sharing other people's experiences. We cannot interpret beyond what we have experienced. How well can an adult male share the experiences of a young girl being sexually harassed? How well can the mathematically able share the experiences of those experiencing math anxiety? The subjective experiences of the researcher become important determinants of what the researcher may understand of other people's minds.

In more traditional 'positivist' approaches, the researchers often avoid the task of interpreting, and simply report categories of behaviour or expressions, and relationships between them. This approach implicitly makes the incorrect assumption that the expressions used in the report embody such cultural conventions that the readers will be able to interpret them unambiguously.

The social level is not only the inevitable field of communication between subjective experiences, but is also an important approach in its own right. After all, mathematics is not an individual endeavour, but is produced by generations of mathematical communities. The social level approaches focus on explaining how old ideas are learned from earlier generations, how such ideas are shared in communities of learning, and also how new ideas emerge through interaction between participants in these mathematical communities.

Connecting the Levels

Affect in mathematics education can be studied as an element of social practice or as an aspect of the individual's thinking and learning. Such a choice could also be seen as an ontological commitment, but rather than trying to firmly fasten the ontology of affect, researchers should pay attention to all aspects:

> "Emotions [...] can be viewed at all levels of analysis between the physiological and cultural levels. In order to understand the role and function of emotion we may need to consider alterations in physiology, the psychological state, the interpersonal signal, and the cultural context." (Power & Dalgleish, 1997, p. xi)

As the quotation aptly summarises, there is value in each approach where research on emotions is concerned. Whichever research paradigm we choose as a starting point, we ought to be sensitive to different levels of analysis.

Dai (2004) discusses the problems of integrating different levels of analysis, yet argues for "integration of neurobiological, psychological-behavioural (functional), and phenomenological levels of analysis"(p. 424). He expects such integration to continue both in global theories of human intelligence and functioning as well as within local analysis of complex human behaviour, such as mathematical problem solving.

Denzin and Lincoln (2000, p. 6) warn that paradigmatic multiperspectivity is difficult to handle and not everyone is prepared to navigate between different paradigms that differ in their ontological, epistemological, and methodological assumptions. We should aim for it anyway. A conceptualisation of affect as subjective experience should not conflict with an understanding of the underlying physiological level or the level of social interactions. For example, the level of human physiology determines the limits for psychology. Physiology enables certain psychological processes (e.g. consciousness, short-term memory) and restricts these processes (e.g. there is no direct consciousness of time and we can hold no more than nine items in short-term memory). On the other hand, many of the psychological phenomena have their primary functionality in social interactions, and can not be fully understood on an individual level.

THE BASIC ELEMENTS TO CONCEPTUALISE AFFECT

Need to Integrate Cognition, Motivation, And Emotion

My own research on affect in mathematics education was based on DeBellis' and Goldin's (1997) classification of affect into emotions, beliefs, attitudes, and values/morals/ethics. In my elaboration of these concepts, the first distinction was between cognition and emotions as aspects of affect. Literature on emotion indicated the importance of goals in relation to emotions and thus pointed to the concept of motivation (Hannula, 2002a, 2004a). Schoenfeld's theory of Teaching-In-Context (1998) includes elements of the same three domains: teachers' decision-making is based on their knowledge (cognitive aspect), goals (motivational aspect), and beliefs (emotional aspect). In addition, some researchers of mathematical beliefs have identified motivational beliefs as an important subcategory of mathematical beliefs (e.g. Kloosterman, 2002; Op 't Eynde, De Corte & Verschaffel, In print).[1]

Coming from a different research tradition, educational psychology, Meyer and Turner (2002) had conducted a study on motivation, conceptualised according to the prevalent tradition to include two components: cognition and motivation. As part of this work, they identified a need to expand their conceptualisation. They summarise their concern for the limitations of the established frameworks as follows:

216

Historically, psychologists have adopted three components to describe human learning: cognition, motivation, and emotion [...]. Yet, theorists and researchers have tended to study these processes separately, attempting to artificially untangle them rather than exploring their synergistic relations in the complexity of real life activities. (Meyer & Turner, 2002)

They called for "new theoretical syntheses and research programs that integrate emotion, motivation, and cognition as equal components in the social process of learning" (ibid. p. 107). Answers to these calls have begun to emerge, for example, a recent book on integrative perspectives on motivation, emotion, and cognition edited by Dai and Sternberg (2004).

Self-regulation as the Systemic Frame

Choice of concepts is not enough; we need to also have an understanding of their relations. The approach taken here is to look at human behaviour from the perspective of self-regulation. Zimmerman and Campillo (2003) have characterised self-regulation as "self-generated thoughts, feelings, and actions that are planned and cyclically adapted for the attainment of personal goals" (p. 238). When the role of unconscious and automatic self-regulation is accepted, planning can not be seen as necessary for self-regulation, but otherwise the characterisation is suitable.

Boekaerts (1999) outlined the three roots of research on self-regulation: "(1) research on learning styles, (2) research on metacognition and regulation styles, and (3) theories of the self, including goal-directed behavior" (p. 451). Based on these schools of thought, she presented a three-layer model for self-regulation:
-   the innermost layer pertains to regulation of the processing modes through choice of cognitive strategies,
-   the middle layer represents regulation of the learning process through use of metacognitive knowledge and skills and
-   the outermost layer concerns regulation of the self through choice of goals and resources.
Most research has focused on the two innermost layers and little effort has been made to integrate motivation control, action control or emotion control into theories of self-regulation (Boekaerts, 1999, p. 445). Boekaerts and Niemivirta (2000) have proposed a broader view for self-regulation that would accept a variety of different control systems, not only metacognition:

[Self-regulation] has been presented as a generic term used for a number of phenomena, each of which is captured by a different control system. In our judgment, self-regulation is a system concept that refers to the overall management of one's behavior through interactive processes between these different control systems (attention, metacognition, motivation, emotion, action, and volition control). ... In the past decade, researchers involved in educational research have concentrated mainly on activity in one control system – the metacognitive control system – thus ignoring the interplay between the metacognitive control system and other control systems. (Boekaerts & Niemivirta, 2000, p. 445)

Clearly, self-regulation is much more than mere metacognition. When we take an overall view of self-regulation, we can distinguish between three different timeframes. One is the rapid self-regulation of actions and thoughts within a given situational context (e.g. solving a given mathematics task). The intermediate timeframe regards self and psychological traits as stable constructs, but allows manipulation of context (e.g. a student solving the problem may start collaborating with a peer). The third timeframe allows psychological traits to be constructed and reconstructed through one's interaction with environment (e.g. the student may become more confident through a series of successful problem solving episodes).

Cognition, motivation and emotion have each a distinctive role in self-regulation, both on the level of traits and on states (see Table 1). Cognition draws on information about self and the situations. Motivation gives direction for behaviour, there are individual needs one wishes to satisfy and goals one wants to reach. The role of emotions is to regulate self towards satisfaction of needs. Emotions may influence physiology to adapt to situation (flight or fight –response) or bias cognition according to the most urgent needs (anxiety biases attention towards threats).

Table 1. Cognition, motivation, and emotion in self-regulation state/trait aspects

Domain \ Concept	Cognition	Motivation	Emotion
Self-regulation	Information about self and environment	Direction for behaviour	Goal-directed self-regulation
State	Thoughts in mind	Active goals	Emotional state
Trait (memory)	Concepts, facts, scripts etc.	Needs, values, desires	Emotional dispositions (attitude)

In cognition, motivation, and emotion, it is important to understand their rapidly fluctuating state and the more stable 'trait' aspect (Table 1). In the cognitive domain of mind, there is the continuously changing 'landscape' on thoughts, which relates to an equally rapidly evolving neural activation pattern of the brain. However, there are also rather stable neural structures in the brain, enabling some neural patterns to activate, disabling others. These more stable structures are reflected in the concepts, facts, scripts and other schemata that are stored in memory. Likewise, there is the continuously evolving emotional state, which is partially embedded in the neural activation patterns of the limbic system, and partially in the biochemical system of hormones and neuropeptides. There is the biologically founded structure of basic emotions in the background, but also an 'emotional memory' that is based on previous experiences. These prime activation of certain emotions in certain situations (e.g. in mathematics class). For motivation, there are rather stable needs, values, and desires, but also more frequently changing goals that influence attention. These issues will be elaborated more thoroughly later on in this chapter, but this integration of emotion, motivation, and cognition is still very much a work in progress.

Emotion

Nowadays, there is general agreement that emotions consist of three processes: physiological processes that regulate the body, subjective experiences that regulate behaviour, and expressive processes that regulate social coordination (e.g. Buck, 1999; Power & Dalgleish, 1997; Schwarz & Skrunik, 2003).

Although researchers have not agreed upon what they mean by emotions, there is agreement on certain aspects. Primarily, emotions are seen in connection to personal goals: they code information about progress towards goals and possible blockages, as well as suggest strategies for overcoming obstacles. Emotions are also seen to involve a physiological reaction, as distinction from non-emotional cognition. Thirdly, emotions are also seen to be functional, i.e. they have an important role in human coping and adaptation. (E.g. Buck 1999, Damasio, 1995; Lazarus 1991, LeDoux, 1998, Mandler 1989, Pekrun, Goetz, Titz & Perry, 2002; Power & Dalgleish 1997)

The three main issues that researchers have not agreed upon are the borderline between emotion and cognition, the number of different emotions, and whether emotions are always conscious. According to Buck, emotions have three mutually independent readouts: adaptive-homeostatic arousal responses (e.g. releasing adrenaline in the blood), expressive displays (e.g. smiling), and subjective experience (e.g. feeling excited) (Table 2). Here, all these readouts are regarded as part of the emotional state. In contrast to its use in mathematics education, the term emotion is not restricted to intensive, 'hot' emotions. Hence, for example, a mildly sad mood is considered as an emotional state.

Table 2. Three readouts of emotion (Buck, 1999)

Readout target	Readout function	Accessibility	Learning
I Autonomic/ endocrine/ immune system responding	Adaptation/ homeostasis	Not accessible	Physiological adaptation
II Expressive behaviour	Communication/ social coordination	Accessible to others (and self)	Social development
III Subjective experience	Self-regulation	Accessible to self	Cognitive development

There are two main routes for emotions to arise (Power & Dalgleish, 1997; LeDoux, 1998). The first route is an automatic, preconscious emotional reaction (often fear) to a relatively simple stimulus (e.g. a sound, an object or a concept). Such automatic emotional reactions form a basis for some emotional traits. They are based on earlier experiences that have left an association (a memory trace) between the emotion experienced in a situation and a specific element of the situation. In the mathematics class, an example of such automatic emotional reaction might be, for example, anxiety generated by the tone of voice of the teacher, by peer's laughter, or through identifying the concept 'fraction'. Such emotional reactions are fast and have evolutionarily provided shorter reaction times to possible threats. On the downside, automatic reactions lack flexibility and are difficult to change once formed (Power & Dalgleish, 1997). For example, Hembree (1990) has identified systematic desensitisation (a slow therapy) to be the most efficient treatment for mathematics anxiety.

The other route to an emotional reaction is based on (possibly unconscious) analyses of personal goals and elements in the situation. This latter reaction is more flexible and possible to affect through conscious deliberations. However, if one's goals and beliefs are relatively stable, the emotional reaction will also remain stable.

Damasio (1995) suggested that automatic emotional reactions include also less intense emotions that function as a preconscious filter to allow decision-making in complex real-life situations (somatic markers). Brown & Reid (forthcoming) have initiated an analysis of the role of somatic markers in teaching and mathematical problem solving.

Motivation

Why do most students put an effort to learn mathematics? In his ICME9 presentation, Shlomo Vinner pointed to the core of all human behaviour: "...human behavior, as well as human thought, is determined by human needs" (Vinner, 2000).

In the motivation literature, one important approach has been to distinguish between intrinsic and extrinsic motivation (e.g. Ryan & Deci, 2000). Another approach to motivation has been to distinguish (usually three) motivational orientations in educational settings: learning (or mastery) orientation, performance (or self-enhancing) orientation, and ego-defensive (avoidance) orientation (e.g. Lemos, 1999; Linnenbrink & Pintrich, 2000). Murphy and Alexander (2000) also see interest (situational vs. individual) and self-schema (agency, attribution, self-competence, and self-efficacy) as important conceptualisations of motivation.

When motivation is conceptualised as a structure of needs, goals and means (Shah & Kruglanski, 2000), we can see that these vary a lot from person to person (Hannula, 2002b). The theoretical foundation of motivation as a structure of needs and goals was further elaborated in Hannula (2004b), where the following definition was introduced for motivation.

Motivation is a potential to direct behaviour that is built into the system that controls emotion. This potential may be manifested in cognition, emotion and/or behaviour. (Hannula, 2004b)

For example, the motivation to solve a mathematics task might be manifested in beliefs about the importance of the task (cognition), but also in persistence (behaviour) or in sadness or anger if failing (emotion). In cognition, the most pure manifestation of motivation is the conscious desire for something, but the manifestation may also take more subtle forms, such as a view of oneself as a good problem solver. Emotions are the most direct link to motivation, being manifested either in positive (joy, relief, interest) or negative (anger, sadness, frustration) emotions. Although emotion and cognition can be observed only partially and are partially inaccessible even to the person him/herself, behaviour is always a trustworthy manifestation of motivation. Even when the person is unable to explain motives for her own behaviour, inferences of the unconscious and subconscious can be drawn from that behaviour.

Needs are specified instances of the general 'potential to direct behaviour'. In the existing literature, psychological needs that are often emphasised in educational settings are autonomy, competency, and social belonging (e.g. Boekaerts, 1999; Covington & Dray, 2002). The difference between needs and goals is in their different levels of specificity (Nuttin, 1984). For example, in the context of mathematics education, a student might realize a need for competency as a goal to solve tasks fluently or, alternatively, as a goal to understand the topic taught. A social need might be realised as a goal to contribute significantly to collaborative project work and a need for autonomy as a goal to challenge the teacher's authority.

INTERACTIONS BETWEEN EMOTION, MOTIVATION, AND COGNITION

Emotion and Cognition

Emotions guide our self-regulated behaviour towards the goals we have. In a non-automatic emotional reaction, cognition has an important role in our evaluation of the situation.

Advances in our understanding of the neuropsychological basis of affect (e.g. Damasio 1995, LeDoux, 1998) have radically changed the prevalent view of the relationship between emotion and cognition. Emotions are no longer seen as peripheral to cognitive processes or as 'noise' to impede rationality. Emotions have been accepted as necessary for rational behaviour.

It is now well established that emotions direct attention and bias cognitive processing. For example, fear (anxiety) directs attention towards threatening information and sadness (depression) biases memory towards a less optimistic view of the past. Emotions also activate action tendencies (e.g. fight or flight – response). (Power & Dalgleish, 1997; for a recent review of affective influences on cognitive processing, see Linnenbrink & Pintrich, 2004)

Research on cognition has studied such feedback loops under the term metacognition, and analogous concepts have been introduced into the affective domain (see Hannula, 2001 for some examples). In mathematics education, DeBellis and Goldin (1997, In print) define meta-affect as affect about affect, affect about and within cognition about affect, and the individual's monitoring of affect through cognition (thinking about the direction of one's feelings) and/or further affect. They claim meta-affect to be the most important aspect of affect:

> It is what enables people, in the right circumstances, to experience <u>fear</u> as <u>pleasurable</u> (e.g., in experiencing a terrifying roller coaster ride as fun), or to distinguish vicarious emotional feelings evoked by books or films from their 'real life' counterparts. Meta-affect helps guide the experience of <u>hypothetical</u> emotions, as these are used for cognitive gain. (DeBellis & Goldin, In print,original emphasis)

This metalevel is essential for understanding affect in real-life settings. However, already the multifaceted definition given by DeBellis and Goldin reveals that the concept is a collection of several somewhat different processes. The concept was further elaborated in Hannula (2001) where the 'metalevel' of mind was divided into four aspects (Table 3). Within each of these four aspects, we can separate the aspects of monitoring and control.

Table 3. The four aspects of the meta-level of mind.

Metacognition (cognitions about cognitions)	Emotional cognition (cognitions about emotions)
Cognitive emotions (emotions about cognitions)	Meta-emotions (emotions about emotions)

This elaborated approach to metalevel of affect and cognition slightly sharpens the definition of metacognition by restricting steering to cognitive steering. In this view direction of attention and bias of cognitive processing is not seen to be part of metacognition, when it is caused by emotions. Instead, they are seen as cognitive emotions.

Emotional cognition is the 'sister' of metacognition. It includes the subjective knowledge of one's own emotional state and emotional processes. Students are aware of the different emotions they have in different situations and they even know of their typical emotional reactions in mathematics classes. The subjective knowledge of one's own emotions is the basis for emotional expectations in different situations, and thereby it directs the approaches one has towards mathematical situations. Emotional cognition also includes the conscious regulation of own emotions, which has been shown to be important in effective problem solving (e.g. Carlson, 2000; Zimmerman & Campillio, 2003).

Emotions exist in relationship with goals and sometimes, (e.g. during problem solving), goals may be cognitive. Emotions relating to cognitive goals are called cognitive emotions. Frustration and curiosity are examples of typical cognitive emotions that are involved in the regulation of problem solving. Cognitive goals may be explicit, like when one wants to remember a fact or a procedure, or when one tries to solve a mathematical problem. Sometimes the goal may be vague, like 'to understand' a topic.

Meta-emotions are emotional reactions to one's own emotions. These meta-emotions code important information about the appropriateness of the emotion in question and they control that emotion. Presumably, all humans share the goal to experience pleasure and avoid unpleasant emotions. Humans have also the capacity to tolerate unpleasant emotions if a reward of pleasure is to be expected later. For example, successful problem solvers are prepared to tolerate frustration on their way towards solution. There are, however, different norms and individual coping strategies concerning emotions. Therefore, the same emotion may be more stressful for one individual than the other.

Motivation and Cognition

The realization of needs into goals in the mathematics classroom is greatly influenced by the students' beliefs about themselves, mathematics, learning, and the social environment. I will review below some results of a three-year longitudinal qualitative study (see e.g. Hannula, 2004a) that indicate the role of beliefs in students' adoption of goals.

Deriving goals from needs is mediated by personal beliefs. One may perceive a single goal to satisfy multiple needs and a need to be satisfied through multiple goals. Goals may also be seen as contradictory in a sense that reaching one goal might prevent achieving another goal. For example, mastery and performance are usually seen as competing motivational orientations (e.g. Linnenbring & Pintrich, 2000; Lemos, 1999). However, in an analysis of Maria and Laura (Hannula, 2002b), mastery and performance were goals that supported each other. Maria was driven by her need for competence and mastery of mathematics was her primary goal. However, performance in mathematics tests was an important subgoal for her evaluation of reaching that goal. Laura, on the other hand, was primarily driven by her desire to gain a high status in class 'hierarchy'. Performance (outsmarting other students) was her main goal, while mastery of mathematics was an important subgoal.

Adopting goals is also influenced by students' beliefs about accessibility of different goals. This is usually discussed under the term 'self-efficacy beliefs' (e.g. Philippou & Christou, 2002). In order for change in motivation to take place there must be a desired goal and one's beliefs must support the change. Earlier (Hannula, 1998a; 2002a), I reported a case study of Rita, where a radical change in beliefs and behaviour included these two aspects. Using the terminology of goals, we may say that Rita had self-defensive goals dominating her behaviour in the beginning ("You don't need math in life"). However, this was later replaced by performance goals ("I will raise my math number"). Behind this change, there was a new awareness of the importance of school success in general (change in goal value) together with more positive self-efficacy beliefs (success is possible). In the case of

Anna and Eva (Hannula, 1998b, 2005), we can also see these conditions for successful goal regulation. Although both students saw mastery of mathematics as a desirable goal that was not accessible by simply listening to the teacher, only Anna managed to act according to this goal. One important difference between Anna and Eva was that Anna had higher self-confidence in mathematics and thus believed that she could learn mathematics through independent studying.

Analogously to emotion, it seems that also motivation has a feedback loop to cognitive processing, although this question has not been studied as intensively. Dweck, Mangels and Good (2004) have studied the educationally important distinction between learning goals and performance goals. They characterise performance goal as a desire to "look smart", and learning goal as a desire to "become smarter". Students' beliefs regarding the nature of intelligence orient towards adoption of specific type of goals. Those who believe that effort can enhance their intelligence are more likely to adopt learning goals, while those who see intelligence as a fixed trait tend to adopt performance goals. Interestingly, that choice between learning and performance goals makes a major difference in cognitive processing, learning behaviour, and outcome. Students with a learning goal show greater attention (indicated by brain activity measured with EEG) towards learning-relevant information, implement more effective cognitive strategies, and gain higher achievement.

Emotions and Motivation

Emotions are intrinsically linked with motivation. Emotions are functional and they code significant information about goal directed behaviour, each basic emotion indicating a specific relation to a goal and activating an appropriate action tendency. Happiness signals that the student is approaching a goal or has reached it, and can relax and previous actions should be remembered in a positive light. Anger signals that something (target of the anger) is perceived to block approaching that goal, and aggressive action may be needed. Fear signals that something is seen to threaten an important goal, and one needs to be cautious and ready to flee. Sadness is an emotion related to a situation, where a goal is seen no longer to be accessible and one needs to reflect upon the situation. (E.g. Power & Dalgleish, 1997)

Automated emotional reactions may also function as an inertial force to students' goal changes. Once formed, these automated emotions associations are difficult to change. During school years, students usually develop some emotional disposition to different mathematical actions and goals. Therefore, emotional associations may prohibit change even when change would be 'rational'.

THEORY INTO PRACTICE

Implications for Teaching

It has been well established that one's affective state has an effect on cognitive processes. How should this inform teaching? Should the teacher regulate the affective climate in the class according to the teaching goals: humour and play to ease adoption of new ideas while practice of rules and routines under less joyful affective climate? There is some evidence that certain emotions facilitate certain type of processing, but the evidence is far from conclusive. Linnenbrink and Pintrich (2004) conclude in their article that

> "As we are yet unsure exactly how moods and emotions relate to cognitive processing in a broad variety of tasks it is difficult to make recommendations for educators regarding the types of affect that may be beneficial for processing." (p. 84)

Yet, some general principles have been widely accepted. Firstly, effective regulation of emotions has been identified as essential for good mathematical problem solving. More generally, fostering emotional intelligence is considered an important educational objective. Emotional intelligence has been defined as

> "the ability to monitor one's own and others' feelings and emotions, to discriminate among them and to use this information to guide one's thinking and actions." (Salovey & Mayer, 1990, p. 189)

Research has confirmed a positive relationship between positive affect and achievement. Although the causal relationship has not been established, positive affective disposition is a worthwhile learning outcome. It seems that the affective outcomes are most important during the first school years, as they are less likely to be altered later on. Two key elements of a desired affective disposition are self-confidence and motivation to learn.

One general principle for promotion of positive affect would be awareness to students' needs. For example, in a teacher-centred mathematics classroom that emphasises rules and routines and individual drilling, there is little room to meet the students' needs for autonomy or social belonging. A classroom that reflects a socio-constructivist view of learning, on the other hand, provides plenty of opportunities to meet different needs and actually relies on students exhibiting their autonomy and social interactions. This would not mean lowering the expectations, quite the contrary. If we manage to find tasks that are engaging and create a learning context where engagement can be sustained, the students will not only stay on task, but they will also work more intensively.

Although mathematics-related beliefs and goals, and especially self-related beliefs are relatively stable, they are not fixed. More cognitive beliefs (e.g. nature of math) can be affected through direct teaching, and automatic emotional reactions are subject to effects of new experiences. Even traumatized students can get help through a therapeutic approach, when they find a safe environment and support for their emotion regulation.

Implications for Research Methodology

There are two main improvements needed in future research. One is the need to go beyond simplistic positive-negative distinction of affect. For example fear and boredom develop under very different conditions and they influence mathematical behaviour differently. The other is the need to pay attention to emotional reactions that may reveal things that are inaccessible to consciousness (and self-reporting) or purposefully hidden from the observer. However, it should be noted that not all emotions have distinctive facial expression (e.g. interest).

Research on affect can be divided into three approaches: observation, interviews and questionnaires. There are research methods that combine several of these approaches (e.g. video based stimulated recall interview). Such approaches are highly recommended for the triangulation they make possible. For example, a forthcoming Special issue of Educational Studies in Mathematics will use one case study with questionnaire data, observation data, and video based stimulated recall interview (Op 't Eynde & Hannula, In print). This case study will then be analysed from different theoretical perspectives, the methodological triangulation making also theoretical triangulation possible.

The most 'natural' way to study affect in classrooms is to use a human observer. Facial expressions, posture and tone of voice tell about emotions in ways that humans are able to interpret more or less naturally. For example, facial expressions of basic emotions have been identified by respondents of unrelated cultures around the world although the accuracy of interpretation is compromised in less familiar (sub)cultures (Elfenbein & Ambady, 2002). Accuracy of interpretations can be increased through training.

The other extreme would be to audio- and video record the events in the classroom and then define exact 'rules' for interpreting the recorded data. For example DeBellis and Goldin (In print), have used the Maximally Discriminative Facial Movement Coding System (Izard, 1983) that includes a score for each of three areas of the face: an eyebrow/forehead movement code, an eyes/nose/cheeks movement code, and a mouth/lips movement code for every hundredth of a second of time on tape. Other frequently used behavioural measures of emotion are Ekman's Facial Action Coding System (FACS; 2003) and Gottman's Specific Affect Coding System (SPAFF; Gottman, 1993). Technical development allows introduction of new measurement instruments into classrooms. For example, Isoda and Nagagoshi (2000) used a heart rate monitor to measure a volunteering student's changing heart rate during mathematics lesson.

In interviews we typically focus on the content of the talk. The student may talk about emotions, beliefs and motivations. However, this is restricted to what the student is aware of and is willing to tell. What the students choose to talk about reflects also the kind of identity they wish to express to the interviewer. In an interview, we can also observe the interviewee's facial expressions, posture, tone of voice, which can tell us about either their emotion in the interview situation or their emotions associated with the content. It is also possible to make a narrative analysis of the interview (e.g. Polkinghorne, 1995, Kaasila, Hannula, Laine & Pehkonen, 2005). The genre, plot, style etc. chosen by the student tell about the identity of the narrator. In a narrative analysis attention should be paid to emphasis, repetition, and telling through negation, which all signal higher personal relevance. It is also important to pay attention to spontaneous talk and silence. Whenever the student brings up a topic spontaneously, it signals relevance or other meaning attributed to the topic. Unwillingness to respond, on the other hand, hints that the interviewee might avoid the topic for some reason.

Much of the research on affect is still based on questionnaires, and they are efficient tools for collecting information from a large group of respondents. However, over- or misinterpreting data collected through a questionnaire is easy. Typically, these tools provide us only with the respondents' surface. However, with a well-designed instrument it is possible to reach the hidden dimensions of affect – at least on a general level of a large sample. Another problem with questionnaire studies is that they typically reach only the relatively stable affective traits, not more rapidly changing affective states. Yet, it is possible to collect data with a questionnaire during any process, for example problem solving (e.g. Vermeer, 1997; Boekarerts, 2002). With such 'on-line' -questionnaires, it is possible to collect data of the fleeting emotions and changing goals in the process.

SUMMARY

Affect in mathematics education has been studied primarily from the point of view of finding variables that might explain and predict future achievement in mathematics. The early studies from the 1970's explored mathematics anxiety and attitude towards mathematics as correlates to overall success in mathematics. Another tradition has been interested in the affective conditions for success and failure in solving mathematical problems. The extensive research on mathematical beliefs has later bridged these two traditions.

Regarding affect in mathematical problem solving, there is a reasonably clear picture of the conditions for success and failure. The critical moment is typically when the process is not straightforward, and a student encounters an initial failure in implementation of their approach. A student, who has confidence and can control the intensity of frustration, will more likely continue efforts and ultimately succeed. On the other hand, lack of confidence and emotion control will lead to wasting cognitive resources on anxiety, and more likely to failure.

Concerning the overall affective disposition of a student, we also have quite a clear image of affective traits that lead to success in mathematics. An optimal student enjoys mathematics and has confidence in it, perceives mathematics as a sense-making activity, and considers effort to be the essential element of success. Furthermore, interest, intrinsic motivation, and learning orientation predict better performance both on a level of a specific task as well as in the long run.

However, when we go into details, there are many unanswered questions. In problem solving, there is a complex relationship between the type of task and the optimal emotional state (nature and intensity of emotion), which is also affected by the type of motivation one has. Positive affective disposition and success do not always go hand in hand, and even in the case of high correlation, we seldom know the direction of the causality.

We need to be more specific. We cannot understand the relationship between emotion and cognition if we classify anger, fear, disgust, boredom, and sadness simply as negative emotions. Nature of motivation will be blurred, if we focus on the strength of the motivation ignoring the goal the student aims at. This work has started, but there are still more questions than answers.

Simple answers cannot satisfy the complexity of classrooms. In order to study affect in mathematics education in contexts of actual classrooms there are three main elements to pay attention to: cognition, emotion, and motivation. Achievement without motivation is not sustainable, and neither is motivation without enjoyment. All three domains have a more rapidly changing state-aspect and more stable trait-aspect. The overall relationship of these components has been sketched, but the work on finer details has barely begun.

Regarding affective traits, there is a need for new longitudinal studies with measurement instruments that would take into account the synergistic relationships between emotion, cognition, and motivation. Such studies might be able to clarify the relationship between affect and achievement and the role of age, gender and ethnicity in the individual development.

Methodologically, questionnaires were the first main tool of research on affect in mathematics education and they still remain as one of the tools. Especially in the 1990's the focus has shifted towards more qualitative methods, such as interviews and observing. The field has also seen more robust physiological measures of affect, and as instruments become less cumbersome and obtrusive, this trend is likely to become stronger. Furthermore, methodological triangulation has become almost a norm for any ambitious research project.

NOTES

[1] Note that beliefs about motivation (motivational beliefs) are not quite the same as motivation.

REFERENCES

Boaler, J. (1997). Reclaiming school mathematics: The girls fight back. *Gender and Education, 9,* 285-305.

Boekaerts, M. (1999). Self-regulated learning: where we are today. *International Journal of Educational Research,* 31, 445 – 457.

Boekaerts, M. (2002). The on-line motivation questionnaire: A self-report instrument to assess students' context sensitivity. In P. R. Pintrich & M. L. Maehr (Eds.) *Advances in Motivation and Achievement, Vol. 12, New directions in measures and methods.* Oxford, UK: Elsevier, 77-120.

Boekaerts, M., & Niemivirta, M. (2000) Self-regulated learning: Finding a balance between learning goals and ego-protective goals. In M. Boekaerts, P. R. Pintrich & M. Zeidner (Eds.) *Handbook of self-regulation*. San Diego, CA: Academic Press, 417-450.

Brown, L. & Reid, D. A. (In print). Embodied cognition: Somatic markers, purposes and emotional orientations. *Educational Studies in Mathematics.*

Buck, R. (1999). The biological affects: A typology. *Psychological Review, 106* (2), 301-336.

Carlson, M. P. (2000). A study of the mathematical behaviours of mathematicians: The role of metacognition and mathematical intimacy in solving problems. In. T. Nakahara & M. Koyama (Eds.) *Proceedings of the 24th Conference of the International Group for the Psychology of Mathematics Education (Vol. 2).* Japan: Hiroshima University, 137-144.

Chapman, J. W., Tunmer, W. E. & Prochnow, J. E. (2000). Early reading-related skills and performance, reading self-concept and the development of academic self-concept: A longitudinal study. *Journal of Educational Psychology, 67*, 145-152.

Covington, M. V. & Dray, E. (2002). The developmental course of Achievement motivation: A need-based approach. In A. Wigfield & J. S. Eccles (Eds.) *Development of achievement motivation.* London: Academic Press, 33-56.

Dai, D. Y. (2004). Epiloque: Putting it all together: Some concluding thoughts. In D. Y. Dai & R. J. Sternberg (Eds.) *Motivation, emotion, and cognition; Integrative perspectives on intellectual functioning and development.* Mahwah, NJ: Lawrence Erlbaum, 419 – 431.

Dai, D. Y. & Sternberg, R. J. (2004). (Eds.) *Motivation, emotion, and cognition; Integrative perspectives on intellectual functioning and development.* Mahwah, NJ: Lawrence Erlbaum.

Damasio, A. R. (1995). *Descartes' error: Emotion, reason, and the human brain.* London: Avon Books.

DeBellis V. A. & Goldin, G. A. (1997). The affective domain in mathematical problem-solving. In E. Pehkonen (Ed.) *Proceedings of the 21st Conference of the International Group for the Psychology of Mathematics Education*, Vol. 26. Lahti, Finland, 209-221.

DeBellis V. A. & Goldin, G. A (In print). Affect and meta-affect in mathematical problem solving: A representational perspective. *Educational Studies in Mathematics.*

Denzin, N. K. & Lincoln, Y. S. (2000). Introduction: The discipline and practice of qualitative Research. In N. K. Denzin & Y. S. Lincoln. (Eds). *Handbook of qualitative research.* Thousand Oaks, CA: Sage, 1-29.

DiMartino, P.& Zan, R. (2001). Attitude towards mathematics, some theoretical issues. In M. van den Heuvel-Panhuizen (Ed.) *Proceedings of the 25th Conference of the International group for the Psychology of Mathematics Education*, Vol. 3. Utrecht, The Netherlands, 351-358.

Dweck, C. S. (2002). The development of ability conceptions. In A. Wigfield & J. S. Eccles (Eds.) *Development of achievement motivation.* London: Academic Press, 57-88.

Dweck, C. S., Mangels, J. A. & Good, C. (2004). Motivational effects on attention, cognition, and performance. In D. Y. Dai & R. J. Sternberg (Eds.) *Motivation, emotion, and cognition; Integrative perspectives on intellectual functioning and development.* Mahwah, NJ: Lawrence Erlbaum, 41-56.

Ekman, P. (2003). *Emotions revealed.* New York: Henry Holt.

Elfenbein, H. A., & Ambady, N. (2002). On the universality and cultural specificity of emotion recognition: A meta-analysis. *Psychological Bulletin, 128*, 203-235.

Evans, J. (2000). *Adults' mathematical thinking and emotions: A study of numerate practices.* London: Routledge Falmer.

Furinghetti, F., & Pehkonen, E. (2002). Rethinking characterizations of beliefs. In. G. C. Leder, E. Pehkonen & G. Törner (Eds.) *Beliefs: A hidden variable in mathematics education.* Dordrecht, The Netherlands: Kluwer, 39–58.

Goldin, G. A. (2000). Affective pathways and representation in mathematical problem solving. *Mathematical Thinking and Learning 2* (3), 209-219.

Gottman, J. M. (1993). Studying emotion in social interaction. In M. Lewis & J. M. Haviland (Eds.) *Handbook of emotions.* New York: Guilford, 475-488.

McLeod, D. (1992). Research on affect in mathematics education: A reconceptualisation. In D. A. Grouws (Ed.) *Handbook of research in mathematics education teaching and learning.* New York: Macmillan, 575-596.

Hannula, M. (1998a). The case of Rita: "Maybe I started to like math more." In A. Olivier & K. Newstead (Eds.) *Proceedings of the 22nd Conference of the International Group for the Psychology of Mathematics Education,* Vol 3. Stellenbosch, South Africa, 33-40.

Hannula, M. (1998b). Changes of beliefs and attitudes. In E. Pehkonen & G. Törner (Eds.) *The state-of-art in mathematics-related belief research; Results of the MAVI activities, Research Report 184.* University of Helsinki, Department of Teacher Education, 198–222.

Hannula, M. S. (2001). The metalevel of cognition-emotion interaction. In M. Ahtee, O. Björkqvist, E. Pehkonen, & V. Vatanen, (Eds.) *Research on mathematics and science education. From beliefs to cognition, from problem solving to understanding.* Finland: University of Jyväskylä, Institute for Educational Research, 55-65.

Hannula, M. S. (2002a). Attitude towards mathematics: emotions, expectations and values. *Educational Studies in Mathematics, 49*(1), 25 – 46.

Hannula, M. S. (2002b). Goal regulation: needs, beliefs, and emotions. In A. D. Cockburn & E. Nardi (Eds.) *Proceedings of the 26th Conference of the International group for the Psychology of Mathematics Education,* Vol. 4. Norwich, UK, 73-80.

Hannula, M. S. (2004a). Affect in mathematical thinking and learning. Turku, Finland: Annales universitatis Turkuensis B 273.

Hannula, M. S. (2004b). Regulating motivation in mathematics. A paper presented at the Topic Study Group 24 of ICME-10 conference. Retrieved September 15th 2005 at http://www.icme-organisers.dk/tsg24/Documents/Hannula.doc

Hannula. M. (2005). A case study of two students' belief systems and goal systems in a conflict over teaching methods. In C. Bergsten & B. Grevholm (Eds.) *Conceptions of mathematics. Proceedings of Norma 01. Third Nordic Conference on Mathematics Education.* Linköping: SMDFs Skriftserie, 140-147.

Hannula, M.S., Maijala, H., & Pehkonen, E. (2004). Development of understanding and self-confidence in mathematics; grades 5-8. In M. J. Høines & A. B. Fuglestad (Eds.) *Proceedings of the 28th Conference of the International Group for the Psychology of Mathematics Education.* Vol 3. Bergen University College, 17-24.

Hembree, R. (1990). The nature, effects, and relief of mathematics anxiety. *Journal for Research in Mathematics Education, 21,* 33–46.

Isoda, M. & Nagagoshi, A. (2000). A case study of a student emotional change using changing heart rate in problem posing and solving Japanese classroom in mathematics. In T. Nakahara & M Koyama (Eds.) *Proceedings of the 24th conference of the international group for the Psychology of Mathematics Education.*Vol 3. Hiroshima, Japan, 87-94.

Izard, C. E. (1983, revised). The maximally discriminative facial movement coding system. Newark: University of Delaware, Instructional Resources Center.

Kaasila, R., Hannula, M. S., Laine, A. & Pehkonen, E. (2005). Autobiograpical narratives, identity and view of mathematics. In *Proceedings of the Fourth Congress of the European Society for Research in Mathematics Education 17. – 21.2. 2005 in Sant Feliu de Guixols, Spain.* Retrieved 3.11.2005 at http://cerme4.crm.es/Papers%20definitius/2/wg2listofpapers.htm

Kloosterman, P. (2002). Beliefs about mathematics and mathematics learning in the secondary school: Measurement and implications for motivation. In. G. C. Leder, E. Pehkonen & G. Törner (Eds.) *Beliefs: A Hidden Variable in Mathematics Education.* Dordrecht, The Neatherlands: Kluwer, 247-269.

Lazarus, R. S. (1991). *Emotion and adaptation.* Oxford, NY: Oxford University Press.

Leder, G. (1995). Equity inside the mathematics classroom: Fact or artifact? In W. G. Secada, E. Fennema & L. B. Adaijan (Eds.) *New directions for equity in mathematics education.* Cambridge: University Press.

LeDoux, J. (1998). *The Emotional Brain.* London: Phoenix/Orion.

230

Lemos, M. S. (1999). Students' goals and self-regulation in the classroom. *International Journal of Educational Researc, 31*, 471-486.

Lincoln Y. S. & Guba, E. G. (2000). Paradigmatic controversies, contradictions, and emerging confluences. In Norman K. Denzin and Yvonna S. Lincoln. (Eds) *Handbook of qualitative research.* Thousand Oaks, CA: Sage,163-188.

Linnanmäki, K. (2002). *Matematikprestationer och självuppfattning, en uppföljninggsstudie I relation till skolspråk och kön.* [Mathematical proficiency and self-concept; a longitudinal study with an attention to language and gender]. Turku: Åbo Akademi University Press.

Liljedahl, P. (2005). Sustained engagement: Preservice teachers' experience with a chain of discovery. In *Proceedings of the Fourth Congress of the European Society for Research in Mathematics Education 17. – 21.2. 2005 in Sant Feliu de Guíxols, Spain.* Retrieved 3.11.2005 at http://cerme4.crm.es/Papers%20definitius/2/wg2listofpapers.htm

Linnenbrink E. A. & Pintrich, P. R. (2000). Multiple pathways to learning and achievement: The role of goal orientation in fostering adaptive motivation, affect, and cognition. In C. Sansone & J. M. Harackiewicz (Eds.) *Intrinsic and extrinsic motivation: The search for optimal motivation and performance.* New York: Academic Press, 195-227.

Linnenbrink, E. A. & Pintrich, P. R. (2004). Role of affect in cognitive processing in academic contexts. In D. Y. Dai & R. J. Sternberg (Eds.) *Motivation, emotion, and cognition; Integrative perspectives on intellectual functioning and development.* Mahwah, NJ: Lawrence Erlbaum, 57-88.

Ma, X. & Kishor, N. (1997). Assessing the relationship between attitude toward mathematics and achievement in mathematics: A meta-analyses. *Journal for Research in Mathematics Education, 28*(1), 26-47.

Mandler, G. (1989). Affect and learning: Causes and consequences of emotional interactions. In D. B. McLeod and V. M. Adams (Eds.), *Affect and mathematical problem solving: A new perspective.* New York: Springer-Verlag, 3-19.

McLeod, D.B. (1992). Research on affect in mathematics education: A reconceptualization. In D.A.Grouws (Ed.) *Handbook of research on mathematics learning and teaching,* 575-596. New York: MacMillan.

Meyer, D. K. & Turner, J. C. (2002). Discovering emotion in classroom motivation research. *Educational Psychologist 37* (2), 107 – 114.

Murphy, P. K. & Alexander, P. A. (2000). A motivated exploration of motivation terminology. *Contemporary Educational Psychology, 25*, 3-53.

Nuttin, J. (1984). *Motivation, planning, and action: A relational theory of behavior dynamic.* Leuven University Press.

Op 't Eynde P., De Corte, E. & Verschaffel, L. (In print). Accepting emotional complexity: A socio-constructivist perspective on the role of emotions in the mathematics classroom. *Educational Studies in Mathematics.*

Op 't Eynde, P. & Hannula, M. S. (In print). The case study of Frank. *Educational Studies in Mathematics.*

Pekrun, R., Goetz, T., Titz, W., & Perry, R. P. (2002). Academic emotions and students' self regulated learning and achievement: A program for qualitative and quantitative research. *Educational Psychologist 37* (2), 91 – 105.

Philippou, G, & Christou, C. (2002). A study of the mathematics teaching, Efficacy beliefs of Primary Teachers. In. G. C. Leder, E. Pehkonen & G. Törner (Eds.) *Beliefs: A hidden variable in mathematics education.* Dordrecht: Kluwer, 211-232.

Polkinghorne, D. (1995). Narrative configuration in qualitative analysis. In J. Hatch & R. Wisniewski (Eds.) *Life history and narrative.* London: Falmer Press, 5-23.

Popper, K. R. & Ecceles, J. C. (1977). *The self and its brain.* Berlin: Springer International.

Power, M. & Dalgleish, T. (1997). *Cognition and emotion: From order to disorder.* UK: Psychology Press.

Reid, D.A. (1996). Enactivism as a methodology. In L. Puig & A Gutiérrez, (Eds.), *Proceedings of the Twentieth Annual Conference of the International Group for the Psychology of Mathematics Education*, Vol. 4. Valencia, Spain, 203-210.

Ryan, R. M. & Deci, E. L. (2000). When rewards compete with nature: The undermining of intrinsic motivation and self-regulation. In C. Sansone & J. M. Harackiewicz (Eds.) *Intrinsic and extrinsic motivation: The search for optimal motivation and performance*. New York: Academic Press, 13-55.

Salovey, P. & Mayer, J. D. (1990). Emotional intelligence. *Imagination, Cognition, and Personality, 9*, 185-211.

Schoenfeld, A. H. (1985). *Mathematical problem solving*. San Diego: Academic Press.

Schoenfeld, A. H. (1998). Toward a theory of teaching-in-context. *Issues in Education, 4* (1), 1-94.

Schwarz, N. & Skrunik, I. (2003). Feeling and thinking: Implications for problem solving. In J. E. Davidson & R. J. Sternberg (Eds.). *The psychology of problem solving*. Cambridge, UK: University Press, 263-290.

Shah, J. Y. & Kruglanski, A. W. (2000). The structure and substance of intrinsic motivation. In C. Sansone & J. M. Harackiewicz (Eds.) *Intrinsic and extrinsic motivation: The search for optimal motivation and performance*. New York: Academic Press, 105-129.

Vermeer, H. J. (1997). Sixth-grade students' mathematical problem solving behavior: Motivational variables and gender differences. Doctoral dissertation, Leiden University.

Vinner, S. (2000). Mathematics education – Procedures, rituals and man's search for meaning. In *ICME 9, Abstracts of plenary lectures and regular lectures, July 31-August 6, 2000*. Tokyo / Makuhari, Japan,120-121.

Yakel, E. & Cobb, P. (1996). Sociomathematical norms, argumentation, and autonomy in mathematics. *Journal for Research in Mathematics Education, 27* (4), 458-477.

Zan, R., Brown. L., Evans, J. & Hannula, M. S. (In print). Affect in mathematics education: an introduction. *Educational Studies in Mathematics*.

Zimmerman, B. J. & Campillio, M. (2003). Motivating self-regulated problem solvers. I J. E. Davidson & R. J. Sternberg (Es.) *The psychology of problem solving*. UK: Cambridge University Press, 233-262.

Zimmerman, B. J. & Schunk, D.H. (2004). Self-regulating intellectual processes and outcomes: A social cognitive perspective. In D. Y. Dai & R. J. Sternberg (Eds.) *Motivation, emotion, and cognition: Integrative perspectives on intellectual functioning and development*. Mahwah, NJ: Lawrence Erlbaum, 323-350.

Marrku S. Hannula
Finnland

NOTES

[1] Note that beliefs about motivation (motivational beliefs) are not quite the same as motivation.

JEFF EVANS

AFFECT AND EMOTION IN MATHEMATICAL THINKING AND LEARNING

The Turn to the Social: Sociocultural Approaches Introduction: Recent Developments in Research on Affect

Twenty to thirty years ago, mathematical affect was considered to comprise basically mathematics anxiety and attitudes to mathematics, typically measured by self-report, paper and pencil measures such as those devised by Richardson and Suinn (1972), and Fennema and Sherman (1976). The former researchers were interested in 'catch-up' programmes for adults intending to return to higher education, and the latter were at the forefront of efforts to increase females' participation in, and achievement in, mathematics courses, especially more advanced ones: in both cases, 'negative' affect towards mathematics was seen as a barrier to their educational goals.[1] In explanations of differences in mathematical outcomes, such as school performance and take-up of mathematics courses, affective variables were considered both to have their own direct effects, and to mediate the effects of social influences (e.g. gender or age) on mathematical outcomes (e.g. Fennema, 1989).

Though it was productive, this early research on affect was constrained by a number of limitations:

- Affect was measured usually by self-report procedures, which limited what could be tapped to what the respondent was conscious of, and also willing to reveal to the researcher.
- Affect was conceived as trait (enduring) measures, rather than state (transitory) measures, thus limiting researchers' ability to trace the dynamics of problem solving, for example.
- Affective responses were conceived as individual characteristics, thus limiting their capacity to be 'situated' in the social (e.g. classroom, family) context.
- Measures were focussed on a limited range of feelings: anxiety, confidence, liking, enjoyment, perceived difficulty, perceived usefulness.
- There was a tendency to see affect as "negative" / debilitating of performance, rather than positive / facilitative (or as anything ambivalent or "in between").

J. Maasz, W. Schloeglmann (Eds.), New Mathematics Education Research and Practice, 233–255.

Since the late 1980s, there have been a number of key developments, some related to broadening the scope of mathematical affect, some related to introducing expanded and/or innovative theoretical frameworks.

In a series of important contributions, McLeod (1989a, 1989b, 1992; McLeod & Adams, 1989) argued for the importance of *emotions*, in addition to attitudes and beliefs, which had been the focus in most previous research in mathematics education. He drew on the work of the psychologist Mandler (1989), to present a 'cognitive-constructivist' model for *transitory* emotions, experienced during the *process* of problem-solving, rather than being restricted to measures of *durable* attitudes and beliefs. DeBellis & Goldin (1997) suggested the addition of *values* to the scheme, which might arguably be placed on the durable, less intense side of the spectrum (though they preferred to place the four categories in unordered form as points of a tetrahedron). Evans (2002) suggested the inclusion of *mood*, on the volatile, more intense side of the spectrum.

Beliefs   (Values)   Attitudes   (Mood)   Emotion

<--->

Trait: More durable   *State*: More transitory

Less intense   More intense

More "cognitive" [reflective]   More "affective" [charged]

Sources: McLeod (1992); DeBellis & Goldin (1997); Evans (2002)

Figure 1. McLeod's Types of Affect

At the same time, there has been continuing interest in mathematics-related *beliefs* both of teachers and of students; see e.g. Leder, Pehkonen & Törner eds. (2002). And although the concept of *attitude* continues to be used in research, it has been subjected to much critical scrutiny (see e.g. Hannula, this volume; DiMartino & Zan, 2001).

The theoretical basis of most research on affect in mathematics education in this period has been mainstream psychology, or (less prominently) mainstream education. There has been only intermittent attention to psychoanalytic approaches; see e.g. Nimier (1977, 1978); Walkerdine (1988); Tahta (1993); Evans (2000); Cabral (2004). All three of these areas share an interest in motivation, which, after years of relative inattention in mathematics education research, is beginning to receive attention by some researchers. This work is summarised by Hannula (this volume); see also Hannula (2006), Mendick (2002), Evans & Wedege (2004).

There has been renewed interest in the biological bases of emotion, in the light of the neuroscientific work of Damasio (1996) and others, which has provided stimulating accounts of the crucial role of emotion in rational procedures, such as decision-making. In mathematics education, see Schlöglmann (2002) and Brown &

234

Reid (2006), who use the concept of *somatic markers*, proposed by Damasio (1996).

There has been some interest in sociological approaches to affect within mathematics education (e.g. Gates, 2006; Evans, Morgan & Tsatsaroni, 2006). But there has been rather more work on developing a somewhat broader grouping of 'sociocultural' approaches. Both of these challenge the psychological emphasis on affect understood as individual characteristics, and emphasise the social basis and *social organisation* of affect.

The key trend in mathematics education research, to which most of the developments described above contribute, is an increasing emphasis on emotions, as compared with earlier periods, when beliefs and attitudes were the main focus. There are a number of reasons for this:

- Mathematics education researchers have tended to take their conceptual frameworks on affect from psychologists (see above), who in turn have tended to focus on 'hotter', more visceral emotion, rather than the whole range of affect in Fig. 1 above (Evans, 2000, pp43-44).
- A focus on emotions allows description of any affect-laden activity, such as mathematical problem-solving, as a *process* which unfolds *dynamically*.
- The activity can be described *in context*, so as to assess the role played by social interaction, classroom culture and pedagogic (and other) discourses in mathematical thinking and performance.
- The more durable forms of affect, attitudes and beliefs can be understood to have a basis in the more transitory emotions (see e.g. Evans, Morgan & Tsatsaroni, 2006).

In the next part of the chapter, I will expand on this emphasis on the emotions, and on how it relates to emphasising the social basis and social organisation of affect in sociocultural approaches. I then go on to describe and to contrast three currently distinguishable types of approach to the study of emotion in mathematics education, all of which can be classified as sociocultural educational research.

EMOTION AS SOCIALLY ORGANISED

A range of social theorists, including the psychologist William James (1890/1950), have considered the different aspects of emotion, and their primacy. When we compare recent analyses from several different disciplines, we find broad agreement on the importance of three aspects of emotional states:

- bodily processes, including the brain, but also nerves and organs (e.g. heart, stomach);
- behavioural (including verbal) expression; and
- subjective experience or "feeling".

We can thus find broadly similar analyses in work by psychologists like Zajonc (1984), Kitayama & Markus (1994), and Buck (1997); by sociologists like Burkitt (1997); by neuroscientists like Damasio (1996)[2]; and by the psychoanalyst Freud (1916-17/1974) on anxiety (see Evans, 2000, pp112-3).

Now, it may seem that all three of these aspects of emotion are individually based – after all, introspection would suggest that they are individual 'experiences'. However, reflection clarifies that certainly (b) methods of self-expression and (c) ways of feeling are at least partly learned in social settings by human beings. Furthermore, social theorists who have argued that the body is the raw material of social and cultural organisation would suggest that (a) bodily processes should be included as social, too (e.g. Grosz, 1994).

This means that there is a wealth of evidence, anecdotal and systematic, that differences, both in modes of behavioural (including verbal) expression and in subjective experience or feeling, are different in different cultures and different social groups (see e.g. Wierzbicka, 1994). Thus it is reasonable to conclude that emotional expression and experience are embedded in social contexts, and thus can be seen as *socially organised* (by the prevailing beliefs and norms, etc.) – just like thinking, learning, or working with mathematics.

So far, we can agree with Markku Hannula (Hannula, this volume) that emotions, emotional states, emotional experience satisfy both of the following:
- they involve physiological reaction, and
- they are functional in human adaptation and social coping.

But we need to question claims made, for example by Markku, that all approaches to the study of emotions need to see them primarily in connection with "personal goals" – *if* the latter are understood in the usual sense as conscious, individually formulated, and/or rationally articulated.

For one thing, emotions may be *unconscious* in the psychoanalytic sense[3] of being pushed into the unconscious, via the operation of *repression*, one of the defence mechanisms. In psychoanalytic approaches, ideas which have strong negative charges, such as anxiety, or which mobilise intrapsychic conflict, have a tendency to meet defences, and thus to be repressed. Therefore, much thought and activity takes place outside of conscious awareness: everyday life is mediated by unconscious images, thoughts and fantasies (Hunt, 1989). This unconscious material is linked to complex webs of meaning (Evans, 2000, Chs.7-10).

In particular, emotions must be understood in connection with *desires* and *fantasies*. There are aspects of these features of human experience that may differentiate them from the characteristics of personal goals, as usually understood. Many desires are unconscious, since they may be felt to be 'unacceptable' or in conflict with the person's desired social image; fantasies are specifically 'unrealistic' or 'irrational' images and narratives that express the desire for some object on the part of the person entertaining them. Both have 'social' aspects, in that desires are connected with social imagery, for example advertising and films, and fantasies can manifestly be shared at the group, professional, or national cultural level (Walkerdine, 1988, Chs. 9 and 10).

- *1ˢᵗ Interlude: an illustration from* Enigma *(2000)*

Both this and the next Interlude present and interpret excerpts from recent films, which portray mathematicians, plus their thinking, and/or their work. This allows me to illustrate the effectivity of films in the way that they articulate powerful elements of social imagery, here discourses about mathematics / mathematicians. In the first excerpt, the themes of desire and fantasy are illustrated in the story of the code-breaking headquarters at Bletchley Park in Britain in World War 2 (Evans, 2003). In this scene, the hero, a mathematician, goes to the home of a woman with whom he had earlier fallen in love. He does not find her there, but he cannot resist entering her room, and recollecting her image, as he smells her perfumes, and, in particular, one earlier meeting with her:

Theme song in the background, they are sitting on a sofa.
She: Why are you a mathematician? Do you like sums?
He, holding a rose: Because I like numbers – because, with numbers, truth and beauty are the same thing ... you know you're getting somewhere, when the equations start looking ... beautiful. *(He looks at her slightly appraisingly / appreciatively.)*
Then you know the numbers are taking you closer to the secret of how things are. A rose is just plain text...
He hands her the rose; she takes it, but, as he passes it over, a thorn pierces his thumb and makes it bleed. She kisses his thumb; they embrace.

In this scene, the beauty of mathematics is intertwined with that of the rose and that of the woman. He exhibits his desire for these beautiful 'objects', and further, in aligning beauty with truth in mathematics, he suggests a 'higher' form of beauty. His desire to follow "the numbers [...] closer to the secret of how things are" suggests a heroic goal shared by many mathematicians, and also attractive to some young mathematics students at school. Others have considered the extent to which this version of 'Reason's dream' can be usefully understood as *fantasy* (e.g. Walkerdine, 1988).

– *Ways that emotions arise*

In the illustration above, the beginning of the scene can be interpreted to show that the male mathematician is experiencing pleasure through entering the room, and smelling the perfume of the woman he loved as these are associated with her. He is also experiencing pleasure through remembering the encounter with her. These re-experienced pleasures derive from the original experience with her, which was imbued with feeling – but they also reformulate that experience, as they reverberate with pleasures experienced in practising mathematics.

In a similar way, many school children and adults would cite experiences in learning and doing mathematics in the classroom, as formative of their 'individual feelings' about mathematics. However we should note the influences at *micro*, *meso* and *macro* levels of the social (see Cobb / Conclusions, this volume). At the meso level, we have the 'socio-mathematical norms' established in the classroom (Cobb et al., 1989), or the form of pedagogic practices (e.g. visible vs. invisible), in which the child is involved (Bernstein, 2000); the latter also have a macro aspect, in that they may be developed and promoted nationally, or even globally, by government policy or other interests. At the micro (face-to-face interactional) level, we can point to examples of experiences in doing mathematics homework within the family; see for example, the case of 'Peter', an undergraduate economics student, who had been constantly 'helped' while at school to do his mathematics homework by his father, and on occasion by one or more of his four 'mathematician' brothers (Evans, 2000).

All of these instances of emotion are experienced by individuals who already have beliefs and attitudes that are to a great extent *culturally transmitted*. This may involve the attention to, and adoption of, views of 'significant others' (Scribner and Cole, 1973). (Thus, three of Fennema & Sherman's (1976) Attitude to Mathematics scales concerned the student's (perception of) her Mother's, Father's, and Teacher's attitudes towards herself as a learner of mathematics.) But there is also a role for the media and other means of communication, which transmit images of mathematics and mathematicians in popular culture (Appelbaum, 1995; Evans, 2003, 2004; Mendick, 2006)[4].

Emotion can also arise through an association with objects or ideas different from those to which it was originally linked. Psychoanalytic approaches see this as happening through the capacity of an affective charge to move from one idea to another along a chain of associations by *displacement*. A number of examples are given by Nimier (1977, 1978; see Evans, 2000, pp116-9). The following excerpt from another film featuring a mathematician also illustrates this displacement.

2nd Interlude: an illustration from Smilla's Feeling for Snow (Bille August, Germany / Denmark / Sweden, 1997)
Here the heroine, who investigates the mysterious death of a young boy in a block of flats in Copenhagen, is also a mathematician. In one scene, where she is having a meal with a man who clearly has strong feelings for her (apparently unreciprocated), she is describing how difficult it was for her to be relocated from Greenland to Denmark, as a young girl:
He: And you were never happy here?
She: The only thing that makes me truly happy is mathematics ... snow ... ice ... numbers [*She smiles.*] To me the number system is like human life. First you have the natural numbers, the ones that are whole and positive, like the numbers of a small child. But human consciousness expands and the child discovers longing. Do you know the mathematical expression for longing? [*He shakes his head.*] Negative numbers, the formalisation of the feeling that you're missing something. Then the child discovers the in-between spaces, between stones, between people, between numbers – and that produces fractions. But, it's, it's like a kind of madness, because it doesn't even stop there.... There are numbers that we can't even begin to comprehend. Mathematics is a vast open landscape: you head towards the horizon, it's always receding ... like Greenland. And that's what I can't live without, that's why I can't be locked up....
He: Smilla, can I kiss you? [*She moves away.*]

This scene again associates mathematics with beauty: here we have a beautiful female mathematician herself talking about mathematics. As we listen to her talk, what comes across most strongly is her longing … for numbers, mathematics, Greenland, and the sense of loss as she sees them "always receding". The original (in this excerpt) feeling of loss and longing appears to relate to Greenland, which itself may stand for another object, such as her dead mother; that feeling is *displaced* onto mathematics, and in turn onto the negative numbers – that part of mathematics which for her "formalises" the feeling of loss, and which she contrasts with the "whole and positive" natural numbers of the young child.

Thus we see that films, and other objects of popular culture are sites for the articulation of discourses within which meanings are defined, images are built up, and hence power is invested. This illustrates another way in which emotions are socially organised.

THE SOCIAL ORGANISATION OF AFFECT: SOCIOCULTURAL APPROACHES

I have argued above that emotion and affect are socially organised, and that a broadly sociocultural approach is needed for investigations in this area. My understanding of developments in this area in mathematics education research at this time is that there are several approaches which certainly have different starting points, but whose trajectories suggest the possibility of developing significant common ground. For the purposes of illustration, I group these sociocultural approaches provisionally under three headings:

- socio-constructivism (SC), based on efforts aiming to bring out a social or 'situated' aspect to work based on the ideas of Piaget and others labelled as "constructivists" (Ernest, 1991; Cobb and Bowers, 1999); see, for example, Op' t Eynde & De Corte (2003), Gomez-Chacon (2000).
- cultural-historical activity theory (CHAT), based on the work of "Soviet psychologists", as developed in the USA and Western Europe over the last fifty years (Leont'ev, 1978); see also Cobb (this volume), van Oers (this volume).
- a discursive practice (DP) approach, which draws on Critical Discourse Analysis (Fairclough, 2003) in socio-linguistics, work on pedagogic discourses in the sociology of education (Bernstein, 2000), and Valerie Walkerdine's poststructuralist analyses, drawing on psychoanalytic concepts (e.g. 1988, 1997); see also Evans (2000), Mendick (2006).

In the following sections, I aim to illustrate the scope of three recent strands of sociocultural work on affect, to highlight theoretical similarities (and to note differences) among these approaches, and to give instances of innovative methodologies. Given space limits, I compare them by referring mainly (but not exclusively) to one 'exemplar' from each. The illustrative reports are:

SC: Op 't Eynde, de Corte & Verschaffel, 'Accepting emotional complexity: a socio-constructivist perspective on the role of emotions in the mathematics classroom' (2006)

CHAT: Roth, 'Motive, Emotion and Identity at Work: a Contribution to Third-Generation Cultural Historical Activity Theory' (2006)

DP: Evans, Morgan & Tsatsaroni, 'Discursive Positioning and Emotion in School Mathematics Practices' (2006).[5]

In order to compare the three approaches to emotion, I use an approach to the analysis of research reports developed by Evans and Zan (2006) [6], drawing on Schoenfeld (2002), and especially Lerman et al. (2002)[7]. Evans and Zan aimed to produce a set of questions and categories that could be used to systematically read and categorise a set of articles from a reasonably homogeneous area, so as to assess commonalities and divergences among different contributions, and the scope of work in the area; see Figure 2.

1. Conceptual framework:
    (a)   What are the key concepts and the basics of the approach used in researching affect?
    (b)   How is emotion characterised?
2. Problems addressed:
    (c)   What are the aims motivating the research at this stage?
3. Methodology:
    (d)   What are the preferred research methods for the approach?
    (e)   What are the key phases in the main study reported, and the research design (the population of interest, etc.)?
4. Outcomes:
    (f)   What uses of the approach are apparent in the main study reported?
    (g)   What findings illustrate the range of the approach, both those which are distinctive to the approach, and those in line with other approaches here classed as sociocultural?

Source: Evans & Zan (2006)

Figure 2. Questions for the Systematic Reading of Research Reports

The categories available for responses to each question, and the way they are applied, are illustrated in the following analyses of each approach.

SOCIO-CONSTRUCTIVIST (SC) APPROACHES

Research Report: Op 't Eynde, DeCorte and Verschaffel (2006); different features of the same main study are reported in Op 't Eynde et al. (2001) and Op 't Eynde & De Corte (2003).

Key concepts and *basics of the approach*: participation; context; situated; appraisal; component systems; beliefs; motivation. Students' learning is perceived as a form of *engagement* (cf. Wenger, 1998) that enables them to realise their identity through *participation* in activities *situated* in a specific *context*. A student's appraisal processes, part of his/her cognitive system (itself one of five mutually influencing *component systems* – see below), are in turn influenced by the student's mathematics-related *beliefs*.

For Op 't Eynde et al., *emotions* are conceptualised as consisting of coordinated feedback from multiple processes, which mutually regulate each other over time in a particular context. These processes are characteristic of five different systems (Scherer, 2000):

- the cognitive system, including appraisal processes
- the autonomic nervous system, the basis for arousal
- the monitor system, the basis for feeling
- the motor system, the basis for (behavioural) expression
- the motivational system, the basis for action tendencies.

Emotions are seen as social in nature and situated in a specific socio-historical context, because of the social nature of an individual's knowledge and beliefs – which play a role in appraisal processes, themselves context-specific and fluid.

Aims of the study: Analysing the relation between students' mathematics-related beliefs, their emotions, and their problem-solving behaviour in the mathematics classroom. Given the close relation between emotions and beliefs, investigation of students' emotions can enhance understanding of their beliefs and therefore behaviour.

Methodology: The basics of the approach imply that *mathematical activity should be studied in context*, and that researchers should *take an actor's perspective* that allows the meaning structure underlying students' behaviours and emotions to become explicit.

Preferred research methods: Following these methodological implications, the main study adopted a multiple approach to collecting data *within* selected classrooms, involving protocols and video tapes of problem solving episodes, questionnaires, interviews.

The *research design* for the study involved selecting four different classrooms within four different schools in the second year of junior high school (aged 14) in Belgium; the four classrooms represented four different secondary education tracks, ranging from classical to vocational "levels" (Op 't Eynde & de Corte, 2003).

There are two *key phases* in the data collection here. First, a beliefs assessment: all students in the four classrooms were presented with the Mathematics-Related Beliefs Questionnaire (MRBQ). Second, problem-solving behaviour and interviews: four students in each class, selected to represent different 'belief profiles', were asked to solve (each of four) mathematical problems, and the process was documented, using a series of records:

- On-line Motivation Questionnaire (OMQ), after the students had skimmed each problem, before actually starting work
- videotaped "thinking aloud" during problem solving

- immediately after finishing, an interview procedure using a Video-Based Stimulated Recall interview (VBSR).

The analysis of the data itself can be divided into four *key phases*. First, the beliefs questionnaires were analysed at the level of the entire sample, using e.g. factor analysis to explore the dimensionality of responses; this provided a basis for each student's responses to be compared with others' and categorised into 'belief profiles' ('negative', 'mildly positive', 'positive' or 'highly positive'). Next, for each student, the 'narrative' describing the process and experiences of each problem-solving episode for each student was produced using the different data sources; these narratives were content analysed. Third, the relations between students' mathematics-related beliefs, their task-specific perceptions and their problem-solving behaviour could be analysed systematically, with a view to producing explanations. Finally, cross-sectional analysis used the results for the sample of student-episodes as a whole.

Outcomes: The research highlights methodological implications of the theoretical framework presented, e.g. the need to study learning and problem solving in the classroom, and to take account of the different component systems constituting an emotion. This methodological approach is applied and illustrated with the data set.

Illustrative findings: The principal component analysis (of 57 beliefs items) produced four components:
- beliefs about the classroom context, specifically the role and functioning of the student's own teacher
- beliefs about the value of mathematics, and the student's competence in it
- beliefs about mathematics as a dynamic and social activity
- beliefs about mathematics as a domain of excellence. (Op 't Eynde & De Corte, 2003).

The narratives provided the basis for 'emotional profiles', plotting over time the changes in emotions (on a positive / negative scale) experienced (or reported) by each student during each episode[8]. The profile for 'Frank' (not his real name) shows a characteristic 'roller-coaster' pattern of alternation of 'positive' emotions like confidence, happiness and relief with 'negative' emotions such as worry, frustration and anger (Op 't Eynde & Hannula, 2006, Fig. 2).

Finally, the cross-sectional analysis (n = 16 students) suggested higher anxiety levels among students from the vocational or traditional humanities classes, compared with those from the humanities reform and traditional classical classes (higher social status). Students with a negative or only mildly positive belief profile were more likely to be classified by the researchers as holding avoidance goals towards the problems than those with more positive belief profiles (who tended to hold 'instructional', task accomplishment, or knowledge building goals) (Op 't Eynde & De Corte, 2003).

To sum up, Op 't Eynde et al. deploy a formidable array of methods to analyse the relation between students' mathematics-related beliefs, their emotions, and their problem-solving behaviour within the mathematics classroom. (Their methodological principles (see above) would certainly seem to raise questions about the appropriateness of studying emotions through out-of-class interviews.) However, the range of measurement instruments used, some fairly 'technological' and obtrusive (e.g. the On-line Motivation Questionnaire) may have limits if one wishes to preserve the ecological validity of the methodology. This concern would gather force, if the researchers were to follow their aim to deploy "a wider variety of instruments" to study component systems concerned with processes ("e.g. hormonal and physiological") in addition to the cognitive, as studied here.

Despite its promise to help in focussing on a wider range of possible measurements, the component systems framework does not yet seem to sit comfortably with the emphasis on the social. While it is plausible to argue that the student's belief structures will provide a 'social' influence on the cognitive (including appraisal) system, or the motivational system (though that has still to be explicated in this work), it is less clear how these beliefs will influence the motor, monitor, or autonomic nervous systems. Overall, the view of the social in this socio-constructivist approach, referring to beliefs and the social contexts of the data, does not analyse sufficiently the social structures relevant to the settings in which the students find themselves, for example the hierarchy of types of secondary schooling, which relates crucially to differences in expectation and resourcing, or indeed the social class backgrounds of the students themselves. This is important, since the interpretation of 'realistic' problems in classroom settings has been shown to depend on the pupils' social background and educational experiences (Cooper & Dunne, 2000).

Socio-constructivist approaches in general are reflected on elsewhere in this book (van Oers, this volume).

CULTURAL - HISTORICAL ACTIVITY THEORY (CHAT)

Research Report: Roth (2006); different features of the same main study are reported in Roth (2003, 2004, in press) and Lee & Roth (2005). Cultural - Historical Activity Theory is discussed elsewhere in this book (van Oers, this volume, and, for an overview, Cobb / Introduction, this volume); see also Engeström (e.g. 2001).

Key concepts: socially organised activity, action, operations, tools, motivation, identity. The *context* for any action is the *activity* in which the subject is engaged; the basic elements of activity include *subject, object, tools, community, rules* and *division of labour*. Activities are oriented toward collective motives, which have arisen in the course of cultural historical development; they are organised in the triplet of *activity / action / operation*: "activities and actions presuppose each other: activities are realized through concrete practical actions, but [conscious, goal-directed] actions are oriented toward the activities" (Roth, 2006). On the other hand, "actions and operations also presuppose each other, as a particular practical action is concretely realized by operations, which are only operated to bring about the action. Among the conditions shaping an operation are the current state of the action and the neurological, biochemical, neuromuscular, and emotional states of the body" (ibid.).

Emotions in this approach come from the body, as described by Damasio (1996), whose findings on the integral role of emotions in decision making are drawn on. Emotion is seen as 'integral to practical action' in two ways: first, 'the general emotional state of a person shapes practical reasoning and practical actions'; second, practical action is generally directed toward "increases in emotional valence" (Roth, 2006, 2004). Here, rather than simply equating to higher levels of pleasure rather than pain, an 'increase in emotional valence' is associated with an increase in 'room for manoeuvre' (a greater choice of actions to choose from) or to being 'better off in the long run'. Emotion is seen as a crucial basis for *motivation* and identity, which derive from it. Motivation is constituted by an "expansion of action possibilities, [which is] loaded [i.e. associated] with an increase in emotional valence in the context of predictable effort, cost and risk" (Roth, in press; see also Turner, 2002). *Identity* is related to an individual's participation in collective activity, and to the 'recognition' received as a member of the community; this relates to individual and collective emotional valences arising from face-to-face interaction with others.

Aims: This paper aims to extend the relatively cognitive approach of '3rd generation CHAT' to encompass emotion, motivation and identity – and to provide evidence of the need for that. This is to provide the basis for a fuller explanation of performance, notably mathematical thinking and modelling, at work (Roth, in press). Thus this work focuses on the mathematical thinking of adults in the workplace, unlike the other two research projects reviewed.

Methodology: The first *key phase* of this study was Roth's full-scale (four-year) ethnography of a salmon fish hatchery in British Columbia. The *preferred research methods* are thus ethnographic (participant observation), as in much work done in the CHAT approach (e.g. Roth, 2005). When the author decided his claims about emotions required more convincing indicators, this was supplemented by systematic measurement of speech intensity and pitch (Roth, 2006).

Outcomes: The study revisits 3rd generation CHAT theory, and contributes to a significant revision, with the illustration of inclusion of conceptions of emotions, motivation and identity.

Illustrative findings: The ethnographic findings described the emotions of pleasure expressed by one of the fish culturists ("Erica") on finding that the fish under her care had grown to satisfactory sizes; these findings were supported further by the measures of the actor's voice pitch. Her use of a PC and a range of mathematical representations (graphs and statistical summaries) allowed her to better monitor the progress of 'her' fish, thus increasing her 'room for manoeuvre' and her feelings of pleasure (positive valence). These actions also help her to be recognised as a bit of a "geek" ("nerd"), an aspect of her identity in the activity system of the fish hatchery. The researcher sees the examples provided by the long-term ethnographic contact as hinting at a "dialectical relation linking individual and collective emotion" (Roth, 2006): for example, he is able to chart the change in *mood* – a moderately volatile type of affect (see Figure 1 above), here experienced *collectively* – in the fishery when operating costs increased, and government funding declined.

To sum up, this series of papers argues firmly for a view in which cognition and emotion are seen not only as mutually influencing, but also as having 'inner connections in activity' (2006). Emotion is seen as a crucial basis for motivation and identity, which derive from it. Including emotion, motivation and identity in 'Third-Generation CHAT' will certainly enhance the theory's ability to contribute to the understanding of practical action. It also provides the basis for dialogue with the other sociocultural approaches examined here.

DISCURSIVE APPROACHES

Research report: Evans, Morgan & Tsatsaroni (2006); see also Evans (2000, 2002, 2003a), Morgan, Tsatsaroni & Lerman (2002), Morgan (1998).

Key Concepts: discourse, practices, positions, positioning, subjectivity, power. Discursive approaches focus on specific societal / institutional *practices*, which are recurrent forms of behaviour / action. A *discourse* then is the system of ideas / signs organising and regulating the related practices, in a way that crucially connects with social relations of *power*. Discourse has several functions:
- defining how certain things are represented, thought about, and practised
- providing resources for constructing meanings, and accounting for actions
- helping to construct identities and subjectivities, which include affective characteristics and processes (Hall, 1997).

Power is exerted in micro social interactions, in 'meso' institutional contexts, and in the wider culture, including by policy-makers and by the media within popular culture (Appelbaum, 1995).

A key concept is that of *positioning*, a process whereby an individual subject takes up and/or is put into one of the *positions* which are *made available* by the discourse(s) at play in the setting. This is how the approach allows for a mutual influencing of social and individual: the social setting makes available specific practices, and individuals retain a degree of agency, to strive to position themselves in available (or 'created') positions. The social produces other effects: different positions are associated with membership of different social groups (class, gender, ethnicity), and with different degrees of power. In this approach, a person's *identity*, which includes more durable affect such as attitudes and beliefs, comes from repetitions of positionings, and the related emotional experiences, in a context of a personal history of positionings in practices.

Emotion is related to desire, which is considered to permeate the workings of language. Thus emotion can be visualised as a charge attached to ideas and the terms in which they are expressed. This charge has a physiological, behavioural (including verbal) expression, and a subjective 'feeling' aspect (see above). This allows emotion to be seen as 'attached' to ideas (cognition), but in ways that are fluid, not fixed. Some of this fluidity can be seen as related to psychic processes of displacement, where meanings and feelings flow along a chain of ideas (or signifiers) and condensation, where meanings and feelings 'pile up' on a single signifier (Evans, 2000). Thus, the psychic / 'individual' and the linguistic / social interconnect.

Aims: This paper aims to "show that emotions are socially organised phenomena, which are constituted in discourse, shaped in relations of power, and implicated in constructing social identity" (Evans et al., 2006). In theoretical terms, the work also has interdisciplinary aims, to bring together ideas on the form of pedagogic discourse from the sociology of education, analyses of the process of positioning from social semiotics, and insights into the dynamics of the unconscious from psychoanalysis. In practical terms, it aims to sensitise teachers, teacher educators and policy makers to the (often neglected) importance of emotions in the learning (and use) of mathematics.

Methodology: Because of the emphasis on detailed semiotic analysis of texts, methods which produce transcripts of social interaction are appropriate. Thus, preferred research methods include classroom observation and also interviews. This study analysed the transcript of interaction in a classroom episode selected by a colleague of the authors as being possibly fruitful for studying emotion9. The episode analysed involved three boys, working together on a mathematical task, in an 8th grade classroom in Lisbon, Portugal. Walkerdine (1988) used transcripts of mothers and daughters discussing everyday tasks at home. Other studies have used interviews with teachers or students (Morgan et al., 2002; Evans, 2000) or questionnaires (Evans, 2000).

Two key phases of analysis of the transcripts (and videotapes), structural and textual, are based on the interdisciplinary theoretical approach. First the structural phase uses Bernstein (2000)'s sociology of education to show how pedagogic discourse(s) make available particular positions to individuals. For example, the discourses at play in school invariably include evaluation practices, which make available positions of evaluator and evaluated. The 'official discourse' (often 'traditional') is contrasted with 'local pedagogy' (in this classroom, relatively 'progressive'), where students may be encouraged to evaluate each other's work. Furthermore, other discourses from 'outside', including those from the peer-group and from the youth culture, are also at play in the classroom. Conflicts between expectations of different practices may elicit emotion.

Second, the textual phase has two functions: (a) showing how positions are actually taken up by subjects as positionings, in social interaction, and (b) providing material for indicators of emotional experience. For these purposes, social interaction is itself represented as text, e.g. via transcripts. Examples of how interpersonal aspects of the text are used to establish particular participants in particular discursive positions include: claims to know or to understand (which are powerful in educational settings), and the use of repetition or hidden agency (passive voice).

Indicators of emotional experience can be divided into (i) those understood within the institutional subculture and/or wider culture, drawing on the everyday 'folk culture' of participants, and (ii) indicators suggested by psychoanalytic insights. Examples of (i) include: verbal expression of feeling; behavioural indicators (facial expression, tone of voice); use of particular metaphors, e.g. a student claiming to be "coasting" in mathematics (Evans, 2000, p214). Examples of (ii) include mainly indicators of defences against strong emotions like anxiety, or conflicts between positionings (see above; Evans 2000), e.g. 'Freudian slips', such as a 'surprising' error in problem solving, behaving 'strangely' (e.g. laughing 'nervously'), denial (e.g. of anxiety), as in 'protesting too much' about how confident one is.

Outcomes: The authors apply their theory to a 'critical case': this is classroom (rather than interview) data, involving several students interacting, and not originally collected for studying emotion; they argue that the results indicate a wider scope for the study of emotions, using this (and other sociocultural) theory than might originally have been expected.

Illustrative findings: At first sight, there is little evidence of the pupils directly *expressing* emotion, though some anxiety is arguably being *exhibited* (cf. Evans, 2000). Yet in one part of the lesson, when the boys are working on their own, in a small group, according to the norms of the local (relatively 'progressive') pedagogy, indicators of several emotions are observed, e.g. excitement on the part of two boys, as well as suggestions of anxiety on the part of all three; the authors argue that these are associated with each participant's positioning in discursive practices. Moreover, when this episode is compared with a later one when the teacher intervenes with a strong suggestion as to how the problem should be addressed mathematically, the traditional pedagogic relations are re-established, with a consequent reduction in the space available for the expression of emotion. In general, the classroom episode shows the importance of evaluation practices – applied to oneself and to others – in establishing an individual's positionings and identity. For example, the authors show how (more durable, less context-specific) *identities* might be produced from *repeated positionings* in this way: one boy ("Mario") in the small group, becomes 'identified' as weak in problem solving, as a result of repeated use of criteria of evaluation that are clearly not from the school mathematics – but rather from 'outside', youth culture discourses. Further, the boy's apparent anxiety, which at first seems to be related to the mathematical task, may be better interpreted as being about being included socially in the group. This illustrates the fluidity with which emotion can be displaced from one 'object' to another (cf. Evans, 2000, Ch.10).

The DP approach shows how meanings and emotions are socially organised in pedagogic contexts. The mathematics and the pedagogic discourses (especially evaluation criteria) interact with other discursive resources and personal histories of individual students, enabling certain positions and creating links and contradictions, thereby opening up spaces within which emotion may occur. The dynamics of the interactional practices lead to ways in which the *positions available* in discourse are realised as *positionings* in practice, thereby allowing space for emotions to be experienced, and sometimes expressed.

The cognitive and the affective are treated as intertwined by showing how discourses and positionings shape both. This avoids the assimilation of the affective into the cognitive – since conceptualising emotion as a charge attached to ideas and the terms in which they are expressed allows the researchers to understand emotion as 'attached' to cognition, but in ways that are not fixed, but fluid.

In connection with the low levels of emotional expression apparent in the classroom studied, it is worth noting that Evans (2000) found many more instances of emotion being expressed, in his interviews with social science undergraduates. However, it can be argued that the difference in levels of emotional expression could be set down to the different discursive constitution of the two contexts, that is, the different positions offered by the classroom and the research interview settings (Evans, 2000, Ch.9; Evans, 2003).

CONCLUSIONS [10]

Common Ground

1. Taken together, the three approaches considered here, as illustrated by the selected studies, show that a sociocultural programme of research focused on a shared problem, the role of emotion in mathematical thinking, can benefit from each of the approaches. Comparison of the three studies on *aims* reveals similar motives for including emotions in the theoretical framework, such as the need of a richer understanding of mathematical thinking and behaviour overall, and its relation to social factors.

All three view mathematical thinking as 'hot', as infused with emotion – in contrast with the commensense view of mathematics as 'cold'. In terms of *key concepts*, the socio-constructivists (SC) understand emotions as related to coordinated feedback from mutually regulating multiple processes based in the person's 'component systems', in particular, the appraisal, monitor and autonomic nervous systems, highlighting, in their work so far, the effect of knowledge and beliefs on this appraisal. The cultural - historical activity theoretical (CHAT) account here sees the person's emotions as related both to relatively conscious efforts to maximise 'emotional valence', and also to the non-conscious "states of the living body" (2006); in this way, it is "reciprocally" (dialectically) related to practical reasoning and action. The discursive practice (DP) approach sees emotion as an affective charge which may be attached to ideas (carried by signifiers), and shows how a range of emotions are associated with each subject's positioning in practices, and especially conflicts in positioning.

These accounts no longer see emotions towards mathematics as largely 'negative' or debilitating, as was the case in earlier research programmes, but often show them as 'positive' / facilitating. Indeed the positive / negative categorisation may be problematical (see also Hannula, this volume), and several types of ambivalence have been shown here, e.g. that due to positioning conflicts of the boys in DP; of 'Frank', torn between the imperatives of stopping to think and performing quickly on the 'test', in SC; or of 'Erica', caught between her drive to do her job "at 300%", and her anxieties about money, once she had been laid off from her job.

2. Further, all three approaches stress the importance of the social, the 'context' of learning. The SC conceptualisation aims to capture this via careful measurement of knowledge and especially beliefs, and also through taking account of the type of course and/or school. However, the effects of these contexts and of social types generally, cannot be captured only by commonsense understandings or 'natural' labels (such as 'school maths' or 'workplace maths'). The DP approach shows how to describe a person's positioning within the discursive practices constituting and regulating their context of action. The CHAT report sees activity within a community, with its collective "motives", and located culturally and historically, as the context. Here any idea of social regulation is so far implicit, or simply assumed, and the role of power less fully sketched.

3. Comparisons of *methodology* reveal multi-phase, multi-method procedures, which differ in specific ways (described briefly above) among approaches. A range of methods has been used, including self-completion questionnaires; systematic physiological measurement; behavioural measurement; several types of interview; participant observation. As is required to deal with dynamic processes, all have methods for capturing the fluidity of emotion: for example, attention both to facial expression and to "thinking aloud" while problem solving in SC; speech intensity and pitch in CHAT; detailed semiotic analysis of verbal interaction transcripts in DP.

Possibilities for Developing a Programme of Research Focused on a Common Problem

4. It is natural to reflect on whether the commonalities among approaches suggest a basis of dialogue and further work, and hence ways of avoiding a proliferation of

approaches to the study of emotion in mathematics education. Here, we can only aim to pose several tentative questions.

(a) Are there any overlaps in the key concepts used, that might allow 'fruitful mutual challenges' among approaches? For example, in what essential ways do 'activities' (CHAT) and 'discursive practices' (DP) differ as a context of thinking? Does CHAT have an analogue of 'positioning'? Can the sets of beliefs so carefully investigated in SC shed any light on the content of different pedagogic discourses (DP), or on the structure of the activity system (CHAT)?

(b) The term 'unconscious' is used in three distinct senses here: (i) *routinised*, not needing conscious attention, as with *operations* (in CHAT); (ii) *'autonomic'* as for physiological processes, such as the heartbeat; and (iii) *repressed* via defence mechanisms into the (Freudian) unconscious (in DP). Distinguishing among these more carefully may allow useful conceptual distinctions in the various approaches.

(c) The SC and CHAT approaches in their current versions focus more strongly on motivation; their conceptions could be of value for developments in DP.

(d) At the same time, the SC and the CHAT approaches are at risk of using an approach to the 'social', which relies on only commonsense or 'natural' labels – and which therefore lacks explanatory power. The DP approach can show how the context is constructed through discourses that give it meaning and that serve to locate participants in positions of power, feeling and capability.

5. Psychoanalytic insights appear to be taken up centrally only in the version of discursive approaches presented here. Nevertheless, they pose a challenge to any strongly cognitivist point of view that emphasises thinking as largely 'conscious' and normally bound by rationality. This is because many emotional reactions, and even beliefs, including those relating to mathematics (etc.) are often not conscious, much less rationally arrived at. Thus, the play of desire and fantasies may invest mathematics and mathematical objects with strong emotional meaning. Feelings like anxiety can be *displaced* to mathematical objects from others, via movement of emotional charge along a *chain of signifiers*: so what seems to be 'mathematics anxiety' may relate to anxiety from other practices. Thus emotion may *transfer* across practices (Evans, 2000), like ideas, perhaps having originated in early relationships, or in images in popular culture (e.g. in films, as illustrated above).

Psychoanalytic insights also suggest that certain beliefs and behaviours are *defensive* (against anxiety and conflict). These insights provide possible explanations for what would otherwise be surprising cognitive 'slips'. These insights may also explain the *transference* of the focus of the student's feelings from parent to teacher.

6. This re-reading of three apparently distinct approaches to broadly 'socio-cultural' research on the role of emotions in mathematical thinking and learning, against an account of developments in this area over the last 25 years, has shown a non-negligible amount of common ground, some possibilities for 'mutual challenging' among the separate approaches, and some promising areas for

development in conceptualisation of several key areas, including 'the social'. Thus this discussion opens several areas for further research.

(a) Both 'motivation' and 'identity' have been marked here as of interest in the affective area; the former in particular has been neglected in mathematics education research until recently, but is featured here in the SC and CHAT reports discussed.

(b) Each of these studies offers suggestions as to how to rethink the links between beliefs and attitudes seen as durable aspects of individual 'identity', and transitory emotions.

(c) The SC approach's emphasis on the cognitive appraisal systems, and their relations with beliefs, provides an impetus to bring in the study of other systems; the indicators of voice pitch and intensity used by the CHAT report may help in this respect.

(d) The CHAT study of working adults raises the issue of child vs. adult differences in affective patterns and emotional experience.

(e) The DP approach especially suggests studies of the ways that popular culture has effects on emotions, e.g. using representations of mathematic(ian)s in films.

(f) These three sociocultural approaches together raise questions like:

- When should there be an emphasis on "enjoying maths" in class – and are there any occasions when it should not be emphasised?
- Should educational policy makers try to control emotions in schools, or require teachers to develop students' 'emotional literacy'?
- In a classroom where 'emotional literacy' is emphasised, which different social categories of student (in terms of gender, social class, ethnicity) would stand to gain or to lose?

REFERENCES

Appelbaum, P. (1995). *Popular culture, educational discourse and mathematics.* Albany NY: SUNY Press.

Bernstein, B. (2000). *Pedagogy, symbolic control and identity: Theory, research, critique*, Rev. ed., Rowman & Littlefield, New York. (Original ed. 1996, Taylor & Francis, London.).

Brown, L. & Reid D. (2006). Embodied cognition: somatic markers, purposes and emotional orientations. *Educational Studies in Mathematics: Affect in Mathematics Education: Exploring Theoretical Frameworks, A PME Special Issue, 63*, 2.

Buck, R. (1999). The biological affects: A typology. *Psychological Review, 106* (2), 301-336.

Burkitt, I. (1997). Social relationships and emotions, *Sociology, 31* (1) 37-55.

Cabral, T. (2004). Affect and cognition in pedagogical transference. In M.Walshaw (Ed.) *Mathematics education within the postmodern.* Greenwich CT: Information Age.

Cobb, P., Gravemeijer, K., Yackel, E., McClain, & Whitenack, J. (1997). Mathematizing and symbolizing: The emergence of chains of signification in one first-grade classroom. In D. Kirshner & J. A. Whitson (Eds.), *Situated cognition. Social, semiotic, and psychological perspectives.* Mahwah: Erlbaum,151 – 233.

Cobb, P., Yackel, E. & Wood, T. (1989). Young children's emotional acts while engaged in mathematical problem solving. In D. McLeod and V. Adams (Eds.) *Affect and mathematical problem solving: A new perspective.* New York: Springer, Ch.9.

Cobb, P., & Bowers, J. (1999). Cognitive and situated learning: Perspectives in theory and practice. *Educational Researcher, 28*(2), 4-15.

Damasio, A. R. (1996). *Descartes' error: Emotion, reason, and the human brain*. London: Papermac.

DeBellis, V. and Goldin, G. (1997). The affective domain in mathematical problem-solving. In E. Pehkonen (Ed.). *Proceedings of the 21st Conference of the International Group for the Psychology of Mathematics Education*, Lahti, Finland, 2-209 - 2-216.

DiMartino, P.& Zan, R. (2001). Attitude towards mathematics, some theoretical issues. In M. van den Heuvel-Panhuizen (Ed.) *Proceedings of the 25th Conference of the International group for the Psychology of Mathematics Education*. Vol. 3. Utrecht, The Netherlands, 351-358.

Engeström, Y. (2001). Expansive learning at work: Toward an activity theoretical reconceptualization. *Journal of Education and Work, 14*, 1, 135-156.

Ernest, P. (1991). *The Philosophy of Mathematics Education*. Basingstoke, UK: Falmer Press.

Evans, J. (2000). *Adults' Mathematical Thinking and Emotions: A Study of Numerate Practices*. London: RoutledgeFalmer.

Evans, J. (2002). Developing research conceptions of emotion among adult learners of mathematics. *Literacy and Numeracy Studies, Special Issue on Adults Learning Mathematics, 11* (2), 79-94.

Evans J. (2003a). Methods and findings in research on affect and emotion in mathematics education. In M. Mariotti et al. (Eds.), *Proceedings of 3rd Conference of European Research in Mathematics Education (CERME-3)*: Topic Group 3 (Affect and Emotion in Mathematics Education), 28 Feb. – 3 Mar., 2003, Bellaria, Italy. [available online]

Evans, J. (2003b). Mathematics done by adults portrayed as a cultural object in advertising and in film. In J. Evans, D. Kaye, V. Seabright & A. Tomlin (Eds.) *Proceedings of 9th International Conference of Adults Learning Mathematics – A research forum (ALM-9), 17-20 July 2002, Uxbridge College, London*. London: ALM and Kings College London.

Evans J. (2004). Mathematics done by adults portrayed as a cultural object in advertising and in film. In J. Maasz and W. Schloegmann (Eds.), *Learning mathematics to live and work in our world. Proceedings of the 10th International Conference on Adults Learning Mathematics (ALM10)*, Strobl, Austria, 29 June – 2 July 2003, Adults Learning Mathematics - a Research Forum (ALM) and University of Linz, Linz, 87-193.

Evans, J., Morgan, C., & Tsatsaroni, A. (2006) Discursive positioning and emotion in school mathematics practices. *Educational Studies in Mathematics: Affect in Mathematics Education: Exploring Theoretical Frameworks, A PME Special Issue, 63*(2).

Evans, J. & Wedege, T. (2004), ICME-10. Motivation and resistance to learning mathematics in a lifelong perspective. Paper contributed to TSG6: Adult and Lifelong Mathematics, ICME-10, Copenhagen, 4-11 July [online http://www.icme10.dk, accessed 12 June 2006].

Evans, J. and Zan, R. (2006). Sociocultural approaches to emotions in mathematics education: Initial Comparisons. *Proceedings of PME-30*.

Fairclough, N. (2003). *Analysing discourse: Textual analysis for social research*. London: Routledge.

Fennema, E. & Sherman, J. (1976). Fennema-Sherman mathematics attitude scales, *Catalogue of Selected Documents in Psychology, 6*.

Freud, S. (1916-17/1974). Anxiety. Lecture 25, in *Introductory lectures on psychoanalysis*, Vol.1, Pelican Freud Library, Harmondsworth: Penguin.

Gates, P. (2006). Going BEYOND BELIEF SYstems: Exploring a model for the social influence on Mathematics teacher beliefs. *Educational Studies in Mathematics* (in press).

Gomez-Chacon, I. (2000). Affective Influences in the knowledge of mathematics. *Educational Studies in Mathematics, 49,* 149-168.

Grosz, E. (1994). *Volatile bodies: Toward a corporeal feminism*. Bloomington and Indianapolis: Indiana University Press.

Hall, S. (1997). *Representations: Cultural representations and signifying practices*. London: Sage / Open University.

Hannula, M. (2006). Motivation in mathematics: Goals reflected in emotions. *Educational Studies in Mathematics: Affect in Mathematics Education: Exploring Theoretical Frameworks, A PME Special Issue, 63*, 2.

Hartley, D. (2004). Management, leadership, and the emotional order of the school. *Journal of Educational Policy, 19* (5), 583-594.

Hunt, J. (1989). *Psychoanalytic aspects of fieldwork*, London: Sage.

James, W. (1890/1950). *The principles of psychology*, 2 vols. New York: Dover.

Kitayama, S. & Markus, H. R. (1994). *Emotion and culture: Empirical studies of mutual influence.* Washington, DC: APA.

Leder, G., Pehkonen, E. and Törner, G. (Eds.) (2002). *Beliefs: A hidden variable in mathematics education?* Dordrecht: Kluwer.

Lee, Y.-J., & Roth, W.-M. (2005). The (unlikely) trajectory of learning in a salmon hatchery. *Journal of Workplace Learning, 17*(4), 243-254.

Leont'ev, A. N. (1978). *Activity, consciousness and personality.* Englewood Cliffs NJ: Prentice-Hall.

McLeod, D. (1989a). The role of affect in mathematical problem solving. In D. McLeod and V. Adams (Eds). *Affect and mathematical problem solving: A new perspective.* New York: Springer, Ch.2.

McLeod, D. (1989b). Beliefs, attitudes, and emotions: New views of affect in mathematics education. In D. McLeod and V. Adams (Eds), *Affect and mathematical problem solving: A new perspective.* New York: Springer, Ch.17.

McLeod, D. (1992). Research on affect in mathematics education: A reconceptualisation. In D.A. Grouws (Ed.) *Handbook of research in mathematics education teaching and learning,* New York: Macmillan,575-596.

McLeod, D. & Adams, V. (Eds.) (1989). *Affect and mathematical problem solving: A new perspective.* New York: Springer.

Mandler, G. (1989). Affect and learning: causes and consequences of emotional interactions. In D. McLeod and V. Adams (Eds). *Affect and mathematical problem solving: A new perspective,* New York: Springer, Ch.1.

Mendick, H. (2002). Why are we doing this? A case study of motivational practices in mathematics classes. In A. D. Cockburn & E. Nardi (Eds.), *Proceedings of the 26th Conference of the International Group for the Psychology of Mathematics Education (PME-26).* Norwich: School of Education and Professional Development, University of East Anglia, 3-329 - 3-336.

Mendick, H. (2006). *Masculinities in mathematics.* Maidenhead: Open University Press.

Morgan, C. (1998), *Writing mathematically: The discourse of investigation.* London: Falmer Press.

Morgan, C., Tsatsaroni, A., and Lerman, S. (2002). Mathematics teachers' positions and practices in discourses of assessment. *British Journal of Sociology of Education, 23*(3), 445-461.

Nimier, J. (1977). Mathematique et Affectivité. *Educational Studies in Mathematics, 8,* 241-250.

Nimier, J. (1978). Mathematique et Affectivité, *Revue Francaise de Pédagogie, 45,* 166-172.

Op 't Eynde, P. & De Corte, E. (2003). Emotions trapped between motivation and cognition?: The integration of trait and state approaches as a promising way out. Paper presented at the 10th Conference of the European Association for Research on Learning and Instruction, Aug. 26-30, Padova, Italy.

Op 't Eynde, P. & Hannula, M. S. (2006). The case study of Frank. *Educational Studies in Mathematics: Affect in Mathematics Education: Exploring Theoretical Frameworks, A PME Special Issue, 63,* 2.

Op 't Eynde, P., De Corte, E., & Verschaffel, L. (2001). What to learn from what we feel?: The role of students' emotions in the mathematics classroom. In S. Volet, & S. Järvelä (Eds.), *Motivation in learning contexts: Theoretical and methodological implications.* EARLI / Pergamon Advances in Learning and Instruction Series, 149-167.

Op 't Eynde, P., De Corte, E., & Verschaffel, L. (2002). Framing students' mathematics-related beliefs: A quest for conceptual clarity and a comprehensive categorization. In G.C. Leder, E. Pehkonen, & G. Törner (Eds.), *Beliefs: A hidden variable in mathematics education?* Dordrecht: Kluwer Academic Publishers, 13-37.

Op 't Eynde, P., De Corte, E., & Verschaffel, L. (2006). Accepting emotional complexity: A socio-constructivist perspective on the role of emotions in the mathematics classroom.

Educational Studies in Mathematics: Affect in Mathematics Education: Exploring Theoretical Frameworks, A PME Special Issue, 63 (2).

Richardson, F. & Suinn, R. (1972). The mathematics anxiety rating scale: Psychometric data. *Journal of Counselling Psychology, 19,* 551-554.

Roth, W.-M. (2003). *Toward an anthropology of graphing.* Dordrecht: Kluwer.

Roth, W.-M. (2004). Emotions, motivation and identity in workplace mathematics and activity theory, paper for International Seminar on Learning and Technology at Work, University of London Institute of Education, London, March 2004.

Online: http://www.lonklab.ac.uk/ltw/seminar.htm. [accessed 5 Dec. 2005].

Roth, W.-M. (2005). *Doing qualitative research: Praxis of method.* Rotterdam: SensePublishers.

Roth, W.-M. (2006). Motive, emotion and identity at work: A contribution to third-generation cultural historical activity theory, *Mind, Culture and Activity, 13,* (3).

Roth, W.-M. (in press). Mathematical modeling 'in the wild': A case of hot cognition. In R. Lesh, J. J. Kaput, E. Hamilton, & J. Zawojewski (Eds.), *Users of mathematics: Foundations for the future.* Mahwah, NJ: Lawrence Erlbaum Associates.

Santos, M., & Matos, J. F. (1998). School mathematics learning: Participation through appropriation of mathematical artefacts. In A. Watson (Ed.), *Situated cognition and the learning of mathematics,* Oxford: University of Oxford Dept. of Educational Studies.

Scherer, K.R. (2000). Emotions as episodes of subsystem synchronization driven by nonlinear appraisal processes. In M.D.Lewis, & I. Granic (Eds.), *Emotion, development, and self-organization: Dynamic systems approaches to emotional development.* Cambridge, UK: Cambridge University Press, 70-99.

Schlöglmann, W. (2002). Affect and mathematics learning. In A. D. Cockburn & E. Nardi (Eds.), *Proceedings of the 26th Conference of the International Group for the Psychology of Mathematics Education (PME-26)* Norwich: School of Education and Professional Development, University of East Anglia, 4-18--4-192.

Scribner, S. and Cole, M. (1973). Cognitive consequences of formal and informal education. *Science, 182,* 553-559.

Tahta, D. (Ed.) (1993) Special Issue on Psychodynamics in Mathematics Education, *For the Learning of Mathematic, 13* (1).

Turner, J. H. (2002). *Face to face: Toward a sociological theory of interpersonal behaviour.* Stanford CA: Stanford University Press.

Walkerdine, V. (1988). *The Mastery of Reason: Cognitive development and the production of rationality.* London: Routledge.

Walkerdine, V. (1997). Redefining the subject in situated cognition theory. In D. Kirshner & J. A. Whitson (Eds.), *Situated cognition: Social, semiotic, and psychological perspectives,* Mahwah NJ: Lawrence Erlbaum Associates, Ch.4.

Wenger, E. (1998). *Communities of practice: Learning, meaning and identity.* Cambridge: Cambridge University Press.

Wierzbicka, A. (1994). Emotion, language, and cultural scripts. In S. Kitayama & H. R. Markus, *Emotion and culture: Empirical studies of mutual influence.* Washington, DC: APA, 33-196.

Zajonc, R. B. (1984). On the primacy of affect, *American Psychologist, 39*(2), 117-123.

Zan, R., Brown, L., Evans, J. & Hannula, M. S. (2006, forthcoming). Affect in mathematics education: An introduction. *Educational Studies in Mathematics: Affect in Mathematics Education: Exploring Theoretical Frameworks, A PME Special Issue, 63* (2).

Jeff Evans
Middlesex University, UK

[1]   Indeed, Fennema and Sherman (1976) produced a whole battery of questionnaires for attitudes towards mathematics, including Attitude to Success in Math, Confidence in Learning Mathematics, Usefulness of Mathematics, and Math as a Male Domain.

[2]   Though, for Damasio (1996), 'emotion' includes only (a) and 'feeling' includes (c)

[3]   For two other senses of the term 'unconscious', see the Conclusions.

[4]   We might even consider the cultural transmission of images and discourses about emotions in other settings in society (e.g. Hartley, 2004).

[5]   Two of the articles, Op 't Eynde et al. and Evans et al., are published in the same journal issue (*Educational Studies in Mathematics: Affect in Mathematics Education: Exploring Theoretical Frameworks, A PME Special Issue,* vol. 63, no.2), and, as part of their analyses, address the same case study, that of 'Frank' (Op 't Eynde & Hannula, 2006).

[6]   This section owes much to collaborative work with Rosetta Zan; see Evans & Zan (2006).

7   Lerman et al. (2002) systematically analysed a sample of research papers published in mathematics education journals and the annual research conference (PME). Their basic idea is that, like any other kind of data, scientific texts need to be systematically read and interpreted. Their approach used a set of questions and categories derived from theoretical resources.

8   These emotional profiles recall the 'Mood maps' presented by Gomez-Chacon (2000), where, however, the students were coding their own emotions.

9   The original data set was collected by Madalena Santos for research with a different focus (Santos & Matos, 1998).

10 These Conclusions have benefited from collaborative work with Rosetta Zan, Anna Tsatsaroni, and Candia Morgan; see Evans & Zan (2006); Evans, Morgan & Tsatsaroni (2006).

GILAH C LEDER

AFFECT AND MATHEMATICS LEARNING

Concluding Comments

There is both congruence and diversity in the contents of the previous two chapters. Both authors convincingly argue that explorations into mathematical thinking and learning need to take account of affective factors beyond simplistically measured attitudes and beliefs about mathematics. Both agree that a focus on emotions will yield new insights into understanding what can promote or inhibit mathematical learning, argue that emotional experiences are reflected in physiological reactions and that they influence and are influenced by human behaviours. However, as can be seen below, there are also differences in the theoretical frameworks, and associated bodies of research, on which Markku Hannula and Jeff Evans draw in their discussions of relevant work. The former places much emphasis on the experiences and behaviours of individual students; the latter on sociocultural approaches which "emphasise the social basis and *social organisation* of affect" (Evans, this volume, emphasis in the original).

Scenario 1: The Landscape Depicted by Markku Hannula

As indicated by the subtitle of his chapter, Markku Hannula's primary aim is to develop a coherent, integrated model of emotion, motivation, and cognition. Parameters guiding the contents of the chapter are established early: affect is defined as comprising "all emotional and motivational phenomena"; throughout the chapter the focus is to be predominantly on students rather than on their interactions with the environment; and psychological rather than biological or sociological theories drive the interpretations and explanations offered – even though affect encompasses all three perspectives.

Given the concentration on attitudes and beliefs in early research on affect, Hannula argues that research on these constructs provides important contextual information and thus warrants attention at the beginning of the chapter. Accordingly, examples of studies highlighting a link between affect and achievement are cited. Various problems emerge at the outset: Can any links identified be described as causal? How can those whose self-concept is persistently low best be helped as they grapple with mathematics? Do highly motivated individuals typically achieve at a higher level than those with lower motivation?

J. Maasz, W. Schloeglmann (Eds.), New Mathematics Education Research and Practice, 257–261.

On the one hand attitudes and beliefs are considered as relatively stable; but on the other there are a multitude of studies exploring the extent to which interventions may modify an individual's attitudes or beliefs. How can this contradiction be handled most effectively? Should attitudes be regarded as more stable than emotions but less stable than beliefs, as some have argued? Or should attitudes be seen as the composite of emotions, beliefs, and behaviours as other have proposed? To what extent has our understanding of affect been constrained by the substantial body of research relying for its measurement on a one-dimensional scale? Just what is the relationship between variables such as self confidence, anxiety, and motivation, components discussed in this early section, and attitudes or beliefs?

To address questions such as these, Hannula sketches the multifaceted dimensions of affect: affect as a subjective experience – typically acknowledged through self report measures, affect as described by physiological changes – able to be measured accurately but offering only limited insights into possible psychological changes, and affect as a social text – classically captured through interviews, observations, or think-aloud protocols – techniques constrained by "limits to sharing other people's experiences. We cannot interpret beyond what we have experienced". By focussing on emotions, Hannula argues, different theoretical perspectives necessarily intertwine to yield richer insights. To elaborate this stance Hannula surveys work on self-regulation, described as having cognitive, motivational, and emotional dimensions – fore- or back-grounded differentially depending on the time frame considered (rapid, intermediate, and longer term).

As discussed earlier, affect has been variously defined and operationalised. Similarly, no consensus definition for emotion has yet been reached although Hannula notes that it is generally agreed that emotions involve "physiological processes that regulate the body, subjective experiences that regulate behaviour and expressive processes that regulate social coordination". Attempts to understand better how emotions arise, how they influence personal goals, and how they influence adaptive behaviours have lead to increased research activity in recent years. Some of this work is described in some detail in both of the chapters in this section. Referenced as well are the writers' own contributions to the field. For Hannula this includes his description of "the four aspects of the meta-level mind" in terms of cognitions about cognitions, cognitions about emotions, emotions about cognitions, and emotions about emotions. Later in the chapter he draws on his own three year longitudinal study to illustrate how students' beliefs influenced and at times modified the goals towards which students strove in mathematics classes. Significantly, reference to students' beliefs featured prominently in the description of this study, despite the professed centrality of emotions highlighted elsewhere.

How, Hannula asks, can research such as that reviewed in his chapter as well as the insights provided by his own work, be utilized to optimize teaching and student achievement in mathematics? His conclusions reinforce those of others in the field: mathematics related beliefs and goal are relatively stable rather than fixed. Thus students should benefit from an instructional environment that is safe, nurturing, sensitive and responsive to their needs. Yet how this is best achieved remains elusive. Appropriately, then, Hannula concludes his chapter with a plea to the field to reject the all too frequent reliance on easily administered questionnaires with their acknowledged limitations for capturing or tracing changes in affect. Instead he advocates the adoption of fine-grained and in-depth data collection methods that, for example, allow valid and reliable human (observer) codings to be supplemented with accurate physiological measures and thus enable both methodological and theoretical triangulation.

More sophisticated methods and measures are indeed needed for more concise descriptions of the interplay and links between emotion, motivation, and cognition. Hannula's chapter has captured strengths and weaknesses in earlier approaches. He has identified areas of research – established and emerging - whose findings can help us understand better what facilitates or inhibits mathematical learning. At the same time it is clear that the journey "*towards* integration of emotion, motivation, and cognition" (the subtitle of Hannula's chapter) is far from complete.

Scenario 2: The Landscape Depicted by Jeff Evans

In his contribution, Evans has chosen to focus on three exemplars of somewhat different sociocultural approaches: socio-constructivism, cultural-historical activity theory, and a discursive practice approach. A brief review of earlier methods and models – and their limitations – serves as a useful advance organizer for the strong focus in the rest of the chapter on emotion and its relation to social factors. Highlighting emotions, Evans argues, enables "affect-laden activity" to be considered within context and as a dynamic process. Important, too, for signalling the thrust of the chapter, is his observation that inhibiting interactions between affect and performance - too often the impetus and topic for earlier research - should be balanced by considering as well the functional or facilitative aspects of affect.

As noted before, Evans – like Hannula - concludes that emotions involve physiological reactions and are determinants of adaptive behaviours and social coping. Material illustrating the many ways in which unconscious images, thoughts and behaviours interweave with daily activities is introduced early in the chapter and acknowledged further in subsequent discussions.

The text of well chosen film excerpts nicely supports Evans assertion that emotions are not only reflected in conscious behaviours but also in conscious and unconscious desires and fantasies. The snapshots illustrate how "films, and other objects of popular culture are sites for the articulation of discourses within which meanings are defined, images are built up, and hence power is invested", exemplifying ways "in which emotions are socially organised" (Evans, this volume). Presented, too, are excerpts of work which demonstrate the ways in which emotions can be generated both through our individual experiences and by our reactions to the beliefs and values of those in our environment, i.e., by cultural transmission. What these examples have in common is a multiple approach to data collection, including qualitative data - participant related as well as referents to aspects of the environment, various techniques for data analysis - including methods of coding sufficiently comprehensive and sensitive to capture both environmental and affective indicators, and a willingness to draw on different theoretical paradigms if this is thought to be meaningful or optimum for constructing new meanings. The commentaries, inferences, and cited sources collectively demonstrate that in contemporary work and theoretical speculations Freud's assertion: "the concept of the unconscious has long been knocking at the gates of psychology and asking to be let in. Philosophy and literature have often toyed with it, but science could find no use for it" (Freud, 1986, p. 286) no longer applies.

In the latter half of the chapter, Evans methodically examines the commonalities of the three sociocultural approaches of particular interest to him under the broad headings of conceptual framework, problems addressed, methodology, and outcomes. These headings cover respectively: key concepts, basic approach, and characterisation of emotion; motivating aims; preferred research methods, key phases, and research design; approach-specific usage and findings. In each of the research studies discussed, mathematical thinking is perceived as "'hot', as infused with emotion". In each, the context in which learning takes place is highlighted rather than ignored. In each, emotions towards and about mathematics are not necessarily assumed to be negative; data analysis also allows positive or ambivalent emotions to be captured. In brief, there is a common assumption that a realistic and functional exploration of mathematical behaviours must include emotions among the variables studied.

The summaries illustrate how aspects of affect are now being captured and traced in ways not previously possible or envisaged. In the socioconstructivist approach adopted by Op 't Eynde and his colleagues this involved the creative use of technology: the administration of an on-line questionnaire to capture the first and immediate affective responses to a series of mathematics problems as well as reliance on videotaped material at different stages of the data gathering process. For Roth, working within a cultural-historical activity theory framework, access to more sensitive instrumentation yielded more objective and reliable data, i.e., the intuitively important but rarely used features of speech intensity and pitch. This, in turn, allowed more convincing inferences to be drawn about the emotions of the participant in his study. In the work of Evans and his colleagues, classroom interactions captured on video and initially gathered for different purposes, were able to be reanalysed through new theoretical lenses which were sensitive not only to the behaviours of individual students but also to the context – situational and personal - which inevitably contributed to the affects aroused and exhibited.

Jointly these studies illustrate just how far the field has moved conceptually and functionally beyond exclusive reliance on the self report scales described at the very beginning of this section. Illustrated, too, is the power of using diverse instruments and methods to capture different aspects of affect which have previously all too often been ignored, thought to be too elusive, or have been inferred from inadequate sources.

Drawing on the different approaches surveyed, Evans points to a number of promising pathways for future investigations on affect and emotions. Less clear, however, are the practical implications for the mathematics classroom. In some ways I see parallels with earlier research on gender and mathematics. There, too, research planned within different theoretical perspectives and access to more refined measures and coding systems yielded insights missing from early work that concentrated on the more readily measured participation and performance data. Yet applying the new found understandings to practical situations in the mathematics classroom has had mixed results. In search of further answers, investigations of mathematical learning still often include gender as a variable of interest. As illustrated so well by the work reported by both Hannula and Evans, individual and contextual differences defy the application of easy recipes to explain the impact of emotions and other affective factors on mathematics learning. To paraphrase just one of the questions raised by Evans: when, and for whom, is it functional to have an emphasis on enjoying mathematics in class – and when not?

REFERENCES

Freud, S. (1986). *Some elementary lessons in psycho-analysis. The standard edition of the complete psychological works of Sigmund Freud, volume XXIII.* London: Hogarth Press. (Original work published in 1940).

Gilah C. Leder
La Trobe University, Australia

C. HOYLES, J.B. LAGRANGE, R. NOSS

DEVELOPING AND EVALUATING ALTERNATIVE TECHNOLOGICAL INFRASTRUCTURES FOR LEARNING MATHEMATICS

FOREWORD

We would like to dedicate this paper to our friend and colleague, Jim Kaput, who was tragically killed in a road accident shortly before the conference. His work on representational infrastructures pointed to a crucial challenge for mathematics education. By situating current representational systems in their historical context, Jim showed the possibilities for designing alternatives. For Jim, and for us, a key concern was to open up, democratise and make more learnable the complex ideas of mathematics, ideas whose complexity often owes as much to the way they are represented, as to the ideas themselves. This paper is the worse for the lack of Jim's critical comments.

INTRODUCTION

The challenge that this chapter addresses is to explore how computers can make it possible for students to engage with mathematics that they either might have failed to engage with in a traditional school setting or which they might not have encountered. We will consider infrastructures for mathematical expression, that is to say systems of representations of mathematical ideas and objects, and the means to manage them to enhance engagement with mathematical ideas.

One focus of our chapter is algebra. Paper/pencil algebraic infrastructures made it necessary for individuals to pay considerable attention to manipulation, and key mathematical topics were only amenable to those who had already been inducted into fluent algebraic representations and calculations. This meant that many never engaged with the mathematical topic at hand and the learning of algebraic notation became a thing-in-itself, rather than a means to an end – learning to play scales without ever playing the music. We will demonstrate that digital technologies can radically change this scenario.

Cultural demands on curricula have encouraged (not always altogether thoughtfully) the use of technology, and stressed its utility for experimentation and exploration. The availability of computers in mathematical research and in the classroom has suggested the development of curricula that urge students and teachers to replicate computer-supported experimental methods used by

J. Maasz, W. Schloeglmann (Eds.), New Mathematics Education Research and Practice, 263–312.

mathematical and scientific researchers. With dynamic media, mathematics can become (and has already become, in parts of the academic field of mathematics) an experimental science, one in which the activities of experiment and observation is as important as logic and proof. So an important question arises as to the kind of assistance technological tools can bring to student experimental activity with dynamic mathematical representations, and under what conditions.

A variety of technological tools, especially Computer symbolic systems (CAS), have been presented as a means to overcome students' difficulties in paper/pencil manipulations, offering them opportunities to develop exploratory approaches inspired from research. These tools stand as candidates for new expressive infrastructures, while maintaining more or less intact the usual representations - including algebraic notation - and using the power of the computer to perform actions on these representations to obtaining diverse graphs, tables and transformations of expressions. Although promising, this approach has not been, in our view, sufficiently discussed from an epistemological point of view, and its 'viability', that is to say the conditions in which it could be effective in actual classrooms, remains problematic. We will have more to say on this below, particularly in section 2.

At the same time, there is a need for new and alternative *representations* for algebra. While the need to think creatively about representational forms arose less obviously in settings where things were mechanical and much more visible (i.e. objects had gears, levers, pulleys etc.), the devolution of processing power to the computer has generated the need for individuals *to represent for themselves* models of how things work, what makes systems fail, and what would be needed to correct them (see Noss, 1998 for an elaboration of this point; see also Hoyles, Morgan and Woodhouse, 1999). In terms of the didactical implications of this trend, perhaps the best known, at least theoretically, has been the *constructionist* proposition (see Harel and Papert 1991) that has emphasised how building and constructing physical and virtual models of situations is an effective means to construct corresponding mental notions.

The authors of this chapter are involved in two distinct projects on which they will draw to exemplify the potential exploitation of technology designed for a more learnable mathematics. These two projects converge in their goal – the design of expressive infrastructures to enhance learnability - yet they adopt different orientations. The first project is the *Casyopée* project (Lagrange 2005b). It is designed to encourage students to use existing mathematical representations with the support of the computer. The second is *WebLabs* (see, for example, Noss & Hoyles, 2006), based on the idea of building new representations for mathematical models. We present an overview of the theoretical approach of both projects, along with some findings and illustrative extracts. Reflecting on the two projects inspired by their different orientations leads us to consider a basis for the evaluation by drawing on a *plurality of dimensions* put forward by Lagrange et al. (2003). Since the classroom is a complex reality, we argue that observation and intervention is needed from a wide range of perspectives, and studies should adopt approaches that span a range of dimensions or themes.

The structure of the chapter will be as follows. First a description and exemplification of the Casyopée project, which is followed by a section about WebLabs. Finally the discussion will compare and contrast the approaches, and point to the different roles that systems like Casyopée and WebLabs can respectively play in the future.

CASYOPÉE: MAKING ALGEBRAIC NOTATION MORE LEARNABLE THROUGH PROBLEM EXPLORATIONS

We identified above two main orientations in which computers can make it possible for young students who have little prior acquaintance or proficiency in paper/pencil algebraic representation to express rich mathematics. The first is to give students an easier and more motivating access to existing algebraic representations; the second is to search for new representations that are easier and more motivating in themselves. In this first orientation, the purpose of the Casyopée project is to offer upper secondary students an open environment for problem solving about functions, with capabilities of formal calculation, and graphic and numerical exploration, encouraging the use of algebraic representations.

Kieran (2006) recalls that difficulties with the algebraic notation has been for many years a major question for mathematics education:

"while arithmetic and algebra share many of the same signs and symbols, such as the equal sign, addition and subtraction signs, even the use of letters, many conceptual adjustments are required of the beginning algebra student as these signs and symbols shift in meaning from those commonly held in arithmetic".

Teaching generally does not deal with these difficulties: algebra is very often taught as procedures disconnected from meaning and purpose. Beyond problem solving "in a narrow sense", authors promoted experimental approaches (or exploration) of problems as a way to reconnect the algebraic activity to meaning and purpose.

For introducing and developing algebra (...) the essential mathematics activity is that of exploring problems in an open way, extending and developing them in the search for more results and more general ones. Hence [all algebraic learning] is based on problem explorations. This is the broad sense of the term. (Bell, 1996, p.167)

The development of computer technology supported this shift towards experimental approaches. For instance, the capacity to carry out many calculations rapidly was thought to assist the transition from an examination of single cases towards the resolution of groups of cases. Graphical and tabular representations or even the possibility of having a spreadsheet recalculate a series of expressions as a particular cell is varied similarly supported this view.

The ambition of the Casyopée project is to contribute to a change towards experimental approaches in classrooms in order to access a meaningful use of algebraic representation. Educational research has stressed the potential of such technology-aided approaches, but this does not mean that actual classroom implementation is straightforward. Considering this objective, the Casyopée team[1] identified three concerns:

1. Students' experimental activity. For a long time, authors and curricula advocated the advantages of classroom problem exploration, often by referring to professional mathematicians' activity and recently to the use of technology. Nonetheless, obstacles persist that cannot be simply attributed to teachers' unfamiliarity with this approach.

2. Students' algebraic activity and the influence of technological tools on this activity. Algebraic activity is multifaceted and involves a plurality of concepts. Technology also offers varied possibilities. A careful examination is necessary to identify the support it might bring to the transition to using algebraic notation.

3. The design of an algebraic software application that can actually be used in classrooms. Many excellent ideas have underpinned the creation of new tools for teaching and learning mathematics, yet it is not so clear that these ideas match the needs and constraints of 'real' classrooms and 'real' teaching.

Any mathematical education research bases its analysis on a theoretical framework. According to Mewborne (2005, p.3 & 4), using a framework brings a researcher two main benefits: "it serves as a sort of binocular that allows one to narrow down the scope of the research site to focus on particular aspects of the situation" and it forces one to "constantly compare and contrast what the data are saying with what the framework is saying."

On the one hand, these advantages have been recognised by researchers in the field of technology. Jones and Lagrange (2003) pointed out:

"there is a range of theoretical frameworks that appear to hold some promise when researching the use and impact of tools and technologies. Theories like embodied cognition and metaphor, cognitive gaps and transitions, situated abstraction, semiotic mediation, instrumentation... help to give relevant account of phenomena arising when students and teachers are using technology."

On the other hand, the technology-rich classroom is a complex reality that necessitates observation and intervention from a wide range of perspectives. We argue, therefore, that it is dangerous prematurely to narrow down the scope of research, leading to a loss of recognition of this complexity. This loss is particularly disadvantageous when the aim of the researcher is to build an application of technology for use in ordinary classrooms. In this case, the framework is not just a means to collect data, but rather has to provide support for a continuous reworking of design, implementation, observation and adaptation. Thus in order to observe how the application works in the classroom, the researcher has to take into account a variety of 'ecological' conditions, or risk a lack of feasibility in the classroom. For example, analysing ten years of development of the E-slate project, Kynygos (2004) explains: "A reason (to take an ecological perspective) was our need for feedback from and interaction with people using E-slate in their daily routines, since we were keen to gain insight as early as possible".

Using a plurality of dimensions is a way to keep a focused view on teaching/learning phenomena and a scientific account of observations, while ensuring a sufficiently wide approach of classroom reality. More precisely, the hypothesis here is that in developing a technological application to teach and learn mathematics, it is possible to conceive a range of dimensions to make sense of the principles on which the development is based and then to anticipate consequences of its use.

How can dimensions be identified that serve to focus on a narrowed scope? Following Mewborne's (*ibid.*) theoretical frameworks may be helpful. Nonetheless, concerns rather than theories are taken here as starting points, since concerns help to achieve a narrowed scope, following which, a theory is needed to investigate the scope and to guide practical choices regarding software development and classroom implementation. A question that then arises is what theory should be used given that several compete: for instance, different theories pointed out by Jones and Lagrange (*ibid.*) adress more or less a similar concern for the interaction between learners, technology and knowledge. Confronting and reconciling theories sensitive to the same concern is a work in itself (see Hoyles *et al.* 2004, on situated abstraction and instrumentation) that will not be undertaken here. Rather the choice of theories to underpin the concerns identified by the Casyopée team, was driven largely by familiarity.

Three dimensions will help in refocussing from each of the above concerns to practical choices regarding software development and the classroom implementation. We now present these dimensions along with two examples of classroom uses of Casyopée to illustrate implementation and how the dimensions helped in its examination.

THREE DIMENSIONS

The anthropological dimension: transposing mathematicians' experimental activity
Introducing students into a "true mathematical activity", giving a significant part to experimentation and conjecture is assumed to be a way into meaningful algebra, and is especially topical, given the development of technology. Many educators, when thinking of a valid mathematical activity and of conjectures has in mind the practices of mathematicians. This reference is also especially present when dealing with technology, because tools and software proposed for classroom use often derive from instruments developed by mathematics research for its own needs, especially to make experimentation more productive. Thus mathematical research practices and tools represent a reference for enhanced classroom activity.

The concern in the Casyopée project for the conditions of a classroom experimental activity takes this reference into account and, in consequence, the first dimension will focus on the phenomenon of *didactic transposition* from research to classroom. The choice of a theoretical approach along this dimension will be the 'anthropological approach', which was initiated precisely by a conceptualisation of the didactic transposition.
Lagrange (2005a) explains:

> The anthropological approach (Chevallard 1985, 1994, 1999) aims to give account of the conditions in which mathematical objects exist and live in institutions or more precisely how they are 'known and understood' as entities arising from practices. The word 'institution' has to be understood in a very broad sense as any social or cultural practice takes place within an institution. (We) will consider (a transposition) between scientific research institutions devoted to producing knowledge and didactic institutions devoted to apprenticeship…
>
> *Other notions of the anthropological approach, especially useful to clarify the influence of technology on teaching/learning are the three components of practices in a institution: a type of task; the techniques used to solve this type of task and the 'theory' which is first the discourse used in order to explain and justify the techniques and then provides a structural basis for this discourse[2]…Chevallard (1999, p.231) explains that praxeologies (i.e. the above components of practices) are the matter of the transposition.*

The anthropological approach helps to identify the challenges that technology-aided experimental praxeologies in teaching/ learning have to meet: to ensure their legitimacy, they must be related to homologous practices in mathematical research and to be viable, they must be compatible with the constraints of the organization of the knowledge in teaching, that is dissimilar to mathematical research.

Let us study the similarities and differences of the experimental practices in research and teaching. In research, praxeologies are characterized by their consistency: mathematicians think of the objects (concepts, properties...) involved in their experimental practices according to the theory they want to build. They know the constraints that their conjectures must satisfy to be included into a deductive production. They try from the beginning to express the conjectures at the more general level, keeping in mind the theoretical apparatus they want to build.

In contrast, in teaching situations, theoretical objects do not come so easily out of experimental practices. As Joshua and Joshua (1987 p. 245) have noted:

The didactic mode (prevalent in the teaching of mathematics) is a rupture between a series of "activities" closed on themselves, and a further axiomatic presentation of a theoretical field that could, abstractedly, correspond.

Even when pupils have an authentic experimental activity in a field of application, it is often difficult for them to establish a link with the theoretical entities modelled by the objects involved in the experimentation. The role of the proof is crucial since theoretical objects find their full relevance only when one goes beyond empirical validation.

What changes does technology bring? Can it cast experimentation as a means to enhance conceptualisation? The possibilities of experimentation are commonly advocated, as illustrated in the extract from the French curriculum for the beginning of algebra:

The computer enlarges considerably the possibilities of observation and manipulation; devoting to the computer a great number of calculations or a multitude of cases makes possible to observe and check empirically various properties.

The idea that increasing the amount of data contributes in itself to the mathematical activity was justly criticized by Lakatos (quoted by Yerushalmy 1999 p. 80): '*If you believe that the longer the table the more conjectures it will suggest, you may waste your time compiling unnecessary data*'. To understand what is really at stake in the transposition of technology-aided experimental praxeologies, it is essential to take into account the practices since, as explained by Lagrange (2000), it is through these practices, where technical work plays a decisive role, that mathematical objects and the connections between them are constructed as a part of developing conceptual understanding. The difficulty is that mathematicians often admit devoting time to tasks of experimental nature, but the methods that made their conjectures possible and the role that these methods play in conceptualisation remain private. Indeed in the mathematical tradition, the way in which the results are conjectured is hidden beneath the deductive presentation of a theoretical structure. Concepts and properties are justified by the consistency of the structure rather than by the conditions of its development.

One branch of professional mathematics has broken with this tradition by expliciting how mathematical activity can take advantage of the computer. This branch —known as 'experimental mathematics'— stresses that using technology to make sense of empirical data and to conjecture and prove, requires to develop specific *methods*, and to build specific *computer environments*. Borwein (2005 p. 76) reports:

At CECM (Centre for Experimental and Constructive Mathematics) we are interested in developing methods for exploiting mathematical computation as a tool (1)in the development of mathematical intuition, (2)in hypotheses building, in the generation of symbolically assisted proofs, and (3)in the construction of a flexible computer environment in which researchers and research students can undertake such research.

There is, however, much more at stake in terms of the transposition in experimental mathematics than simply using the computer to produce more data. With this transposition in view, the Casyopée project set out to be a contribution to the construction and study of viable and legitimate 'techno-experimental praxeologies'. Its work involved (1) thinking of techniques that could help students to benefit from the computer's possibilities of data production, (2) developing the use of the computer's processing capabilities to facilitate the search of conjectures and proof, and (3) thinking of an appropriate software environment.

THE EPISTEMOLOGICAL DIMENSION: SCHOOL ALGEBRA ACTIVITIES WITH TECHNOLOGY.

In the Casyopée project, experimentation should be designed to help students access algebraic activity or to progress in this domain. This is a significant aspiration. Whereas basic numerical proficiency progresses - at least in 'developed' societies - a majority of citizens encounter difficulties at school in algebra and give up all practice after school. Thinking of a tool to enhance students' algebraic activity, highlights the concern about the relationship between mathematical knowledge and tools. This concern refers to the epistemology of algebra as a second dimension.

The choice for a theoretical approach in this dimension has been the "model for conceptualising algebraic activity" that Kieran (2006) introduced as a synthesis of a stream of research about school algebra. This model classifies school algebra activities into three categories: generational – becoming aware of a functional relationship and finding ways of expressing and exploring this relationship; transformational –changing the form of an expression in order to maintain equivalence; and global / meta-level – modelling, searching for structures and generalizing. The model was used for the conception of Casyopée as well as for the design of the associated classroom activities. Kieran (2004 p.23) suggests that there are two main frameworks – generalised arithmetic and functions – providing a "unique transversal thread to these three categories". The focus in Casyopée is on functions, because functions are objects and tools in many algebraic activities at upper secondary level.

This choice of functions had consequences on the objects that Casyopée handles:
a) letters identify the variable, values of the variable (*abscissas*), functions and parameters,
b) graphs and tabular representations of functions complement symbolic expressions,
c) equations correspond to the search for a value of the variable for a given value of the function or they can be about the equality of two functions, or the search for a value of a parameter. They can also be interpreted in the graphic register (intersection of curves).

Parameters are introduced in order to enrich the set of literals (beyond the variable and the functions names). They help the global / meta-level category of activity, because, in these activities, dependency has to be expressed at a sufficiently general level. For instance, (Lagrange 2005b p. 173) searching for a rectangle of maximum area on a triangle, the functional dependency between the area and the length of the rectangle includes, as parameters, the lengths of the sides of the triangle, giving a more general signification to the problem.

In problems about functions depending on parameters, the search for conjectures on graphic or numeric (tabular) representations has to be conducted more methodically (see the first example below) and empirical evidence is less convincing than in 'ordinary' one-variable functions, which provides an advantage to symbolic proof. In Casyopée, each parameter can exist symbolically or it can be instantiated and dynamically animated. This capability helps to explore and generate empirical evidence on numerical examples in parallel with the symbolic study of a generic case (see the example of the maximum area rectangle, (Lagrange *ibid* p. 175).

In its present state, Casyopée does not contribute to the category of generational activities, while software such as dynamic geometry would. That is why embedding dynamic geometry features into Casyopée, postponed until now, will be undertaken at a later stage, as the Casyopée teams would like to offer an 'all in one' software that offers support for all three categories of activities[3].

In the Casyopée project, transformational activities were considered significant. They are consistent with the objectives of the French curriculum:

Students should be able to recognize the form of an expression (sum, product, square, difference of two squares), to recognize various forms of an expression and to choose the most relevant form for a given work

These objectives do not put at stake the technique of transformation itself, but rather the understanding of the multiplicity of equivalent forms and the role that a form can play in a proof. That is why computer symbolic calculation capabilities have been chosen in Casyopée to help students to easily obtain various forms for expressions of functions, their sub-expressions, and their values.

Proof is important to give sense to the transformational activities, keeping students away from unmotivated manipulation. Casyopée favours an approach to proving through meta-global activities. Casyopée also supports the building of a proof by offering students a set of elementary proofs (justifications) that a student can use to build his/her proof, justifying a property by a relevant form of the expression of the function. This set is designed to be an aid to students, rather than a constraint, by exploiting the "transformational knowledge" of computer symbolic calculation.

THE THIRD DIMENSION: DESIGNING A SYMBOLIC ENVIRONMENT

After choosing computer symbolic calculation as the means to support students' transformational activities, it was decided to build Casyopée as a new environment rather than to use a standard symbolic application (like Derive or Maple). The team who started the Casyopée project, after trying to develop classroom uses of these applications found strong disadvantages.

A first disadvantage was the design of the interface. The power and openness of these applications imply a multiplicity of modes, menus, objects, and keywords, which is a cause of difficulties and erratic behaviours by students. Standard symbolic application's main window is a 'history' of the calculation and definition. It provides no direct information about the present state of the application and the status of the objects and it is hard for a newcomer to have a proper representation of these. For instance, a very common difficulty for students arises when they have used a letter to name a value and then try to use the same letter as a formal parameter in a calculation. Actually, these applications are designed to be a powerful 'scratch paper' rather than a learning environment where students could develop methodical and reflective approaches to problem solving. The team felt the need for a working environment with a better balance between simplicity and power, where objects would have a clear status, and where their present state would be visible at the interface.

A second disadvantage with standard symbolic applications is that little care is taken for consistency with the curriculum. The consequence is that phenomena that students cannot understand (like complex values for 10th graders) constantly occur, complicating the task of the teacher. Inconsistencies between the way objects are handled in these applications and the way recommended by the curriculum also cause deep misunderstanding, for example when formal calculation simplifies x^2/x into x without warning or gives $\{0\}$ as the set of solutions for $zeros(x^2/x, x)$.

The following example shows inconsistencies that would cause no difficulty to mathematicians but led to serious problems among students.

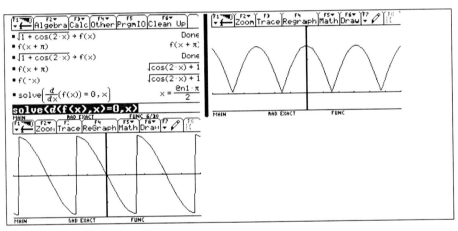

Figure 2.1: *Using the TI-92 to discuss a trigonometric function*

The task was to study the function $\mathbf{f(x)} = \sqrt{1 + \cos(2 \cdot x)}$. It was set to 11th graders at the end of the year. The students used a TI-92[4] throughout the year within a research project (Lagrange 1999).

We expected that students would easily find periodicity and symmetry by observing the graph (figure 2.1, middle) and confirm their conjecture using the symbolic module (figure 2.1, left), then detect that the derivative is not defined at the points where the curve reaches the x-axis by observing that the curve has different non-zero gradients at these points. (S)he would conclude that the function has an 'ordinary maximum' (i.e. null derivative) every $\mathbf{k\pi}$ and a 'special minimum' (i.e. no derivative) every $\pi/2 + k\pi$.

Observation showed that parity was not a problem for students. In contrast, they had difficulty in finding a period, because of the phenomenon on the screen (left): the curve seemed not to reach the x axis for $\pm\ 3\pi/2$.

Interpreting accurately the behaviour of the function at the points where the curve reaches the x-axis was not possible. Students persisted to think of an 'ordinary minimum', wondering why repeated zooming in did not show a null gradient. They were reinforced in this idea by the false solution of the equation $f'(x)=0$ by the symbolic module, giving zeros of the derivative for every $k\pi/2$. Students thought this resolution was a reliable means to get extrema and had no reason to mistrust the result. Even the graph of the derivative (figure 2.1, right) was misleading because of the irrelevant line across the discontinuity. The reason for this behaviour was that the TI-92, like other symbolic systems, does not consider that functions are defined on a domain. Thus, solving the equation, it just looks for zeros of the numerators without considering possible zeros of the denominator.

These observations drew our attention towards the importance of a careful design that took into account the multiple constraints of classroom use: this is why *design* is a third dimension in the framework. Human Computer Interaction (HCI) researchers stressed for ten years that '*Laboratory-based usability studies are (only) part of the solution,*' and are best preceded by "*careful field studies*" to address question like: '*how technology can fit into users' actual social and material environments; the problems users have that technology can remedy; the applications that will promote creativity and enlightenment...*' (Nardi 1996).

As Yerushalmy (1999, p. 184) puts it, software design should give the learner control over experimentation by helping him/her to develop methods. It should also support the organization of the curriculum by being consistent, using "the same language of objects and actions that form the grid along which the curriculum is mapped".

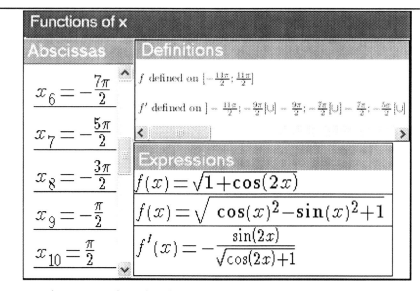

A main function window identifies an independent variable (here x), "abscissas" that will be critical values of this variable (here zeros of the function which are also discontinuities of the derivative), the definition of the functions (union of intervals where they exist) and their expressions. Here the user created the function f by entering the definition and an expression. The symbolic kernel calculated an equivalent expression, the zeros and the derivative.

Figure 2.2 : A main function window of Casyopée.

This is how the Casyopée team tried to take this dimension into account. First, the environment's interface displays windows that help to organize objects of different status (figure 2.2): values of the variable defining the intervals in which functions are defined and where properties can be proven or conjectured, functions with proven or conjectured properties, expressions with various algebraic equivalent definitions of the same function, equations. This organization is dynamic (as in a spreadsheet) by recalculation of the objects after instantiation of the parameters, and after modification of the functions. The history exists as a 'notebook', designed to be used as a basis for writing a report or a proof.

Objects are designed to be consistent with the usual repertory of secondary mathematics. For example, a basic choice was to define the functions on a domain (interval or union of intervals), rather than by just an expression as in symbolic systems. Casyopée evaluates the existence of the function on the domain and, on request, calculates the greatest domain. It is an example of assistance that the environment brings to various steps of the algebraic activity.

Finally, the properties of the functions – sign, variations and existence of zeros – are obtained as results of proofs. The elementary steps of proof (justifications) correspond to theorems familiar at secondary level and to properties of 'reference functions'. Casyopée can directly take for granted properties that, because of their simplicity, are not explicitly justified in usual practice.

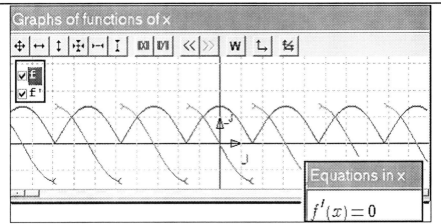

Figure 2.3: *Child windows*
From a "main function windows" a user can open five "child windows" : properties of functions involved in proof processes, exact and approximate values, graphs and equations. Each change in a main window is reflected in the child windows. Graphs and equations take the definition into account.

NotePad

resolution $f'(x) = 0$ in x

$$S = \{\pi, 0, -\pi, -2\pi, 2\pi, -3\pi, 3\pi, -4\pi, 4\pi, -5\pi, 5\pi\}$$

Figure 2.4: *The Notepad window*

Data resulting of actions (creation, computation, justification, equation solving) are automatically recorded in the Notepad (here solutions of the equation). Facilities for editing the Notepad and copying graphs are available.

CLASSROOM SITUATIONS

This section presents two examples of classroom use of Casyopée. The first is a situation intended to help students progress towards a method for experimenting on algebraic expressions. It corresponds to our first concern (experimental activity) while also addressing the issue of a genuine algebraic activity especially at a global meta level. The second example is a situation where students used Casyopée to perform algebraic proof more effectively. The main concern is then the algebraic activity, especially *transformational* activity. These examples also provide insight into the influence of Casyopée's design on students' classroom activity, our third concern.

TOWARDS A METHOD FOR EXPERIMENTING

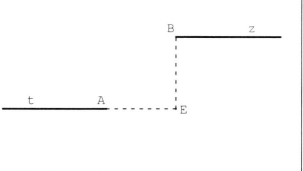

You have to build a track for skateboarding. At one point the track is horizontal, and two meters farther it has to be horizontal again, but one meter higher. The goal is to find a function whose graph could be a track. The track has to be smooth. Try to make it as smooth as possible.

1° What axes can we choose? Which are the most interesting? Why?
2° What types of functions can we choose?
3° Use Casyopée to find functions whose graph could be a smooth track. Write a report on your work.

Figure 2.5 *The skateboarding track problem.*

The problem of figure 2.5 was proposed in a twelve-grade class, scientific stream, at the beginning of the year. The goal was consistent with the curriculum, that is to "motivate the study of functions by problem solving", especially problems whose solution uses the relationship between the properties of a function and its derivative. The session was two hours long in a computer room. The teacher had introduced the problem in a session before. Nineteen students were in this class. As often happens now in France even in the scientific stream, they had difficulties in algebraic manipulations and did not easily tackle problems by themselves but rather waited for the teacher's solution.

Mathematically, after choosing axes, a student has to look for a function f satisfying four conditions:

$$f(x_A) = y_A, \ f(x_B) = y_B \text{ and } f'(x_A) = f'(x_B) = 0.$$

He/she can think of cubic, piecewise quadratic and sine functions (figure 2.6). Depending on the type of function, the values of three or four parameters are to be found to satisfy the above conditions. Searching for these values can be done by animating parameters to adjust the curve and/or by algebraic calculations. In the team's *a priori* analysis, students would have not much trouble satisfying the first two conditions by animating parameters, but would less easily deal with conditions about the derivative. It was expected that the students could not obtain a solution just by animating parameters and thus the situation would bring to light algebraic conditions about the derivative necessary to get a 'smooth graph'. The use of Casyopée, was expected to help students to work by themselves in the session. Students were free to choose axes and a type of function (among those identified by collective discussion in the preceding session) to give them some sense of autonomy.

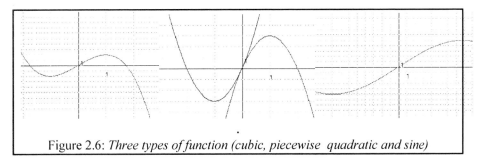

Figure 2.6: *Three types of function (cubic, piecewise quadratic and sine)*

REPORT ON THE SESSION

–   *Choosing Axes*

In the preceding session, students proposed axes with four different origins (A, B E and the middle of [AB]) and they usually searched for solutions in their own axes. After this session, classroom discussion made clear that setting the origin at the middle of [AB] helped to reach a solution more efficiently.

The team analysed this as an indication of the students' developing autonomy over decisions in their mathematical activity. This is a difference with another experiment of a similar problem (Artigue 2005, p.279) where students used the quite complex TI-92 calculator, and the teacher had to decide a common axis for all students, in order to engage students in a productive resolution.

–   *Types of Functions*

Students found functions of different types. No type was chosen more frequently, which seems again to be an indication of students' developing autonomy. When a cubic function was chosen, the difficulty lay in the complexity of animating four parameters. The role of a parameter, like the 0-degree coefficient, is easily grasped, whereas the effect of changing other parameters confers little insight. The role of the parameters in a trigonometric function is more visible. Students nevertheless had difficulties in recognising the value $\pi/2$ after they found 1.6 by animating a parameter.

– *Animating Parameters Versus Considering Algebraic Conditions*

We observed very varied student behaviour. Some students persisted in randomly animating parameters, although it did not lead them to a solution. Most students organised the animation, giving constant values to some parameters and animating others. The remaining students discovered by themselves that writing algebraic conditions helped to decrease the number of parameters. Nearly all solutions were found by reflective animation. Seven students found solutions by themselves. The others could not reach a solution alone in the two hours, but most did personal and productive work that they could reuse after a collective synthesis to write a solution.

It seemed that Casyopée helped to make a relatively complex research situation 'live' in a class with students likely to be passive in normal lessons, with a clear integration into the curriculum[5]. Moreover, decreasing the number of parameters appeared as a generic method to solve this type of problem.

– *Building an Algebraic Proof*

This is an example of a session for 11th grade vocational students in electronics. As mentioned earlier, proving is a way to give meaning to transformational activity. Proof, however, is thought irksome and irrelevant by many students, because in ordinary cases, conjectures can be validated through a graph or a table. Students experience difficulties calculating algebraic transformations, but also in organising and writing proof. The hypothesis for this session was that studying a function with a parameter could bring them towards a symbolic proof, and that Casyopée could help them not only by performing algebraic calculations, but also by providing for the means to build a proof.

In the vocational part students were learning about band-pass filters. These electronic devices attenuate all signals below a given frequency and all signals above another given frequency. Students considered a practical device made of resistors and capacities of given values R and C using an oscilloscope to observe for a given input tension V_{in}, the evolution of the output tension V_{out} against the frequency. They also calculated the transfer function that is the absolute value of the complex quotient V_{out}/V_{in}, which depends on a parameter *T*, product of the device's resistance and capacity (Figure 2.7). They characterized the filter as band-pass because the limits of this function are zero for frequencies approaching zero and infinity.

In the mathematics classroom they had to go further in the study of transfer functions. Using Casyopée, after entering the function, students could perform algebraic transformations by means of the "Compute" menu (Fig. 2.8) and elementary proofs by way of the "Justify" menu. (Fig. 2.9) These actions have a result in the functions windows (new functions or expressions, properties and so on) and also produce information in the 'Notepad' (Fig. 2.10). A standard study begins by using the "Compute" menu to obtain the derivative. Then it is to get the factorised form and finally to select a sub-expression informative of the sign of the derivative by way of the same menu. Then the proof consists in the justification of the sign of this sub-expression and of the derivative. Note that Casyopée, as in ordinary practice 'admits' that a 'visibly positive' factor (for instance a square) does not change the sign of a product. The study is classically achieved by justifying the variation of the function by way of the derivative's sign.

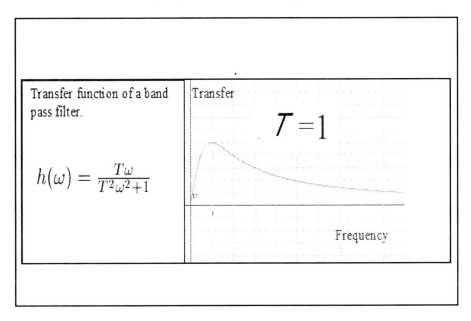

Figure 2.7 : *The band pass filter.*
Transfer function and curve for a value of the resistor and capacitor

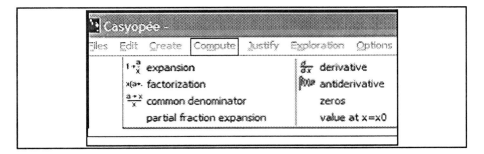

Fig 2.8: *The 'Compute' menu*

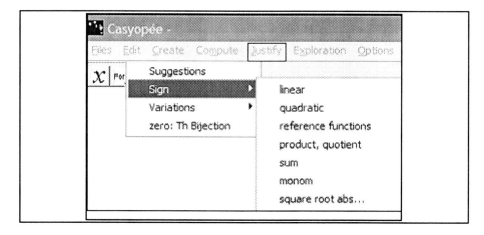

Fig 2.9: *The 'Justify' menu*

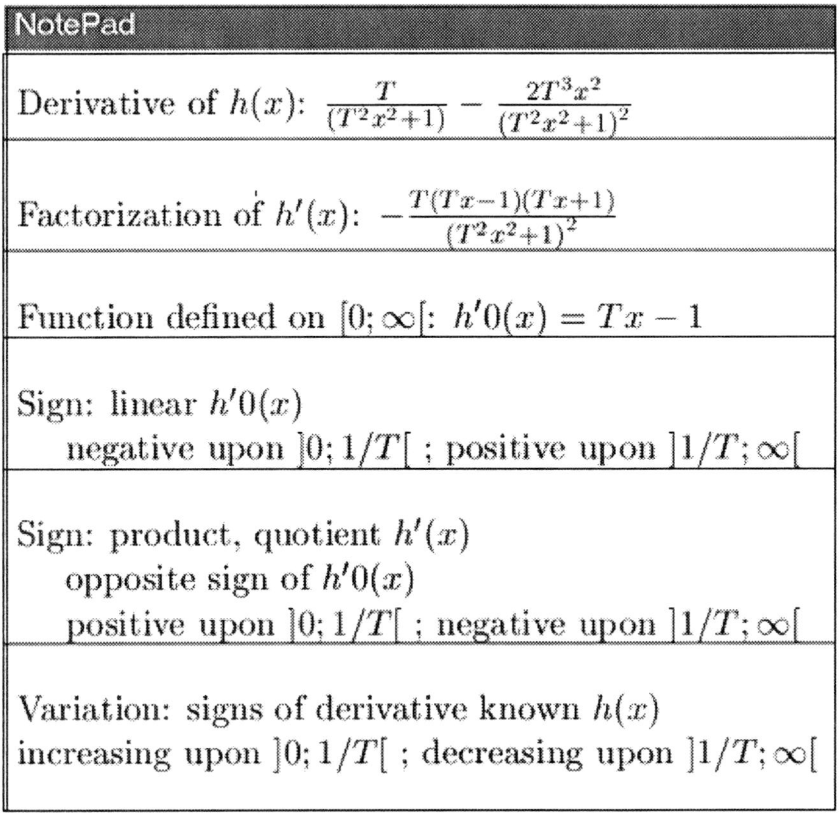

NotePad
Derivative of $h(x)$: $\frac{T}{(T^2x^2+1)} - \frac{2T^3x^2}{(T^2x^2+1)^2}$
Factorization of $h'(x)$: $-\frac{T(Tx-1)(Tx+1)}{(T^2x^2+1)^2}$
Function defined on $[0;\infty[$: $h'0(x) = Tx - 1$
Sign: linear $h'0(x)$ negative upon $]0;1/T[$; positive upon $]1/T;\infty[$
Sign: product, quotient $h'(x)$ opposite sign of $h'0(x)$ positive upon $]0;1/T[$; negative upon $]1/T;\infty[$
Variation: signs of derivative known $h(x)$ increasing upon $]0;1/T[$; decreasing upon $]1/T;\infty[$

Fig 2.10: Indications given by Casyopée in the NotePad after
(1) calculating the derivative, (2) factoring this derivative, (3) selecting a sub-expression,
(4)justifying by 'sign: linear' (5) justifying by 'product-quotient' (6) justifying by 'signs of the
Derivative'

Students were familiar with the study of function, but here it was presented as a new task because of the parameter T. The 'electronics' context contributed, however, in providing sense to this 'generalized' study. Students were asked to do this study and then to use the information given in Casyopée's notepad to write a solution. For instance, students were expected to motivate their choice of a factored form of the derivative by a comment such as: *the factorisation is the form that permits to study the sign of the function.*

The team analysed the record of the students' actions and their written productions with the aim of evaluating how Casyopée helped them find and write proofs. Nearly all students correctly did the first part of the study, using the 'Compute' menu; most justified correctly the derivative's sign and half of them interpreted correctly the solution relatively to the nature of the filter. Globally, this is satisfying, because even students who did not totally succeed had a consistent approach to developing a proof.

Differences were observed in the written productions that students completed from Casyopée's notepad. Half of them merely added informative subtitles to the successive steps of proof while the other half produced results that were of better quality, especially when compared with their usual written work. Some productions were very personal, detailing the steps they had gone through in a narrative way, or, conversely, synthesising the proof by reorganising and rewriting the notebook. So there is some justification for acknowledging Casyopée's potential as an aid to writing a proof.

SUMMARY OF SECTION 2

This Section set out to explain how the development of a digital tool and associated classroom situations could usefully start from a selection of concerns, and is summarised in the table below. Aiming to make the algebraic representation more learnable brought about three concerns (third row) that defined three dimensions. In each dimension, a theoretical approach (fourth row) brought central ideas and concepts. The five central rows of the table show how basic choices made in the Casyopée project are related to each dimension and the two last lines put the two described classroom situations into relation with the three dimensions above.

The three dimensions are based on distinctive approaches of teaching learning and software development. Each of them helps to focus on specific aspects of the project, informing basic choices. Nearly all rows corresponding to basic choices have more than one empty cell, showing that choices in software development cannot be informed by a single dimension.

Intersecting the two examples of classroom activity with the dimensions has helped to evaluate how the work with Casyopée contributed to situations taking into account the three concerns. There is an obvious gap as generational activities were not involved in the present state of Casyopée. Casyopée works on functions given by algebraic representations and till now provides no enactive representation for non-algebraic functional exploration. One consequence has been limitations in the students' experimental activity, especially when modelling phenomena: except when the phenomenon is directly described by a curve, like in the skateboarding problem, students cannot build and try models by themselves.

This summary gives pointers to additional work: to develop features allowing students to work with enactive non-algebraic representations of phenomena and to pass fluidly between algebraic and non-algebraic representations[6]. Thus we argue that an analysis around dimensions provides a basis for future work in design, implementation, observation, and adaptation.

	Dimensions		
Concerns	Classroom experimental activity	Students' algebraic activity	Software environment for classroom use
Ideas, concepts	<u>Anthropological approach</u> Transposition Techno-Experimental praxeologies	<u>Epistemology</u> Categories of algebraic activity	**Design** Users' social and material environment Problems that technology can remedy
Basic choices in the Casyopée project			
Symbolic calculation	Relationship with mathematicians' tools	Transformational activity	Difficulties with standard symbolic systems
Proof	Methods for proving	Transformational and global meta level activities	Help to search conjectures and write proofs
Interface	Methods for experimenting		Students' control over experimentation
Objects			Consistency with the curriculum
Dynamic parameters		Global meta level activity	
Examples of classroom situation			
Smooth track	Methods for experimenting	Global meta level activity	Organisation of objects and actions at the interface
Filter transfer function	Help to find and write proofs	Transformational activity	

Table 2.1: Summary of dimensions, concerns, choices and classroom situations

THE WEBLABS PROJECT: DEVELOPING AN ALTERNATIVE INFRASTRUCTURE

WebLabs was a three-year project (http://www.lkl.ac.uk/kscope/weblabs/) whose overarching aim was to create an alternative infrastructure with which students (age 13-15 years) in 6 different European countries could construct, share, comment on and evaluate representations of their evolving mathematical and scientific ideas[7]. There were two main focal points of our design effort. First, to construct a set of tools and activities, based on *ToonTalk* – a programming language in the style of a videogame - that allowed students to address various knowledge domains in mathematics in ways that resonated with the activities of an experimental lab: to do 'experiments', test conjectures, look for counterexamples, and share their evolving ideas. We designed and built a series of toolsets of working models of mathematical objects and relationships for students to think about and manipulate, which were transparent in the sense that it was easy to look not only at what the models *did,* but how they *worked*, through expressing them in a programming language rather than with standard numerical or algebraic notation. By making their thoughts 'visible' in the form of working models or programs, we hoped to leverage students' intuitions and add to them a formalism that would become generative in developing their understandings. Alongside this development we designed sequences of activities to explore several mathematical domains using the toolkits.

The second focus of the project involved the construction of *WebReports*, a web-based system that included simple mechanisms for uploading and downloading models to form a basis of collaboration, co-construction and comment. *WebReports* also afforded us a window on the ways students could share their models of evolving knowledge at a distance, what they felt was important to discuss, to change and manipulate, providing a way to assess how the new representational structures influenced the trajectories of student thinking (for a discussion of the role of expressive tools, see Noss & Hoyles, 2006).

Thus the twin objectives of the work were iteratively to design, develop and evaluate tools both for *constructing* and *sharing* evolving knowledge of mathematical relationships. The key idea was that learners could not only discuss, conjecture with and comment upon each others' ideas, but they could inspect and edit each others' *working models* of ideas, computer programs – rather than in algebraic notation - that instantiated the state of their current knowledge.

An objective of the WebLabs project was to explore the extent to which some of the apparent complexity and difficulties of mathematical and scientific ideas is due to the symbols and language used to express them. Such a hypothesis has a strong design implication, namely to develop a system and an activity structure in which students could express their ideas in novel ways, *without* sacrificing what makes the ideas powerful and rigorous. Our theoretical framework is based on two distinct and interrelated themes. The first is *Constructionism,* an 'orienting framework' (Cobb *et al.*, 2003) suggested by Papert in the late nineteen-eighties as a pedagogical counterpart of *constructivism.* The idea is that students learn by building with appropriate tools, virtual 'external' realities that mirror their developing mathematical or scientific meanings, and by sharing this public or semi-public entity with a community. The second orienting idea that guided our design decisions was to exploit the benefits for learning mathematics and science of collaborative interaction, by including (mainly asynchronous) discussion and evaluation at a distance as part of the programme of activities, as well as face-to-face interchange.

To support the work of WebLabs, we designed sequenced activities in five knowledge domains: *Sequences*, *Infinity*, *Collisions*, *Lunar Lander* and *Models, Systems and Randomness*:

a) In *Sequences* students construct and analyse number sequences, which after common introductory activities focussed either on the Fibonacci sequence or on explorations of sequences that converge and diverge.

b) In *Infinity*, students explore the cardinality of infinite sets and the relationships between different infinite sets.

c) In *Collisions*, students build models of objects colliding in 1-dimension, iteratively test them against reality and refine their models to cover more cases of collision.

d) In *Lunar Lander*, students control the motion of virtual objects, record data and plot the resulting position-time and velocity-time graphs, thereby investigating acceleration and the relationships between different representations of motion.

e) In *Models, Systems and Randomness* students build computational models that represent and explore various real-world phenomena, and investigate the concept of randomness, and how it could be understood and used.

In each domain, we expended considerable effort in iteratively designing these sequences of activities; starting from distinguishing the core epistemological ideas of the domain, predicting potential obstacles and then building tools that would assist exploration and problem solving. The activity sequences were also designed to fit into, complement or extend the present mathematics curriculum for secondary school students. We are unable here to deal with more than a small fraction of these activities: the interested reader may wish to consult www.lkl.ac.uk/kscope/weblabs/. In what follows, we distinguish between *design* outcomes – a main focus in this chapter – and then report on general *learning* outcomes, which we illustrate with specific examples of what some students achieved with our system.

THE METHODOLOGICAL APPROACH

We provide a brief overview of our methodological approach. In order to research both technological design and learning, our methodology fits the paradigm of the *iterative design experiment* - theory-based interventions that aim for specific learning goals alongside the development of theoretical frameworks for learning, in general and within a particular knowledge domain (diSessa & Cobb, 2004). We have sought to discover how different aspects of learning are supported and mediated by the toolsets and the activity systems we designed. Our approach was iterative, in the sense that initial evaluations of the research team, collaborating teachers and partners in other countries fed into subsequent phases of design. Technical development, assessment of engagement with the core ideas proceeded in tandem and informed further design cycles.

This methodology was challenging. It inevitably drew on inter-disciplinary expertise as well as requiring systematic evaluations of learning based on prior research, while remaining open to the potential of the new tools. Our evaluation of learning was almost entirely qualitative, largely because of the small numbers of students (a maximum of two classrooms in each country) and their diversity in terms of language and prior attainment. We stress, therefore, that this research aimed to provide proof of concept – to describe the conditions (technical, cultural, pedagogical) in which learning took place, and the specific kinds of domain-specific learning that could occur. In what follows we give examples of the design outcomes of the project; we then briefly describe our pedagogical approach and activity structures, illustrate them by one example of an extended interaction; finally, we summarise the learning outcomes of WebLabs and suggest its limitations.

DESIGN OUTCOMES

We chose for our modelling environment, *ToonTalk*, a concurrent constraint-based programming language, in which the source code consists of actions of animated cartoon-like characters. ToonTalk is an object-oriented language so that tools can be attached to the back of any object to give it functionality and reused, inspected, or combined. The basic idea of ToonTalk is that it provides a rich programming environment capable of supporting the construction of, for example, games, simulations and animations: it is a general-purpose computation engine with an interface that is concrete and playful. We will give a flavour of what is involved in what follows: for the moment, we should simply note that there is no textual editing involved in ToonTalk programming, that it involves manipulating animated characters rather than, say, static icons (more information can be gained at www.toontalk.com).

From a design point of view, a programming environment provided a necessary but far from sufficient basis for our system. By analogy with, say, Lego bricks, construction of complex structures is substantially facilitated if one is provided with ready-made working parts of modules that can be combined into larger more complex structures, but which can also be broken apart to their elements to see how each works. This idea of *layering* turned out to be an important design criterion, and as the project developed, we sought to understand how the different *layers of interaction* that characterised student engagement with the system and its related activities, could engender learning at different structural layers of knowledge – what students came to express and know about specific pieces of knowledge.

Before such layers could be developed, we faced the challenge of tuning the substrate on which they could be built; that is, to enhance ToonTalk in many different ways so that the representational infrastructure could support innovative expression. We begin, therefore, by pointing to three examples of how ToonTalk was tuned to provide learners with the right kinds of functionalities required for their activities.

EXTENDING TO VERY LARGE NUMBERS

Standard ToonTalk only supported the standard computer programming size for integer numbers. Yet as our activities developed, it became natural to encourage learners to imagine what would happen if their robots continued to run forever, generating larger and larger integers. Accordingly, we devised a means by which programs could produce *very* large numbers, supporting integers of *any* size within memory limitations. At one level, of course, very big integers behave just like small ones: the laws of combination are the same, checking whether a number is divisible by, say, 3 involves the same algorithm and so on. But there are possibilities that open up with very large numbers that generate a sense of surprise – an unexpected pattern in the final digits of 100! for example – and a sense of engagement that accrues from being able to – literally – hold in one's hand and integer that has tens of thousands of digits.

There are dangers too. We intended that such activities would be part of a transitional set of activities during which it became logical to ask what would happen if the number of digits (or the number itself) actually became infinite. Of course, gaining a sense of what happens "at infinity" could easily be seen as being at odds with what happens when the integers are 'merely large'. Plenty of scope, here, for what mathematics educators could label as "misconceptions"! But there is also a sense in which very large numbers almost demand questions about infinitely large ones: if one has a sense of a number taking longer and longer to write, then it becomes acceptable to ask whether one could write one just a little bit longer, or a lot longer.

Writing, of course, has its own limitations. It is easy to imagine that 100, 1000, 10000 is a sequence that could go on for a *very* long time. After a few terms, it seems rather cumbersome to apply pen to paper. But supposing one could go for a walk along a number, looking at patterns or, looking *for* patterns? See Figure 3.1 for a possible view of the situation, which involves looking at – actually walking along –100!.

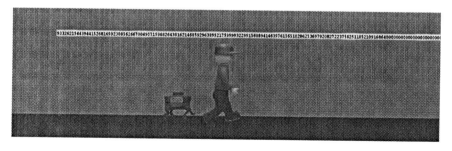

Figure 3.1: The result of a process that computes 100!. The programmer can literally "walk along" the length of the number to get a sense of its size.

It is worth asking what kind of affordances this (relatively small) change in representational form might make? Consider a simple example. Any teacher of mathematics knows that students routinely confuse squaring with doubling. 3 squared is 9; 3 * 2 is 6. There is not much difference! More seriously, there is no real sense of what squaring does (as a function), particularly when examples are routinely confined to small numbers less than 10. Now consider programming a ToonTalk "robot" to produce 1,000,000,000 squared. Laying the result out as in Figure 3.1 will soon reveal how much "longer" it is than the same number doubled. "How much longer?" becomes a sensible question, and one that generalises to cubes and so on. Merely being able to walk up and down numbers, and get a sense of their size makes – potentially at least – a huge difference to the kinds of questions it is natural to ask, and the sorts of knowledge that are likely to be developed.

One last point. While we remarked that walking along a number is rather a different way to think of it compared to writing it down, we might ask how else we could "view" such an object. In ToonTalk it is possible to zoom out and look at any object from above, in a helicopter. This revealed a surprising (to students) fact about a very large number (in this case 10000!): namely that there was a large number of zeros at the end, a fact that would have been rather time-consuming to reveal if one was confined to walking!

INFINITE DECIMAL REPRESENTATION

Part of our evolving set of activities involved students interacting with rational numbers. For example, in our work on infinite sequences and series, we engaged students with the sum of sequences like 1, ½, ¼, $^1/_8$, ... and 1, ½, $^1/_3$, ¼, ... In such a scenario, there are several difficulties with the conventional representation. The first is evident with the use of ellipsis to denote "and so on". Not all students see that, for example, 0.1428571... as an infinite decimal, preferring instead to seeing 1 as the "last" digit. Indeed, the fact that it takes an infinite number of digits to represent a tangible entity like $^1/_7$ is a paradoxical situation for many students – the difference between a number and its (various) representations is far from obvious! So a second difficulty – more serious than the first – is that it is, in conventional representations, *impossible* to write down an equation like $^1/_7 = 0.1428571$ without some convention peculiar to the representational infrastructure (such as judicious placing of dots either at the end, or above some of the digits).

Our challenge, therefore, was to eliminate rounding errors. We achieved this by the implementation of exact rational arithmetic in ToonTalk. In ToonTalk, it really is the case that there is an exact decimal expansion of a rational number, and moreover, that this is recognised by the system ($^1/_7 = 0.1428571...$ is "true").

But how to represent the "..." to the right of the decimal expansion? Clearly this is a serious design challenge: no truncation should return 'true', yet there *is* a decimal expansion of $^1/_7$ that is *exactly* equal to it. We remark in passing that we met this situation many times in our iterative design process: solving one problem of representation threw up a new problem.

Our solution was to invent the idea of *shrinking digits*. Digits are displayed in gradually decreasing size until they reach the size of a pixel. In this way the idea that an infinite number of digits follow the decimal point is conveyed visually. By using the ToonTalk 'pumping' tool for increasing the size of an object, a student can view more and more of the digits that initially were too small to see. This process can take place indefinitely: there is a theoretical size limit based on the memory of the computer, although there is nothing to stop the process being transferred to a second computer when the memory is full! Figure 3.2 provides an illustration of a decimal representation of the rational number $^5/_{49}$.

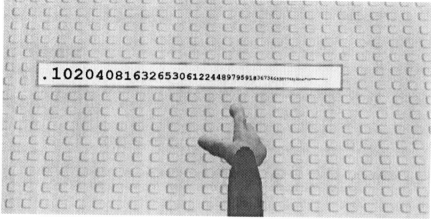

Figure 3.2: An example of the new shrinking digit display, showing the result of dividing 5 by 49.

Once shrinking digits were implemented, we could incorporate in activities discussions of the equivalence of different representations of the same number. Figures 3.3 shows how ToonTalk tests for equality and inequality by showing a balance between any two numbers, regardless of how they are represented (as rationals, infinite decimals or mixed fractions).

Fig 3.3: a) The fraction 54/49 is the same regardless of whether it is displayed as a proper fraction or an infinite decimal expansion.

Fig 3.3: b) If both sides are multiplied by 49 the results are exactly 54.

Fig 3.3: c) If the decimal is approximated then it is not equal to the original fraction.

Fig 3.3: d) If the original fraction and the approximation are multiplied by 49 the approximated decimal expansion no longer becomes exactly 54.

THE WEBREPORT SYSTEM

We now turn to the collaborative dimension of the work. As we explained above, we designed a web-based collaboration system, called *WebReports*. The primary aim of this system was to allow learners to reflect on each others' work by sharing working models of their ideas. To help the students navigate the system, it was organised around the different knowledge domains each with a repository of tools, and online guidance as to how to use the system in general as well as hints to support both teacher and students in their exploration of the knowledge domain. Figure 3.4 shows the front page of the system.

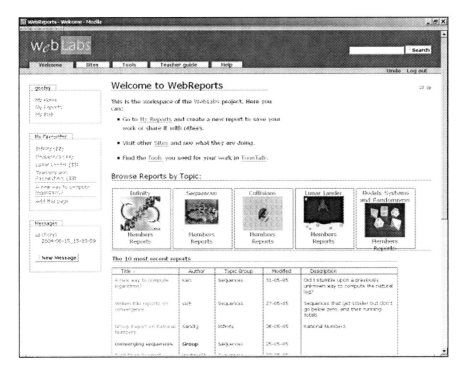

Fig 3.4: Front page of the Webreport system showing the topics available, the 10 most recent reports and the link to the repository of tools

WebReports could include formatted text, comments, diagrams and multi-media objects, and most importantly – ToonTalk models. These models were embedded in the report as images, which linked to the actual code object. When clicked, they automatically opened in the reader's ToonTalk environment – which could be in another classroom or another country. The reader could then manipulate the object, modify it, and respond with a comment that might include her own model.

Interaction between groups and individuals was promoted by a layered commenting facility, inspired by Knowledge Forum and the work of Scardamalia and Bereiter (2006). We wanted, like them, to build a community of learners of mathematics who would increasingly take control of monitoring their own learning, sharing and building on ideas and raising counter examples to refute conjectures. Thus each report ended with a selection of comment options, which included "Can you explain?", "What if...", "I have a conjecture..", and "This doesn't work because..." as well as a box to insert a new custom comment type or an unclassified comment. Commenting on someone else's report provided the same functionality as posting a report – a *wysiwyg* editor and the facility to include images, embedded ToonTalk objects and external links. Comments could also be posted as replies to other comments so that threads of discussion could be created (in much the same way as in internet newsgroups) and monitored.

The idea was that after discussion of a phenomenon in a group at one site, the group would publish a report of their collective observations, models, conjectures and conclusions. The key idea was that they would focus on the *process* of reasoning (the construction and then running of ToonTalk programs) and then illustrate this with outcomes that might be, for example, sequences of numbers, or spreadsheet graphs, that could then become the subject of discussion and further experimentation. Finally when a task sequence was completed, we planned that groups would publish a concluding report devised after extensive within-site negotiation to achieve a consensus and through this report they would share conclusions with remote peers. Thus in order maximally to exploit the collaborative dimension, we developed a common frame for activities that evolved iteratively – these focused on intra- and inter-classroom collaboration (see Figure 3.5). For some background to the theoretical rationale for such an approach, see Hoyles *et al.* (1992).

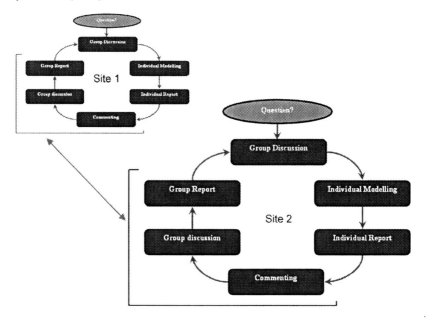

Figure 3.5: The common frame for WebLabs activities

So the innovative component of WebReports is that in addition to students talking to each other about what they *think*, they can discuss what they have *done*: the models they upload with their discussion become objects to argue about, modify, reconstruct and build upon. Building on the success we achieved with students sharing each others' ToonTalk models, we found a way to pipe data from running programs directly into Excel, so that students could easily generate and upload graphical representations where appropriate: see Simpson *et al.* (2005; 2006) for detailed examples of this functionality and the way students appropriated it.

Our focus so far has been on the design of tools for construction and collaboration and a general framework into which they were inserted. We now turn to describe the activity sequences we iteratively devised after experimentation with students and the pedagogical approach we planned to adopt.

PEDAGOGY AND ACTIVITY

Having set up our general framework, we designed, again iteratively, sequences of activities in each knowledge domain that sought to exploit the representational system we had designed. Each activity sequence had explicit overarching learning aims as well as aims for each of its component tasks, each taking into account the mathematical background of the students and the curriculum they would have followed. Each sequence also focussed on the tools to be used, the need to encourage prediction and reflection, and our intention to capitalise on collaborative exchange, both face-to-face and at a distance, as relevant to the knowledge domain. Rather than describe the process in general, we present part of one activity sequence with respect to one knowledge domain, *sequences, cardinality and infinity*, which is particularly relevant to a discussion of an alternative infrastructure for algebra. Finally, we provide an illustrative example of the implementation of one activity.

SEQUENCES, CARDINALITY AND INFINITY

In many countries pattern recognition and generalisation are considered fundamental to mathematical thinking, and a fruitful pathway into algebraic thinking. Yet at the same time, a number of researchers have pointed to the difficulties students encounter in shifting from pattern spotting to structural understanding (Stacey 1989; Lee and Wheeler 1987; MacGregor and Stacey 1992; Arzarello 1991; Hoyles & Noss, 1996).

A set of activities was designed for students to investigate number sequences with the main aim being for them to learn to reason and argue about the structure of number sequences. Students started by modelling the most basic sequence: the natural numbers. However, the way we encouraged them to model in ToonTalk afforded easy generalisation to any arithmetic sequence, and later to any iterative sequence, developing a shared language for describing their sequences that formed the basis for mathematical discussion. How was the sequence generated? Were different generating rules mathematically equivalent? Could different sequences be generated by the same programs? We tried to produce situations that generated surprises and we then formulated two different directions – one pointing toward Fibonacci sequences, and the other to an exploration of convergence and divergence – which were both tried with students in different classrooms. Figure 3.6 outlines the structure of the activities in the number sequences domain.

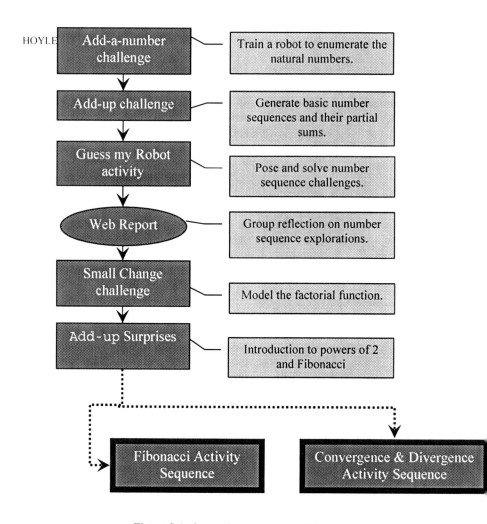

Figure 3.6: the number sequence activities.

From the point of view of this chapter, our focus is on how the representational infrastructure shaped – and was shaped by – our intention to highlight the collaborative dimension. We now illustrate this by reference to one episode of student interaction during one activity, the *Guess my Robot* activity.

AN EPISODE FROM GUESS MY ROBOT

The key players in the story were Rita, a 12-year old girl in a school near Lisbon, and Nasko, a 12-year-old boy in Sofia[8]. The Sofia group consisted of 6 boys and girls, aged 11-12, working with *WebLabs* researchers. They had been working with *ToonTalk* for several months, approximately once a week for a couple of hours. The second group was from a village south of Lisbon. Paula, a teacher and researcher in the *WebLabs* team, worked with a school group there (aged 12-13) during the first project year. Researchers in both groups acted as teachers, guiding the students through the mathematical ideas and activities as well as through the programming skills. At the same time, the researchers facilitated collaborative interaction, by pointing children to interesting and relevant peer Webreports and helping them to add a few words in English to their own reports.

The activity was based on the well-known "Guess my rule" game, which has been used in many classrooms over many years to provoke children to discuss and compare the formulation of rules. In its classical form, it was used as an introduction to functions and to formal algebraic notation. As Carraher and Earnest (2003) have recently reported, even children in younger grades enjoy participating in this game, and can be drawn into discussions of an algebraic nature through playing it.

Our version of the game was somewhat different. The idea was that a student set out a challenge, in the form of a sequence produced by a robot (a ToonTalk computer program) he or she has built, and posted it on the *Webreport* system in the form of the first few terms. The challenge was for the second player to produce a robot that resulted in *the same* sequence. Responders had to build a robot that would produce this sequence, and in doing so work out an underlying rule for its generation. The new element in our variant of the game was that "rules" had to be encoded as programs: one responded to a challenge sequence by posting a program that produced "the same" sequence. Managing to reproduce someone else's sequence by training a robot was the way to show that a learner had grasped *how* the sequence might have been originally generated. As one girl said:

"So, like, the robot is my proof that I got it?"

Rita found the 'guess my robot' activity, and decided to pose her own challenge. The sequence she posted was *2, 16, 72, 296, 1192 ...* (see Figure 3.7).

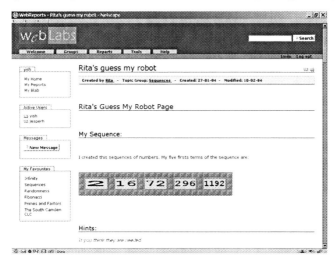

Figure 3.7: Rita's "Guess My Robot" challenge. The five numbers in the boxes were produced by Rita's program (a ToonTalk robot).

A few days after she had posted her Webreport, the Sofia *WebLabs* group held a session, and some of the students tried to solve Rita's challenge. Nasko posted his response. He had built a robot that produced Rita's five terms, but the robot turned out to be different from Rita's. Nasko also realised that the same robot could be used to generate other sequences by changing its initial inputs. So, he posed a two-part challenge back at Rita:

• Could she use *his* robot to generate a new sequence of five terms?
• Could she use *her* robot to generate the same sequence?

We remark in passing, how questions of uniqueness and existence arose as part of the collaborative exchange, apparently naturally – if one *sees* a set of numbers being generated by two robots, it is natural to ask whether each robot is doing the same thing (and conversely, if two robots are each generating different sequences, whether they must necessarily be different).

After a few days, Rita came to her next session to find comments on her page – and from children on the other side of Europe! She immediately clicked on the *ToonTalk* robots in the responses, and watched them step through the process of rule-generation. She was totally surprised: Nasko and Ivan had solved her challenge, but their robots seemed completely different from hers. We will suppress details of the evolving story. Here we will focus on just one 'ending', which involved Rita's response to Nasko. She worked out what inputs Nasko must have given his robot, and showed that *her* robot could in fact generate the same output as his. Her response nicely captured the way the structure of the programming system shaped her thinking.

Later we asked Rita again: "How did you know that the two robots generated the same sequence"? The next day, Rita surprised us. She had generated two robots, one was hers and the other Nasko's. Then she has made a new robot that subtracted one stream of outputs from the other and had watched the robots create a stream of zeros. She had generated thousands of zeros in this way and was convinced that this was a 'proof' of her conjecture that the sequences were the same.

Well, not quite a proof, at least not in any conventional sense, but one that was generated by the tools available and became acceptable in the community of students engaged with the activity. If Rita had found that there were 6000 terms that were equal to zero, she was as likely to wonder if the 6001st would be zero, as to assume that *all* terms to infinity would be zero. The point is not that Rita had constructed a proof for her community of the equality of the robots (incidentally, she has implicitly defined two robots as equal if they generate the same output for ever). She had developed a tacit situated abstraction: "For any two corresponding actions of the two original robots, my robot will produce a zero." From a pedagogical point of view, the construction of large but finite streams of zeros *raises the question* of equality in a natural way, which could provide the basis for a conventional proof in some future pedagogical scenario.

We end this section by highlighting some issues illustrated by this episode. First, we point to the way in which the responses made by the children was shaped by the models and by their medium of communication. This was particularly visible in Rita's unexpected (by us) construction of a new robot to generate the differences. In fact several times in this activity sequence when their mathematical argument was challenged, students initiated programming a model to support it or reject it. They displayed the confidence to reflect on their own errors either individually or collectively and were able to compare or accept algorithms and use counterexamples to refute theories, a remarkable focus on the processes by which the sequences were generated, and in rather stark contrast to usual interactions with algebra.

Second, we recognised the substantive possibility opened up by the imperatives of asynchronous discourse. The formality required for articulation in Webreports was shaped by the need to communicate unambiguously. We also note the power of sharing models and ideas in a dynamic medium when embedded in this game like situation. This undoubtedly provided a strong affective component, to respond to challenges, to build on them or rebut them and then finally to decide if there were any equivalences in the responses provided. This method of interacting at a distance was generative in developing similar activities in other domains, and we referred to them collectively as *Guess my X* activities. Guess my X seemed to attract more sustained participation than, for example, the development of group webreports, by providing a good balance of competition and consensus; the need to negotiate the criteria for assessing equivalence.

LEARNING OUTCOMES

While the focus of this chapter is on the design of an expressive alternative infrastructure of constructing and sharing, we turn – very cursorily in the form of a brief summary - to report some general learning outcomes of the project, based on an evaluation methodology that was essentially qualitative, although supported by some quantitative data.

Developing a rigorous language: Students developed a model-based language and symbols to express ideas rigorously that served at least in the limited domains under investigation as an alternative to algebra. Judged by the criteria of the quality of WebReport interactions, and the nature of classroom discussion, we saw an emergence of structural reasoning based on models, and an improved awareness of mathematical ways of thinking, including fundamental ideas such as generalisation, invariance, consistency and proof.

Layered learning: Students worked at different layers: running ready-made models/programs; inspecting programs and changing parameters; modifying programs and programming from scratch. The depth at which the students interacted with the system influenced the quality of their engagement with the topic.

Motivation and engagement leading to enhanced responsibility for learning: Having built models around a long-term motivational challenge, learners became committed to them, and were willing to argue about the correctness of the models posted by others. They did not always change their mind when confronted with conflicting models and arguments but nonetheless engaged in extended argumentation, and took responsibility for their own and their group's learning, quite unlike normal classroom interactions. Students' awareness of their audience was a strong motivational factor, provoking them to invest great efforts in articulating and illustrating their arguments.

Interpreting and comparing representations: We found students better able to make connections between different representations through constructing and sharing them, by identifying with the structure of the   representational   system. The facility to share comments and hypotheses together with working models was a valuable tool for critiquing and sharing representations of mathematical and scientific phenomena.

Collaboration and formalisation: Asynchronous communication through the WebReports encouraged formalisation, since the normal contextual cues were absent from the interaction. But for collaboration to be effective, we needed to design carefully for it. We identified the need for the distributed group to sign up to a joint enterprise, which could be the development of a shared product, but could also be engagement in a game or series of challenges, such as in Guess my Robot, which was extended to a more general category 'Guess my X'. We also recognized the importance of a group facilitator to ensure sustained interchange.

Effective inter-site collaboration: When inter-site collaboration was successful it tended not to be about group knowledge building but evolving products or cumulative challenges. Final group products as originally conceived, were rarely achieved, largely due to pragmatic reasons of language and curricular organisation and the fact that the production of an inter-site group product tended to be counter to traditional school culture in terms of the long-term engagement necessary and the requirement to pursue collaborative rather than individual goals.

Time to develop fluency with tools: Substantial time and effort was necessary before students could become fluent enough with the programming tools and with the WebReports system to engage with the tools and to express their ideas to each other. Nevertheless, particularly with the students of 13 or 14 years, we found a surprising readiness to learn and become fluent with the interface and the tools.

SUMMARY OF SECTION 3

In this section, we have outlined what becomes possible with a radically different infrastructure from the standard algebra which was developed with static media. Nevertheless, such an innovation brings with it new and often unforeseen difficulties. From the research point of view, the most challenging element has been to explore the sustainability of an online community. This is a far from trivial enterprise. We saw from the example above that students were beginning to develop autonomy and to be able to manage their own learning, listen to, challenge

298

and learn from others from diverse backgrounds, as well as manage multiple technologies. Yet sustained interactions of this nature were rather rare and for the most part, only happened with appropriate facilitation from a teacher or researcher: thus students did not necessarily engage with the distributed community spontaneously. We should not be surprised: the teacher's role does not disappear in this new scenario, although it certainly changes. In fact, there is a research agenda here. This should include studying the mentoring role, which becomes necessary to balance the trend towards student self-managed mathematical work and the need for guidance and instruction, the kinds of support that foster collaborative engagement and, perhaps most challenging of all, the extent to which *some* of the 'functionality' of the teacher might, with the necessary computational support, be devolved to the system.

COMPARING AND CONTRASTING CASYOPÉE AND WEBLABS: A CONTRIBUTION TO CONVERGENCE IN MATHEMATICS EDUCATION

The ambition of this book is to combat the fragmentation of knowledge in Mathematics Education arising from the wealth of research undertaken in many different countries and situations. Although the authors of this chapter share many ideas and conceptualisations, the differing approaches of Casyopée and WebLabs could be interpreted as instances of this fragmentation arising from the different research cultures and contexts in which the two projects were developed. Casyopée was much influenced by the work around the classroom implementation of computer symbolic computation and associated theoretical reflection in terms of instrumentation and praxeologies whose genesis was analysed by Artigue (2002) and more recently by Monaghan (2005). WebLabs was derived from constructionism[9] and more than two decades of research in this tradition from which notions such as situated abstraction and webbing had been derived (Noss & Hoyles 1996).

There are, however, points of convergence. The first point was articulated in section one: most students do not have access to interesting and complex mathematical problems because the traditional school setting does not allow them to master the symbolism necessary to express solutions. A second point is that both projects consider that creating new representational infrastructures for mathematical expression is essential for the future. A third point is that both projects emphasised the process of design on the basis of carefully selected criteria, both focussed carefully on key mathematical objects and relationships (related, perhaps, to what Schweiger – this volume – calls 'fundamental ideas') and both adopted iterative trialling to adapt designs on the basis of feedback from trials with students.

From this starting point, this last section will try in more depth to compare and contrast the two projects with the aim of drawing common trends linked to technology use in mathematics teaching and learning and more generally to mathematics education. Before this, we develop the idea of a plurality of dimensions as a tool to analyse educational uses of technology.

A META-STUDY OF PUBLICATIONS ABOUT DIGITAL TECHNOLOGY IN MATHEMATICS

The idea of a plurality of dimensions as a tool to analyse educational use of technology came, at the end of the nineties, from a contract that researchers in France had with the Ministry of Research to do a meta-study of publications in the educational use of digital technology. The Ministry wanted to know what were really the efficient uses of technology for teaching and learning. It initially appeared that it was an impossible task, since from reading all the literature about ICT and Education, it appeared that although researchers found a substantial amount of interesting potential uses of technology, this contrasted with what they knew of the poor classroom integration of technology (Lagrange et al. 2003).

Thus the researchers found it more useful to search for reasons for this discrepancy. Assuming that the classroom situation is complex and that technology introduces even more complexity, the hypothesis was that much research and innovation failed to take this complexity into account because it tended to restrict its focus to only a few dimensions. The first step of the methodology was to take a broad view of all publications (nearly 800) we could access from the years 1994 to 1998 in order to identify dimensions of analyses from questions or concerns that authors put forward to justify an innovation or a research study. Then, a set of 79 research papers was selected on the basis of representativity and quality. This set was analysed statistically to specify how these dimensions were taken into account by research and to identify trends. Finally, the analysis focused on ten papers representing these trends.

The first step produced six dimensions. The second step led to a classification into three groups: two dimensions were widely considered, two had limited consideration and two were 'embryonic' in a sense that will be explained later.

WIDELY CONSIDERED DIMENSIONS

A first dimension (epistemological and semiotic) considered the influences of ICT on the mathematical knowledge taught and on the way mathematical objects could be represented and manipulated. Most papers considered this influence, generally seeing advantages to new meanings and new ways of representing mathematics that technology fostered.

The second dimension dealt with cognition: many papers offered a cognitive framework within which to explain how the student might learn with ICT, referring to general mathematics education frameworks or to more specifically technology-oriented theorizations, using a wealth of concepts. Jones and Lagrange (*ibid.*) pointed out some of these and stressed that further work needed to be done to understand their connections and specificities.

DIMENSIONS GIVEN LIMITED CONSIDERATION

The meta-study had prepared two dimensions that were thought important while reading literature in the first step. The first is the situational dimension. 'Situational' refers to the work of Brousseau (1997) but, in our meaning, this dimension was not necessarily linked to a specific didactic theorization. We meant that a learning situation had an 'economy', that is a specific organization of the many different components intervening in the classroom and that technology brings changes and specificities in this economy. For instance, technological tools have a deep impact on the 'didactical contract', which is a continually evolving agreement between teacher and students about this organization. Thus one would have anticipated a need for 'situational' analysis given the wealth of new situations provided by the literature. Surprisingly, very few research papers were identified that took such an approach.

We also prepared a dimension of analysis of the role of the teacher, because it appeared to us that benefits or disadvantages of technology reported or assumed in the literature could not be explained without considering the many aspects of the teacher's classroom preparation and management. Again, very few papers investigated research questions related to this aspect.

"EMBRYONIC" DIMENSIONS

We designated as "embryonic" the two remaining dimensions, because they were not explicitly mentioned but concerns and analyses that could be interpreted in these frames were found in some research papers.

INSTRUMENTAL DIMENSION

The instrumental approach (Lagrange 1999, Artigue 2003, Trouche 2005) takes a tool first as an artifact. For instance a scientific calculator is at a material level just plastic and silicon. A human being has to elaborate an instrument from this artifact. The following ideas are important in this dimension :

- the instrument is built during human activity;
- this activity is dependent on features of the artifact: precisely, its constraints and potentialities;
- it has two components, the first one –instrumentalization-- is directed toward the artifact, when the human being creates uses of the tool for himself: the second --instrumentation-- is directed towards the human himself when he builds understanding of the tool's operation[10] .

The instrument is therefore a mixture of features of the artifact and a mental construct of the user. The process of elaboration is what Rabardel names 'instrumental genesis'. In the case of tools to do mathematics, a student learns mathematics while instrumenting the tool. That is why we speak of interwoven mathematical and instrumental genesis, which means that mathematical understanding will be dependent on features of the tool and that schemes of use of the tool will be dependent on mathematical knowledge. This notion complements the idea of situated abstraction, in which the tool shapes the evolving conceptions of learning while, at the same time, being shaped by learners *in use*. In Hoyles, Noss and Kent (2004), we address the complementarity between the theory of instrumental genesis and the ideas of situated abstraction. In that paper, we suggest the importance of this complementarity as follows:

> This is what the notion of situated abstraction seeks to address, by providing a means to describe and validate an activity from a mathematical vantage point but without *necessarily* mapping it onto standard mathematical discourse. The notion is particularly pertinent in computational environments, since the process of instrumental genesis involving the new representational infrastructure supported by the computer will tend to produce individual understandings and ways of working that are divergent from standard mathematics. (*ibid* p. 314).

We give an illustrative example. When students graph functions in a computer environment (or with a graphic calculator), they are faced with the fact that a function graph depends on parameters of the 'graphing window' and they have to develop specific 'framing schemes', typically interweaving knowledge in mathematics and on the calculator. This is far from a spontaneous and immediate process.

ANTHROPOLOGICAL DIMENSION

This dimension was introduced in section 2. Here the notion of praxeology will be explained in more detail. Analyzing the transposition of mathematicians' experimental activity into education helped in section 2 to make clear that knowledge cannot be seen independently of institutions. Bosch et al. (2004, p. 4) explain: "The process of didactic transposition highlights the institutional relativity of knowledge and situates didactic problems at an institutional level, beyond individual characteristics of the institutions' subjects". Section 2 pointed out that 'institution' has to be taken in a very broad sense: a school system in a country is an institution, but a branch of this system is also one. Then, mathematical activity can be modeled as a human institutionally-situated activity among others. In a given institution, among many problems or questions, some are recognized as a 'type of task' and 'techniques' are identified as specific ways to do these tasks. Tasks and techniques together make up the practical component of "know-how"; the praxeologies (*praxis* + *logos*) integrate into a theoretical component.

Techniques have a central role in this model. They cannot be seen just as 'skills'. Certainly, they sometimes mean routines, especially when the purpose is to perform a sub-task in a problem, but they also imply reasoning about mathematical entities, especially during their creation and when questioning their consistency and their domain of validity. As Artigue (2002) pointed out, techniques have both a pragmatic and an epistemic value. The pragmatic value is related to the technique's usefulness and efficiency. It is directed towards tasks. The epistemic value is the light that the technique sheds on properties of mathematical objects. It is directed towards the theoretical component[11].

The following example presents a problem to show how considering this level of the techniques helps us to understand the impact of technology on classroom mathematical practices. The following problem was taken from a 10th grade textbook and is representative of a type of task existing at this level: reducing an expression with radicals. The task was to prove the equality:

$$\frac{1}{1+\sqrt{2}}+\frac{1}{\sqrt{2}+\sqrt{3}}+\frac{1}{\sqrt{3}+\sqrt{4}}=1$$

It is motivating because the expression on the left side is quite complicated and on the right side it is quite simple. Without technology, students should rewrite each term on the left side without surds in the denominator and there is a technique for that. In the textbook, it is written like this.

If a denominator is $a+\sqrt{b}$ then multiply numerator and denominator by $a-\sqrt{b}$

If a denominator is $a-\sqrt{b}$ then multiply numerator and denominator by $a+\sqrt{b}$.

The textbook also provides for a number of exercises for training, numerical or more theoretical.

Write with an integer denominator $\dfrac{1}{\sqrt{5}-1}$ and $\dfrac{\sqrt{3}-\sqrt{2}}{\sqrt{3}+\sqrt{2}}$

Show the equality $\dfrac{\sqrt{x}-\sqrt{y}}{\sqrt{x}-y}=\dfrac{\sqrt{x-y}}{\sqrt{x}+\sqrt{y}}$

With this technique, the problem can be solved, albeit with careful and accurate manipulation. A question is why teachers ask students to learn and practice this technique, to train in its application and to use it to solve problems. A first reason is pragmatic. The technique helps a learner to obtain canonical expressions that are easier to handle in calculations. If this technique would have only this pragmatic role, teaching would be too much oriented towards skills and training. But this technique has also an epistemic role relative to more theoretical knowledge. When practising the technique, a student has to reflect on the structure of an expression to consider, for instance, the denominator and its structure. He (she) has to use properties of equivalent quotients and of the square of surds. He (she) has to also to consider algebraic facts like the factorisation of the difference of two squares. Questions like "does this technique work for every expression?" can begin to develop a student's appreciation of the structure of sets of these expressions.

When students use technology the problems and the exercises become (almost) trivial. Even an ordinary numeric calculator (Fig. 4.1 top) computes the sum into 1. It is a numerical approximation but to students, it is a strong indication that the equality is true. A symbolic calculator also simplifies the sum into 1. It also transforms the expressions of the exercises just in the form a teacher would expect. The equality with x and y is not directly proved, but the proof can be done by a simple transformation (see Fig. 4.1 bottom).

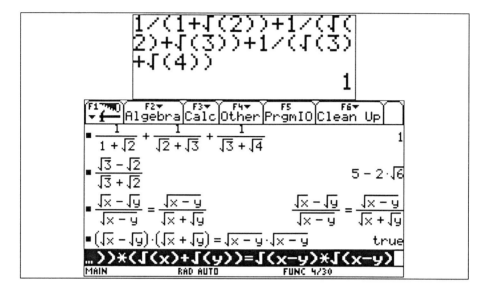

Fig 4.1: *Contrasting a numerical and symbolic calculater*

This means that a valuable praxeology has been destroyed by the use of technology because calculators do computations that could be done before only at the cost of a laborious but potentially epistemic technique. Such a phenomenon can be easily explained: technology was developed precisely to help people perform smoothly algorithmic techniques. As valuable praxeologies disappear, teaching has to create new praxeologies in which techniques performed using technologies retain an epistemic value. New types of tasks have to be thought of and evaluated by considering the possible techniques to solve them and their epistemic value.

Lagrange (2005a) showed that this is a realistic challenge, not least because of the variety of new tasks and techniques and of their epistemic potentialities that technology, especially symbolic calculation, brings about: CAS, for example, aided pattern discovery, problems and techniques to access generalization and the management of expression by way of symbolic calculation.

NEW DIMENSIONS

The meta-study was undertaken in 2000 and was derived from a corpus of papers published up to 1998. Now, some years later, two other dimensions should be added. One is collaboration. We are seeing rapid developments in the ways that it is possible to interact and collaborate through technological devices and many papers now stress the dimension of interactive and collaborative learning, especially when dealing with web-based applications: as we saw, WebLabs attempted to exploit these technological possibilities with some success. A wealth of new questions opens, especially about the contribution to mathematics learning of different levels and modalities of interactivity and collaboration, and about the potential of virtual communities, and how they might be fostered and sustained.

The other new dimension is design. There is growing awareness that, as educators, we cannot simply orchestrate software applications that industry or computer science creates. Yerushalmy (*ibid.*) developed artefacts to experiment with classroom use of technology as a part of her research activity and she reflected on principles that could orientate design. She sees a discrepancy between encouraging evidence about the impact of various specific software capabilities and discouraging evidence about work with educational software that does not always act as the idea generator it was designed to be. She asks designers for more work, not just having good ideas, but also to realize and articulate their perhaps unconscious decisions and turn them into conscious design considerations. Design also needs to be iterative: to have clear aims and criteria but also to be flexible enough so as to be adaptive to and support student learning requirements during mathematical activities.

TOWARDS A SYNTHESIS

The dimensions were conceived so as to encompass the varied aspects of the educational use of digital technologies in an analytic approach. To move closer towards a synthesis, it is useful to consider what dimensions have in common, and to group them around centres of interest, as shown in table 4.1.

The epistemological and semiotic, cognitive and instrumental dimensions are principally concerned with new ways of representing and manipulating objects supported by digital technologies. The epistemological and semiotic dimensions privilege the relationship to mathematical knowledge, while the cognitive dimension focuses on the learner. The instrumental dimension takes into account the user's operative knowledge related to the representations and manipulations.

The 'situational' and 'design' dimensions share a common interest for the 'economy' of the learning situation in the sense described earlier, recognizing that technological tools shape mathematical activity and trying to predict as much as possible the ways they do so. The notion of *scenario of use* should encompass both the design dimension in the narrow sense of software development and implementation in teaching/learning.

Sensitivity to contexts of learning brings together the anthropological, 'teacher' and 'collaboration' dimensions. These dimensions recognize the complexity of human thinking and learning, emphasizing the social aspects of these activities where technology is seen as providing cultural artifacts supplementing language and written expression. While the anthropological dimension considers institutions and the transposition of practices between these, the teacher dimension takes into account the process of mediation in teaching/learning practices and its necessary adaptation to new artifacts. Through software and networks, digital technologies can afford a means to develop collaboration in social activities, creating new contexts and dramatically changing existing ones.

Dimensions	Common centre of interest
Epistemological & semiotic	Influence of digital representations on conceptualisations
Cognitive	
Instrumental	
Situations	Influence of tools on teaching/learning situations
Design	
Anthropological	Sensitivity of technology use to contexts of learning
Teacher	
Collaboration	

Table 4.1: *Grouping Dimensions*

COMPARING AND CONTRASTING THE APPROACHES IN CASYOPÉE AND WEBLABS

As indicated in the introduction to this section, approaches to technology use in the research contexts where Casyopée and WebLabs were developed seem, at first sight, rather distinct. Reflection on the use of computer symbolic computation, which is the context of Casyopée, comes from experiments of the introduction of technology into educational settings that can tolerate from some adaptation, but are not supposed to change fundamentally. In contrast, the central orientation of WebLabs was a design experiment to test out conditions for more or less radical change.

In this concluding section we will see how a comparison between the two projects helps to draw common trends linked to technology use in mathematics teaching/learning and more generally to mathematics education. The above centres of interest, or groups of dimensions, will help to organize the comparison.

The Influence of Digital Representations on Conceptualisations

In both projects, the influence of digital representations on conceptualisations is seen from an epistemological point of view. Both projects share a common concern for students' access to formal thinking and to formal objects, and recognise that formal representations should be learnt as part of a culture of empowerment. They also share a common motivation: to use technology to provide students with representational infrastructures to help them make sense of mathematical ideas and over time to take responsibility for their activity using these infrastructures.

Starting from this common assumption and motivation, Casyopée's and WebLabs' position towards standard mathematical notation differ. Casyopée keeps to this notation as one which proved powerful for mathematicians for centuries. It postulates that technology in the form of symbolic calculation offers a means for more fruitful problem solving with the more or less standard algebraic notation and thus could contribute to make this notation more accessible and learnable.

WebLabs, on the other hand, choose to explore the extent to which some of the apparent complexity and difficulties of mathematical and scientific ideas is due to symbols and language that were the only ones available in the pre-computer age. Thus, technology is seen as a means to broaden mathematical knowledge, either by opening access to problems for Casyopée and by new linkages with mathematical content for WebLabs.

Both authors are concerned with proof. Casyopée focuses on formal proof, principally for epistemological reasons: formal proof is what gives sense to transformational activity. In the WebLabs example, proof is grounded on, first an emphasis on making explicit the processes of reasoning, and second on students deriving situated abstractions rather than on explicit (algebraic) formal reasoning. The motivation for proving is in the social relationship when students want to compare different models. In WebLabs, the technology helps to create situations where students feel the need for a proof and find informal approaches to it. Proof in WebLabs is a way to convince each other of the validity of a property. In Casyopée, technology is an aid, principally when students have to write a proof: here proof is more a written text conforming to institutional standards. As the literature on proof abundantly reports, these two aspects of proof are complementary.

The instrumental dimension is important in both examples, although not developed here: the difficulty of instrumenting standard Computer Algebra Systems has been a strong motivation to design a new environment (Lagrange 2005b).

The Influence of Tools on Teaching/Learning Situations

Both projects take design as a very central dimension. Sections 2 and 3 showed how the design of an application has a deep impact on the way teachers and students can use it and what they learn from its use. The authors of this chapter consider the design of new environments as a crucial dimension of their work as mathematics educators, by opening windows on all elements of the teaching/learning process: situational, cognitive and didactical. A further common orientation is iterative design, starting from initial reflection of a research team and taking advantage of collaborating teachers and partners' feedback during subsequent phases of design. Designers of computer environments for learning should be aware that, in many aspects, the impact of new software on classroom practices can never be totally anticipated. This is particularly the case in environments providing for new representational infrastructure, because, as we remarked in section 3, solving one problem of representation often throws up new unexpected problems. There is evidence that trying small-scale implementations and studying the effect on teachers and students in successive iterations is a way to take account of epistemological relevance and classroom complexity.[12]

Casyopée and WebLabs are mathematical educational applications developed on an underlying "general purpose" platform. In Casyopée, this platform was a computer symbolic kernel and in WebLabs a programming language. In both projects a first task was to "tune" the platform to provide learners with just the right functionalities. In WebLabs the platform is seen as a first level of a layered design, with layers that structure not only the tool but also student engagement with the system and finally the knowledge that he (she) develops. Casyopée, in fact, might also be analysed as a layered tool. It would help students to situate the idea of symbolic computation, of general forms of expressions and of symbolic rules inside strategies of exploration and proof. Tuning the layers and organising them consistently with the knowledge at stake are important principles.

Transparency is another important principal of design. In the WebLabs project, this implies "that it is easy to look not only at what the models *do,* but how they *work*". In Casyopée, the most important design principle, consistent with Yerushalmy's idea of tools supporting the curriculum, is that teachers and students should easily recognise objects manipulated in the environment by referring to standard mathematical objects. Thus, Casyopée and WebLabs do not privilege transparency in the same sense. In Casyopée transparency is 'external': it is in the relationship that users perceive between the functioning the environment and the ordinary mathematics. By contrast, WebLabs' transparency is 'internal' referring to the representation itself rather than to standard mathematical representations. For WebLabs, curriculum support is linked to the appropriate design of activity sequences using the new tools to achieve the learning aims. Both understandings of transparency seem important when dealing with formal representations, although it is not so clear how they can be reconciled.

Contexts of Use

Regarding the contexts of use, the legitimacy of technology in the mathematics classroom is an important issue for Casyopée. Many authors stress the idea of experimental approaches for pedagogical reasons loosely referring to mathematicians' practices. The idea underlying the development of Casyopée is that, to develop viable implementations of this idea, it is necessary to discuss how mathematical practices can be transposed to students. The link between experimentation and conceptualisation appears critical. Technology can help to make this link if it promotes methods and tools for conjecturing and proving.

WebLabs focuses on collaboration between students: distance is taken as an opportunity to allow students to share their models of evolving knowledge, discuss, change and manipulate them. Computer programs are seen as formal objects, by which students operationalise their ideas and edit each others', instantiating the state of their current knowledge and at the same time beginning to appreciate the need for a shared formal language. While WebLabs does not consider the idea of transposition from professional to classroom mathematics, and Casyopée does not involve collaboration, it is interesting to note that distance collaboration is now a growing dimension of mathematicians' work and thus this might form an interesting basis for reconciliation. The idea of alternative systems of representation could also be considered from the perspective of the intermediate systems mathematicians use when investigating a new problem (especially with computers) before having recourse to the standard notation.

Finally, we should consider the relationship between theoretical frameworks and the dimensions. Research on the use of technology in mathematics education exploits many frameworks to help to interpret many aspects of a complex reality. This does make it difficult for researchers to communicate their goals and findings cumulatively. The relationship of dimensions to theoretical frameworks is, therefore, not uniform. In the epistemological, semiotic and cognitive dimensions, a researcher can choose among frameworks that reflect the research emphasis on these dimensions, while in others the choice is limited.

This chapter presents, through a comparison of two projects, the considerable potential in seeking out convergences among existing frameworks using structuring dimensions as a tool. It also points to both practical and theoretical research around those dimensions that are, until now, under-researched.

REFERENCES

Artigue, M. (2005). The integration of symbolic calculation into secondary education: some lessons from didactical engineering. In Guin D. & Trouche L., *The integration of symbolic calculators*. Ch. 9. Dordrecht: Kluwer.

Artigue, M. (2002). Learning mathematics in a CAS environment: The genesis of a reflection about instrumentation and the dialectics between technical and conceptual work. *International Journal of Computers for Mathematical Learning*, 7(3), 254-274.

Arzarello, F. (1991). Pre-algebraic Problem Solving. Paper presented at a seminar on problem-solving. Viana do Castelo, Portugal.

Bell A. (1996). Problem solving approaches to algebra: Two aspects. Bednarz, N., Kieran, C. and Lee, L. (Eds) *Approaches to Algebra: Perspectives for Research and Teaching*. Dordrecht, The Netherlands: Kluwer Academic Publishers.

Borwein, J.,(2005),The experimental mathematician: the pleasure of discovery and the role of proof, *International Journal of Computers for Mathematical Learning*, 10 (2), 75–108.

Bosch, M., Chevallard, Y. & Gascòn, J. 2005 - Science or magic? The use of models and theories in didactics of mathematics. *Proceedings of CERME 4, European research in mathematics education - cerme4.crm.es*

Brousseau, 1997, *Theory of didactic situations*, Kluwer.

Carraher D. & Earnest D. (2003). *Guess my rule revisited. Proceedings of the 27th. conference of the International Group for the Psychology of Mathematics Education*. Honolulu.

Chevallard, Y. (1985). *La transposition didactique*, Editions La Pensée Sauvage, Grenoble.

Chevallard, Y. (1994). Les processus de transposition didactique et leur théorisation. In Arsac, Martinand, Tiberghien (Eds.) *La Transposition didactique à l'épreuve des faits*, Editions La Pensée Sauvage, Grenoble.

Chevallard, Y. (1999). L'analyse des pratiques enseignantes en théorie anthropologique du didactique. *Recherches en Didactique des Mathématiques*, 19, 221-266

Cobb, P., Confrey J., diSessa, A., Lehrer R. and Schauble, L. (2003). Design experiments in educational research. *Educational Researcher*, 32 (1), 9–13.

diSessa, AA, & Cobb, P. (2004). Ontological innovation and the role of theory in design experiments. *Journal of the Learning Sciences, 13*(1), 77-103.

Harel, I. and Papert, S. (1991). *Constructionism.* Norwood, NJ: Ablex.

Hoyles, C., Healy, L. & Pozzi, S. (1992). Interdependence and autonomy: Aspects of groupwork with computers. In Mandel, H., De Corte, E., Bennett S.N. and Friedrich H.F (Eds.), *Learning and instruction: European research in international context.* Vol. 2, pp. 239-257.

Hoyles C. & Noss R. (1996). The visibility of meanings: Modelling the mathematics of banking, *International Journal of Computers for Mathematical Learning. 1* (1) 3-31.

Hoyles C., Noss R. & Kent, P. (2004). On the integration of digital technologies into mathematics classrooms. *International Journal of Computers for Mathematical Learning, 9* (3), 309-326.

Hoyles, C. Morgan and G. Woodhouse (Eds.). *Rethinking the mathematics curriculum.* London: Falmer Press, 22-28.

Hoyles, C., Noss, R. and Kent, P. (2004). On the integration of digital technologies into mathematics classrooms. *International Journal of Computers for Mathematical Learning, 9* (3), 309-326.

Jones and Lagrange (2003). Tools and technologies in mathematical didactics: Research findings AND future directions. In Mariotti (Ed.). CERME3 Proceedings, ermeweb.free.fr.

Joshua, S., Joshua, M.A. (1988). Les fonctions didactiques de l'expérimental dans l'enseignement scientifique. *Recherches en Didactique des Mathématiques, 9* (1), 5-27.

Kieran (2006). Research on learning and teaching algebra. In Angel Gutierrez and Paolo Boero (Eds.). *Handbook of research on the psychology of mathematics education.* Rotterdam/Taipe: Sense Publishers, 11-40.

Kieran, C. (2004). The core of algebra: Reflections on its main activities. In Stacey et al. (Eds.). *The future of the teaching and learning of algebra: The 12th ICMI study.* Springer.

Kynigos, C. (2004). A 'Black-and-White Box' approach to user empowerment with component computing, *Interactive Learning Environments, 12*(1–2), 27–71.

Lagrange , J.B., (1999). Techniques and concepts in pre-calculus using CAS: A two year classroom experiment with the TI-92, *International Journal for Computer Algebra in Mathematics Education, 6,* (2).

Lagrange, J.B. (2005b). Curriculum, classroom practices and tool design in the learning of functions through technology-aided experimental approaches. *International Journal of Computers for Mathematical Learning, 10* (2), 143–189.

Lagrange, J.B. (2005a). Using symbolic calculators to study mathematics. The case of tasks and techniques. Chapter 5 in Guin D., Trouche L. (Eds.), *The integration of symbolic calculators.* Dordrecht: Kluwer.

Lagrange, J.B. (2000). L'intégration d'instruments informatiques dans l'enseignement : Une approche par les techniques. *Educational Studies in Mathematics, 43*(1).

Lagrange, J.-B., Artigue, M., Laborde, C. and Trouche, L.(2003). Technology and mathematics education: A multidimensional study of the evolution of research and innovation. In A. Bishop, M.A. Clements, C. Keitel, J. Kilpatrick and F.K.S. Leung (Eds.). *Second international handbook of mathematics education.* Dordrecht :Kluwer Academic Publishers, 239-271.

Lee, L., & Wheeler, D. H. (1987). *Algebraic thinking in high school students: Their conceptions of generalisation and justification.* Montreal: Concordia University.

MacGregor, M., & Stacey, K. (1992). Seeing a pattern and writing a rule. *Proceedings of the Sixteenth International Conference for the Psychology of Mathematics Education,.* 181-188. New Hampshire: Program Committee of the 16th PME Conference.

Mewborne (2005). Framing our work. In G. M. Lloyd, M. R. Wilson, J. L. M. Wilkins, & S. L. Behm (Eds.). *Proceedings of the 27th annual meeting of the North American Chapter of the International Group for the Psychology of Mathematics Education.* Retrieved October 31, 2005, from http://convention2.allacademic.com/index.php?cmd=pmena_guest

Monaghan, J. D. (2005). Computer algebra, instrumentation and the anthropological approach. *CAME 2005 - The Fourth CAME Symposium.* http://www.lonklab.ac.uk/came/events/CAME4

Mor, Y., Hoyles, C., Simpson G. & Noss R. (in press). Designing to see and share structure in number sequences. *International Journal for Technology in Mathematics Education*

Nardi, B. A. (1996). Introduction to context and consciousness: activity theory and human- computer interactions. Cambridge MA: MIT Press.

Noss R. & Hoyles C. (1996). *Windows on mathematical meanings: Learning cultures and computers.* Dordrecht: Kluwer.

Noss R. & Hoyles, C. (2006). Exploring mathematics through construction and collaboration. In K.R. Sawyer (Ed). *Cambridge handbook of the learning sciences.* Cambridge: CUP.

Noss, R. (1998). New numeracies for a technological culture. *For the Learning of Mathematics, 18* (2), 2-12.

Papert, S., and Harel, I. (1991). Situating constructionism. In Harel & Papert (Eds.) *Constructionism.* Norwood, NJ: Ablex.

Scardamalia, M. & Bereiter, C. (2006). Knowledge building: Theory, pedagogy and technology. In: Sawyer, K. (Ed.). *Cambridge handbook of the learning sciences.* Cambridge UK: C.U.P, 97-118.

Simpson, G., Hoyles, C. & Noss, R. (2005). Designing a programming-based approach for modelling scientific phenomena. *Journal of Computer Assisted Learning, 21*, 143–158.

Simpson, G., Hoyles, C. & Noss, R. (2006). Exploring the mathematics of motion through construction and collaboration. *Journal of Computer Assisted Learning, 22,*1-23.

Stacey, K. (1989). Finding and using patterns in linear generalising problems.

Trouche, L. (2005). An instrumental approach to mathematics learning. In Guin D., Trouche L. (Eds.). *The integration of symbolic calculators.* Dordrecht: Kluwer.

Vergnaud, G., (1985). Concepts et schèmes dans une théorie opératoire de la représentation. *Psychologie Française, 30* (3/4), 245-251.

Yerushalmy, M. (1999). Making exploration visible: On software design and school algebra curriculum. *International Journal of Computers for Mathematical Learning, 4*, 169-189.

Celia Hoyles
University of London, UK

Jean-Baptiste Lagrange
IUFM centre de Reims, France

Richard Noss
University of London, UK

NOTES

[1] The team includes two teachers of the Institute for Research in Mathematical Education (IREM) of Rennes and the author. The project is supported by the French National Institute for Pedagogical Research (INRP).

[2] See Lagrange (2000, 2005a) for developments about the notion of praxeology when using technology and Monaghan (2005) for a discussion.

[3] See the conclusion of this section.

[4] This Texas Instrument calculator (very similar to other calculators sold by this company: TI-89 ad Voyage 200) integrates symbolic calculation. The company claims that it has been designed for upper secondary level mathematics learning, but most of the remarks we address to standard symbolic application are relevant for this calculator (complexity, relationship to curriculum...)

[5] In France, the 12th grade is the 'Terminale', i.e. a class preparing to the baccalaureate and the curriculum's pressure cannot be ignored.

6 This objective will be pursued inside the European project ReMath (Representing Mathematics with Digital Media http://remath.cti.gr/).

7 We acknowledge the support of Grant IST 2001-3220 of the Information Society Technologies Programme of the European Commission. We also acknowledge the contribution of all the *WebLabs* team (from participating countries, Portugal, Bulgaria, Sweden, Cyprus, Italy as well as UK), and notably the UK researchers, Y. Mor and G. Simpson. See http://www.weblabs.eu.com.

8 This episode is based on a description that is due to appear in Mor, Hoyles, Simpson & Noss (submitted).

9 For Harel & Papert (1991) "constructionism shares constructivism's connotation of learning as "building knowledge structures" (and) then adds the idea that this happens especially effectively when learners are engaged in construction for a "public" audience".

10 This understanding is not just declarative knowledge. That is why authors referring to the instrumental approach generally use the notion of scheme in Vergnaud (1985)'s acceptation: "A scheme is an invariant organization of activity for a given class of situations. It has an intention and a goal and constitutes a functional dynamic entity". In this chapter I do not want to enter into a detailed conceptualization of the mental activity in instrumented situations: scheme can be taken as a mental construct pre-organizing the subject's activity.

11 This block has two levels. One is 'technological' —in the etymological acceptation of 'discourse about techniques'—and the other theoretical. Considering the 'technological' level in the context of use of 'technology' —in the ordinary acceptation— is useful because as the example below will show, classroom conceptualization of mathematical objects and properties is aimed through a 'discussion about the techniques'.

12 Iterative design in Weblabs is explained in section 3 above. For Casyopée, see Lagrange (2005b p. 173).

CONTRIBUTORS

Paul Cobb's research interests focus on instructional design, the classroom microculture, and the broader institutional setting of mathematics teaching and learning. He has participated in a series of classroom design experiments and has used the methodology more recently to investigate the process of supporting a group of mathematics teachers learning as it is situated in the institutional settings in which they work.

Willi Dörfler, PhD (Mathematics) University of Vienna, has been, since 1974 Full Professor of Mathematics and Mathematics Education at the University of Klagenfurt, Vice-Rector and Rector 1990-1999. Editor Journal für Mathematikdidaktik (1986-1990) and Educational Studies in Mathematics (1990-1995). Research: Abstraction and generalization, semiotics of mathematics, philosophy of mathematics.

Jeff Evans is Reader in Adults' Mathematical Learning at Middlesex University, UK. His career work has emphasised the teaching and public understanding of statistics and research methodology. Current research focuses on mathematics, the emotions, and popular culture; and the transfer / transformation of knowledge across academic and everyday contexts, including work.

Roland Fischer is professor for mathematics and didactics at the Klagenfurt University in Vienna. Fields of research: didactics and philosophy of mathematics and the sciences in general.

Markku S. Hannula works as a lecturer at the University of Helsinki, Finland, and as a professor in mathematics education in Tallinn University, Estonia. His main interests in mathematics education are affect, gender, and teacher change.

Celia Hoyles has been a Professor of Mathematics Education since 1984. Her research includes using computers to enhance mathematical learning, how mathematics is used in the workplace, and students' developing conceptions of proof. In 2004, ICMI awarded her the first Hans Freudenthal medal as recognition of a cumulative programme of research.

Christine Keitel's major research areas are comparative studies on the history and current state of mathematics education in various European and Non-European countries, on social practices of mathematics, on values of teachers and students, on "mathematics for all" and "mathematical literacy", on equity and social justice, on learners' perspectives of classroom practice, on internationalization and globalization of mathematics education.

Jean-Baptiste Lagrange is a Professor in Mathematics Education at the Institute for Teacher Education in Reims and a member of the Research Team in Didiactique at University Paris 7. His main research interest is in the use of technological tools to teach and learn Mathematics. His present research is centered on the development of new tools and the professional situation of teachers using technology.

Gilah Leder is foundation Director of the Institute for Advanced Study and Director of Graduate Studies at La Trobe University. She is Past President of the Mathematics Research Group of Australasia [MERGA] and of the International Group for the Psychology of Mathematics Education [PME]. In 2001 she was elected a Fellow of the Academy of the Social Sciences in Australia.

Stephen Lerman was a secondary school teacher of mathematics for many years before commencing doctoral research and moving into teacher education and further research. He is now Professor of Mathematics Education, responsible for the doctoral programmes in mathematics education and Director of the Centre for Mathematics Education. He is a past President of PME (International Group for the Psychology of Mathematics Education) and a former Chair of the British Society for Research in Learning Mathematics.

Juergen Maasz's main areas of research and activity are concentrated on mathematics education (teaching real word problems (MUED, ISTRON), adults learning mathematics (ALM), computer and learning – Maaß & Stöckl Consulting). Other interdisciplinary areas are ethics (ETHICA), social competence (CSCC), computer(games) and children (ACOS).

Hermann Maier has been "Professor für Didaktik der Mathematik" at the university of Regensburg for 40 years and trained future mathematics teachers for all levels of schooling. My main research interest was in language in the mathematics classroom, and in the learners' understanding of mathematical concepts. I tried to contribute to the development of an effective interpretation research in the field of mathematics education.

Mogens Niss is Professor of Mathematics and Mathematics Education at Roskilde University, Denmark, of which he was one of the founding staff members since 1972. He served as a member of the Executive Committee of ICMI 1987-1998, the Secretary General 1991-1998. His research interests include applications and modelling, the justification problem in mathematics education, the nature and development of research on the teaching and learning of mathematics, and assessment.

Richard Noss is Professor of Mathematics Education and co-director of the London Knowledge Lab. Richard holds a PhD in mathematics education from King's College, University of London, and a Masters degree in pure mathematics from the University of Sussex.

314

Bert van Oers is Professor for Culturalhistorical Theory of Education at the Vrije Universiteit, Amsterdam. His research interests are emergent mathematics and literacy, play, psychosemiotic analysis of learning, activity theory. Publications: (among others): Narratives of childhood (Amsterdam VU press, 2003); co-editor of: Symbolizing.modelling and tool use in mathematics education (Gravemijer et al.; Kluwer 2002).

Michael Otte was born in Riga in 1938. He studied Mathematics and German literature at the universities of München and Göttingen. In 1973 he established an interdisciplinary research group on mathematical epistemology, history and cognition at the University of Bielefeld.

Wolfgang Schlöglmann is Professor of Mathematics Education at the Johannes Kepler University of Linz. His research interest focuses in mathematics learning of adults and the influence of affect to cognitive processes.

Fritz Schweiger studied mathematics and physics at the University of Vienna. In 1969 he became professor of mathematics at the University of Salzburg. His broad research interests cover mathematics, mathematical education and linguistics.

Anna Sfard's research is focused on the development of mathematical discourse, with the word development referring both to learning and to the historical evolution of this discourse. The results of her studies are now being summarized in a book due to appear in 2007. She holds a joint appointment as Lappan-Phillips-Fitzgerald Professor of Mathematics Education in Michigan State University in US and in the University of Haifa, Israel.

Ole Skovsmose has a special interest in critical mathematics education. Recently he has published Travelling Through Education, which investigates the notions of mathematics in action, students' foreground, globalisation, ghettoising with particle reference to mathematics education. He is professor at Aalborg University, Department of Education, Learning and Philosophy.